I0877797

Critical Survey of Long Fiction

African American Culture

Editor

Carl Rollyson
Baruch College, City University of New York

Salem Press
Ipswich, Massachusetts • Hackensack, New Jersey

Cover photo:
Alice Walker (© Bonnie Schiffman/Corbis)

978-1-4298-3687-6

CONTENTS

Contributors iv

African American Long Fiction 1
James Baldwin 14
Toni Cade Bambara. 33
George Washington Cable 39
Charles Waddell Chesnutt 50
Ralph Ellison 61
Jessie Redmon Fauset 74
Ernest J. Gaines. 80
Chester Himes 91
Zora Neale Hurston. 98
William Melvin Kelley 109
Nella Larsen. 116
Harper Lee 122
Claude McKay 128
Terry McMillan 134
Toni Morrison 140
Gloria Naylor 154
Ishmael Reed 163
Harriet Beecher Stowe 175
Alice Walker 190
Colson Whitehead. 205
John Edgar Wideman 211
John A. Williams 222
Richard Wright 230
Frank Yerby 244

Bibliography 254
Glossary of Literary Terms 257
Guide to Online Resources 269
Category Index 274
Subject Index 276

CONTRIBUTORS

Timothy Dow Adams
Original Contributor

Heather Russell Andrade
Florida International University

Jane L. Ball
Yellow Springs, Ohio

Paula C. Barnes
Hampton University

Kate Begnal
Original Contributor

Jacquelyn Benton
Metropolitan State College of Denver

Mary A. Blackmon
Hardin-Simmons University

Harold Branam
Savannah, Georgia

Carl Brucker
Original Contributor

Robert P. Ellis
Original Contributor

Howard Faulkner
Original Contributor

Dennis Goldsberry
Original Contributor

Charles A. Gramlich
Xavier University of Louisiana

Cynthia Packard Hill
University of Massachusetts Amherst

Nika Hoffman
Crossroads School for Arts and Sciences

Deborah Kaplan
Original Contributor

Mabel Khawaja
Hampton University

Rebecca Kuzins
Pasadena, California

Barbara A. McCaskill
Original Contributor

Edythe M. McGovern
West Los Angeles College

Joseph McLaren
Hofstra University

Charles E. May
California State University, Long Beach

Laurence W. Mazzeno
Alvernia College

Holly L. Norton
University of Northwestern Ohio

David Peck
Laguna Beach, California

Frank W. Shelton
Original Contributor

Charles L. P. Silet
Iowa State University

Rebecca G. Smith
Barton College

Sherry G. Southard
Original Contributor

Theresa L. Stowell
Adrian College

Bernice Larson Webb
Original Contributor

Shawncey Webb
Taylor University

Craig Werner
Original Contributor

Tyrone Williams
Xavier University

Judith Barton Williamson
Sauk Valley Community College

AFRICAN AMERICAN LONG FICTION

SLAVE NARRATIVES

Nineteenth century American fiction influenced the form and content of many of the slave narratives of the time, while nineteenth and twentieth century African American fiction owes a great debt, in form and content, to the slave narrative. Thus, the development of African American fiction can be traced to nineteenth century American fiction only by way of the slave narrative.

Just as Africans arriving in the Americas staked their claims to humanity on the basis of the cultural models available to them—European Enlightenment and Christian values—so too did the first "authors" of the slave narrative model their testimonies on the Christian confessionals of Jonathan Edwards and the sentimental fiction of Harriet Beecher Stowe. Despite these debts to Puritanism and sentimentality, the best and most influential narratives transcended their origins to create an entirely new prose genre. Thus, an achievement such as Frederick Douglass's *Narrative of the Life of Frederick Douglass, an American Slave, Written by Himself* (1845) is instructive, if rare.

Because the slave narrative was, by definition, a collaborative effort between white and free black abolitionists, political or social supporters, and the slave, a great number of reputed slave narratives were outright frauds concocted by abolitionists to fan the flames of the antislavery movement or, occasionally, by proslavery forces determined to demonstrate the slaves' satisfaction with their lives. Yet even in those slave narratives that have been generally authenticated by meticulous historical research, the voice of the slave is often muffled under letters of support, prefaces, introductions, reproductions of bills of sale, and appendixes, all deployed to assure the reader of the truthfulness of the tale. Indeed, insofar as many of the slave narratives are careful to depict the slave's freedom as having been the result of the aid of sympathetic white people, the narrative moral reinforces its collage format: The story of a slave's flight to freedom is inconceivable without the support and aid of northern and, occasionally, southern whites.

Narrative of the Life of Frederick Douglass, an American Slave, Written by Himself is distinguished, however, by both its literary élan and political independence. This well-known narrative boldly rises above its encumbering supplementary materials to depict one man, one slave, fighting his way to freedom. Of course, both luck and friendly white hands play a role in Douglass's flight to freedom, just as they do in every other slave narrative. However, the thrust of Douglass's narrative is that he, and he alone, took his life into his hands and forged for himself a new destiny. This theme also was evident in Olaudah Equiano's *The Interesting Narrative of the Life of Olaudah Equiano: Or, Gustavus Vassa, the African, Written by Himself* (1789).

Such independence and bravado were not always available for enslaved African American women, as demonstrated in Harriet Jacobs's narrative, written under the pseudonym Linda Brent. *Incidents in the Life of a Slave Girl* (1861) has many parallels with

Harriet E. Wilson's novel, *Our Nig: Or, Sketches from the Life of a Free Black, in a Two-Story White House, North. Showing That Slavery's Shadows Falls Even There* (1859). Wilson's protagonist, Alfrado, submits to a marriage with a fugitive slave who abandons her while she is pregnant, forcing her to work for an abusive white female employer. For Jacobs, affirming her gender means that she will be forced to submit to her sexual identity as an African American woman to escape sexual exploitation by her white master. The central psychological crisis for Jacob occurs when she decides to take a white man as a lover in order to block the predatory sexual advances of her master. For Jacobs, the submission to sexuality as a form of power over her circumstances is humiliating, but it is a humiliation redeemed, if only in part, by her choice to decide with whom she will have illicit sexual relations. Having learned that literacy is not enough to affirm and defend her humanity (her freedom), she must affirm her racial and sexual difference—her status as a black woman—by a decision that ironically ensures her identity as both a woman and a human.

The narratives escape the limitations of their origins and their utility as propaganda for the antislavery cause precisely because they emphasize specific individuality rather than a vague "humanity." That they differ in terms of gender stereotypes—physical prowess for the men, sexual wiliness for the woman—only underscores the narrow band of options available for those attempting to escape slavery. More important, Douglass and Equiano can demonstrate their humanity with a number of virile activities, while Jacobs has only one way to demonstrate her humanity: sexuality. This imbalance in the range of choices, along with the stereotypical, sentimental, and fiction-derived narrative of flight, disguise, concealment, near discovery, and final freedom, orients the trajectory of the African American novel along lines that consistently wed identity to gender, which then orient the positions authors take on issues such as class, caste, and skin-color distinctions; individualism and integration; and cultural nationalism.

Before these themes are considered, however, it is necessary to examine a subgenre of the slave narrative known as the narrative of revolt. *The Confessions of Nat Turner* (1832) is a peculiar document of some twenty pages, a reputed record of Nat Turner's descriptions of the revolt he launched against white Virginian men, women, and children in 1831. Augmented with the usual preface attesting the truthfulness of what follows, *The Confessions of Nat Turner* resembles in form the stereotypical slave narrative. However, the witnesses in question are proslavery white men, and the content of the narrative is indeed a "confession" of the conception, planning, and execution of the revolt. This slave narrative is thus not an attempt to affirm the humanity of the "author." Instead there is only the justification of righteous violence, the inspired zealot wreaking judgment upon the sinners—that is, the slave owners. Thus, just as white abolitionists created the format of the slave narrative to depict the horrors of slavery, so too was *The Confessions of Nat Turner* created to justify not only the continuation of slavery but also the ruthless suppression of the few privileges permitted selected slaves.

The Confessions of Nat Turner may well have benefitted the proslavery cause, but it also inspired other slave revolts, as well as the first protest novel in the African American literary tradition, *Blake: Or, The Huts of America* (serial 1859), by Martin Delany, himself an African American. *Blake* did not appear as a book until 1970, but it first ran serially in a black abolitionist newspaper. *Blake* is a call to arms, an explicit justification for open slave revolt and the establishment of a black sovereignty. It is, in some respects, the novelistic version of *Walker's Appeal, in Four Articles* (1830), by David Walker, judged to be so inflammatory that a large number of people called for its suppression; it also allegedly cost the author his life a short time after its publication. Like *Walker's Appeal, in Four Articles*, *Blake* rejects the possibility of slaves integrating into American society. Instead, Delany imagines a black-ruled Cuba as the only viable option for the enslaved Africans. Both *The Confessions of Nat Turner* and *Blake* imagine violence as the only solution to slavery and link this violence to masculinity.

Post-Reconstruction

Francis E. W. Harper's *Iola Leroy: Or, Shadows Uplifted* (1892), Charles Waddell Chesnutt's *The Marrow of Tradition* (1901), and Paul Laurence Dunbar's *The Sport of the Gods* (1902) represent three different reactions in the African American novel to the post-Reconstruction United States, although Harper's idealized treatment of injustice, suffering, and redemption stands in marked contrast to the bitterness evident in the works by Chesnutt and Dunbar.

Harper's *Iola Leroy* is the story of a woman who is, unknown to herself and others, a mulatto (of mixed race). Iola Leroy believes she is white until the unexpected death of her father spurs her uncle, who has long resented his brother's interracial marriage, to sell Iola and her mother separately into slavery. Aside from the search for her mother and abolitionist arguments that function as subplots, the novel focuses on Iola's courtship by two men, one a white abolitionist doctor, the other a mulatto like herself. Though tempted by the doctor's offer to "pass" into white society, Iola steadfastly rejects the opportunity. Instead, she weds herself to the cause of abolition by agreeing to marry the mulatto. The novel's happy ending suggests that Harper preferred to invoke the nineteenth century sentimental novel of manners rather than the "tragic mulatta," a figure who had already appeared in William Wells Brown's *Clotel: Or, The President's Daughter: A Narrative of Slave Life in the United States* (1853; revised as *Miralda: Or, The Beautiful Quadroon*, 1860-1861; *Clotelle: A Tale of the Southern States*, 1864; and *Clotelle: Or, The Colored Heroine*, 1867).

On the other hand, Chesnutt's *The Marrow of Tradition* and Dunbar's *The Sport of the Gods* are much darker assessments of African American life during the so-called decades of disappointment. Based loosely on the Wilmington, North Carolina, riot of 1898, Chesnutt's novel follows the lives of several white and black characters whose unacknowledged but intertwined lives culminate in a literal "revelation" amid a murderous riot. Ostensibly a depiction of the end of Reconstruction—the riot is fomented by white people who want to "take back" their town—*The Marrow of Tradition* is also a morality tale concerning the futility of hate and violence, themes that Chesnutt links to the obsession with racial purity. For Chesnutt, miscegenation is the only viable solution to the race problem.

If Chesnutt offers some hope to his audience, Dunbar's vision of the destiny of the newly freed slaves is relentlessly desolate. *The Sport of the Gods* concerns the dissolution of a postslavery African American family forced to flee to New York City after the father is jailed on trumped-up burglary charges. Every family member ends up losing his or her moral integrity in the urban landscape; even when the parents are reunited near the end of the novel, it is clear that their lives will be cheap imitations of their shattered dreams. Dunbar's dismal vision of the urban landscape, a vision anticipated by *Our Nig*, looks forward to those novelists of the Harlem Renaissance whose portraits of city life effectively undermine any romantic notions of what it might mean to have come "up from slavery."

THE HARLEM RENAISSANCE

The concern with skin color, particularly with miscegenation, became particularly urgent during the Harlem Renaissance (1919-1929), as the possibility of an "authentic" African American culture began, however tentatively, to take shape. Insofar as the fledgling culture had to partake of the culture of its former oppressors, the tensions and arguments over who and what was, in fact, "Negro" took on a certain urgency. However, not every African American writer treated this issue with morbid seriousness. Wallace Thurman's *Infants of the Spring* (1932) is an excoriating roman à clef about the central figures of the Harlem Renaissance. Its vicious attacks on the petty prejudices of the leading personages of the day echo themes developed in his first and most popular novel, *The Blacker the Berry* (1929), which concerns skin-color prejudice within African American culture.

Less known but in many respects a better work, George Schuyler's *Black No More: Being an Account of the Strange and Wonderful Workings of Science in the Land of the Free, A.D. 1933-1940* (1931) is a hilarious send-up of the obsession with "race advancement" among members of newly formed organizations such as the National Association for the Advancement of Colored People (NAACP) and the obsession with racial purity among members of the Ku Klux Klan. Thurman's and Schuyler's satires on race, class, and gender mock the absurdities of politicians and artists identified with the Harlem Renaissance.

James Weldon Johnson's *The Autobiography of an Ex-Coloured Man* (1912), for example, represents a logical extension of the reconciliation themes evident in the novels of Harper and Chesnutt. If, in their works, the mulatto or mulatta appears to embody the race's best chance for advancement, then passing—mulattoes and mulattas "disappearing" into white society—would obviously be the next logical step. Johnson's novel idealizes the passing motif even as it rehearses its tragedy: the mulatto as a wanderer between separate cultures, never at home in either.

At the opposite end of the spectrum is Nella Larsen. Her two novels, *Quicksand* (1928) and *Passing* (1929), contain depictions of the tragic mulatta. In *Quicksand*, Helga Crane, a mulatta never at ease among African Americans or Caucasians, marries and has children. In *Passing*, Clare Kendry is a mulatta passing for Caucasian while her friend, Irene Redfield, is both disgusted and envious of her freedom. Kendry's sudden death offers her escape from the humiliation of being unveiled as a "nigger" by her white, racist husband.

Larsen's analyses of middle-class mulattas represents an extension of Jean Toomer's *Cane* (1923), a collage of poetry and fiction centered on multiple themes in early twentieth century African American life: the juxtaposition of urban and rural lifestyles, tensions between the North and the South, and "purebred" or "mixed-blood" characteristics. As with Harper, Chesnutt, and others, Toomer links the resolution of these oppositions to the mulatto. Like Larsen, however, Toomer is not optimistic about this figure, who is shunned and scorned by both African Americans and whites.

Between Johnson's idealism and Larsen's cynicism lie authors such as Claude McKay and Zora Neale Hurston on one hand and Jessie Redmon Fauset on the other. McKay's novel *Home to Harlem* (1928) was a commercial success, which some critics, including W. E. B. Du Bois, attributed to its exotic treatment of Harlem nightlife. Richard Wright made similar criticisms of Hurston's novel *Their Eyes Were Watching God* (1937), arguing that Hurston created laughable caricatures of African Americans.

Like the novels of Larsen, Fauset's three best novels, *There Is Confusion* (1924), *Plum Bun: A Novel Without a Moral* (1928), and *The Chinaberry Tree: A Novel of American Life* (1931), concern the plight of middle- and upper-class African American women struggling with racial passing, material possessions, marital prospects, and self-worth. Unlike Larsen, and in some respects more like Johnson, Fauset delineates the pitfalls of racial confusion without the melodrama of tragedy. At the same time, Fauset's protagonists are clearly more sensitive to, and more psychologically damaged by, the perplexing anxieties of the color caste system in African American culture.

Post-Renaissance realism

If the problem of the color caste system dominated African American fiction as a concern before and during the Great Depression, perhaps it was because of the effects of post-Reconstruction migrations of African Americans from the South to the North. Although writers such as Dunbar attempted to unmask the urban dreamscape, the struggle by so many writers to confront color prejudice among African Americans is linked to the social problems associated with mass migrations: poverty, joblessness, overcrowding, and, in the case of African Americans, class distinctions tied to the presence or absence of "white" blood. Underlying the tendency to privilege or castigate on the basis of miscegenation was a belief that becoming white was either a way to escape the stigma attached to African blood or a way to delude oneself that white America would accept African Americans if they acted less "African."

Richard Wright's groundbreaking first novel, *Native Son* (1940), changed the terms of the debate, dramatizing the conflict between race and class. Wright's portraits of communists—the naïve Mary, the careless Jan, and the rough-hewn Max—were augmented by his negative portraits of both liberal Caucasians, such as the Daltons, and African American women, such as Bigger's mother, sister, and girlfriend. Wright's realist novel was widely criticized, and in this respect Dunbar's equally desolate, if less brutal novel, *The Sport of the Gods*, can be seen as its most immediate ancestor. A similar combination of gritty realism and broad criticism can be seen in two other writers of the period: Chester Himes and Ann Petry.

Himes's postwar work is an effective combination of the hard-boiled detective fiction of Raymond Chandler and the protest fiction of Wright. His best novel, *If He Hollers Let Him Go* (1945), is a masterful hybrid of these two genres. On one hand, as Wright does in *Native Son*, Himes compresses his story into a short time frame (four days) that allows him to explore the effects of unrelenting racism on the consciousness of his narrator-protagonist, Bob Jones. At the same time, Himes pays tribute to the detective story as Jones struggles to figure out why a Caucasian coworker has fabricated a rape charge against him. His later novels, such as *Retour en Afrique* (1964; *Cotton Comes to Harlem*, 1965), owe more to the detective genre than to the protest novel, perhaps because Himes wrote them after his expatriation to France.

Petry's fame rests primarily on the basis of her novel *The Street* (1946), the first novel by an African American woman to sell more than one million copies. While some critics have compared the novel to Wright's *Native Son* because of its intense focus on urban decay and squalor, a case could also be made for linking it to Dunbar's *The Sport of the Gods* and Hurston's pioneering *Their Eyes Were Watching God.* Just as Hurston's novel concerns Janie's triumph over the patriarchal traditions of white male racism and black male chauvinism, so, too, does Petry's novel focus on Lutie Johnson's attempts to eke out a meager living away from the brutality of her father. Like those of the mother in Dunbar's novel, Lutie's dreams to provide for herself and her son are driven by a naïveté that drags her even further down the social ladder. If Hurston's Janie seems like an idealized role model for all women to emulate, Petry's Lutie is a grim reminder of what so many black women actually go through in their daily lives.

Compared to the grim urban realism of Wright, Himes, and Petry, the fiction of

Told in a flashback by an unnamed narrator, *Invisible Man* chronicles the misadventures of a naïve high school graduate in the grand tradition of the episodic, picaresque novel. Boiled down to its essential themes, the novel traces the gradual awakening of a potential leader who believes that the key to the salvation of his community is organized group action, the most notorious of which turns out to be the Brotherhood, a political organization loosely based on the Communist Party of America. In the epilogue, however, the narrator realizes that individualism is the answer to his, and his community's, problems, that all groups are, to one degree or another, straitjackets of intolerance.

Ellison's novel was thus read as a direct rebuke to *Native Son*, though Wright himself saw more affinities than differences between the two works. Nevertheless, Ellison was heralded as the successor to Wright, whose commitment to the communist cause, if not the Communist Party, isolated him and his later work in the context of, and fallout from, McCarthyism. Moreover, a chorus of new voices began to declaim their relevancy and militancy, a phenomenon that had the effect of elevating Wright while demoting Ellison.

The writer who not only functions as a transitional figure between the 1950's and 1960's but also inherited all the contradictions and conflicts between the two decades, represented by the trajectories of Wright's and Ellison's careers, is James Baldwin. Baldwin authored six novels, but his fame rests almost entirely on his provocative essays, especially "Everybody's Protest Novel," which signaled his aesthetic break from his mentor, Wright. Just as Baldwin slays his literary father in the essay, so too does his first novel, *Go Tell It on the Mountain* (1953), a depiction of the Oedipal struggle between a religious father and an unconventional young son, seem to be directed at his real-life stepfather, David Baldwin.

Baldwin's next two novels, *Giovanni's Room* (1956) and *Another Country* (1962), explore homosexuality and black pride as avenues toward individualism. More ominous, the tone of these novels is a little more high-strung than that of the first novel, and in his subsequent novels—*Tell Me How Long the Train's Been Gone* (1968), *If Beale Street Could Talk* (1974), and *Just Above My Head* (1979)—the pitch is harsh and loud, developments reflected in the essays. In one of those ironies that permeate African American literary history, Baldwin also wrote the same kind of protest novels, articles, and essays for which he criticized Wright and others. How did this happen? To answer this question, it is necessary to examine the effects that the developing Civil Rights movement, the black power spinoffs, the antiwar protests, and the Black Arts movement had on Baldwin's growth as an artist. That is, it is necessary to examine the cultural, social, and political upheavals of the 1960's and 1970's through the lenses of the African American writers who would emerge as distinctive literary voices.

The 1960's, 1970's, and 1980's

The counterculture movements of the 1960's and 1970's affected all American artists, and African American novelists were no exception. Though his first two novels and various essays had gained him some notoriety, Baldwin had written himself into an aesthetic corner not unlike that inhabited by Ellison. Just as Ellison's essays after *Invisible Man* would put distance between his nineteenth century genteel aesthetics and the politicized aesthetics of the new African American writers, so, too, would Baldwin's criticism of Wright's *Native Son* as mere "protest" fiction alienate Baldwin from a new generation of African Americans anxious to relate literature to social concerns. For writers attempting to forge a black aesthetic based on the values of working-class African Americans, Baldwin was aesthetically and politically irrelevant. Worse, Baldwin's homosexuality only confirmed the suspicions of the largely homophobic Black Arts movement.

In 1967, one of the few novelists of the Black Arts movement, John A. Williams, penned *The Man Who Cried I Am*, a kind of roman à clef of African American literary history featuring Langston Hughes, Wright, and Baldwin under pseudonyms. Williams's novel, about a somewhat famous African American male writer who struggles with illness, the envy of his peers, and rampant racism, is composed with the crude urban realism of Himes and Wright, but its value is primarily archival.

It was during the same year, 1967, that John Edgar Wideman's first novel, *A Glance Away*, first appeared, presenting Wideman as a transitional figure between Ellison and Baldwin on one hand and the Black Arts movement on the other. Perhaps influenced by Baldwin's interest in the contingencies of sexuality and race, *A Glance Away* is a concentrated study—the narrative covers a single day—of the lives of an African American drug addict and a gay white professor. *Hurry Home* (1970), Wideman's second novel, focuses on the attempt of an African American to unite his European and African cultural heritages. Both novels are less concerned with racial issues per se than with philosophical ones. However, by the publication of his third novel, *The Lynchers* (1973), Wideman was under the influence of the Black Arts movement, though aesthetically the book remains outside its camp, a stance evident in Wideman's subsequent work such as *Damballah* (1981) and *Sent for You Yesterday* (1983).

Finally, 1967 saw yet a third auspicious debut. The most important male African American novelist to follow Ellison was Ishmael Reed. Eschewing the simplistic posturing of much of the Black Arts movement, *The Free-Lance Pallbearers* (1967) was a remarkable first novel, as Reed laid claim to being the best African American satirist since Schuyler. The form of his avant-garde novel was inspired as much by experimental jazz and film as James Joyce and Ellison. *Yellow Back Radio Broke-Down* (1969), his second novel, was an even greater triumph, a full-blown parody of the American Western as portrayed in dime-store novels and black-and-white films. Subsequent novels during the 1970's—such as *Mumbo Jumbo* (1972), *The Last Days of Louisiana Red* (1974), and *Flight to Canada* (1976)—reinforced Reed's reputation as one of the most innovative comic spirits of his generation.

Ernest J. Gaines inaugurated the 1970's as the first major African American regional novelist since Jean Toomer, though he was soon followed by the equally talented Leon Forrest. Like Toomer, Gaines situates his novels in the complicated racial, sexual, and class mixtures of Cajun culture in Louisiana, Gaines's birthplace. His early novel, *The Autobiography of Miss Jane Pittman* (1971), was a major literary (and, later, television) event, as its 108-year-old narrator interweaves her personal history with that of the United States, allowing her to witness and comment on American history from nineteenth century slavery to the Civil Rights movement. Other significant novels would follow, including *In My Father's House* (1978); *A Gathering of Old Men* (1983), which was also made into a television movie; and *A Lesson Before Dying* (1993).

Forrest has staked a claim as the most important regional novelist of the North, as his four historical novels are all set in Forrest's native home, "Forest County"—that is, Cook County, Illinois. Focusing on the life and development of one central character, Nathaniel Turner Witherspoon, *There Is a Tree More Ancient than Eden* (1973), *The Bloodworth Orphans* (1977), *Two Wings to Veil My Face* (1983), and *Divine Days* (1992) trace the interrelated histories of two families by way of collage as Forrest draws on traditional oral storytelling, dream sequences, and mythological allusions to dramatize the intrinsic uncertainties of knowledge.

Forrest's redeployment of the serial novel—interrelated novels that follow a central theme, character, or family (for example, the Snopeses and Compsons in William Faulkner's fiction)—was mimicked by a number of other novelists, including Albert Murray. Unlike Faulkner, who used the serial novel to trace the disintegration of southern gentility, African American novelists such as Forrest and Murray used its epic possibilities to depict male heroism. Thus, Murray's trilogy of novels—*Train Whistle Guitar* (1974), *The Spyglass Tree* (1991), and *The Seven League Boots* (1995)—celebrate the spirit of adventure by linking the travels of an African American musician to those of the Greek hero Odysseus.

The serial novel has even been used by avant-garde writers such as the poet and novelist Nathaniel Mackey. His ongoing series of novels, From a Broken Bottle Traces of Perfume Still Emanate, has manifested itself in two epistolary novels: *Bedouin Hornbook* (1986) and *Djbot Baghostus's Run* (1993). Focusing on an ensemble of experimental jazz musicians, Mackey plays with polar oppositions usually taken for granted, especially those that supposedly define cultural borders, gender differences, racial and class biases, and natural and supernatural events.

The traditional novel, however, has not lost its viability among African American male writers. Yoking together the sophistication of northern urbanity and the penetrating eccentricity of southern folklore, David Bradley published *The Chaneysville Incident* (1981), a tour de force of historical guilt, murder, and atonement very much in the tradition of Dante's *La divina commedia* (c. 1320; *The Divine Comedy*, 1802).

Myth plays a fundamental role in the fiction of Charles Johnson. Like the early Wideman, Johnson was and remains essentially a philosophical writer. Johnson's first novel, *Faith and the Good Thing* (1974), is a good but unremarkable effort, though it already intimates the philosophical and theological concerns that would become more central to his next novel. *Oxherding Tale* (1982) could not be more different from the first book. Written under the influence of Zen Buddhism, *Oxherding Tale* revisits the slave narrative from an Asian philosophical perspective. Though not as pronounced in subsequent works such as the short-story collection *The Sorcerer's Apprentice* (1986) and the award-winning novel *Middle Passage* (1990), Johnson's Buddhist perspective tempers all his writings, both fiction and nonfiction. Oddly enough, Johnson's use of myth and philosophy has more in common with the experimental work of Mackey than it does with the mainstream novels ofToni Morrison, whose unique blend of myth, philosophy, folklore, and political outrage is unique, not only among African American women writers but also among all African American novelists.

AFRICAN AMERICAN WOMEN

Paule Marshall, the literary predecessor of the better known Morrison and Alice Walker, has labored in relative obscurity, perhaps, in part, because of her ethnicity. Born in New York City to Caribbean parents, Marshall draws on myriad cultural influences. Independent girls and women dominate her fiction, and when they are not strong, Marshall's narratives lead them back to healing sources, which are invariably African (as opposed to American) or pan-African in nature. Her novels—including *Brown Girl, Brownstones* (1959), *The Chosen Place, the Timeless People* (1969), *Praisesong for the Widow* (1983), and *Daughters* (1991)—counterpose, to varying degrees, American materialism and individualism to African American, Caribbean, and African spiritual ideals; these themes are also present in the writing of Marshall's literary descendant, Jamaica Kincaid.

Still, Morrison, who was awarded the Nobel Prize in Literature in 1993, was the most important African American novelist between the 1970's and 1990's. She has plumbed the depths of African American history with much insight, eloquence, and passion. Along with Walker, she takes seriously the feminist aphorism that the personal is political and redefines the relationship between African American women and their culture.

Like Walker, Gloria Naylor, Gayl Jones, and Toni Cade Bambara, Morrison focuses on the relationships between African American women and white women, African American women and African American men, and African American women and white America in general from a gendered and politically engaged perspective. Her novels—including *The Bluest Eye* (1970), *Sula* (1973), *Song of Solomon* (1977), *Tar Baby* (1981), *Beloved* (1987), *Jazz* (1992), *Paradise* (1998), *Love* (2003), and *A Mercy* (2008)—range across the landscape of African American culture. For example, while most of her novels—*Song of Solomon* is an important exception—feature women as central protagonists, none of the novels is determinedly feminist.

Morrison's work is primarily concerned with class and caste distinctions and divisions within African American culture; while slavery and racism, along with sexism, frame all the novels, Morrison's work cannot be deemed protest fiction because it is not addressed primarily to either male or white readers. Nevertheless, it certainly can be said that the novels have become increasingly political insofar as slavery, sexism, and racism loom larger in each succeeding novel. Although this process has been gradual, many critics, both detractors and proponents, cite *Beloved*, Morrison's best-known work and most controversial novel, as her representative work. The novel won a Pulitzer Prize in fiction in 1988.

Beloved, like *Jazz*, is based on a true story. It centers on Sethe, a former slave and a mother who attempts to escape from the South but pays a tremendous personal price. Trapped by slave hunters, she tries to kill both of her baby daughters rather than see them sold to slavery, succeeding only with the youngest, unnamed daughter. Years later, free in Ohio but ostracized from the African American community because of the murder, Sethe and Denver, her surviving daughter, are visited by the ghost of Sethe's dead daughter, Beloved, as well as Paul D., Sethe's lover, who wants to start a new life with her. Thus, the novel centers on the tug-of-war Sethe endures as she is alternately pulled back by the past (Beloved's claim of birthright) and toward the future (Paul D.'s claim on her as his wife).

The controversy over the novel centered on the question of the murder of Beloved. Was it indeed better to kill oneself or one's children than submit to the horrors of slavery? Or was it better to live, knowing that those who survived the ordeal would pass their indomitable genes and traditions on to a hoped-for, but unforeseeable, future of freedom? Morrison herself never directly addressed the issue, and readers are not helped by the ambivalence of the novel's last pages, which assert that the "story" was one "to pass on" and "not pass on." This ambivalence, a feature of all Morrison's novels, tempers the heightened political profiles of the stories. None of Morrison's contemporaries has achieved this precarious balance between political outrage and human complexity.

Walker's first novel, *The Third Life of Grange Copeland* (1970), appeared in the same year as Morrison's *The Bluest Eye*. *The Third Life of Grange Copeland* is a well-written, harrowing account of women who are not only physically and psychologically abused but also driven to madness by men. To this extent, Walker's writing is much more explicitly feminist than that of Morrison. However, *The Third Life of Grange Copeland* is also concerned with racism and class bias, as well as their relationship to violence against women.

Walker is best known, however, for her second novel, the controversial *The Color Purple* (1982), which won a Pulitzer Prize in fiction (1983) and the National Book Award (1983). An epistolary novel also made into a successful, award-winning film, *The Color Purple* explores the gradual sexual and feminist awakening of a young teenager, Celie, who has been abused by both her family and her husband, whom she calls Mister. Although she writes letters addressed to God, Celie is actually saved by Mister's mistress, Shug. The narrative of the novel implies that Shug's lesbian relationship with Celie is sparked, in part, by the oppression both undergo from Mister. This implication understandably angered feminist critics, who argued that Celie and Shug's relationship appeared to be simply a counter to Mister's misogyny and sexism instead of a willing relationship of attraction and desire. At the same time, the portrait of a misogynist and abusive Mister angered writers such as Ishmael Reed and Amiri Baraka, who believed that Walker and other African American feminists were unwittingly perpetuating the traditional demonization of African American men's sexuality. Largely unheard in the debate, however, was Walker's attempt to remind her critics that Celie is complicit in her own abuse and oppression and that Mister is transformed by the novel's end into a humane father and friend to Celie.

Walker sold the screen rights of the novel to director Steven Spielberg, whose 1985 film essentially deleted the sexual politics and romanticized the South, dismaying supporters and critics of the book. Although Walker continued to produce readable and successful novels, such as *The Temple of My Familiar* (1989) and *Possessing the Secret of Joy* (1992), she was made a marginal literary and cultural figure for focusing much of her work on black women's lesbian sexuality, a fate not unlike that suffered by James Baldwin (who was gay) for writing about gay men, and by lesbian poet and writer Audre Lorde, among many others.

Other black women writers, including Toni Cade Bambara, followed the lead of Morrison and Walker. Bambara, who died in 1995, was a brilliant short-story writer and a promising novelist. Her 1980 novel *The Salt Eaters* showcased complex narrative textures and jazz influences similar to those in Reed's early novels.

Gloria Naylor's first novel, *The Women of Brewster Place: A Novel in Seven Stories* (1982), was a major success that was made into an even more successful film for television. However, it was published in the same year as *The Color Purple* and, similarly, it suffered critically because of its depiction of black lesbian sexuality and black men's misogyny. Naylor rewrote and updated Baraka's *The System of Dante's Hell* (1965) with her second novel, *Linden Hills* (1985), revived the novel of manners in the vein of Jessie Redmon Fauset in *Mama Day* (1988), and, in *Bailey's Café* (1992), echoed the improvisational experiments of Morrison's *Jazz.*

Gayl Jones, author of *Corregidora* (1975) and *Eva's Man* (1976), among other novels, is, in many ways, the most interesting of the "new" African American writers. Her interest in the abnormalities of psychological profiles and their link to linguistic modes suggests an intelligence only partially realized in her first two novels. Jones, however, suffered a series of personal and professional traumas, and it was more than two decades before she published her next novel, *The Healing* (1998). This novel, along with her fourth, *Mosquito* (1999), suggests a return to creative and psychological health for Jones, and to the continuing development of African American fiction.

Tyrone Williams
Updated by David Peck

BIBLIOGRAPHY

Beaulieu, Elizabeth Ann. *Black Women Writers and the American Neo-Slave Narrative: Femininity Unfettered.* Westport, Conn.: Greenwood Press, 1999. Beaulieu discusses the efforts of African American women writers to redefine the slave narrative in the twentieth century. Among the novels discussed is Toni Morrison's *Beloved.*

Bell, Bernard W. *The Contemporary African American Novel: Its Folk Roots and Modern Literary Branches.* Amherst: University of Massachusetts Press, 2004. Broad, expansive history of African American literature. Focuses on distinctive elements and outlines the role of political and social influences in changing the focus of African American novels over time.

Braxton, Joanne M., and Andree Nicola McLaughlin. *Wild Women in the Whirlwind: Afra-American Culture and the Contemporary Literary Renaissance.* New Brunswick, N.J.: Rutgers University Press, 1990. Excellent anthology of critical writings on African American women writers of several generations. The range of writers covered is impressive, and the language is free of jargon.

Butler, Robert. *Contemporary African American Fiction: The Open Journey.* Madison, Wis.: Fairleigh Dickinson University Press, 1998. Butler's book, as the subtitle suggests, covers a wide range of subject matter, from a study of the picaresque in the fiction of Zora Neale Hurston and Richard Wright to a discussion of Octavia E. Butler's vision of the twenty-first century.

Callahan, John F. *In the African-American Grain: Call-and-Response in Twentieth-Century Black Fiction.* Middletown, Conn.: Wesleyan University Press, 1988. Callahan examines the way novelists and short-story writers from Charles Waddell Chesnutt to Alice Walker have insisted on the importance of call-and-response in the creation of a personal identity that remains bound to larger ideals of African American culture.

Dickson-Carr, Darryl. *The Columbia Guide to Contemporary African American Fiction.* New York: Columbia University Press, 2005. Valuable reference work on the growth of the African American novel since 1970.

Gates, Henry Louis, Jr. *The Signifying Monkey: A Theory of African-American Literary Criticism.* New York: Oxford University Press, 1988. Ambitious, concise text that argues for the importance of the trickster figure in African American literature and its link to the problem of literacy and identity. For advanced readers.

Graham, Maryemma, ed. *Cambridge Companion to the African American Novel.* New York: Cambridge University Press, 2004. Scholarly essays examining "The Long Journey: The African American Novel and History," "Search for a Form: The New American Novel," and "African American Voices: From Margin to Center." Covers topics such as the Harlem Renaissance and the blues novel, as well as writers Richard Wright, Toni Morrison, John Edgar Wideman, and many others.

Joyce, Ann. *Warriors, Conjurers, and Priests: Defining African-Centered Literary Criticism.* Chicago: Third World Press, 1994. Joyce examines the work of neglected African American writers such as Ann Petry and Sonia Sanchez while taking on antifeminist critics such as Ishmael Reed. Joyce also provides the first tentative assessments of emerging writers such as Terry McMillan and E. Ethelbert Miller.

Kostelanetz, Richard. *Politics in the African-American Novel: James Weldon Johnson, W. E. B. Du Bois, Richard Wright, and Ralph Ellison.* New York: Greenwood Press, 1991. This investigation of the development of the African American novel charts the movement from the protest fiction of Johnson and Du Bois to the more complex and thus "better" work of Wright and Ellison.

Schwarz, A. B. Christa. *Gay Voices of the Harlem Renaissance.* Bloomington: Indiana University Press, 2003. Schwarz examines the work of four leading writers from the Harlem Renaissance—Countée Cullen, Langston Hughes, Claude McKay, and Richard Bruce Nugent—and their sexually nonconformist, or gay, literary voices.

JAMES BALDWIN

Born: New York, New York; August 2, 1924
Died: St. Paul de Vence, France; December 1, 1987
Also known as: James Arthur Baldwin

PRINCIPAL LONG FICTION

Go Tell It on the Mountain, 1953
Giovanni's Room, 1956
Another Country, 1962
Tell Me How Long the Train's Been Gone, 1968
If Beale Street Could Talk, 1974
Just Above My Head, 1979

OTHER LITERARY FORMS

Before he published his first novel, James Baldwin had established a reputation as a talented essayist and reviewer. Many of his early pieces, later collected in *Notes of a Native Son* (1955) and *Nobody Knows My Name: More Notes of a Native Son* (1961), have become classics; his essays on Richard Wright, especially "Everybody's Protest Novel" (1949) and "Many Thousands Gone" (1951), occupy a central position in the development of "universalist" African American thought during the 1950's. Culminating in *The Fire Next Time* (1963), an extended meditation on the relationship of race, religion, and the individual experience in America, Baldwin's early prose demands a reexamination and redefinition of received social and cultural premises. His collections of essays *No Name in the Street* (1971) and *The Devil Finds Work* (1976) reflected a more militant stance and were received less favorably than Baldwin's universalist statements. *The Evidence of Things Not Seen* (1985) is a book-length essay on the case known as the Atlanta child murders, and *The Price of the Ticket* (1985) includes all of Baldwin's essay collections as well as a number of previously uncollected pieces. Less formal and intricate, though in some cases more explicit, reflections of Baldwin's beliefs can be found in *A Rap on Race* (1971), an extended discussion between Baldwin and anthropologist Margaret Mead, and *A Dialogue* (1975), a conversation with poet Nikki Giovanni.

Baldwin also wrote children's fiction (*Little Man, Little Man*, 1975), the text for a photographic essay (*Nothing Personal*, 1964, with Richard Avedon), an unfilmed scenario (*One Day, When I Was Lost: A Scenario Based on "The Autobiography of Malcolm X,"* 1972), dramas, and short stories. Most critics prefer Baldwin's first play, *The Amen Corner* (pr. 1954), to his *Blues for Mister Charlie* (pr. 1964) despite the latter's four-month Broadway run. Although he published little short fiction after the collection *Going to Meet the Man* (1965), Baldwin was an acknowledged master of the novella form. "Sonny's Blues" (1957), the story of the relationship of a jazz musician to his "respect-

James Baldwin
(Library of Congress)

able" narrator-brother, anticipates many of the themes of Baldwin's later novels and is widely recognized as one of the great American novellas.

Achievements

James Baldwin's role as a major spokesman on race guarantees his place in American cultural history. Although not undeserved, this reputation more frequently obscures than clarifies the nature of his literary achievement, which involves his relationship to African American culture, existential philosophy, and the moral tradition of the world novel. To be sure, Baldwin's progression from an individualistic, universalist stance through active involvement with the integrationist Civil Rights movement to an increasing sympathy with militant pan-Africanist thought parallels the general development of African American thought between the early 1950's and the mid-1970's. Indeed, Baldwin's novels frequently mirror both the author's personal philosophy and its social context. Some, most notably *Another Country*, attained a high degree of public visibility when published, leading to a widely accepted vision of Baldwin as a topical writer. Consideration of Baldwin primarily as a racial spokesman, however, imposes a stereotype that distorts many of his most penetrating insights and underestimates his status as a literary craftsman.

More accurate, although ultimately as limited, is the view of Baldwin primarily as an exemplar of the African American presence in the "mainstream" of the American tradition. Grouped with Ralph Ellison as a major "post-Wright" black novelist, Baldwin represents, in this view, the generation that rejected "protest literature" in favor of "universal" themes. Strangely at odds with the view of Baldwin as racial spokesman, this view emphasizes the craftsmanship of Baldwin's early novels and his treatment of "mainstream" themes such as religious hypocrisy, father-son tensions, and sexual identity. Ironically, many younger African American novelists accept this general view of Baldwin's accomplishment, viewing his mastery of Jamesian techniques and his involvement with continental literary culture as an indication of alienation from his racial identity. Recasting political activist Eldridge Cleaver's political attack on Baldwin in aesthetic terms, the African American writer Ishmael Reed dismisses Baldwin as a great "white" novelist. A grain of truth lies in Reed's assertion; Baldwin rarely created new forms. Rather, he infused a variety of Euro-American forms, derived from Wright and William Faulkner as well as from Henry James, with the rhythms and imagery of the African American oral tradition.

Like the folk preacher whose voice he frequently assumed in secular contexts, Baldwin combined moral insight with an uncompromising sense of the concrete realities of his community, whether defined in terms of family, lovers, race, or nation. This indicates the deepest level of Baldwin's literary achievement; whatever his immediate political focus or fictional form, he possessed an insight into moral psychology shared by only a handful of novelists. Inasmuch as the specific circumstances of this psychology involve American racial relations, this insight aligns Baldwin with Wright, Faulkner, Mark Twain, and Harriet Beecher Stowe. Inasmuch as Baldwin's insight involves the symbolic alienation of the individual, it places him with American romantics such as Nathaniel Hawthorne and European existentialists such as Albert Camus. Since his insight recognizes the complex pressure exerted by social mechanisms on individual consciousness, it reveals affinities with James Joyce, George Eliot, and Ellison. As a writer who combined elements of all of these traditions with the voice of the anonymous African American preacher, Baldwin cannot be reduced to accommodate the terms of any one of them. Refusing to lie about the reality of pain, he provided realistic images of the moral life possible in the inhospitable world that encompasses the streets of Harlem and the submerged recesses of the mind.

BIOGRAPHY

James Arthur Baldwin once dismissed his childhood as "the usual bleak fantasy." Nevertheless, the major concerns of his fiction consistently reflect the social context of his family life in Harlem during the Depression. The dominant figure of Baldwin's childhood was clearly that of his stepfather, David Baldwin, who worked as a manual laborer and preached in a storefront church. Clearly the model for Gabriel Grimes in *Go Tell It on the Mountain*, David Baldwin had moved from New Orleans to New York City, where he married Baldwin's mother, Emma Berdis. The oldest of what was to be a group of nine children in the household, James assumed a great deal of the responsibility for the care of his half brothers and half sisters. Insulated somewhat from the brutality of Harlem street life by his domestic duties, Baldwin, as he describes in *The Fire Next Time*, sought refuge in the church. Undergoing a conversion experience, similar to that of John in *Go Tell It on the Mountain*, at age fourteen in 1938, Baldwin preached as a youth minister for the next several years. At the same time, he began to read, immersing himself in works such as Harriet Beecher Stowe's *Uncle Tom's Cabin* (1852) and the novels of Charles Dickens. Both at his Harlem junior high school, where the African American poet Countée Cullen was one of his teachers, and at his predominantly white Bronx high school, Baldwin contributed to student literary publications. The combination of family tension, economic hardship, and religious vocation provides the focus of much of Baldwin's greatest writing, most notably *Go Tell It on the Mountain*, *The Fire Next Time*, and *Just Above My Head*.

If Baldwin's experience during the 1930's provided his material, his life from 1942 to 1948 shaped his characteristic approach to that material. After he graduated from high school in 1942, Baldwin worked for a year as a manual laborer in New Jersey, an experience that increased both his understanding of his stepfather and his insight into American economic and racial systems. Moving to Greenwich Village in 1943, Baldwin worked during the day and wrote at night for the next five years; his first national reviews and essays appeared in 1946. The major event of the Village years, however, was Baldwin's meeting with Richard Wright in the winter of 1944-1945. Wright's interest helped Baldwin secure first a Eugene F. Saxton Memorial Award and then a Rosenwald Fellowship, enabling him to move to Paris in 1948.

After his arrival in France, Baldwin experienced more of the poverty that had shaped his childhood. Simultaneously, he developed a larger perspective on the psychocultural context conditioning his experience, feeling at once a greater sense of freedom and a larger sense of the global structure of racism, particularly as reflected in the French treatment of North Africans. In addition, he formed many of the personal and literary friendships that contributed to his later public prominence. Baldwin's well-publicized literary feud with Wright, who viewed the younger writer's criticism of Wright's novel *Native Son* (1940) as a form of personal betrayal, helped establish Baldwin as a major presence in African American letters. Although Baldwin's first novel, *Go Tell It on the Mountain*, was well received critically, it was not so financially successful that he could devote all of his time to creative writing. As a result, Baldwin continued to travel widely, frequently on journalistic assignments, while writing *Giovanni's Room*, which is set in France and involves no black characters.

Returning to the United States as a journalist covering the Civil Rights movement, Baldwin made his first trip to the American South in 1957. The essays and reports describing that physical and psychological journey propelled Baldwin to the position of public prominence that he maintained for more than a decade. During the height of the movement, Baldwin lectured widely and was present at major events such as the March on Washington and the voter registration drive in Selma, Alabama. In addition, he met with most of the major African American activists of the period, including Martin Luther King, Jr., Elijah Muhammad, James Meredith, and Medgar Evers. Attorney General Robert F. Kennedy asked Baldwin to bring together the most influential voices in the black community; even though the resulting meeting accomplished little, the request testifies to Baldwin's image as a focal point of African American opinion.

In addition to this political activity, Baldwin formed personal and literary relationships—frequently tempestuous ones—with numerous white writers, including William Styron and Norman Mailer. A surge in literary popularity, reflected in the presence of *Another Country* and *The Fire Next Time* on best-seller lists throughout most of 1962 and 1963, accompanied Baldwin's political success and freed him from financial insecurity for the first time. He traveled extensively throughout the decade, and his visits to Puerto Rico and Africa were to have a major influence on his subsequent political thought.

Partly because of Baldwin's involvement with prominent whites and partly because of the sympathy for gays evinced in his writing, several black militants, most notably Eldridge Cleaver, attacked Baldwin's position as "black spokesman" beginning in the late 1960's. As a result, nationalist spokesmen such as Amiri Baraka and Bobby Seale gradually eclipsed Baldwin in the public literary and political spotlights. Nevertheless, Baldwin, himself sympathetic to many of the militant positions, continued his involvement with public issues, such as the fate of the group of North Carolina prisoners known as the Wilmington 10, which he addressed in an open letter to Jimmy Carter shortly after Carter's election to the U.S. presidency. In his later years, though he returned periodically to the South, Baldwin lived for much of the time in France and Turkey. He died in St. Paul de Vence, France, on November 30, 1987.

ANALYSIS

Uncompromising in his demand for personal and social integrity, James Baldwin from the beginning of his career charged the individual with full responsibility for his or her moral identity. Both in his early individualistic novels and in his later political fiction, he insisted on the inadequacy of received definitions as the basis for self-knowledge or social action. Echoing the existentialist principle "existence precedes essence," he intimated the underlying consistency of his vision in the introductory essay in *Notes of a Native Son*: "I think all theories are suspect, that the finest principles may have to be modified, or may even be pulverized by the demands of life, and that one must find, therefore, one's own moral center and move through the world hoping that this center will guide one aright."

This insistence on the moral center and movement in the world cautions against associating Baldwin with the atheistic or solipsistic currents of existential thought. Never denying the possibility of transcendent moral power—which he frequently imaged as the power of love—he simply insisted that human conceptions must remain flexible enough to allow for the honest perception of experience. Fully recognizing the reality of existential pain and despair, Baldwin invoked honesty and self-acceptance as the necessary supports for the love capable of generating individual communication and at least the groundwork for political action.

Baldwin's social vision, reflecting his experience in a racist culture, acknowledges the forces militating against self-knowledge and moral responsibility. Each of his novels portrays a series of evasive and simplifying definitions built into religious, economic, and educational institutions. These definitions, which emphasize the separation of self and other, control the immediate contexts of individual experience. As a result, they frequently seem to constitute "human nature," to embody the inevitable limits of experience. While sympathizing with the difficulty of separating the self from context without simultaneously denying experience, Baldwin insists that acquiescing to the definitions inevitably results in self-hatred and social immorality. The individual incapable of accepting his or her existential complexity flees to the illusion of certainty provided by the institutions that assume responsibility for directing moral decisions. This cycle of institutional pressure encouraging existential evasion ensuring further institutional corruption recurs in each of Baldwin's novels. On both personal and social levels, the drive to deny the reality of the other—racial, sexual, or economic—generates nothing save destruction. Derived from the streets of Harlem rather than from Scripture, Baldwin's response echoes Christ's admonition to "love thy neighbor as thyself." The derivation is vital; in Baldwin's novels, those who extract the message from the Bible rather than from their lives frequently aggravate the pain that makes evading reality seem attractive.

The immediate focus of Baldwin's attention gradually shifted from consciousness to context, creating the illusion of a change in his basic concerns. While he always worked in the realistic tradition of the novel, his choice of specific forms paralleled this shift in thematic focus, though again his later work indicates an underlying unity in his fiction. His first novel, *Go Tell It on the Mountain*, employs a tightly focused Jamesian form to explore the developing awareness of the adolescent protagonist John Grimes, who is not yet aware of the evasive definitions conditioning his experience. After a second Jamesian novel, *Giovanni's Room*, Baldwin adapted the relatively unstructured Dreiserian mode in *Another Country* and *Tell Me How Long the Train's Been Gone*. Characters such as Rufus Scott and Vivaldo Moore in *Another Country* continue to struggle for individual awareness, but Baldwin's new narrative stance emphasizes the impact of the limiting definitions on a wide range of particular social circumstances. Attempting to balance the presentation of consciousness and context, Baldwin's last two novels, *If Beale Street Could Talk* and *Just Above My Head*, synthesize the earlier technical approaches. Returning to the immediate focus on the individual consciousness in these first-person narratives, Baldwin creates protagonists capable of articulating their own social perceptions. Consciousness and context merge as Baldwin's narrators share their insights and, more important, their processes with their fellow sufferers.

These insights implicitly endorse William Blake's vision of morality as a movement from innocence through experience to a higher innocence. Beginning with an unaware innocence, individuals inevitably enter the deadening and murderous world of experience, the world of the limiting definitions. Those who attempt to deny the world and remain children perish alongside those who cynically submit to the cruelty of the context for imagined personal benefit. Only those who plunge into experience, recognize its cruelty, and resolve to forge an aware innocence can hope to survive morally. Specifically, Baldwin urges families to pass on a sense of the higher innocence to their children by refusing to simplify the truth of experience. This painful honesty makes possible the commitment to love despite the inevitability of pain and isolation. It provides the only hope, however desperate, for individual or social rejuvenation.

To a large extent, Baldwin's career developed in accord with the Blakean pattern. John Grimes begins his passage from innocence to experience in *Go Tell It on the Mountain*; Rufus Scott and Vivaldo Moore, among others, struggle to survive experience in *Another Country*, which intimates the need for the higher innocence. Baldwin's last two novels portray the entire process, focusing on the attempt first to find and then to pass on the higher innocence. *Just Above My Head*, with its middle-aged narrator and his teenage children, clearly represents a more highly developed and realistic stage of the vision than *If Beale Street Could Talk*, with its teenage-mother narrator and her newborn infant.

GO TELL IT ON THE MOUNTAIN

Go Tell It on the Mountain centers on the religious conversion and family relationships of John Grimes, whose experience parallels that of Baldwin during his youth. Although he believes himself to be the natural son of Gabriel Grimes, a preacher who, like Baldwin's stepfather, moved to New York after growing up in the South, John is actually the son of Gabriel's wife, Elizabeth, and her lover, Richard, who committed suicide prior to John's birth. Growing up under the influence of his hypocritical and tyrannical stepfather, John alternately attempts to please and transcend him. Gabriel expends most of his emotional energy on his openly rebellious son Roy, whose immersion in the violent life of the Harlem streets contrasts sharply with John's involvement with the "Temple of the Fire Baptized," the storefront church where his conversion takes place.

To the extent that Baldwin organizes *Go Tell It on the Mountain* around John's attempt to come to terms with these pressures, the novel appears to have a highly individualistic focus. The overall structure of the novel, however, dictates that John's experience be viewed in a larger context. Of the three major sections of *Go Tell It on the Mountain*, the first, "The Seventh Day," and the third, "The Threshing Floor," focus directly on John. The long middle section, "The Prayers of the Saints," a Faulknerian exploration of history, traces the origins of John's struggle to the experience of his elders, devoting individual chapters to Elizabeth, Gabriel, and Gabriel's sister Florence. Together the prayers portray the Great Migration of African Americans from South to North, from rural to urban settings. Far from bringing true freedom, the movement results in a new indirect type of oppression. As Elizabeth recognizes,

> There was not, after all, a great difference between the world of the North and that of the South which she had fled; there was only this difference: the North promised more. And this similarity: what it promised it did not give, and what it gave, at length and grudgingly with one hand, it took back with the other.

Even in his most individualistic phase, Baldwin is aware of the power of institutional pressures. The origins of John's particular struggle against the limiting definitions go back to their impact on both Elizabeth and Gabriel.

Elizabeth's relationship with John's true father, at least in its early stages, appears to offer hope for at least a limited freedom from external definition. Highly intelligent and self-aware, Richard struggles to transcend the limitations imposed on black aspiration through a rigorous program of self-education, which he shares with Elizabeth. Despite his intelligence and determination, however, Richard maintains a naïve innocence concerning the possibility of self-definition in a society based on racist assumptions. Only when arrested on suspicion of a robbery he had nothing to do with does he recognize that his context defines him as simply another "nigger." Unable to reconcile this imposed definition with his drive for social transcendence, he despairs and commits suicide. This act, in turn, destroys Elizabeth's chance for obtaining a greater degree of freedom. She is not, however, simply a victim. Fearing that Richard will be unable to cope with the responsibility of a family, she fails to tell him of her pregnancy. Far from protecting him, this evasion contributes to his destruction by allowing Richard to view his situation as purely personal. Elizabeth's own choice, conditioned by the social refusal to confront reality, combines with the racist legal system to circumscribe her possibilities. Forced to care for her infant son, she marries Gabriel, thus establishing the basic terms for John's subsequent struggle.

Seen in relation to John in "The Seventh Day," Gabriel appears to be one of the most despicable hypocrites in American literature. Seen in relation to his own history in "The Prayers of the Saints," however, he appears victimized by the institutional context of his youth. In turn, he victimizes his family by attempting to force them into narrowly defined roles. The roots of Gabriel's character lie in the "temple-street" dichotomy of his southern childhood. Encouraged by his religious mother to deny his sensuality, Gabriel undergoes a conversion experience and immerses himself in the role of preacher. As a result, he enters into a loveless, asexual marriage with his mother's friend Deborah, herself a victim of the racist psychology—enforced by blacks and whites—that condemns *her* after she has been brutally raped by a group of whites.

Eventually, Gabriel's repressed street self breaks out and he fathers a son by the sensual Esther. Again attempting to deny his sensuality, Gabriel refuses to acknowledge this son, Royal. Like John's half brother Roy, the first Royal immerses himself in the street life that Gabriel denies; he dies in a Chicago barroom brawl. Gabriel fears that Roy will share Royal's fate, but his attempt to crush his second son's street self merely strengthens the resulting rebellion. Faced with the guilt of Royal's death and the sense of impending doom concerning Roy, Gabriel retreats into a solipsism that makes a mockery of his Christian vocation. Far from providing a context for moral responsibility, the church—both in the South and in the North—simply replaces the original innocence of religious fervor with a cynical vision of religion as a source of the power needed to destroy the innocence of others.

Against this backdrop, John's conversion raises a basic question that will recur in slightly different circumstances in each of Baldwin's novels: Can an individual hope to break the cycle of evasion that has shaped his or her personal and social context? In John's case, the problem takes on added dimensions, since he remains ignorant of many of the events shaping his life, including those involving his own birth. By framing the prayers with John's conversion, Baldwin stresses the connection between past and present, but the connection can be perceived as either oppressive or liberating. The complex irony of "The Threshing Floor" section allows informed readings of John's conversion as either a surrender to evasion or a movement toward existential responsibility. Focusing primarily on John's internal experience as he lies transfixed on the church floor, "The Threshing Floor" revolves around a dialogue between an "ironic voice" that challenges John to return to the street and the part of John that seeks traditional salvation. Throughout John's vision, the narrative voice shifts point of view in accord with John's developing perception. As John accepts the perceptions implied by his vision, the ironic voice shifts its attention to yet deeper levels of ambiguity. To the extent that John resolves these ambiguities by embracing the Temple, his experience seems to increase the risk that he will follow Gabriel's destructive example.

Several image patterns, however, indicate that John may be moving nearer to a recognition of his actual complexity. Chief among these are those involving the curse of Ham, the rejection of the father, and the acceptance of apparent opposites. From the beginning of the vision, the ironic voice ridicules John for accepting the curse of Ham, which condemns him both as son and as "nigger." Manipulating John's sense of guilt for having indulged his street self by masturbating, the ironic voice insists that John's very existence "proves" Gabriel's own sexual weakness. If Gabriel condemns John, he condemns himself in the process. As a result, John comes to view himself as the "devil's son" and repudiates his subservience before his "father." Without this essentially negative, and ultimately socially derived, definition of himself, John finds himself in an existential void where "there was no speech or language, and there was no love."

Forced to reconstruct his identity, John progresses from this sense of isolation to a vision of the dispossessed with whom he shares his agony and his humanity. John's vision of the multitude whose collective voice merges with his own suggests suffering as the essential human experience, one obliterating both the safety and the isolation of imposed definitions. Significantly, this vision leads John to Jesus the Son rather than God the Father, marking an implicit rejection of Gabriel's Old Testament vengeance in favor of the New Testament commitment to an all-encompassing love. The son metamorphoses from symbol of limitation to symbol of liberation. Near the end of his vision, John explicitly rejects the separation of opposites—street and temple, white and black—encouraged by his social context: "The light and the darkness had kissed each other, and were married now, forever, in the life and the vision of John's soul." Returning to his immediate environment from the depths of his mind, John responds not to the call of Gabriel but to that of Elisha, a slightly older member of the congregation with whom he has previously engaged in a sexually suggestive wrestling match reminiscent of that in D. H. Lawrence's *Women in Love* (1920). John's salvation, then, may bring him closer to an acceptance of his own sensuality, to a definition of himself encompassing both temple and street. Baldwin ends the novel with the emergence of the newly "saved" John onto the streets of Harlem. His fate hinges on his ability to move ahead to the higher innocence suggested by his vision of the dispossessed rather than submit to the experiences that have destroyed and deformed the majority of the saints.

ANOTHER COUNTRY

Another Country, Baldwin's greatest popular success, analyzes the effects of deforming pressure and experience on a wide range of characters, black and white, male and female, homosexual and heterosexual. To accommodate these diverse consciousnesses, Baldwin employs the sprawling form usually associated with political rather than psychological fiction, emphasizing the diverse forms of innocence and experience in American society. The three major sections of *Another Country*—"Easy Rider," "Any Day Now," and "Toward Bethlehem"—progress generally from despair to renewed hope, but no single consciousness or plot line provides a frame similar to that of *Go Tell It on the Mountain*. Rather, the novel's structural coherence derives from the moral concerns present in each of the various plots.

Casting a Melvillean shadow over the novel is the black jazz musician Rufus Scott, who is destroyed by an agonizing affair with Leona, a white southerner recently arrived in New York at the time she meets him. Unable to forge the innocence necessary for love in a context that repudiates the relationship at every turn, Rufus destroys Leona psychologically. After a period of physical and psychological destitution, he kills himself by jumping off a bridge. His sister Ida, an aspiring singer, and his friend Vivaldo Moore, an aspiring white writer, meet during the last days of Rufus's life and fall in love as they console each other over his death. Struggling to overcome the racial and sexual definitions that destroyed Rufus, they seek a higher innocence capable of countering Ida's sense of the world as a "whorehouse." In contrast to Ida and Vivaldo's struggle, the relationship of white actor Eric Jones and his French lover Yves seems edenic. Although Baldwin portrays Eric's internal struggle for a firm sense of his sexual identity, Eric and Yves's shared innocence at times seems to exist almost entirely outside the context of the pressures that destroyed Rufus. The final major characters, Richard and Cass Silenski, represent the cost of the American Dream. After Richard "makes it" as a popular novelist, the couple's personal relationship decays, precipitating Cass's affair with Eric. Their tentative reunion after Richard discovers the affair makes it clear that material success provides no shortcut to moral responsibility.

Baldwin examines each character and relationship in the context of the institutional pressures discouraging individual responsibility. His portrait of Rufus, the major accomplishment of *Another Country*, testifies to a moral insight and a raw artistic power resembling that of Wright and Émile Zola. Forgoing the formal control and emotional restraint of his earlier novels, Baldwin opens *Another Country* with the image of Rufus as a man who "had fallen so low, that he scarcely had the energy to be angry." Both an exceptional case and a representative figure, Rufus embodies the seething anger and hopeless isolation that render Baldwin's United States a landscape of nightmare. Seeing his own situation as unbearable, Rufus meditates on the fate of a city tormented by an agony like his own: "He remembered to what excesses, into what traps and nightmares, his loneliness had driven him; and he wondered where such a violent emptiness might drive an entire city." Forcing readers to recognize the social implications of Rufus's situation, Baldwin emphasizes that his specific situation originates in his own moral failure with Leona. Where Gabriel Grimes remained insulated from his immorality by arrogance and pride, Rufus feels the full extent of his self-enforced damnation. Ironically and belatedly, his destitution clarifies his sense of the extent of his past acceptance of the social definitions that destroy him.

Wandering the streets of Manhattan, Rufus feels himself beyond human contact. Desperately in need of love, he believes his past actions render him unfit for even minimal compassion. His abuse of Leona, who as a white woman represents both the "other" and the source of the most obvious social definitions circumscribing his life as a black male, accounts for his original estrangement from family and friends, who find his viciousness uncharacteristic. All, including Rufus, fail to understand soon enough that his abuse of Leona represents both a rebellion against and an acceptance of the role dictated by racial and sexual definitions.

Separated from the psychological source of his art—jazz inevitably rejects the substructure of Euro-American definitions of reality—Rufus falls ever further into a paranoia that receives ample reinforcement from the racist context. Largely by his own choice, he withdraws almost entirely from his acquaintances, both black and white. Once on the street following Leona's breakdown, he begins to recognize not only his immediate but also his long-term acceptance of destructive definitions. Thinking back on a brief same-sex affair with Eric to which he submitted out of pity rather than love, Rufus regrets having treated his friend with contempt. Having rejected the "other" in Eric and Leona, Rufus realizes he has rejected a part of himself. He consigns himself to the ranks of the damned, casting himself beyond human love with his plunge off the bridge.

While not absolving Rufus of responsibility for his actions, Baldwin treats him with profound sympathy, in part because of his honesty and in part because of the enormous power of the social institutions that define him as the "other." Throughout *Another Country*, Baldwin emphasizes that white heterosexual males possess the power of definition, although their power destroys them as surely as it does their victims. Television producer Steve Ellis, a moral cripple embodying the basic values of the American economic system, nearly destroys Ida and Vivaldo's relationship by encouraging Ida to accept a cynical definition of herself as a sexual commodity. Vivaldo, too, participates in the cynicism when he visits the Harlem prostitutes, indirectly perpetuating the definitions that reduce black people to sexual objects and thus implicating himself in Rufus's death. In fact, every major character with the exception of Eric bears partial responsibility for Rufus's destruction, since each at times accepts the definitions generating the cycle of rejection and denial. The constituting irony, however, stems from the fact that only those most actively struggling for moral integrity recognize their culpability. Vivaldo, who attempts to reach out to Rufus earlier on the night of his suicide, feels more guilt than Richard, who simply dismisses Rufus as a common "nigger" after his mistreatment of Leona.

This unflinching portrayal of moral failure, especially on the part of well-meaning liberals, provides the thematic center of *Another Country*. Baldwin concludes the novel with the image of Yves's reunion with Eric, who is apparently on the verge of professional success with a starring role in a film of a Fyodor Dostoevski novel. This combination of personal and financial success seems more an assertion of naïve hope than a compelling part of the surrounding fictional world. The majority of the narrative lines imply the impossibility of simple dissociation from institutional pressure. Ultimately, the intensity of Rufus's pain and the intricacy of Ida and Vivaldo's struggle overshadow Eric and Yves's questionable innocence. As Ida tells Vivaldo, "Our being together doesn't change the world." The attempt to overcome the cynicism of this perception leads to a recognition that meaningful love demands total acceptance. Ida's later question "How can you say you loved Rufus when there was so much about him you didn't want to know?" could easily provide the epitaph for the entire society in *Another Country*.

JUST ABOVE MY HEAD

In *Just Above My Head*, Baldwin creates a narrator, Hall Montana, capable of articulating the psychological subtleties of *Go Tell It on the Mountain*, the social insights of *Another Country*, and the political anger of *Tell Me How Long the Train's Been Gone*. Like other observer-participants in American literature, such as Nick Carraway in F. Scott Fitzgerald's *The Great Gatsby* (1925) and Jack Burden in Robert Penn Warren's *All the King's*

Men (1946), Hall tells both his own story and that of a more publicly prominent figure, in this case his brother Arthur, a gospel singer who dies two years prior to the start of the novel.

Significantly, *Just Above My Head* also reconsiders Baldwin's own artistic history, echoing countless motifs from his earlier writings. Though not precisely a self-reflexive text, *Just Above My Head* takes on added richness when juxtaposed with Baldwin's treatment of religious concerns in *Go Tell It on the Mountain*, the homosexuality theme in *Giovanni's Room*, the relationship between brothers and the musical setting in "Sonny's Blues," racial politics in *Blues for Mister Charlie* and *Tell Me How Long the Train's Been Gone*, the Nation of Islam in *The Fire Next Time* and *No Name in the Street*, and, most important, the intermingled family love and world politics in *If Beale Street Could Talk*. Baldwin's reconsideration of his own history, which is at once private like Hall's and public like Arthur's, emphasizes the necessity of a continual reexamination of the nature of both self and context in order to reach the higher innocence.

Similarly, Hall's resolve to understand the social and existential meaning of Arthur's experience originates in his desire to answer honestly his children's questions concerning their uncle. Refusing to protect their original innocence—an attempt he knows would fail—Hall seeks both to free himself from the despair of experience and to discover a mature innocence he can pass on to the younger generation. Tracing the roots of Arthur's despair to pressures originating in numerous limiting definitions and failures of courage, Hall summarizes his, and Baldwin's, social insight:

> The attempt, more the necessity, to excavate a history, to find out the truth about oneself! is motivated by the need to have the power to force others to recognize your presence, your right to be here. The disputed passage will remain disputed so long as you do not have the authority of the right-of-way. . . . Power clears the passage, swiftly: but the paradox, here, is that power, rooted in history, is also, the mockery and the repudiation of history. The power to define the other seals one's definition of oneself.

Recognizing that the only hope for meaningful moral freedom lies in repudiating the power of definition, Hall concludes: "Our history is each other. That is our only guide. One thing is absolutely certain: one can repudiate, or despise, no one's history without repudiating and despising one's own."

Although Baldwin recognizes the extent to which the definitions and repudiations remain entrenched in institutional structures, his portrayal of Hall's courage and honesty offers at least some hope for moral integrity as a base for social action. If an individual such as Hall can counteract the pressures militating against personal responsibility, he or she may be able to exert a positive influence on relatively small social groups such as families and churches, which in turn may affect the larger social context. Nevertheless, Baldwin refuses to encourage simplistic optimism. Rather than focusing narrowly on Hall's individual process, he emphasizes the aspects of the context that render that success atypical.

Although Hall begins with his immediate context, his excavation involves the Korean War, the Civil Rights movement, the rise of Malcolm X, and the role of advertising in American culture. Hall's relationships with his family and close friends provide a Jamesian frame for the Dreiserian events of the novel, somewhat as John's conversion frames the historical "Prayers of the Saints" in *Go Tell It on the Mountain. Just Above My Head*, however, leaves no ambiguity concerning the individual's ability to free him- or herself from history. Only a conscious decision to accept the pain and guilt of the past promises any real hope for love, for the higher innocence. Similarly, Baldwin reiterates that, while the desire for safety is understandable, all safety is illusion. Pain inevitably returns, and, while the support of friends and lovers may help, only a self-image based on existential acceptance rather than repudiation makes survival possible.

Arthur's death, occupying a thematic and emotional position similar to the death of Rufus in *Another Country*, provides the point of departure for Hall's excavation. A gifted gospel singer as a teenager, Arthur rises to stardom as the "emperor of soul." Despite his success, however, he never frees himself from doubts concerning his own identity or feels secure with the experience of love. Even though his parents offer him a firm base of love and acceptance, Arthur feels a deep sense of emotional isolation even as a child, a sense reinforced by his observations of life in Harlem and, later, in the South. Though he accepts his own homosexuality with relatively little anxiety, his society refuses him the freedom necessary for the development of a truly satisfying emotional life. The edenic innocence of Eric and Yves in *Another Country* clearly fails to provide a sufficient response to the institutional context of *Just Above My Head*.

Arthur's childhood experiences provide clear warnings against the attempt to maintain innocence through simplistic self-definition. Julia Miller, like John in *Go Tell It on the Mountain*, undergoes a salvation experience and embarks on a career as a child evangelist. Encouraged by her parents, friends of the Montanas who rely on their daughter for economic support, she assumes a sanctimonious attitude, which she uses to manipulate her elders. Arthur's parents deplore the indulgence of Julia, unambiguously rejecting the idea that her religious vocation lifts her beyond the "naughty" street side of her personality. Ultimately, and in great pain, Julia confronts this truth. After her mother's death, she discovers that her father, Joel, views her primarily as an economic and sexual object. His desire to exploit her earning potential even when she says she has lost her vocation reflects his underlying contempt for the spirit. This contempt leads to an incestuous rape that destroys Julia's remaining innocence and drives her to a life as a prostitute in New Orleans. Eventually, Julia recovers from this brutalization, but her example provides a clear warning to Arthur against confusing his vocation as a gospel singer with a transcendence of human fallibility.

The experiences of the members of Arthur's first gospel group, the Trumpets of Zion, reveal how institutions infringe even on those not actively committed to simplifying definitions. At one extreme, the social definitions establish a context that accepts and encourages murder—symbolic and real—of the other. Peanut, a member of the Trumpets and later Arthur's companion on the road, vanishes into the Alabama night following a civil rights rally, presumably murdered by whites seeking to enforce the definition of blacks as "niggers." Equally devastating, although less direct, is the operation of the context on Red, another member of the Trumpets, who turns to drugs in an attempt to relieve the pain of the Harlem streets.

Even Hall finds himself an unwilling accomplice to the imposition of social definitions when he is drafted and sent to Korea. Powerless to alter the institutional structure, Hall recognizes, and tells Arthur, that the American military spreads not freedom but repudiation in the developing world. Hall's subsequent employment by an advertising agency involves him in another aspect of the same oppressive system. Viewed as an anomaly by his employers, as an atypical high-class "nigger," Hall nevertheless participates in the creation of images designed to simplify reality for economic gain, which will be used to strengthen the oppressive system. The juxtaposition of Julia's false innocence with the destructive experiences of Peanut, Red, and Hall protects Arthur against the urge to dismiss any aspect of his awareness. A large part of his power as a singer derives from his recognition of the reality of both street and temple, expressed in his ability to communicate sexual pain in gospel songs and spiritual aspiration in the blues.

Arthur, then, appears ideally prepared for the responsible exercise of existential freedom. His failure even to survive underscores the destructive power of the corrupt institutional context. The roots of Arthur's doom lie in his homosexual relationship with Crunch, the final member of the Trumpets. Highly desirable physically, Crunch feels locked into a definition of himself as a sexual object prior to his involvement with Arthur. In its early stages, Arthur and Crunch's love, like that of Yves and Eric in *Another Country*, seems an idyllic retreat, a spot of innocence in the chaos of experience. The retreat, however, proves temporary, in part because Crunch cannot free himself from the urge for self-simplification and in part because of the continuing presence of the outside world. Uneasy with his sexual identity, Crunch becomes involved with Julia when he discovers the extent of her father's abuse. Arthur recognizes that Crunch is not abandoning him by reacting to Julia's pain and accepts the relationship. Granted sufficient time for adjustment, Arthur and Crunch seem capable of confronting their experience and forging a higher innocence as the basis for a lasting love. The time does not exist, however. Crunch is drafted and sent to Korea. Separated from Arthur's reassurance and tormented by self-doubt, Crunch never fully accepts his sexuality. After his return to Harlem, he and Arthur gradually lose contact.

The repeated losses—of Peanut, Red, and Crunch—create a sense of isolation that Arthur never overcomes. The expectation of loss periodically overpowers his determination to communicate, the determination that makes him a great singer. Even during periods of real joy, with his French lover Guy in Paris or with Julia's brother Jimmy, who is both his pianist and his lover, Arthur suffers acute emotional pain. Attempting to survive by rededicating himself to communication, to his artistic excavation of history, Arthur drives himself past the limits of physical and psychological endurance. He dies in the basement bathroom of a London pub after a lovers' quarrel, clearly only temporary, with Jimmy. By concluding Arthur's life with an image of isolation, Baldwin emphasizes the power of limiting definitions to destroy even the most existentially courageous individual.

Arthur's death, however, marks not only a conclusion but also the beginning of Hall's quest for the higher innocence that he, along with his wife Ruth, Julia, and Jimmy, can pass on to the younger generation. This higher innocence involves both individual and social elements, ultimately demanding the mutual support of individuals willing to pursue excavation of their own histories. This support expresses itself in the call-and-response dynamic, a basic element of African American oral culture that Arthur employs in his interaction with audiences while singing. As Baldwin re-creates the traditional form, the interaction begins with the call of a leader who expresses his own emotional experience through the vehicle of a traditional song that provides a communal context for the emotion. If the members of the community recognize and share the experience evoked by the call, they respond with another traditional phrase that provides the sense of understanding and acceptance that enables the leader to go on. Implicitly, the process enables both individual and community to define themselves in opposition to dominant social forces. If the experience of isolation is shared, it is no longer the same type of isolation that brought Rufus to his death. In *Just Above My Head*, the call-and-response rests on a rigorous excavation requiring individual silence, courage, and honesty expressed through social presence, acceptance, and love. Expressed in the interactions between Arthur and his audiences, between Hall and his children, between Baldwin and his readers, this call-and-response provides a realistic image of the higher innocence possible in opposition to the murderous social definitions.

As in John's vision in *Go Tell It on the Mountain* and Rufus's self-examination in *Another Country*, the process begins in silence, which throughout Baldwin's novels offers the potential for either alienation or communication. The alienating silence coincides thematically with institutional noise—mechanical, social, political. The majority of Americans, Baldwin insists, prefer distracting and ultimately meaningless sounds to the silence that allows self-recognition. Only individuals sharing Arthur's willingness to remove himself from the noise can hope to hear their own voices and transform the silence into music. Every moment of true communication in *Just Above My Head* begins in a moment of silence that effectively rejects the clamor of imposed definitions. The courage needed for the acceptance of silence prepares the way for the honest excavation of history that must precede any meaningful social interaction. The excavation remains a burden, however, without that interaction. No purely individual effort can alter the overwhelming sense of isolation imposed by social definitions. The individual stage of the process merely heightens the need for acceptance, presence, and love. Arthur sounds the call amid the noise; he cannot provide the response. Perhaps, Baldwin indicates, no one, not even

Jimmy, can provide a response capable of soothing the feeling of isolation emanating from early experiences. Nevertheless, the attempt is vital. Julia recognizes both the necessity and the limitation of presence when she tells Hall of her relationship with Jimmy: "I don't know enough to change him, or to save him. But I know enough to be there. I *must* be there."

If presence—being there—is to provide even momentary relief, it must be accompanied by the honest acceptance underlying love. Refusing to limit his acceptance, Hall answers his son Tony's questions concerning Arthur's sexuality with complete honesty. Understanding fully that his acceptance of Arthur entails an acceptance of the similar complexity in himself and in Tony, Hall surrenders his voice to Jimmy's, imaginatively participating in a love that repudiates social definition, that rises up out of the silence beyond the noise. Implicitly, Hall offers both Tony and his daughter Odessa the assurance of presence, of acceptance, of love. They need not fear rejection if they have the courage to accept their full humanity. The assurance cannot guarantee freedom, or even survival. It can, and does, intimate the form of mature innocence in the world described by the composite voice of Baldwin, Jimmy, and Hall, a world that "doesn't have any morality. Look at the world. What the world calls morality is nothing but the dream of safety. That's how the world gets to be so fucking moral. The only way to know that you are safe is to see somebody else in danger—otherwise you can't be sure you're safe."

Against this vicious safety, a safety that necessitates limiting definitions imposed on others, Baldwin proposes a responsibility based on risk. Only by responding to the call sounding from Arthur, from Jimmy and Hall, from Baldwin, can people find freedom. The call, ultimately, emanates not only from the individual but also from the community to which he or she calls. It provides a focus for repudiation of the crushing definitions. Hall, using Jimmy's voice, describes the call: "The man who tells the story isn't *making up* a story. He's listening to us, and can only give back, to us, what he hears: from us." The responsibility lies with everyone.

Craig Werner

OTHER MAJOR WORKS

SHORT FICTION: *Going to Meet the Man*, 1965.

PLAYS: *The Amen Corner*, pr. 1954; *Blues for Mister Charlie*, pr., pb. 1964; *A Deed from the King of Spain*, pr. 1974.

POETRY: *Jimmy's Blues: Selected Poems*, 1983.

SCREENPLAY: *One Day, When I Was Lost: A Scenario Based on "The Autobiography of Malcolm X,"* 1972.

NONFICTION: *Notes of a Native Son*, 1955; *Nobody Knows My Name: More Notes of a Native Son*, 1961; *The Fire Next Time*, 1963; *Nothing Personal*, 1964 (with Richard Avedon); *No Name in the Street*, 1971; *A Rap on Race*, 1971 (with Margaret Mead); *A Dialogue*, 1975 (with Nikki Giovanni); *The Devil Finds Work*, 1976; *The Evidence of Things*

Not Seen, 1985; *The Price of the Ticket*, 1985; *Conversations with James Baldwin*, 1989; *Collected Essays*, 1998; *Native Sons: A Friendship That Created One of the Greatest Works of the Twentieth Century—"Notes of a Native Son,"* 2004 (with Sol Stein).

CHILDREN'S LITERATURE: *Little Man, Little Man*, 1975.

BIBLIOGRAPHY

Balfour, Lawrie Lawrence, and Katherine Lawrence Balfour. *The Evidence of Things Not Said: James Baldwin and the Promise of American Democracy*. Ithaca, N.Y.: Cornell University Press, 2001. Explores the political dimension of Baldwin's essays, stressing the politics of race in American democracy.

Campbell, James. *Talking at the Gates: A Life of James Baldwin*. New York: Viking Press, 1991. Good narrative biography is organized into five sections, each focusing on a particular period of Baldwin's life. Places Baldwin's work within the context of his times. Includes detailed notes and bibliography.

Fabré, Michel. "James Baldwin in Paris: Love and Self-Discovery." In *From Harlem to Paris: Black American Writers in France, 1840-1980*. Chicago: University of Illinois Press, 1991. Discusses Baldwin's Paris experiences. Brings biographical details to the European experiences of the bicontinental playwright, who owed France "his own spiritual growth, through the existential discovery of love as a key to life." The notes offer interview sources of quotations for further study.

Harris, Trudier, ed. *New Essays on "Go Tell It on the Mountain."* New York: Cambridge University Press, 1996. Collection of essays examines the composition, themes, publication history, public reception, and contemporary interpretations of Baldwin's first novel. Some of the essays discuss Baldwin's treatment of God, the American South, and homosexuality in the novel.

Kinnamon, Keneth, ed. *James Baldwin: A Collection of Critical Essays*. Englewood Cliffs, N.J.: Prentice Hall, 1974. A good introduction to Baldwin's early work featuring a collection of diverse essays by such well-known figures as Irving Howe, Langston Hughes, Sherley Anne Williams, and Eldridge Cleaver. Includes a chronology of important dates, notes on the contributors, and a select bibliography.

Leeming, David. *James Baldwin: A Biography*. New York: Alfred A. Knopf, 1994. A biography of Baldwin written by one who knew him and worked with him for the last quarter century of his life. Provides extensive literary analysis of Baldwin's work and relates his work to his life.

McBride, Dwight A., ed. *James Baldwin Now*. New York: New York University Press, 1999. Collection of essays reevaluates Baldwin's work, stressing the usefulness of interdisciplinary approaches in understanding Baldwin's appeal, political thought and work, and legacy. The contributors maintain that Baldwin was not an exclusively gay, expatriate, black, or activist writer but instead was a complex combination of all of those things.

Miller, D. Quentin, ed. *Re-viewing James Baldwin: Things Not Seen*. Philadelphia: Temple University Press, 2000. Collection of essays explores the ways in which Baldwin's writing touched on issues that confront all people, including race, identity, sexuality, and religious ideology. Works analyzed include the novels *Giovanni's Room*, *Another Country*, and *Just Above My Head*.

Scott, Lynn Orilla. *James Baldwin's Later Fiction: Witness to the Journey*. East Lansing: Michigan State University Press, 2002. Analyzes the decline of Baldwin's reputation after the 1960's, the ways in which critics have often undervalued his work, and the interconnected themes in his body of work.

Sylvander, Carolyn Wedin. *James Baldwin*. New York: Frederick Ungar, 1980. Good overview of Baldwin's work provides an aesthetic perspective, a bibliographical summary, and an analysis of individual works, with greatest emphasis given to Baldwin's plays, novels, and short stories.

Troupe, Quincy, ed. *James Baldwin: The Legacy*. New York: Simon & Schuster, 1989. Contains eighteen essays by and about Baldwin, five of which were written for this collection, and homage and celebration from many who were profoundly influenced by him, including Pat Mikell's account of Baldwin's last days in St. Paul de Vence. With a foreword by Wole Soyinka.

Weatherby, W. J. *James Baldwin: Artist on Fire*. New York: Donald I. Fine, 1989. Lengthy personal reminiscence of Baldwin by a close friend who calls his biography a portrait. Based on conversations with more than one hundred people who knew Baldwin. Rich in intimate detail; reveals the man behind the words.

TONI CADE BAMBARA

Born: New York, New York; March 25, 1939
Died: Philadelphia, Pennsylvania; December 9, 1995
Also known as: Miltona Mirkin Cade

PRINCIPAL LONG FICTION
The Salt Eaters, 1980
Those Bones Are Not My Child, 1999

OTHER LITERARY FORMS

Toni Cade Bambara (bam-BAHR-ah) is best known for her short stories, which appear frequently in anthologies. She has also received recognition as a novelist, essayist, journalist, editor, and screenwriter, as well as a social activist and community leader. Her stories depict the daily lives of ordinary people who live in the African American neighborhoods of Brooklyn, Harlem, and other sections of New York City and the rural South. Although she wrote in other genres, her short stories established her reputation. In *Gorilla, My Love* (1972), a collection of fifteen stories, Bambara focuses on the love of friends and neighborhood as she portrays the positive side of black family life and stresses the strengths of the African American community. These fast-paced stories, characterized by her use of the black dialect of the street, are full of humorous exchanges and verbal banter. *The Sea Birds Are Still Alive* (1977) is a collection of short stories that reflect Bambara's concern with people from other cultures; the title story focuses on the plight of Vietnamese refugees at the end of the Vietnam War. *Deep Sightings and Rescue Missions: Fiction, Essays, and Conversations*, a collection of Bambara's writings, most of which never appeared before in print, was published posthumously in 1996.

ACHIEVEMENTS

Toni Cade Bambara received the Peter Pauper Press Award in Journalism from the *Long Island Star* in 1958, the John Golden Award for Fiction from Queens College in 1959, and the Theater of Black Experience Award in 1969. She was also the recipient of the George Washington Carver Distinguished African American Lecturer Award from Simpson College, *Ebony*'s Achievement in the Arts Award, and the American Book Award, for *The Salt Eaters*, in 1981. *The Bombing of Osage Avenue* won the Best Documentary of 1986 Award from the Pennsylvania Association of Broadcasters and the Documentary Award from the National Black Programming Consortium in 1986.

As an editor of anthologies of the writings of African Americans, Bambara introduced thousands of college students to the works of these writers. She was a founder of the Southern Collective of African American Writers and played a major role in the 1984 Conference on Black Literature and the Arts at Emory University.

BIOGRAPHY

Miltona Mirkin Cade was born in New York City on March 25, 1939, to Helen Brent Henderson Cade. She grew up in Harlem, Bedford-Stuyvesant, and Queens, where she lived with her mother and her brother, Walter. She credited her mother with "cultivating her creative spirit and instilling in her a sense of independence and self-sufficiency." In 1970, after finding the name Bambara written in a sketchbook in her grandmother's trunk, she legally changed her surname to Bambara. She received a bachelor's degree in theater arts and English literature from Queens College in 1959, and that same year her first short story, "Sweet Town," was published in *Vendome* magazine. After studying in Italy and Paris, she earned a master's degree in American literature at City College of New York and completed additional studies in linguistics at New York University and the New School for Social Research. She was a social worker for the Harlem Welfare Center and director of recreation in the psychiatric division of Metro Hospital in New York City. She also taught in the Search for Education, Elevation, Knowledge (SEEK) program at City College.

In 1970, under the name Toni Cade, she published *The Black Woman: An Anthology*, a collection of essays, short fiction, poetry, and letters exploring the experiences of black women, with emphasis on their involvement with the Civil Rights movement and the women's movement. In 1971 she edited *Tales and Stories for Black Folks*, a collection of writings from students in her composition class along with works of well-known authors.

As an assistant professor at Livingston College at Rutgers University from 1969 to 1974, Bambara was active in black student organizations and arts groups. She was a visiting professor in Afro-American Studies at Emory University and an instructor in the School of Social Work at Atlanta University. In 1973, on a visit to Cuba, Bambara met with the Federation of Cuban Women, and in 1975 she traveled to Vietnam. These experiences served to broaden Bambara's view of the importance of community involvement and political action and provided subject matter for the stories in *The Sea Birds Are Still Alive.*

Bambara and her daughter, Karma, lived in Atlanta from 1974 to 1986, during which time Bambara continued to be active in community political and artistic organizations, hosting potluck dinners in her home and organizing writers and artists in the community. In 1986 Bambara moved to Philadelphia, where she continued her active participation in the community and worked on *The Bombing of Osage Avenue*, a 1986 documentary film about the bombing of a house where a group of black nationalists lived. She also worked on a film about African American writer Zora Neale Hurston.

Bambara was known as a writer, civil rights activist, teacher, and supporter of the arts. Her work represents her dedication to the African American community and her desire to portray the ordinary lives of the people who live in those communities. As a lecturer and teacher she worked to raise the consciousness of other African Americans and to encourage a sense of pride in their heritage. Bambara died of cancer in a suburb of Philadelphia on December 9, 1995.

ANALYSIS

Toni Cade Bambara's work reflects her experiences with political action committees and her belief in the necessity for social responsibility. The political activism of the 1960's and 1970's provides the subject matter for her work, as she explores the consequences of the Civil Rights movement and divisions in the African American community. In describing this community, Bambara portrays the individual characters with affection and humor.

THE SALT EATERS

Set in the 1970's, Bambara's novel *The Salt Eaters* focuses on the effects of the Civil Rights movement on the inhabitants of the small town of Claybourne, Georgia. The plot centers on the attempted suicide of the novel's main character, Velma Henry, a community activist who has tried to kill herself by slitting her wrists and sticking her head in an oven. The other major character is Minnie Ransom, a conjure woman who uses her healing powers to restore Velma to health. Minor characters include Fred Holt, the bus driver; Obie, Velma's husband; and Dr. Julius Meadows. These members of the African American community are suffering from the fragmentation and alienation that have occurred in the wake of the Civil Rights movement. Velma has been so filled with rage that she has sought death as an answer to her pain. The novel traces Velma's journey from despair to mental and spiritual health. Bambara's own experiences with political activism provided her with the background for the events of the novel.

Throughout the novel, Bambara stresses the importance of choice. In the opening line, Minnie Ransom asks Velma, "Are you sure, sweetheart, that you want to be well?" Freedom of choice requires acceptance of responsibility. If Velma is to heal herself, she must make a conscious choice of health over despair. Characters in the novel are seen in relationship to the larger community. Godmother Sophie M'Dear reminds Velma that her life is not solely her own, but that she has a connection and obligation to her family and community. Other characters are reminded of their responsibility to others. When Buster gets Nadeen pregnant, her uncle Thurston arrives with a gun, ordering Buster to attend parenting classes. Doc Serge tells Buster that abortion is not a private choice but a choice that involves the whole community. The characters echo Bambara's belief that membership in a community entails responsibilities to that community.

For most of the novel Velma sits on a stool in a hospital, suffering from depression, overwhelming fatigue, and mental collapse. She remains immobile and seemingly frozen as scenes from the past and present play in her mind in no particular order. Other characters seem to whirl past Velma and blend into one another, reflecting the problems that have brought Velma to this hospital room. Bambara shows that these problems are a result of alienation from the community. Because of his light skin, education, and profession, Dr. Julius Meadows has lost touch with his roots. Through a chance encounter with two young black men, Julius begins his journey back to the black community. Reflecting on the encounter, Julius feels that "whatever happened, he wasn't stumbling aimlessly around the streets anymore, at loose ends, alone."

Meadows's journey back into the black community parallels Velma's journey to health. Alienation from the community had brought Velma to the brink of destruction, and realignment with the community heals her. Velma's journey is similar to the spiritual journey of Tayo, the Native American protagonist in Leslie Marmon Silko's *Ceremony* (1977). The horrors Tayo experienced as a prisoner of the Japanese during World War II and the sense of alienation he experiences when he returns to his Laguna reservation have nearly destroyed his will to survive. Through immersion in the Native American culture, traditions, beliefs, and stories, Tayo finds his way back to health. Like Tayo, as Velma embraces her cultural heritage, she begins to heal.

The predominant image in the novel is the vision of the mud mothers painting the walls of their cave. This recurring vision haunts Velma until she sees the cave as a symbol of cultural history and identity. Other characters reflect on the responsibility of the older generation to educate and nurture the children of the community. If the children are forgetting the values of the community, it is because the elders have failed in their responsibility to instill community values in the young.

Bambara demonstrates in the novel that to keep traditions alive, every generation has to be nurtured and educated, has to be taught the old stories. At times the novel seems to be a catalog of African American cultural history, which includes African tribal customs and rituals, slave ships, and names of famous leaders. In the early part of the novel, Ruby, one of the most politically active characters, laments the loss of leaders and causes: "Malcolm gone, King gone, Fanni Lou gone, Angela quiet, the movement splintered, enclaves unconnected." Near the end of the novel, Velma realizes how much she has learned from the leaders and influences that are part of her background, "Douglass, Tubman, the slave narratives, the songs, the fables, Delaney, Ida Wells, Blyden, Du Bois, Garvey, the singers, her parents, Malcolm, Coltrane."

Bambara enriches the novel with background from folk legends and literary works. At times she merely mentions a name, such as Shine, the famous African American trickster, or the legendary Stagolee, who killed a man for his hat. Fred's friend Porter, borrowing a term from Ralph Ellison's novel *Invisible Man* (1952), explains his feelings about being black: "They call the Black man the Invisible Man. . . . Our natures are unknowable, unseeable to them." The following lines show how Bambara packs cultural, historical, and political history into one sentence: "Several hotheads, angry they had been asleep in the Sixties or too young to participate, had been galvanized by the arrival in their midst of the legless vet who used to careen around Claybourne fast and loose on a hot garage dolly."

In contrast to the positive images, Bambara shows the negative side of society in describing the "boymen" who hang around women in grocery stores begging for money in a ritual she calls "market theater." In another scene, Ruby complains about the way women have had to carry the burden of improving society, "taking on . . . drugs, prisons, alcohol, the schools, rape, battered women, abused children," while the men make no contribution.

One of the most distinctive aspects of Bambara's style is her use of black dialect, with its colorful vocabulary, playful banter, and unique phrasing and speech patterns. At times the rhythm and rhyme of phrases give a musical quality to the prose: "Cause the stars said and the energy belts led and the cards read and the cowries spread." At other times Bambara describes the atmosphere in musical terms: "the raga reggae bumpidity bing zing was pouring out all over Fred Holt" and "the music drifted out over the trees . . . maqaam now blending with the bebop of Minnie Ransom's tapes."

The major theme of the novel is that identification with one's cultural history can be liberating and empowering. In *The Salt Eaters*, loss of cultural identity has brought despair. Bambara provides flashbacks to the civil rights struggles of the 1960's and the legacy of slavery. As they fight for political power, African Americans must remember the past and maintain their best traditions. As Velma begins to heal, she thinks that she knows "how to build resistance, make the journey to the center of the circle . . . stay centered in the best of her people's traditions."

Judith Barton Williamson

Other Major Works

Short fiction: *Gorilla, My Love*, 1972; *The Sea Birds Are Still Alive: Collected Stories*, 1977; *Raymond's Run: Stories for Young Adults*, 1989.

Screenplays: *The Bombing of Osage Avenue*, 1986 (documentary); *W. E. B. Du Bois: A Biography in Four Voices*, 1995 (with Amiri Baraka, Wesley Brown, and Thulani Davis).

Nonfiction: "What It Is I Think I'm Doing Anyhow" in *The Writer on Her Work*, 1981.

Edited texts: *The Black Woman: An Anthology*, 1970; *Tales and Stories for Black Folks*, 1971; *Southern Exposure*, 1976 (periodical; edited volume 3).

Miscellaneous: *Deep Sightings and Rescue Missions: Fiction, Essays, and Conversations*, 1996.

Bibliography

Alwes, Derek. "The Burden of Liberty: Choice in Toni Morrison's *Jazz* and Toni Cade Bambara's *The Salt Eaters*." *African American Review* 30, no. 3 (Fall, 1996): 353-365. Compares the works of Morrison and Bambara, arguing that whereas Morrison wants readers to participate in a choice, Bambara wants them to choose to participate. Asserts that Bambara's message is that happiness is possible if people refuse to forget the past and continue to participate in the struggle.

Butler-Evans, Elliott. *Race, Gender, and Desire: Narrative Strategies in the Fiction of Toni Cade Bambara, Toni Morrison, Alice Walker.* Philadelphia: Temple University Press, 1989. In the first book-length study to treat Bambara's fiction to any extent, Butler-Evans uses narratology and feminism to explore Bambara's works as well as those of two other important female African American writers.

Collins, Janelle. "Generating Power: Fission, Fusion, and Post-modern Politics in Bambara's *The Salt Eaters*." *MELUS* 21, no. 2 (Summer, 1996): 35-47. Examines nuclear power as a key metaphor in the novel, noting how Bambara raises ecological and ethical concerns about nuclear energy. Argues that Bambara's nationalist and feminist positions inform the novel's text as the author advocates political and social change.

Evans, Mari, ed. *Black Women Writers (1950-1980): A Critical Evaluation*. Garden City, N.Y.: Anchor Press/Doubleday, 1984. In the essay "Salvation Is the Issue," Bambara says that the elements of her own work that she deems most important are laughter, use of language, sense of community, and celebration.

Holmes, Linda J., and Cheryl A. Wall, eds. *Savoring the Salt: The Legacy of Toni Cade Bambara*. Philadelphia: Temple University Press, 2007. Collection of insightful essays commemorates Bambara's life, her writings, and the importance of her contributions to African American literature. Contributors include Toni Morrison, Amiri Baraka, Ruby Dee, Nikki Giovanni, and Audre Lorde.

Shinn, Thelma J. "Orbiting Home: Toni Cade Bambara." In *Women Shapeshifters: Transforming the Contemporary Novel*. Westport, Conn.: Greenwood Press, 1996. Chapter on Bambara's novels is included in a larger examination of how twentieth century women authors transformed the novel's structure by combining the traditions of Romantic and realistic fiction.

Taylor, Carole Anne. "Postmodern Disconnection and the Archive of Bones: Toni Cade Bambara's Last Work." *Novel: A Forum on Fiction* 35 (Spring/Summer, 2002): 258-280. Discusses Bambara's self-referential storytelling in *Deep Sightings and Rescue Misions*, where the stories refer to their own creation, and in her last novel, *Those Bones Are Not My Child*, which refers to Bambara's own life as a mother, writer, activist, and filmmaker.

Vertreace, Martha M. *Toni Cade Bambara*. New York: Macmillan Library Reference, 1998. The first full-length resource devoted to the entirety of Bambara's career. Provides information useful for students of the author's works.

Willis, Susan. "Problematizing the Individual: Toni Cade Bambara's Stories for the Revolution." In *Specifying: Black Women Writing the American Experience*. Madison: University of Wisconsin Press, 1987. Clear and informative essay analyzes Bambara's work, focusing largely on *The Salt Eaters* while also commenting on her most important short fiction.

GEORGE WASHINGTON CABLE

Born: New Orleans, Louisiana; October 12, 1844
Died: St. Petersburg, Florida; January 31, 1925

PRINCIPAL LONG FICTION

The Grandissimes, 1880
Madame Delphine, 1881
Dr. Sevier, 1884
Bonaventure, 1888
John March, Southerner, 1894
The Cavalier, 1901
Bylow Hill, 1902
Kincaid's Battery, 1908
Gideon's Band, 1914
Lovers of Louisiana, 1918

OTHER LITERARY FORMS

In addition to nine novels, George Washington Cable published a novella, *Madame Delphine*, and four collections of short stories: *Old Creole Days* (1879), *Strong Hearts* (1899), *Posson Jone' and Père Raphaël* (1909), and *The Flower of the Chapdelaines* (1918). He also wrote a dramatized version of one of his novels, *The Cavalier*. His eight books of nonfiction cover miscellaneous subjects. *The Creoles of Louisiana* (1884) is a collection of history articles, and *Strange True Stories of Louisiana* (1889) is a collection of factual stories; both collections are set in Cable's native state. *The Silent South* (1885) and *The Negro Question* (1890) are collections of essays on southern problems. *The Busy Man's Bible* (1891) and *The Amateur Garden* (1914) grew out of Cable's hobbies of Bible teaching and gardening. *A Memory of Roswell Smith* (1892) is a memorial tribute to a friend, and *The Cable Story Book: Selections for School Reading* (1899) is a book of factual and fictional material for children. Cable also wrote magazine articles and a newspaper column.

ACHIEVEMENTS

In his 1962 study of the author, Philip Butcher shows the high position that George Washington Cable held in American literature in the last years of the nineteenth century. In 1884, the *Critic* ranked him ahead of fourteenth-place Mark Twain on its list of "Forty Immortals." A cartoon in the May 27, 1897, issue of *Life* magazine depicted Cable among the ten most popular authors of the day. In the American edition of *Literature* in 1899, he was tenth on the list of greatest living American writers.

Popular both with critics and with the reading public in his own time, Cable is little

George Washington Cable
(Library of Congress)

known today. His reputation as a writer of fiction rests on three works: the novel *The Grandissimes*, the novella *Madame Delphine*, and the collection of short stories *Old Creole Days*, later editions of which include *Madame Delphine* as the lead story. Although *Dr. Sevier* and *John March, Southerner* contain serious commentary, the three novels that followed in the first decade of the new century are trivial romances. His last two novels, *Gideon's Band* and *Lovers of Louisiana*, signal only an incomplete return to the artistic level and social worth of his first three books. Because much of his energy went into provocative social essays on southern racial problems, into humanitarian reforms in such areas as prisons and insane asylums, into cultural projects, and, as a major source of income, into platform tours, Cable found insufficient time for the fiction he might otherwise have created. Nevertheless, as late as 1918 he published a collection of short stories and a novel, and up to his death in 1925 he was working on still another novel.

Cable was much admired by his contemporaries. William Dean Howells praised him privately and in print. Twain took him as a partner on a reading tour, and for four months (1884-1885) the two shared the stage as they read from their respective works. Cable also read on programs that included Hamlin Garland, James Whitcomb Riley, Eugene Field, and other popular writers of the day.

Cable was invited to England by Sir James Barrie for the first of two trips abroad (1898, 1905). For nearly three months in 1898, he traveled and visited in the homes of Barrie, Arthur Conan Doyle, Rudyard Kipling, Henry James, and other well-known figures. His friends arranged for him to read his fiction, play a guitar, and sing Creole-black songs in their homes and in public halls. Andrew Carnegie was so impressed with Cable's personality and writing that he later bestowed a lifetime pension on him. Among his honorary degrees was the doctorate of letters given by Yale University in 1901 to Cable, Twain, Howells, Theodore Roosevelt, Woodrow Wilson, and other contemporary notables.

Cable's reputation began to decline before his death and has never recovered. In the 1980's he was considered too important a writer to be omitted from southern literature anthologies and American literature textbooks, but by the end of the twentieth century he had yet to be deemed worthy of widespread revival.

BIOGRAPHY

George Washington Cable was born in New Orleans, Louisiana, on October 12, 1844. Ancestors of his mother, Rebecca Boardman Cable, had lived in New England since the seventeenth century and had moved to Indiana in 1807. The background of his father, the elder George Washington Cable, dates back to pre-Revolutionary times in Virginia. The elder Cable lived in Virginia and Pennsylvania with his parents before moving to Indiana, where he married Rebecca in 1834. The Cable family migrated to New Orleans in 1837, where George, their fifth child, was born.

In the 1840's, the Cables lived a comfortable existence, owning several household slaves until the father's business failed. Through the 1850's, the elder Cable worked at a series of jobs until, weakened in health, he died on February 28, 1859. Because young George's older brother, along with an older sister, had died of scarlet fever, his father's death required him, not yet fourteen, to leave school to support the family. Until the third year of the Civil War, he held his father's former position as a clerk at the customhouse.

Slight in size—only five feet five inches and weighing one hundred pounds—and deceptively youthful in features, Cable enlisted in the Confederate Army on October 9, 1863, three days before his nineteenth birthday. Incurring two slight wounds during his service, he was discharged in 1865.

After the war, Cable worked as an errand boy, as a store clerk, and, until malaria stopped him, as a rodman with a surveying party on the Red River. In 1868, he became a bookkeeper for two cotton firms in New Orleans. He married Louise Stewart Bartlett on December 7, 1869, and soon fathered the first of a large family of children. At one time, he worked simultaneously for the cotton house of William C. Black and Company, the New Orleans Cotton Exchange, and the National Cotton Exchange.

Newspaper work provided Cable's first opportunity to see his writing in print. While continuing as an accountant, he worked for newspapers as a freelance contributor and then as a full-time reporter. For eighteen months, beginning February 27, 1870, he wrote the column "Drop Shot" weekly, and then daily, for the New Orleans *Picayune*. While working for the *Picayune*, his research into Louisiana history at city hall, the cathedral, and the Cabildo, former seat of colonial government, led him to factual stories later to be shaped into fiction. In addition, his newspaper reports on contemporary local affairs interested him in reform on civic, regional, and national levels.

Appearing in *Scribner's Monthly*, Cable's stories were based on his knowledge of the people and activities of New Orleans and of events in Louisiana history. Six of the stories appearing in *Scribner's Monthly* and a seventh story, "Posson Jone'," which was published in *Appleton's Journal*, were later collected as *Old Creole Days*, published by Scribner's. His first novel, *The Grandissimes*, also based on the people and history of Louisiana, was serialized in *Scribner's Monthly* over a twelve-month period and then published in book form in 1880. Next came the novella *Madame Delphine*, first printed in *Scribner's Monthly* as a three-part serial, and then published in book form in 1881.

In 1881, Cable gave up his position as an accountant, depending for the rest of his life on lectures and public readings of his fiction to supplement his income as a writer. One of his successes was a series of six lectures at Johns Hopkins University in 1883, and he continued to find himself in demand on platforms in many cities. In 1884, his regional history *The Creoles of Louisiana* appeared, and in the same year his second novel, *Dr. Sevier*, was published. In 1884-1885, he went on a successful reading tour with Mark Twain.

Cable, son of a slaveholding family, was a loyal Confederate soldier during the Civil War and apparently remained unchanged in political stance for some time thereafter. Later, however, he began to express feeling against racial injustice. Although criticism of discrimination is present in his fiction, it was only through the direct statements of his magazine articles and public lectures that fellow southerners became fully aware of his radical stance. The publication of a volume of his essays, *The Silent South* (1885), made his stand clear. Newspaper editorialists who had acclaimed his fiction now began to attack his social and political views.

Cable had two households to support—one including his wife and children, and the other his mother, his sisters, and the children of his widowed sister. His wife, who traced her ancestry back to the Mayflower, was born and reared in New England. Cable believed that a return to the climate of New England would be beneficial for his wife's frail health. In addition, the attraction that a location near his publishers in New York held for him, and a sensitivity to the criticism aimed at him in the South, influenced his decision to leave New Orleans after forty years of residence there. Having previously visited Northampton, Massachusetts, he moved his wife and children to a home there in 1885, and his mother, sisters, and cousins followed soon thereafter.

Despite his desire to write fiction, Cable allowed other interests to take much of his time. In 1885, he championed black rights in an essay read nationwide, "The Freedman's

Case in Equity." In 1886, he founded the first of the Home Culture Clubs, in which he would be involved for the next thirty-five years. Through his Open Letter Club (1888-1890), in the name of which he lectured, wrote, and published, Cable completed the period identified as his greatest effort for reform in the South. From 1887 to 1889, he undertook an extensive program of religious writing and teaching; he conducted a large Bible class in Northampton each Sunday, traveling to Boston on Saturdays to hold a similar class.

For five years, Cable published a book annually: *Bonaventure*, *Strange True Stories of Louisiana*, *The Negro Question*, *The Busy Man's Bible*, and *A Memory of Roswell Smith* were all published during this period. At the same time, he was giving readings and lectures from coast to coast. A popular speaker, he was frequently invited to deliver commencement addresses and to give talks on literary subjects, southern problems, and Creole history. Despite his endeavors, however, he remained constantly in debt—receiving advances on royalties from his publishers, obtaining loans, repaying old debts, and incurring new ones.

By this time, Cable had ceased actively campaigning for civil rights, and his writing developed a noncontroversial tone. His third novel, *John March, Southerner*, although concerned with Reconstruction problems, avoided racial issues, as did his collection of short stories *Strong Hearts*. *The Cable Story Book*, needless to say, offended no one. The following novels, *The Cavalier* and *Bylow Hill*, veered even more sharply from controversy to entertainment, their artistic value diminishing proportionately.

Meanwhile, in 1898, Cable had made a triumphal reading tour in Britain. Philanthropist Andrew Carnegie, with whom Cable became friends while in Scotland, donated money to one of Cable's long-enduring projects. In 1903, Carnegie agreed to give fifty thousand dollars for a building for the Home Culture Clubs on the condition that five thousand dollars a year be guaranteed locally for five years.

Dimming Cable's good fortune, his beloved wife died on February 27, 1904, ending a devoted marriage of nearly thirty-five years. Cable continued to write, although without immediately readying a book for publication. Two years and nine months after Louise's death, he married Eva C. Stevenson. In 1908, he published the novel *Kincaid's Battery*, and in 1909 he put two of his short stories (one of them selected from the *Old Creole Days* collection) into book form, *Posson Jone' and Père Raphaël*. In 1911, Carnegie began sending Cable one thousand dollars a year to support his writing. Three years later, *Gideon's Band* and *The Amateur Garden* were published.

Despite his debts, Cable managed to travel outside the United States even before Carnegie began to subsidize him. When traveling, he often carried with him an unfinished manuscript, working on it when he had time. In later years, no longer dependent on the platform circuit, he began staying in Northampton in the summer, spending the winter in New Orleans, Florida, and Bermuda. In 1918, at the age of seventy-four, he published two books—*The Flower of the Chapdelaines*, a collection of short stories, and *Lovers of Louisiana*.

When Carnegie died in 1919, his will provided Cable with five thousand dollars a year for life, the annuity to be transferred to Eva if she survived her husband. Eva, however, died on June 7, 1923. Six months after her death, Cable married his third wife, Hanna Cowing. A little more than a year later, on January 31, 1925, he died. Among his literary papers was an unfinished novel on which he had been working.

ANALYSIS

Although George Washington Cable's reputation rests primarily on one collection of short stories and two pieces of longer fiction, his total output includes twenty-two books. For an understanding of Cable as a writer of fiction, one should first consider his nonfiction and his reasons for writing it. Cable's interest in history is shown in two books centered on Creole culture, *The Creoles of Louisiana*, a collection of history articles, and *Strange True Stories of Louisiana*, a collection of factual stories about the Creoles. On a juvenile level, *The Cable Story Book* is a combination of factual and fictional material that emphasizes the same Creole subjects as his fiction. *The Silent South* and *The Negro Question*, his best-known works of nonfiction, are collections of essays on controversial southern problems, notably the problem of racial discrimination. Characteristic of Cable's prose is a moral posture and a humanitarian zeal, openly stated in his nonfiction and imaginatively expressed in the most important of his fiction. He worked for the reform of people and institutions and for a reversal in racial attitudes.

THE GRANDISSIMES

Cable's first novel, *The Grandissimes*, is his unqualified masterpiece. Louis D. Rubin, Jr., has called it the first "modern" southern novel, dealing realistically as it does with the role of the black in American society. Added to the rich portrayal of aristocratic Creole settings and family problems, a panoramic array of characters of Native American, black, and mixed bloods vivify problems of social castes and racial discrimination in Louisiana in 1803, the year of the Louisiana Purchase. Using the historical actuality of racially tangled bloodlines as the theme for dramatic episodes, Cable emphasizes the ramifications of black-white relationships. The free quadroon caste, for example, had its special role in southern society, as shown historically in the New Orleans "quadroon balls." Beautiful young women of one-quarter black blood (quadroons) or, perhaps, one-eighth (octoroons) danced at these balls with white men, were chosen by them as mistresses, and were set up in separate households in the city.

Two principal quadroons interact in *The Grandissimes*. A male quadroon is the identically named half brother of the aristocratic Creole Honoré Grandissime. The darker Honoré Grandissime flouts the law by refusing to inscribe the letters "f.m.c." (free man of color) after his name. Educated in Paris along with his half brother and heir to most of their deceased father's wealth, the quadroon nevertheless remains unrecognized as a legitimate member of the Grandissime family. The Creoles' acceptance of an American Indian chieftain as ancestor is introduced to point up their unwonted prejudice against the taint of black blood. The main female quadroon is Palmyre Philosophe, a freed slave who bears a hopeless love for the all-white Honoré Grandissime and, in turn, is loved by his quadroon half brother. To illustrate the injustices perpetrated against blacks, Cable inserts the episode of the black Bras-Coupé, a historical figure used earlier in Cable's unpublished short story "Bibi." Palmyre hates Agricola Fuselier, her former owner and uncle to Honoré Grandissime, who forced her unconsummated marriage to Bras-Coupé.

The character who serves throughout the novel as spokesman for Cable is Joseph Frowenfeld, a German American newcomer to New Orleans, who observes, participates in, and comments critically on the action. Honoré Grandissime, the leading male character, is a Creole who recognizes the faults of his society and works with moderation to correct them. He provides a liberal Creole viewpoint, supplementary to the rigid moral judgment of Frowenfeld. Agricola Fuselier, in direct contrast to Frowenfeld, represents the proud old Creoles who insist on purity of race.

Action antecedent to the yearlong events of the novel goes back to 1673, the year of the birth of the American Indian girl whose choice of a De Grapion suitor began a feud between two Creole families, the De Grapions and the Grandissimes. Preceding the main plot by eight years comes the tale of Bras-Coupé. Otherwise, the action takes place between September, 1803, and September, 1804.

The leading female character, Aurora Nancanou, daughter of a De Grapion, is the young widow of a man killed by Agricola Fuselier in a duel over a card game. Agricola took Nancanou's estate in payment for the gambling debt, passing the estate on to his nephew, the white Honoré, and leaving Aurora and her daughter Clotilde without land or money. The novel opens at a masked ball in New Orleans where Aurora and Honoré meet, unaware of each other's identity, thus beginning a romantic complication. Paralleling the love triangle of Palmyre and the Grandissime half brothers, Joseph Frowenfeld falls in love with Clotilde, who, at the same time, is desired by Frowenfeld's friend Dr. Charlie Keene.

Honoré Grandissime, as leader of the Grandissime family and as Cable's symbol of right-thinking Creoles, upsets his relatives on several occasions: Endangering the Grandissime finances, he returns Aurora Nancanou's property to her; in an act socially degrading to the family, he becomes a partner with the quadroon Honoré, under the business title "The Grandissime Brothers"; on an uneasy political level, he cooperates with Claiborne, the newly appointed territorial governor.

Romance, realism, and melodrama are mingled in *The Grandissimes.* In a romantic resolution, the De Grapion-Grandissime feud is ended, and marriage is imminent for two sets of lovers—Aurora and the white Honoré Grandissime, Clotilde and Frowenfeld. On the realistic side—with an admixture of melodramatic incidents—the two leading quadroons of the story are defeated. After Palmyre's several attempts to get revenge on the object of her hate, Agricola Fuselier, and after he is stabbed by the quadroon Honoré, she is forced to flee for safety to Paris. She is accompanied by her fellow refugee, Honoré Grandissime (f.m.c.), who commits suicide by drowning because of her final rejection of him.

Intentional obscurity is a characteristic of Cable's style in *The Grandissimes*. Lack of direct statement and slow revelation of relationships mark the progress of the plot. Facts are given through hints and implication; full information is withheld in a dense accumulation of incidents. This technique, typical of his early and best works, has been praised for its artistry and criticized for its lack of clarity.

Cable's portrayal of slaveholders, slaves, and the stubbornly held traditions of French Louisiana added a new dimension to southern literature. Succeeding in his aim as a novelist, Cable found that fame brought a painful backlash. His radical views caused this native son to be identified as a traitor to New Orleans and the South.

MADAME DELPHINE

In 1881, Cable published the novella *Madame Delphine*, the third in the three-year sequence of Cable's finest literary works (after the short-story collection *Old Creole Days* and the novel *The Grandissimes*). First published as a three-part novelette in *Scribner's Monthly* from May to July, 1881, *Madame Delphine* was published by Scribner's in book form later that year. In editions of *Old Creole Days* succeeding its initial publication, *Madame Delphine* is included and given lead position in the book.

The story begins with beautiful Olive Delphine returning from France on a ship that is boarded by the Creole pirate Ursin Lemaitre. Confronted by Olive's piety and charm, Lemaitre is struck with repentance for his sinful life and with love for the unidentified stranger. Settling in New Orleans, the reformed Lemaitre changes his name to Vignevielle and turns from piracy to banking. When not in his banker's office, he wanders through the streets, searching for the mysterious young woman.

Eventually, the lovelorn banker and Olive develop a friendship and marriage becomes their intention. Olive, however, is not legally able to become Lemaitre's wife, for she has black ancestry. Her mother, Madame Delphine, is a quadroon, the mistress to a white man, Olive's father. Madame Delphine, despite the laws against miscegenation, approves of the marriage. Indeed, she has made it clear that she is seeking a white husband for her daughter.

Vignevielle's relatives and friends, knowing that Madame Delphine is a quadroon, attempt to stop the illegal marriage, going so far as to threaten to turn him over to government agents who are searching for him. Madame Delphine meanwhile puts forth the ultimate effort to make the union possible. Producing fabricated evidence, she perjures herself by swearing that she is not the girl's blood mother. After Vignevielle and Olive are married, Madame Delphine goes for confession to the priest Père Jerome, admits her lie, and dies. Père Jerome speaks the closing line: "Lord, lay not this sin to her charge!"

The style of *Madame Delphine* is leisurely. Little mysteries cling to characters and actions, with revelation coming in glimpses, suggestions, and half-expressed statements. Early reviewers compared Cable to Nathaniel Hawthorne in achievement of mood, atmosphere, and ambiguity. Adverse criticism of *Madame Delphine*, however, finds the work excessively obscure; most troubling to critics is the needlessly complicated unfolding of the plot.

Furthermore, the characterization of the lovers is weak. Vignevielle's switch from dashing pirate to banker is inadequately motivated. Olive is a shadowy figure without distinguishable traits. Madame Delphine, despite her maneuvers, approaches the stereotype of the helpless mother. The only strong character is Père Jerome, a compassionate observer and spokesman for Cable. Père Jerome sees that society deserves blame, both for its actions and for its failure to act. Society acquiesces in evil—from its unprotesting profit in Lemaitre's smuggled goods to its deliberate manipulation of the lives of mulattoes.

More significant than the style of *Madame Delphine* is its portrayal of the southern attitude toward miscegenation. Although romanticism embellishes the outwardly happy ending of the story, Cable's recognition of the female mulatto's untenable position is clear. Looking beyond the temporary bliss of the wedding day, the reader realizes that prospects for Olive in New Orleans are not favorable. Madame Delphine's perjury has made the marriage legally permissible, but in the eyes of Lemaitre's friends, Olive is not and will never be an acceptable member of their aristocratic society.

The developing social consciousness revealed by Cable in *Madame Delphine* gives the work a lasting value. After this novella, however, he confined the most telling of his indictments to essays, disappointing readers who waited for his familiar critical tone in future novels. He was never able to duplicate the blend of artistic craftsmanship, authentic local color, and social commentary that distinguishes *Madame Delphine*, *The Grandissimes*, and *Old Creole Days*.

Bernice Larson Webb

Other major works

SHORT FICTION: *Old Creole Days*, 1879; *Strong Hearts*, 1899; *Posson Jone' and Père Raphaël*, 1909; *The Flower of the Chapdelaines*, 1918.

NONFICTION: *The Creoles of Louisiana*, 1884; *The Silent South*, 1885; *Strange True Stories of Louisiana*, 1889; *The Negro Question*, 1890; *The Busy Man's Bible*, 1891; *A Memory of Roswell Smith*, 1892; *The Amateur Garden*, 1914.

MISCELLANEOUS: *The Cable Story Book: Selections for School Reading*, 1899.

Bibliography

Biklé, Lucy Leffingwell Cable. *George W. Cable: His Life and Letters*. New York: Charles Scribner's Sons, 1928. This biography, written by Cable's daughter, has the advantage of immediacy to, and intimacy with, the subject. Covers the life of Cable primarily through the many letters that he wrote.

Butcher, Philip. *George W. Cable*. New York: Twayne, 1962. Literary biography provides a good general introduction to Cable, examining his life in the context of his work and vice versa. Discusses the major phases of Cable's life—from New Orleans and *Old Creole Days* to his friendship with Mark Twain to his social and political involvement—in an honest, engaging fashion.

Cleman, John. *George Washington Cable Revisited*. New York: Twayne, 1996. Critical introduction to Cable's life and work discusses the author's major works and the social context within which they were created. Includes chapters devoted to Cable's advocacy of civil rights for African Americans, his political writing, and his later works of "pure fiction."

Ekstrom, Kjell. *George Washington Cable: A Study of His Early Life and Work*. New York: Haskell House, 1966. Focuses on Cable's Creole fiction, giving much historical, literary, and cultural background to Cable's early work. In addition to biographical information on Cable's early years, provides discussion of the literary and nonliterary sources for the Creole short stories and novels.

Foote, Stephanie. "'The Shadow of the Ethiopian': George Washington Cable's *The Grandissimes*." In *Regional Fictions: Culture and Identity in Nineteenth-Century American Literature*. Madison: University of Wisconsin Press, 2001. Examination of Cable's novel explains the book's place in American regional fiction. This chapter is part of a larger study that focuses on how Cable's work and other regional fiction shaped Americans' ideas about the value of local identity.

Jones, Gavin. "Signifying Songs: The Double Meaning of Black Dialect in the Work of George Washington Cable." *American Literary History* 9 (Summer, 1997): 244-267. Discusses the interaction of African American and French Creole culture in Cable's works. Argues that African American dialect, song, and satire were transmitted to the white community subversively.

Ladd, Barbara. *Nationalism and the Color Line in George W. Cable, Mark Twain, and William Faulkner*. Baton Rouge: Louisiana State University Press, 1996. Demonstrates how the works of Cable and the other writers were influenced by the cultural legacy that French and Spanish colonialism embedded in the Mississippi River Valley and the Deep South.

Rubin, Louis D., Jr. *George W. Cable: The Life and Times of a Southern Heretic*. New York: Pegasus, 1979. By Rubin's own admission, the biography in this book is dependent on the work of Arlin Turner (cited below), but Rubin's comments on Cable's works are insightful and informative. Includes complete chapters on the novels *The Grandissimes*, *Dr. Sevier*, and *John March, Southerner*.

Schmidt, Peter. "Romancing Multiracial Democracy: George Washington Cable's *Lovers of Louisiana*." In *Sitting in Darkness: New South Fiction, Education, and the Rise of Jim Crow Colonialism, 1865-1920*. Jackson: University Press of Mississippi, 2008. Chapter on Cable's last novel is included in an exploration of how southern fiction published from the time of Reconstruction through the end of World War I affected societal reform in the South in regard to race, politics, and education.

Turner, Arlin. *George W. Cable: A Biography.* Durham, N.C.: Duke University Press, 1957. Thoroughly researched biography in many ways set the standard for further Cable studies. Discusses in great detail not only Cable's life but also his literary work, his political involvement, the geographical contexts of his work, and the important historical events that affected his life and work. Includes extensive bibliography and index.

CHARLES WADDELL CHESNUTT

Born: Cleveland, Ohio; June 20, 1858
Died: Cleveland, Ohio; November 15, 1932

PRINCIPAL LONG FICTION

The House Behind the Cedars, 1900
The Marrow of Tradition, 1901
The Colonel's Dream, 1905
Mandy Oxendine, 1997 (wr. 1897)
Paul Marchand, F.M.C., 1998 (wr. 1921)
The Quarry, 1999 (wr. 1928)
A Business Career, 2005 (wr. 1898; Matthew Wilson and Marjan van Schaik, editors)
Evelyn's Husband, 2005 (wr. 1903; Wilson and van Schaik, editors)

OTHER LITERARY FORMS

Charles Waddell Chesnutt published two major collections of short stories: *The Conjure Woman* (1899) and *The Wife of His Youth, and Other Stories of the Color Line* (1899). Some critics view both of these collections as novels. William Andrews, in *The Literary Career of Charles W. Chesnutt* (1980), has explained the reasons some critics have asserted these two collections should be approached as novels. At the heart of *The Conjure Woman* is former slave Uncle Julius McAdoo, whose reminiscences in black dialect present a picture of plantation life in the Old South. His tales in turn center on old Aunt Peggy, the plantation conjure woman, and each has a moral, although the primary purpose of the stories is supposed to be entertainment. Another major character is a midwestern businessman who has come to North Carolina for his wife's health and who describes rural life in the South after the Civil War. The businessman's loosely connected descriptions serve as a frame for the tales of Uncle Julius, who is the businessman's coachman and unofficial family entertainer. In the stories in *The Conjure Woman*, Chesnutt follows the dialect/local-color tradition.

The stories in *The Wife of His Youth, and Other Stories of the Color Line* are issue-oriented. In them, Chesnutt is concerned with the special difficulties that those of mixed blood had in the pervasively racist environment in the United States after the Civil War. He asserted in a letter to his publisher, Houghton Mifflin, that while the stories are not unified by a character such as Uncle Julius in *The Conjure Woman*, they are unified by a theme—what Chesnutt calls "the color line." The collection is made up of various fictional case studies of social problems caused by the color consciousness of Americans. Some stories are addressed to blacks, some to those of mixed blood, and others to whites. Aside from having all the stories deal with the common subject of "the color line," Chesnutt attempted to unify the stories in another way: In all of them, he sought to revise the public's conception of blacks, to counter the stereotypes found in American fiction at that time.

Chesnutt also wrote a biography (*The Life of Frederick Douglass*, 1899), a play (*Mrs. Darcy's Daughter*), and a few poems. In addition, he wrote essays and speeches that were published in national magazines. Representing a dominant concern of his, these writings were primarily political and didactic; some titles include "A Plea for the American Negro," "The White and the Black," and "What Is a White Man?" His essay "The Disfranchisement of the Negro" appeared as part of a book titled *The Negro Problem* (1903), the subtitle of which announced that it was *A Series of Articles by Representative American Negroes of Today*; other contributors to the volume included such men as Booker T. Washington, W. E. B. Du Bois, T. Thomas Fortune, and Paul Laurence Dunbar.

In the early twenty-first century, new collections of Chesnutt's works appeared: *Stories, Novels, and Essays* (2002), and *The Portable Charles W. Chesnutt* (2008). Chesnutt's correspondence and many of his writings have not been published, however. Most of these unpublished works, as well as many of the published ones, are housed in the Charles Waddell Chesnutt Collection of the Erastus Milo Cravath Memorial Library, Fisk University, Nashville, Tennessee.

Achievements

In 1872, when he was fourteen years old, Charles Waddell Chesnutt saw his first story published serially in a local black weekly. The publication of "The Goophered Grapevine" in August, 1887, in *The Atlantic Monthly* marked Chesnutt's first appearance in a major American literary magazine. Three more short stories followed: "Po' Sandy," "The Conjurer's Revenge," and "Dave's Neckliss." The publication of these four Uncle Julius stories were his entering wedge into the literary world—a world of which Chesnutt had long dreamed of being a part as a novelist. The two collections of his short stories, *The Conjure Woman* and *The Wife of His Youth*, were moderately successful. Containing virtually all his best writing during the period 1887-1899, these collections are ultimately the basis for Chesnutt's reputation as a short-story writer. With these stories, he moved up from literary apprenticeship to a respected position among American short-story writers. The stories must be viewed within the context of Chesnutt's total contribution to the traditional dialect/local-color story and the issue-oriented problem story.

In 1900, Chesnutt published his first novel, *The House Behind the Cedars*, which sold about two thousand copies in its first two months. His next two published novels (*The Marrow of Tradition* and *The Colonel's Dream*) were not as well received. Although he was honored as a writer by being asked to be a guest at Mark Twain's seventieth birthday party, Chesnutt retired from writing as a profession in 1905; no more of his creative work was published during the remainder of his lifetime.

Chesnutt achieved a great deal for his fellow African Americans in nonliterary areas. He was active politically and socially, and he wrote many controversial essays and speeches on the race issue. In 1913, he received an honorary LL.D. degree from Wilberforce University. In 1928, he was awarded the National Association for the Advancement of Colored People (NAACP) Spingarn Medal, an award given to African Americans who distinguish themselves in their fields. The medal honored Chesnutt for his "pioneer work as a literary artist depicting the life and struggles of Americans of Negro descent and for his long and useful career as a scholar, worker, and freeman of one of America's greatest cities [Cleveland]."

BIOGRAPHY

Charles Waddell Chesnutt was born on June 20, 1858, in Cleveland, Ohio. When he was nine years old, his family moved to Fayetteville, North Carolina, where he spent his youth. Although he was of African American descent, his features barely distinguished him from Caucasians. He learned, however, that family blood was very important in determining a person's social and economic prospects.

Chesnutt's mother died in 1871, when he was thirteen years old. Two years later, he left school to take a teaching job, in order to supplement the family income. In 1878, he married Susan Perry, a fellow teacher and daughter of a well-to-do black barber in Fayetteville. He had begun teaching in 1877 at the new State Colored Normal School in Fayetteville, and in 1880 he became principal of that school.

On a job-hunting trip to Washington, D.C., in 1879, Chesnutt was unable to find work. He had been studying stenography and hoped to obtain a job on a newspaper. In 1883, he was able to begin a new career as a stenographer and reporter in New York City, and shortly afterward he moved to Cleveland, where he was first a clerk and then a legal stenographer. Two years later, he began studying law, and in 1887, he passed the Ohio bar examination with the highest grade in his group. He opened his own office as a court reporter in 1888.

Between 1887 and 1899, beginning with the publication of "The Goophered Grapevine" by *The Atlantic Monthly*, he achieved some success as a short-story writer. In 1899, when Houghton Mifflin published two collections of his short stories, he gave up his profitable business and began writing novels full time—something he had dreamed of doing for many years.

His first published novel, *The House Behind the Cedars*, had some commercial success, but the next, *The Marrow of Tradition*, did not. In 1901, two years after he had closed his stenographic firm, he reopened it. Deciding to write short stories once more in 1903 and 1904, he sent them to *The Atlantic Monthly*, where he had found success earlier, but only one, "Baxter's Procrustes," was accepted. His novel *The Colonel's Dream*, published in 1905, failed to attract the attention of the public. The public of the early 1900's was not ready for the controversial subject matter of Chesnutt's novels and later short stories or for the works' sympathetic treatment of black characters. Americans in general did not want to read literature that featured African Americans as the main characters, that presented their problems in a predominantly white world, and that were written with sympathy for blacks rather than for whites. Chesnutt retired from creative writing as a profession in 1905, and thereafter he published only nonfiction.

During the rest of his life, Chesnutt concentrated on managing his business affairs, on participating in civic affairs, and on working on behalf of African American causes. He was an active member of the Rowland Club, an exclusive male literary group in Cleveland, although at first he was denied membership because of his race. During the last twenty-seven years of his life, he managed to find time to travel in Europe and to help educate his three children. He was a member of the Cleveland Chamber of Commerce and the National Arts Club; he also helped establish the Playhouse Settlement (now Karamu House) in Cleveland.

Before 1905, Chesnutt had been politically and socially active in helping to advance the cause of black people, and he continued to be active throughout his life. In 1901, he contributed greatly to having William Hannibal Thomas's controversial work *The American Negro* withdrawn from circulation. That same year, he chaired the Committee on Colored Troops for the Thirty-fifth National Encampment of the Grand Army of the Republic in Cleveland. In 1904, he became a member of the Committee of Twelve, a group organized by Booker T. Washington, and in 1905, he was a member of the Cleveland Council of Sociology. He addressed the National Negro Committee, which later became the NAACP, and served as a member of that organization's general committee. He protested the showing of the film *The Birth of a Nation* (1915), which glorified the Ku Klux Klan, and, more important, he protested the treatment of black American soldiers. He participated in the first Amenia Conference, called by Joel Spingarn in 1916, and he was awarded the Spingarn Medal by the NAACP in 1928.

ANALYSIS

Charles Waddell Chesnutt wrote three novels that were published during his lifetime and several that were not published until much later. He was a much more skillful short-story writer than a novelist, and although he developed most of his novels from short stories, one of the novels is exceptional as a literary work. Those reading his novels should remember, however, that some of the matters for which Chesnutt is criticized today—thin, idealized characters and the use of plot manipulations such as foreshadowing and coincidence—were standard in the fiction of the late 1800's and were accepted by the readers of the day.

Chesnutt dreamed of being a novelist, and he believed that racial issues such as the problems of passing, miscegenation, and racial assimilation had to be addressed in serious fiction. He found, however, that if he tried to write novels that would be commercially successful, publishers would not accept them, and if he tried to write works that examined racial issues honestly and with sympathy for blacks, the public would not accept these topical but controversial novels.

Chesnutt is notable for being the first African American fiction writer to gain a reputation for examining honestly and in detail the racial problems of black people in the United States after the Civil War. Many Americans in the last part of the nineteenth century preferred to ignore the problems of African Americans and especially did not want to read works of fiction that displayed sympathetic attitudes toward blacks, such as those written by Chesnutt.

His most successful years as a novelist, if they can be called successful, were from 1900 to 1905. During that time, his three published novels appeared: *The House Behind the Cedars, The Marrow of Tradition*, and *The Colonel's Dream*. Chesnutt believed that the only way to change the attitudes of Caucasians toward African Americans was to do so slowly and through fiction that expressed ideas indirectly. He believed too that preaching was not art, yet with each novel he became more of a crusader. After giving up writing in 1901, he decided that he could help his people best by achieving in a field other than writing. Chesnutt may have been a victim, just as his characters sometimes are. The themes that he could present most effectively and that he felt compelled to present were ones that the public would not accept; thus he did not continue to write novels and so did not develop further as a literary artist.

Any study of Chesnutt's three published novels should begin with an understanding of the author's views concerning racial issues of the late 1800's and early 1900's. One of the racial situations with which he was most concerned was that of the mulatto. The mulatto shared many of the problems of the full black person but was also confronted with two additional issues—those of passing for white and miscegenation. (Chesnutt himself was a mulatto who appeared white and who considered trying to pass for white.) Those passing might achieve social, economic, and professional opportunities, but they also had to make emotional sacrifices by giving up their families and friends. Furthermore, they faced certain limitations; for example, they had to avoid becoming too well known or distinguished because their pasts might be revealed.

Chesnutt believed that Americans had an unnatural fear of miscegenation. Because of this fear, persons of mixed black and white blood were outcasts in society and were almost forced to try to pass for white to obtain the American Dream. Ironically, those forced into passing and marrying whites began again the miscegenation cycle that was so feared by whites. Anglo-Saxon racial purity was something that should not be preserved, Chesnutt believed. He asserted that intermingling and integration would improve humanity biologically, but, more important, such mixing would result in African Americans' gaining the rights they should have as human beings. Only through the elimination of laws against intermarriage and social interaction between the races would African Americans gain true social, economic, and political equality.

Chesnutt's three published novels are all problem novels that treat his characteristic theme of the effects of color consciousness in American life. The first one, a novel of miscegenation and passing, is written from the point of view of "the socially alienated, ambitious young mulatto," as William Andrews has put it. The second novel takes the viewpoint of "a conscientious Southern social critic," and in it, Chesnutt analyzes the political aspects and the caste structure of the small town in the South after the Civil War. The last one, in the vogue of the muckraking novel, is an economic problem novel told from the viewpoint of "the progressive northern reformer."

The House Behind the Cedars

Between 1890 and 1899, Chesnutt greatly expanded and revised his short story "Rena Walden" until it became *The House Behind the Cedars*. He focused first on how color consciousness can destroy an interracial marriage and then on the predominant issue of whether a mulatto should cross the "color line." In March, 1899, he stated in a letter to Walter Hines Page that the Rena Walden story was the strong expression of a writer whose themes dealt primarily with the American color line. When he wrote to his daughters in the fall of 1900, he indicated that he hoped for "a howling success" from *The House Behind the Cedars*, "a strong race problem novel." The story of Rena Walden and her brother was the first in which the problems of Americans concealing their African heritage were studied with a detached and compassionate presentation of individuals on various sides of the issue.

The novel can be divided into two parts: Rena in white society, in which her brother is the major focus, and Rena in black society, in which she becomes the focus. The novel is set in Patesville, North Carolina, a few years after the Civil War. John Warwick, who has changed his name from Walden, has left Patesville and gone to South Carolina, where he has become a lawyer and plantation owner, acquiring wealth and position. He and his sister Rena are the children of a quadroon mother, Molly, and a white man who has died. John has returned to Patesville to help his beautiful sister escape the restrictions of color by teaching her how to pass for white. She is a success at the boarding school in South Carolina to which he takes her. Proof of her success in passing is seen when George Tryon, a good friend of John and a white, wants to marry Rena. Rena is not sure she should marry him, however, without telling him of her mixed blood. John and Rena indirectly discuss the pros and cons of passing and intermarriage. A series of coincidences leads to an unexpected meeting between George and Rena; he learns of her heritage, and the engagement is broken. Rena returns home to her mother and the house behind the cedars.

A chapter interlude that gives the Walden family history separates the first part of the novel from the second. John tries to persuade his sister to return to South Carolina with him or to take money and go to the North or the West, where she can pass for white and marry someone even better than George, but she refuses to leave Patesville. She has decided to accept her destiny and be of service to her people, whom she has rediscovered. After this point, the reader is told little more about John.

Rena meets Jeff Wain, an influential and prosperous mulatto from a rural county for which he is seeking a schoolteacher. Rena accepts the position, not realizing Jeff has a personal as well as a professional interest in her. Jeff is not as admirable a character as he first appears. As he pays Rena more and more attention, she becomes upset and repulsed. Once again, coincidence plays a part in the plot. George Tryon happens to learn of Rena's presence near a place he is visiting. When he sees her, he realizes that he loves her and that his love is stronger than his racial prejudice. The same day that George decides to declare his love to Rena, Jeff also decides to do so. Rena fears both of the men and leaves hastily for her mother's house behind the cedars. After Rena is overcome by exposure and fatigue, Frank Fowler, a childhood friend and a conscientious black workman, finds her and carries her to her home, where she dies. Rena realizes before she dies that Frank loved her the best.

In his fiction before *The House Behind the Cedars*, Chesnutt did not directly condemn passing and miscegenation, but neither did he directly call for them. Primarily, he wanted the public to be aware of the issues and to feel sympathy for those of mixed blood. In this novel, he makes passing and miscegenation acts deliberately chosen by mature African Americans. Such choices were justified because they were the only means by which blacks could gain and enjoy the social, economic, and political rights due them as citizens of the United States. Rather than lecturing, Chesnutt seeks to lead his readers to share his perspective. He delays revealing that John and Rena are mulattoes. To create sympathy for them first, he presents them simply as persons of humble origins who are attempting to achieve prosperity and happiness. Chesnutt passes John and Rena for white with the reader before he lets the reader know that they are mulattoes who have chosen or will deliberately choose to pass for white.

John Walden is the first black character in American fiction to decide to pass for white and, at the same time, to feel that his decision is legally and morally justified. Believing that the color of his skin tells him that he is white, he has no psychological problems concerning his choice to pass. He is not a stereotype. Intelligent and industrious, he patiently trains himself so that he can achieve the American Dream. At the beginning of the novel, the reader learns that he has become a prosperous lawyer and plantation owner after leaving Patesville; in the second part of the novel, after he has not been successful in helping Rena pass for white, he returns to South Carolina to regain his position.

The characters are not fully developed; they remain stick figures, although Chesnutt is partially successful in creating human interest for them. While Chesnutt attempts to create pity for her, Rena is simply a victim who accepts her fate, like other antiassimilationist mulattoes of the time. Another character, Dr. Green, is no more than a vehicle to present the traditional southern viewpoint. Two figures, Molly Walden and George Tryon, retain some individuality. Molly, as an unprotected free black woman in the slave South, is a product of her environment. With the circumstances that she faces, she can do little other than be the kept mistress of the white plantation owner, who has died but left her the house behind the cedars. Chesnutt does not want the reader to feel contempt for her or to be repulsed by her actions; her position is rendered dispassionately. George Tryon, on the other hand, undergoes great emotional upheaval and has a change of view that is probably meant to be instructive. He is tied to the traditional code of the southern gentleman but is not deluded about his prerogatives as a southern aristocrat. Rather, he is meant to be the best of the new South. His realization that he loves Rena and that her racial heritage is not important comes too late; she dies before he is able to do anything about it. He does not blame her for passing, and Chesnutt expects the reader not to blame her.

In *The House Behind the Cedars*, Chesnutt tries to present a mulatto that is not a prop or stereotype, one who deserves interest and sympathy apart from his position on the miscegenation issue. Furthermore, he treats the theme of color consciousness in post-Civil War American life honestly, in contrast to the sentimentalizing of other authors of the time. This novel, the one for which Chesnutt will be best remembered, should be read for its historical place in American literature.

THE MARROW OF TRADITION

Immediately after finishing *The House Behind the Cedars*, Chesnutt began working on his next novel. Events in Wilmington, North Carolina, gave him a race problem for the novel. In November, 1898, during city elections, a bloody race riot had taken place in which more than twenty-five black persons were killed, after which white supremacists took over the town government. Chesnutt followed events in the city after this incident. He learned graphic details when a local Wilmington physician visited him in Cleveland and described what he had seen when the violence was at its peak. Chesnutt also sought information from other friends in the area, and, in 1901, he went on a fact-finding trip to Wilmington and Fayetteville.

The Marrow of Tradition is the story of two families: The Carterets stand for the aristocracy of the "new South," with its pride and prejudice, and the Millers, who are of mixed blood, represent the qualities of the new black. The lives of the families are intertwined because the wives are half sisters. Janet Miller, however, has been cheated of her inheritance by Olivia Carteret, and Olivia constantly struggles with the problem of accepting Janet as her rightful sister.

The novel's study of white supremacist politics in a small southern town after the Civil War is more relevant to the problems encountered by the husbands than to those facing the wives. Dr. Adam Miller is a brilliant young surgeon denied opportunity in his hometown of Wellington (Wilmington, North Carolina). Major Philip Carteret, editor of the town's newspaper, seeks to seat a white supremacist regime in the local government. If he is successful, Adam Miller's position will be even more intolerable than it has been.

At the end of the novel, Major Carteret stirs up a riot during which Dr. Miller's son is killed. Immediately after the death of the Millers' child, the son of the Carterets becomes ill, and Adam Miller is the only person who can perform the surgery necessary to save the child's life. At first Miller refuses, but after Olivia Carteret humbles herself before her half sister and pleads with her to help save the Carterets' son, Janet Miller convinces her husband to change his mind and operate. The child is saved.

The Marrow of Tradition was too controversial a novel for the public when it was published. Americans were not ready for the subject of white supremacist politics and the political injustice existing in the South. Chesnutt himself was concerned that the novel approached fanaticism. He believed that it might not be wise for him to speak so plainly concerning such matters if he hoped to succeed as a fiction writer.

The Colonel's Dream

Like Chesnutt's previous two novels, *The Colonel's Dream* seems to have come from a long story that became a novel; however, no manuscript evidence for such a history exists. This novel deals with the economic status quo in the South, where caste and class prejudice prevented the rise of nonwhites. Muckraking novels were popular at this time, but none had been published about the new South. Chesnutt tends to become didactic in this novel, and he relies on overused novelistic machinery such as melodramatic subplots that involve interracial love and a lost inheritance. The novel is almost an economic parable.

The main character in the novel is Colonel Henry French, who, though born and reared in the South, has become a successful businessman in the North. His wife has died, and he has returned to Clarendon, North Carolina, where he hopes his son's health will improve. During the first part of the book, Colonel French, who is respected and admired by the townspeople, successfully reenters southern life. Although he is a white moderate, he comes to believe that he can unite the races into one society. He is especially concerned with improving the economic situation of African Americans. As he and the people of Clarendon become further and further apart in their understanding of the situation, he finds all of his efforts nullified by racial bigotry, and he must leave in failure. The novel was not successful commercially and is not very satisfying as a work of literature. After the failure of *The Colonel's Dream*, Chesnutt decided to stop writing novels and devoted himself to helping his people in other ways.

None of Chesnutt's three published novels was widely popular with the reading public of the early twentieth century, although *The House Behind the Cedars* enjoyed a modest commercial success. Furthermore, none of the novels can be considered successful artistic endeavors. Chesnutt sought to reveal his views slowly and indirectly so as to lead his readers to the feelings he wanted them to have. Too often, however, his "message" dominates, and he is didactic despite his intentions. His characters are not fully developed, even though Chesnutt attempts to present characters, especially mulattoes and African Americans, who are not stereotypes. It may be his strong concern with conveying his views and instructing his readers that prevents his characters from achieving depth. All of these novels are important, however, because Chesnutt was one of the first American novelists to create black characters who were not stereotypes and to deal honestly with racial issues that most Americans of the time preferred to ignore.

Sherry G. Southard

OTHER MAJOR WORKS

SHORT FICTION: *The Conjure Woman*, 1899; *The Wife of His Youth, and Other Stories of the Color Line*, 1899.

NONFICTION: *The Life of Frederick Douglass*, 1899; *The Journals of Charles W. Chesnutt*, 1993; *"To Be an Author": The Letters of Charles W. Chesnutt, 1889-1905*, 1997; *Charles W. Chesnutt: Essays and Speeches*, 1999; *Selected Writings*, 2001 (Sally Ann H. Ferguson, editor); *An Exemplary Citizen: Letters of Charles W. Chesnutt, 1906-1932*, 2002.

MISCELLANEOUS: *Stories, Novels, and Essays*, 2002; *The Portable Charles W. Chesnutt*, 2008.

BIBLIOGRAPHY

Chesnutt, Charles Waddell. *"To Be an Author": Letters of Charles W. Chesnutt, 1889-1905*. Edited by Joseph R. McElrath, Jr., and Robert C. Leitz III. Princeton, N.J.: Princeton University Press, 1997. Collection of letters is organized into sections in a manner particularly useful to students of Chestnutt's fiction and his career development: "Cable's Protégé in 1889-1891," "A Dream Deferred, 1891-1896," "Page's Protégé in 1897-1899," "The Professional Novelist of 1899-1902," "Discontent in 1903-1904," "The Quest Renewed, 1904-1905." Includes an informative introduction and a detailed index.

Heermance, Noel. *Charles Chesnutt: America's First Great Black Novelist*. Hamden, Conn.: Archon Books, 1974. Provides a good introduction to Chesnutt's life and to the themes of his fiction. Discusses Chesnutt's novels, short fiction, and other writings.

Keller, Frances Richardson. *An American Crusade: The Life of Charles Waddell Chesnutt*. Provo, Utah: Brigham Young University Press, 1978. One of the most helpful and important biographical resources on Chesnutt. Describes how Chesnutt refused to accept the segregation of his time, choosing to participate in both the black and white worlds.

McElrath, Joseph R., Jr., ed. *Critical Essays on Charles W. Chesnutt*. New York: G. K. Hall, 1999. Broad compilation of materials includes reviews of Chesnutt's works that appeared at the time of their initial publication as well as essays and articles, written between 1905 and 1997, analyzing his writings. Also contains overviews of his work and discussions of individual novels, including *The Colonel's Dream* and *The House Behind the Cedars*.

McWilliams, Dean. *Charles W. Chesnutt and the Fictions of Race*. Athens: University of Georgia Press, 2002. Examines Chesnutt's novels and short stories, describing how his fiction changed Americans' assumptions about race. Devotes separate chapters to analysis of the novels *The House Behind the Cedars*, *The Marrow of Tradition*, *The Colonel's Dream*, *The Quarry*, and *Mandy Oxendine*.

Pickens, Ernestine Williams. *Charles W. Chesnutt and the Progressive Movement*. New

York: Pace University Press, 1994. Provides both historical and literary analysis of two of Chesnutt's novels: *The Marrow of Tradition* and *The Colonel's Dream*. Chronicles Chesnutt's involvement in the Progressive movement and points out elements of the movement's philosophy in these works.

Render, Sylvia. *Charles W. Chesnutt*. Boston: Twayne, 1980. Good general introduction to the life and writing of Chesnutt. Discusses Chesnutt's major concerns with narrative technique, social justice, and the place of the African American in U.S. society.

Simmons, Ryan. *Chesnutt and Realism: A Study of the Novels*. Tuscaloosa: University of Alabama Press, 2006. Defines Chesnutt as a realist and describes how he was influenced by the literary realist movement. Points out elements of literary realism in Chesnutt's novels and explains how Chesnutt used the techniques and concepts of realism to depict race in his works.

Wilson, Matthew. *Whiteness in the Novels of Charles W. Chesnutt*. Jackson: University Press of Mississippi, 2004. Examines Chesnutt's novels with the aim of understanding the peculiar problems the African American author confronted in writing books for a predominantly white readership. Analyzes how Chesnutt constructed novels that appealed to this white audience while also examining racial issues that were not traditionally addressed in mainstream American fiction.

RALPH ELLISON

Born: Oklahoma City, Oklahoma; March 1, 1914
Died: New York, New York; April 16, 1994
Also known as: Ralph Waldo Ellison

PRINCIPAL LONG FICTION

Invisible Man, 1952

Juneteenth, 1999 (John F. Callahan, editor; revised and expanded as *Three Days Before the Shooting*, 2010, Callahan and Adam Bradley, editors)

OTHER LITERARY FORMS

Ralph Ellison's reputation rests primarily on *Invisible Man*, but *Shadow and Act* (1964), a collection of nonfiction prose, established Ellison as a major force in the critical theory of pluralism and in African American aesthetics. Arranged in three thematically unified sections, the essays, most of which appeared originally in journals such as *Antioch Review, Partisan Review*, and *The New Republic*, emphasize the importance of folk and popular (especially musical) contributions to the mainstream of American culture. Several of the essays from *Shadow and Act* are recognized as classics, notably "Richard Wright's Blues," "Change the Joke and Slip the Yoke," and "The World and the Jug." In addition, Ellison published several excellent short stories, including "Flying Home" and "Did You Ever Dream Lucky?" Collections of his essays include *Going to the Territory* (1986), *The Collected Essays of Ralph Ellison* (1995), and *Living with Music: Ralph Ellison's Jazz Writings* (2001).

ACHIEVEMENTS

Ralph Ellison occupies a central position in the development of African American literature and of contemporary American fiction. Equally comfortable with the influences of Fyodor Dostoevski, Mark Twain, Louis Armstrong, Igor Stravinsky, James Joyce, and Richard Wright, Ellison was the first African American writer to attain recognition as a full-fledged artist rather than as an intriguing exotic. Whereas Caucasian critics had previously, and unjustly, condescended to African American writers such as Langston Hughes, Zora Neale Hurston, and Wright, most granted Ellison the respect given Euro-American contemporaries such as Norman Mailer and Saul Bellow. A 1965 *Book World* poll identifying *Invisible Man* as the most distinguished postwar American novel simply verified a consensus already reflected in the recurrence of the metaphor of invisibility in countless works by both Caucasians and African Americans during the 1950's and 1960's.

Within the African American tradition itself, Ellison occupies a similarly prominent position, although his mainstream acceptance generates occasional reservations among some African American critics, particularly those committed to cultural nationalism. A

Ralph Ellison
(National Archives)

Black World poll, reflecting these reservations, identified Wright rather than Ellison as the most important black writer. The discrepancy stems in part from the critical image in the late 1960's of Ellison and James Baldwin as leading figures in an anti-Wright "universalist" movement in African American culture, a movement that some critics viewed as a sellout to Euro-American aesthetics. In the late twentieth century, however, both Euro-American and African American critics recognized Ellison's synthesis of the oral traditions of black culture and the literary traditions of both his black and his white predecessors. The consensus of that time viewed Ellison as clearly more sympathetic than Wright to the African American tradition. As a result, Ellison seems to have joined Wright as a major influence on younger black fiction writers such as James Alan McPherson, Leon Forrest, Toni Morrison, and David Bradley.

Ellison's most profound achievement, his synthesis of modernist aesthetics, American romanticism, and African American folk culture, embodies the aspirations of democratic pluralists such as Walt Whitman, Twain, and Hughes. His vernacular modernism earned Ellison an international reputation while exerting a major influence on the contemporary mainstream. With a reputation resting almost entirely on his first novel, Ellison's career is among the most intriguing in American literary history.

Biography

Despite Ralph Ellison's steadfast denial of the autobiographical elements of *Invisible Man* and his insistence on the autonomy of the individual imagination, both the specific details and the general sensibility of his work clearly derive from his experience of growing up in a southern family in Oklahoma City, attending college in Alabama, and residing in New York City during most of his adult life. Ellison's parents—whose decision to name their son Ralph Waldo Ellison, for American philosopher and essayist Ralph Waldo Emerson, reflected their commitment to literacy and education—moved from South Carolina to the comparatively progressive Oklahoma capital several years before their son's birth. Reflecting on his childhood, which was characterized by economic hardship following his father's death in 1917, Ellison emphasized the unusual psychological freedom provided by a social structure that allowed him to interact relatively freely with both whites and blacks. Encouraged by his mother, Ida, who was active in socialist politics, Ellison developed a frontier sense of a world of limitless possibility rather than the more typically southern vision of an environment filled with dangerous oppressive forces.

During his teenage years, Ellison developed a serious interest in music, both as a trumpet player and as a composer-conductor. Oklahoma City offered access both to formal classical training and to jazz, which was a major element of the city's nightlife. The combination of Euro-American and African American influences appears to have played a major role in shaping Ellison's pluralistic sensibility. After he graduated from high school in 1933, Ellison accepted a scholarship to the Tuskegee Institute, where he remained for three years, studying music and literature, until financial problems forced him to drop out. Although he originally planned to finish his studies, his subsequent relocation to New York City marked a permanent departure from the South.

Arriving in the North in 1936, Ellison established contacts with African American literary figures, including Hughes and Wright, who encouraged him to develop his knowledge of both the African American literary world and Euro-American modernism, especially that of T. S. Eliot and James Joyce. Never as deeply involved with leftist politics as Wright, Ellison nevertheless began developing his literary ideas in reviews and stories published in radical magazines such as *New Masses*. In 1938, Ellison, who had previously supported himself largely as a manual laborer, worked for the Federal Writers' Project, which assigned him to collect urban folklore, providing him direct contact with northern folk culture to complement his previous knowledge of southern folkways. Ellison's short fiction began appearing in print in the late 1930's and early 1940's. After a short term as managing editor of *Negro Quarterly* in 1942, he briefly left New York, serving in the merchant marine from 1943 to 1945. Awarded a Rosenwald Fellowship to write a novel, Ellison returned to New York and married Fanny McConnell in 1946.

Invisible Man, which took Ellison nearly seven years to write, was published in 1952, bringing him nearly instantaneous recognition as a major young writer. The novel won the National Book Award in 1953, and its reputation has continued to grow. Starting in 1952,

Ellison taught at Bard College, Rutgers University, New York University, and other institutions. From 1955 to 1957, he was the American Academy Fellow in Rome. In addition, he delivered public lectures, wrote essays, and worked on a second novel.

Less inclined to direct political involvement than contemporaries such as Amiri Baraka and James Baldwin, Ellison participated in the Civil Rights movement in a relatively quiet manner. He nevertheless attracted political controversy during the rise of the African American nationalist movements in the mid-1960's. Refusing to endorse any form of cultural or political separatism, Ellison was attacked as an aesthetic European and a political reactionary, especially after he accepted appointments to the American Institute of Arts and Letters (1964) and to the National Council on the Arts and Humanities, acts that were interpreted as support for the Lyndon B. Johnson's presidential administration's Vietnam policy. During the mid-1970's, however, these attacks abated as nationalist critics such as Larry Neal rose to Ellison's defense and a new generation of African American writers turned to him for aesthetic inspiration.

From 1970 to 1980, Ellison was Albert Schweitzer Professor of Humanities at New York University. He then retired from full-time teaching and continued to work on his second novel, *Juneteenth*, which was delayed both by his own perfectionism and by a house fire that destroyed much of the manuscript. The novel was incomplete at the time of his death on April 16, 1994, in New York.

ANALYSIS

Ellison's artistic vision is not impaired by blind spots related to racially divided cultures. While he acknowledges the expression of racial divisions in the works of such authors as Richard Wright and Langston Hughes, he is also critical of stereotyped images of blacks in fiction by white authors. Ellison's mature attitude toward American pluralism made him aware that racism is a common phenomenon that both whites and blacks need to transcend in order to coexist.

A masterwork of American pluralism, Ralph Ellison's *Invisible Man* insists on the integrity of individual vocabulary and racial heritage while encouraging a democratic acceptance of diverse experiences. Ellison asserts this vision through the voice of an unnamed first-person narrator who is at once heir to the rich African American oral culture and a self-conscious artist who, like T. S. Eliot and James Joyce, exploits the full potential of his written medium. Intimating the potential cooperation between folk and artistic consciousness, Ellison confronts the pressures that discourage both individual integrity and cultural pluralism.

INVISIBLE MAN

Invisible Man is a story about the gradual awakening of an African American man concerning his role in a multicultural democracy. The novel's narrator-protagonist introduces Ellison's central metaphor for the situation of the individual in Western culture in the first paragraph: "I am invisible, understand, simply because people refuse to see me." As the novel develops, Ellison extends this metaphor: Just as people can be rendered invisible by the willful failure of others to acknowledge their presence, so by taking refuge in the seductive but ultimately specious security of socially acceptable roles they can fail to see *themselves*, fail to define their own identities. Ellison envisions the escape from this dilemma as a multifaceted quest demanding heightened social, psychological, and cultural awareness.

The style of *Invisible Man* reflects both the complexity of the problem and Ellison's pluralistic ideal. Drawing on sources such as the blindness motif from William Shakespeare's *King Lear* (pr. c. 1605-1606), the underground man motif from Fyodor Dostoevski, and the complex stereotyping of Wright's *Native Son* (1940), Ellison carefully balances the realistic and the symbolic dimensions of *Invisible Man*. In many ways a classic *Künstlerroman*, the main body of the novel traces the protagonist from his childhood in the deep South through a brief stay at college and then to the North, where he confronts the American economic, political, and racial systems.

This movement parallels what Robert B. Stepto in *From Behind the Veil* (1979) calls the "narrative of ascent," a constituting pattern of African American culture. With roots in the fugitive slave narratives of the nineteenth century, the narrative of ascent follows its protagonist from physical or psychological bondage in the South through a sequence of symbolic confrontations with social structures to a limited freedom, usually in the North. This freedom demands from the protagonist a "literacy" that enables him or her to create and understand both written and social experiences in the terms of the dominant Euro-American culture. Merging the narrative of ascent with the *Künstlerroman*, which also culminates with the hero's mastery of literacy (seen in creative terms), *Invisible Man* focuses on writing as an act of both personal and cultural significance.

Similarly, Ellison employs what Stepto calls the "narrative of immersion" to stress the realistic sources and implications of his hero's imaginative development. The narrative of immersion returns the "literate" hero or heroine to an understanding of the culture he or she symbolically left behind during the ascent. Incorporating this pattern in *Invisible Man*, Ellison emphasizes the protagonist's links with the African American community and the rich folk traditions that provide him with much of his sensibility and establish his potential as a conscious artist.

The overall structure of *Invisible Man*, however, involves cyclical as well as directional patterns. Framing the main body with a prologue and epilogue set in an underground burrow, Ellison emphasizes the novel's symbolic dimension. Safely removed from direct participation in his social environment, the invisible man reassesses the literacy gained through his ascent, ponders his immersion in the cultural art forms of spirituals, blues, and jazz, and finally attempts to forge a pluralistic vision transforming these constitutive elements. The prologue and epilogue also evoke the heroic patterns and archetypal cycles described by Joseph Campbell in *The Hero with a Thousand Faces* (1949). After undergoing tests of his spiritual and physical qualities, the hero of Campbell's "monomyth"—usually a person of mysterious birth who receives aid from a cryptic helper—gains a reward, usually of a symbolic nature involving the union of opposites. Overcoming forces that would seize the reward, the hero returns to transform the life of the community through application of the knowledge connected with the symbolic reward.

To some degree, the narratives of ascent and immersion recast this heroic cycle in specifically African American terms: The protagonist first leaves, then returns to his or her community bearing a knowledge of Euro-American society potentially capable of motivating a group ascent. While it emphasizes the cyclic nature of the protagonist's quest, the frame of *Invisible Man* simultaneously subverts the heroic pattern by removing the protagonist from his community. He promises a return, but the implications of the return for the life of the community remain ambiguous.

This ambiguity superficially connects Ellison's novel with the classic American romance that Richard Chase characterizes in *The American Novel and Its Tradition* (1975) as incapable of reconciling symbolic perceptions with social realities. The connection, however, reflects Ellison's awareness of the problem more than his acceptance of the irresolution. Although the invisible man's underground burrow recalls the isolation of the heroes of the American romance, he promises a rebirth that is at once mythic, psychological, and social:

> The hibernation is over. I must shake off my old skin and come up for breath. . . . And I suppose it's damn well time. Even hibernations can be overdone, come to think of it. Perhaps that's my greatest social crime, I've overstayed my hibernation, since there's a possibility that even an invisible man has a socially responsible role to play.

Despite the qualifications typical of Ellison's style, the invisible man clearly intends to return to the social world rather than light out for the territories of symbolic freedom.

The invisible man's ultimate conception of the form of this return develops out of two interrelated progressions, one social and the other psychological. The social pattern, essentially that of the narrative of ascent, closely reflects the historical experience of the African American community as it shifts from rural southern to urban northern settings. Starting in the deep South, the invisible man first experiences invisibility as a result of casual but vicious racial oppression. His unwilling participation in the "battle royal" underscores the psychological and physical humiliation visited upon southern blacks. Ostensibly present to deliver a speech to a white community group, the invisible man is instead forced to engage in a massive free-for-all with other blacks, to scramble for money on an electrified rug, and to confront a naked white dancer who, like the boys, has been rendered invisible by the white men's blindness.

Escaping his hometown to attend a black college, the invisible man again experiences humiliation when he violates the unstated rules of the southern system—this time imposed by blacks rather than whites—by showing the college's liberal northern benefactor,

Mr. Norton, the poverty of the black community. As a result, the black college president, Dr. Bledsoe, expels the invisible man. Having experienced invisibility in relation to both blacks and whites and still essentially illiterate in social terms, the invisible man travels north, following the countless southern blacks involved in the "Great Migration."

Arriving in New York, the invisible man first feels a sense of exhilaration resulting from the absence of overt southern pressures. Ellison reveals the emptiness of this freedom, however, stressing the indirect and insidious nature of social power in the North. The invisible man's experience at Liberty Paints, clearly intended as a parable of African American involvement in the American economic system, emphasizes the underlying similarity of northern and southern social structures. On arrival at Liberty Paints, the invisible man is assigned to mix a white paint used for government monuments. Labeled "optic white," the grayish paint turns white only when the invisible man adds a drop of black liquid. The scene suggests the relationship between government and industry, which relies on black labor. More important, however, it points to the underlying source of racial blindness/invisibility: the white need for a black "other" to support a sense of identity. White becomes white only when compared to black.

The symbolic indirection of the scene encourages the reader, like the invisible man, to realize that social oppression in the North operates less directly than that in the South; government buildings replace rednecks at the battle royal. Unable to mix the paint properly, a desirable "failure" intimating his future as a subversive artist, the invisible man discovers that the underlying structure of the economic system differs little from that of slavery. The invisible man's second job at Liberty Paints is to assist Lucius Brockway, an old man who supervises the operations of the basement machinery on which the factory depends. Essentially a slave to the modern owner/master Mr. Sparland, Brockway, like the good darkies of the plantation tradition, takes pride in his master and will fight to maintain his own servitude. Brockway's hatred of the invisible man, whom he perceives as a threat to his position, leads to a physical struggle that culminates in an explosion caused by neglect of the machinery. Ellison's multifaceted allegory suggests a vicious circle in which blacks uphold an economic system that supports the political system that keeps blacks fighting to protect their neoslavery. The forms alter, but the battle royal continues. The image of the final explosion from the basement warns against passive acceptance of the social structure that sows the seeds of its own destruction.

Although the implications of this allegory in some ways parallel the Marxist analysis of capitalist culture, Ellison creates a much more complex political vision when the invisible man moves to Harlem following his release from the hospital after the explosion. The political alternatives available in Harlem range from the Marxism of the "Brotherhood" (loosely based on the American Communist Party of the late 1930's) to the black nationalism of Ras the Exhorter (loosely based on Marcus Garvey's pan-Africanist movement of the 1920's). The Brotherhood promises complete equality for blacks and at first encourages the invisible man to develop the oratorical talent ridiculed at the battle royal. As his effectiveness increases, however, the invisible man finds the Brotherhood demanding that his speeches conform to its "scientific analysis" of the black community's needs. When he fails to fall in line, the leadership of the Brotherhood orders the invisible man to leave Harlem and turn his attention to the "woman question."

Without the invisible man's ability to place radical politics in the emotional context of African American culture, the Brotherhood's Harlem branch flounders. Recalled to Harlem, the invisible man witnesses the death of Tod Clifton, a talented coworker driven to despair by his perception that the Brotherhood amounts to little more than a new version of the power structure underlying both Liberty Paints and the battle royal. Clearly a double for the invisible man, Clifton leaves the organization and dies in a suicidal confrontation with a white policeman. Just before Clifton's death, the invisible man sees him selling Sambo dolls, a symbolic comment on the fact that blacks involved in leftist politics in some sense remain stereotyped slaves dancing at the demand of unseen masters.

Separating himself from the Brotherhood after delivering an extremely unscientific funeral sermon, the invisible man finds few political options. Ras's black nationalism exploits the emotions the Brotherhood denies. Ultimately, however, Ras demands that his followers submit to an analogous oversimplification of their human reality. Where the Brotherhood elevates the scientific and rational, Ras focuses entirely on the emotional commitment to blackness. Neither alternative recognizes the complexity of either the political situation or the individual psyche; both reinforce the invisible man's feelings of invisibility by refusing to see basic aspects of his character.

As he does in the Liberty Paints scene, Ellison emphasizes the destructive, perhaps apocalyptic, potential of this encompassing blindness. A riot breaks out in Harlem, and the invisible man watches as DuPree, an apolitical Harlem resident recalling a number of African American folk heroes, determines to burn down his own tenement, preferring to start again from scratch rather than even attempt to work for social change within the existing framework. Unable to accept the realistic implications of such an action apart from its symbolic justification, the invisible man, pursued by Ras, who seems intent on destroying the very blackness he praises, tumbles into the underground burrow. Separated from the social structures, which have changed their facade but not their nature, the invisible man begins the arduous process of reconstructing his vision of America while symbolically subverting the social system by stealing electricity to light the 1,369 lightbulbs on the walls of the burrow and to power the record players blasting out the pluralistic jazz of Louis Armstrong.

As his frequent allusions to Armstrong indicate, Ellison by no means excludes the positive aspects from his portrayal of the African American social experience. The invisible man reacts strongly to the spirituals he hears at college, the blues story of Trueblood, the singing of Mary Rambro after she takes him in off the streets of Harlem. Similarly, he recognizes the strength wrested from resistance and suffering, a strength asserted by the broken link of chain saved by Brother Tarp. These figures, however, have relatively little power to alter the encompassing social system. They assume their full significance in relation to the second major progression in *Invisible Man*, that focusing on the narrator's psychological development.

As he gradually gains an understanding of the social forces that oppress him, the invisible man simultaneously discovers the complexity of his own personality. Throughout the central narrative, he accepts various definitions of himself, mostly from external sources. Ultimately, however, all definitions that demand he repress or deny aspects of himself simply reinforce his sense of invisibility. Only by abandoning limiting definitions altogether, Ellison implies, can the invisible man attain the psychological integrity necessary for any effective social action.

Ellison emphasizes the insufficiency of limiting definitions in the prologue when the invisible man has a dream-vision while listening to an Armstrong record. After descending through four symbolically rich levels of the dream, the invisible man hears a sermon on the "Blackness of Blackness," which recasts the "Whiteness of the Whale" chapter from Herman Melville's *Moby Dick* (1851). The sermon begins with a cascade of apparent contradictions, forcing the invisible man to question his comfortable assumptions concerning the nature of freedom, hatred, and love. No simple resolution emerges from the sermon, other than an insistence on the essentially ambiguous nature of experience. The dream-vision culminates in the protagonist's confrontation with the mulatto sons of an old black woman torn between love and hatred for their father. Although their own heritage merges the "opposites" of white and black, the sons act in accord with social definitions and repudiate their white father, an act that unconsciously but unavoidably repudiates a large part of themselves. The hostile sons, the confused old woman, and the preacher who delivers the sermon embody aspects of the narrator's own complexity. When one of the sons tells the invisible man to stop asking his mother disturbing questions, his words sound a leitmotif for the novel: "Next time you got questions like that ask yourself."

Before he can ask, or even locate, himself, however, the invisible man must directly experience the problems generated by a fragmented sense of self and a reliance on others. Frequently, he accepts external definitions, internalizing the fragmentation dominating his social context. For example, he accepts a letter of introduction from Bledsoe on the assumption that it testifies to his ability. Instead, it creates an image of him as a slightly dangerous rebel. By delivering the letter to potential employers, the invisible man participates directly in his own oppression. Similarly, he accepts a new name from the Brotherhood, again revealing his willingness to simplify himself in an attempt to gain social acceptance from the educational, economic, and political systems. As long as he accepts external definitions, the invisible man lacks the essential element of literacy: an understanding of the relationship between context and self.

His reluctance to reject the external definitions and attain literacy reflects both a tendency to see social experience as more "real" than psychological experience and a fear that the abandonment of definitions will lead to total chaos. The invisible man's meeting with Trueblood, a sharecropper and blues singer who has fathered a child by his own daughter, highlights this fear. Watching Mr. Norton's fascination with Trueblood, the invisible man perceives that even the dominant members of the Euro-American society feel stifled by the restrictions of "respectability." Ellison refuses to abandon all social codes, portraying Trueblood in part as a hustler whose behavior reinforces white stereotypes concerning black immorality. If Trueblood's acceptance of his situation (and of his human complexity) seems in part heroic, it is a heroism grounded in victimization.

Nevertheless, the invisible man eventually experiments with repudiation of all strict definitions when, after his disillusionment with the Brotherhood, he adopts the identity of Rinehart, a protean street figure who combines the roles of pimp and preacher, shifting identities with context. After a brief period of exhilaration, the invisible man discovers that "Rinehart's" very fluidity guarantees that he will remain locked within social definitions. Far from increasing his freedom at any moment, his multiplicity forces him to act in whatever role his "audience" casts him. Ellison stresses the serious consequences of this lack of center when the invisible man nearly becomes involved in a knife fight with Brother Maceo, a friend who sees only the Rinehartian exterior. The persona of "Rinehart," then, helps increase the invisible man's sense of possibility but lacks the internal coherence necessary for psychological, and perhaps even physical, survival.

Ellison rejects both acceptance of external definitions and abandonment of all definitions as viable means of attaining literacy. Ultimately, he endorses the full recognition and measured acceptance of the experience, historical and personal, that shapes the individual. In addition, he recommends the careful use of masks as a survival strategy in the social world. The crucial problem with this approach, derived in large part from African American folk culture, involves the difficulty of maintaining the distinction between external mask and internal identity. As Bledsoe demonstrates, a protective mask threatens to implicate the wearer in the very system he or she attempts to manipulate.

Before confronting these intricacies, however, the invisible man must accept his African American heritage, the primary imperative of the narrative of immersion. Initially, he attempts to repudiate or to distance himself from the aspects of that heritage associated with stereotyped roles. He shatters and attempts to throw away the "darky bank" he finds in his room at Mary Rambro's. His failure to lose the pieces of the bank reflects Ellison's conviction that stereotypes, major aspects of the African American social experience, cannot simply be ignored or forgotten. As an element shaping individual consciousness, they must be incorporated into, without being allowed to dominate, the integrated individual identity. Symbolically, in a scene in which the invisible man meets a yam vendor shortly after his arrival in Harlem, Ellison warns that one's racial heritage alone cannot provide a full sense of identity. After first recoiling from yams as a stereotypical southern food, the invisible man eats one, sparking a momentary epiphany of racial pride. When he indulges the feelings and buys another yam, however, he finds it frost-bitten at the center.

The invisible man's heritage, placed in proper perspective, provides the crucial hints concerning social literacy and psychological identity that allow him to come provisionally to terms with his environment. Speaking on his deathbed, the invisible man's grandfather offers cryptic advice that lies near the essence of Ellison's overall vision: "Live with your head in the lion's mouth. I want you to overcome 'em with yeses, undermine 'em with grins, agree 'em to death and destruction, let 'em swoller you till they vomit or bust wide open." Similarly, an ostensibly insane veteran echoes the grandfather's advice, adding an explicit endorsement of the Machiavellian potential of masking:

> Play the game, but don't believe in it—that much you owe yourself. Even if it lands you in a straitjacket or a padded cell. Play the game, but play it your own way—part of the time at least. Play the game, but raise the ante, my boy. Learn how it operates, learn how *you* operate. . . . that game has been analyzed, put down in books. But down here they've forgotten to take care of the books and that's your opportunity. You're hidden right out in the open—that is, you would be if you only realized it. They wouldn't see you because they don't expect you to know anything.

The vet understands the "game" of Euro-American culture, while the grandfather directly expresses the internally focused wisdom of the African American community.

The invisible man's quest leads him to a synthesis of these forms of literacy in his ultimate pluralistic vision. Although he at first fails to comprehend the subversive potential of his position, the invisible man gradually learns the rules of the game and accepts the necessity of the indirect action recommended by his grandfather. Following his escape into the underground burrow, he contemplates his grandfather's advice from a position of increased experience and self-knowledge. Contemplating his own individual situation in relation to the surrounding society, he concludes that his grandfather "*must* have meant the principle, that we were to affirm the principle on which the country was built but not the men." Extending this affirmation to the psychological level, the invisible man embraces the internal complexity he has previously repressed or denied: "So it is that now I denounce and defend, or feel prepared to defend. I condemn and affirm, say no and say yes, say yes and say no. I denounce because though implicated and partially responsible, I have been hurt to the point of abysmal pain, hurt to the point of invisibility. And I defend because in spite of all I find that I love. In order to get some of it down I *have* to love."

"Getting some of it down," then, emerges as the crucial link between Ellison's social and psychological visions. In order to play a socially responsible role—and to transform the words "social responsibility" from the segregationist catchphrase used by the man at the battle royal into a term responding to Louis Armstrong's artistic call for change—the invisible man forges from his complex experience a pluralistic art that subverts the social lion by taking its principles seriously. The artist becomes a revolutionary wearing a mask. Ellison's revolution seeks to realize a pluralist ideal, a true democracy recognizing the complex experience and human potential of every individual. Far from presenting his protagonist as a member of an intrinsically superior cultural elite, Ellison underscores his shared humanity in the concluding line: "Who knows but that, on the lower frequencies, I speak for you?" Manipulating the aesthetic and social rules of the Euro-American "game," Ellison sticks his head in the lion's mouth, asserting a blackness of blackness fully as ambiguous, as individual, and as rich as the whiteness of Herman Melville's whale.

JUNETEENTH

Forty-seven years after the release of *Invisible Man*, Ellison's second novel was published. Ellison began working on *Juneteenth* in 1954, but his constant revisions delayed its publication. *Juneteenth* is about a black minister, Hickman, who takes in and raises a little boy as black, even though the child looks white. The boy soon runs away to New England and later becomes a race-baiting senator. After he is shot on the Senate floor, he sends for Hickman. Their past is revealed through their ensuing conversation. The title of the novel, appropriately, refers to a day of liberation for African Americans. June 19, 1865, which came to be known as Juneteenth, was the day on which Union forces announced the emancipation of slaves in Texas. The title applies to the novel's themes of evasion and discovery of identity, themes that Ellison explores so masterfully in *Invisible Man*.

Although the novel was unfinished at the time of Ellison's death, only minor edits and revisions were necessary to publish the book, first in 1999 with some chapters previously published in various magazines and in a more complete edition, retitled *Three Days Before the Shooting*, in 2010.

Craig Werner
Updated by Mabel Khawaja

OTHER MAJOR WORKS

SHORT FICTION: *Flying Home, and Other Stories*, 1996.

NONFICTION: *Shadow and Act*, 1964; *The Writer's Experience*, 1964 (with Karl Shapiro); *Going to the Territory*, 1986; *The Collected Essays of Ralph Ellison*, 1995 (John F. Callahan, editor); *Conversations with Ralph Ellison*, 1995 (Maryemma Graham and Amritjit Singh, editors); *Trading Twelves: The Selected Letters of Ralph Ellison and Albert Murray*, 2000; *Living with Music: Ralph Ellison's Jazz Writings*, 2001 (Robert O'Meally, editor).

BIBLIOGRAPHY

Applebome, Peter. "From Ellison, a Posthumous Novel, with Additions Still to Come." *The New York Times*, February 11, 1999. Provides information on the origins of *Juneteenth*, both historical and personal to Ellison.

Benston, Kimberly, ed. *Speaking for You: The Vision of Ralph Ellison*. Washington, D.C.: Howard University Press, 1987. Useful resource reprints critical responses to Ellison's fiction and essays. Also includes an extensive bibliography of his writings.

Busby, Mark. *Ralph Ellison*. Boston: Twayne, 1991. Provides a concise, excellent introduction to Ellison's life and work.

Hill, Michael D., and Lena M. Hill. *Ralph Ellison's "Invisible Man": A Reference Guide*. Westport, Conn.: Greenwood Press, 2008. Analytical study addresses the content of the novel, the context in which it was written, its critical reception, and the work's artistic merit.

Jackson, Lawrence. *Ralph Ellison: Emergence of Genius*. New York: John Wiley & Sons, 2002. First book-length study of Ellison's life is a good source of information on the novelist's early life and career. Jackson, however, ends his study in 1953, shortly after the publication of *Invisible Man*.

O'Meally, Robert G., ed. *New Essays on "Invisible Man."* New York: Cambridge University Press, 1988. Collection of essays includes the responses of many critics and scholars to questions raised by earlier commentators on Ellison's novel.

Posnock, Ross, ed. *The Cambridge Companion to Ralph Ellison*. New York: Cambridge University Press, 2005. Collection of essays offers analysis of Ellison's life and interests. Includes a biographical chronology.

Rampersad, Arnold. *Ralph Ellison: A Biography*. New York: Alfred A. Knopf, 2007. Definitive biography draws extensively on Ellison's correspondence.

Rice, William H. *Ralph Ellison and the Politics of the Novel*. Lanham, Md.: Lexington Books, 2003. Addresses an unanswered question implied in *Invisible Man* regarding the politics of redefining the American novel and whether it is possible to ignore an author's ethnicity.

Schor, Edith. *Visible Ellison: A Study of Ralph Ellison's Fiction*. Westport, Conn.: Greenwood Press, 1993. Excellent study of all of Ellison's fiction that was generally available at the time, including his short fiction, which had not yet been collected in book form. A good starting place for any study of Ellison's work.

JESSIE REDMON FAUSET

Born: Snow Hill, New Jersey; April 27, 1882
Died: Philadelphia, Pennsylvania; April 30, 1961

PRINCIPAL LONG FICTION

There Is Confusion, 1924
Plum Bun: A Novel Without a Moral, 1928
The Chinaberry Tree: A Novel of American Life, 1931
Comedy, American Style, 1933

OTHER LITERARY FORMS

In addition to her four novels, Jessie Redmon Fauset wrote short stories, poems, nonfictional pieces, and works for children. She also translated the works of some Haitian writers.

ACHIEVEMENTS

Jessie Redmon Fauset was one of the most prolific novelists of the Harlem Renaissance of the 1920's, when her works were highly praised for introducing the reading public to a class of African Americans unknown to whites. Perhaps more important than her own works was her publishing and nurturing of other Harlem Renaissance writers as literary editor of *The Crisis*, the journal of the National Association for the Advancement of Colored People (NAACP), from 1919 to 1926. In that capacity, she published works by Langston Hughes, Claude McKay, Nella Larsen, Jean Toomer, and Countée Cullen. In 1920, Fauset also became the managing editor of the short-lived *The Brownies' Book*, writer W. E. B. Du Bois's magazine for children. Her first novel, *There Is Confusion*, was nominated for the Harmon Award in Literature in 1928.

BIOGRAPHY

Jessie Redmon Fauset, the youngest of seven children born to Redmon Fauset, an African Methodist Episcopal minister, and Annie Seamon Fauset, was born in South Hill, New Jersey, on April 27, 1882. She attended the public schools in Philadelphia and graduated as an honor student from the Philadelphia School for Girls. When she sought admission to Bryn Mawr College, rather than admit her, the college supported her application to Cornell University. Fauset graduated Phi Beta Kappa from Cornell in 1904. Whether she was the first black woman to attend Cornell or to be elected to Phi Beta Kappa, both of which are often speculated, Fauset "was one of the best educated Americans of her generation."

Denied employment in Philadelphia's integrated schools, Fauset began teaching high school in New York in 1905. After a year there and a year in Baltimore, she moved to the M Street High School (later named Dunbar High School) in Washington, D.C., where she taught for fourteen years. In 1921, a few months after receiving her master's degree from the University of Pennsylvania, Fauset joined the staff of *The Crisis* as literary editor. In 1924 she published her first novel. Fauset left *The Crisis* and returned to teaching in 1926. In 1929, she married a businessman, Herbert Harris, and between 1929 and 1933, she completed three other novels. When her husband died in 1958, Fauset returned to Philadelphia, where she died in 1961.

Analysis

Although she had been writing for *The Crisis* since her undergraduate days, it was not literary aspiration that spurred Jessie Redmon Fauset to write novels, but rather the 1922 publication of T. S. Stribling's novel about a middle-class mulatto, *Birthright*. Realizing that there was "an audience waiting to hear the truth about" African Americans, Fauset felt that those who were better qualified than whites to present the truth should do so. In presenting such truth, Fauset wrote about characters she knew best: educated African Americans from respectable family backgrounds who in their values and goals were, as she stated, "not so vastly different from other Americans." Fauset used traditional literary forms in her writing, such as the sentimental novel, Greek tragedy, and fairy tales, and she was criticized for offering nothing innovative during a time when African American writers were experimenting with cultural forms and themes. In addition, because Fauset's novels focused on women and women's issues, they were dismissed in the 1930's by both white and black male critics. With the burgeoning interest in African American women's literature in the 1970's, female critics began to discover the complexity of Fauset's novels and to note her treatment of gender, class, and race issues. As a result, Fauset's works have become the focus of increased critical attention.

There Is Confusion

Fauset's first novel, *There Is Confusion*—a tale of two families—is structured by three separate but connected plot lines, the first of which focuses on the Marshalls, a well-to-do family. Joanna, the youngest of the four children, encouraged by her father's thwarted dreams of greatness, wants to become a dancer. The second plot line focuses on Peter Bye, the fourth-generation descendant of a family whose lives are intertwined with the lives of their wealthy white former owners. While Peter's grandfather, Isaiah, refuses to accept his relative's offer to serve as their coachman and goes on to found a school for black youths in Philadelphia, Peter's dreams of becoming a surgeon are thwarted because he longs to be recognized by the white Byes and is not. Meriwether, Peter's father, deciding instead that "the world owes [him] a living," does nothing. Influenced by his father's attitude, Peter becomes entangled in the legacy of racial hatred and aspires to nothing. It is only when he becomes attracted to Joanna and is influenced by her goals of greatness that he decides, in order to win her love, to become a doctor.

The third plot line, the story of Maggie Ellersley, the daughter of a washerwoman, involves a conventional marriage. Aspiring to the middle class, Maggie begins working for

Joanna's father, where she meets and takes an interest in his son, Philip. The interest appears to be mutual; however, Joanna intervenes and tells Maggie that she should marry someone in her own class. A hurt Maggie does so, then becomes a successful businesswoman when the marriage fails. After a second failed marriage, Maggie goes to France to volunteer during World War I and encounters the dying Philip. They marry, and she takes care of him until his death. Within each plot line, Fauset heavy-handedly reveals the obstacles to the achievement of each character's dreams: Joanna's dream of becoming a professional dancer is thwarted by race; Peter's dream (or lack thereof) is influenced by family legacy; Maggie's dream is hindered by class. Fauset also reveals how each character achieves despite the obstacles. Unable to dance in a white theater troupe, Joanna starts her own dance class but is asked to dance the role of the colored American in "The Dance of the Nations" when the white woman chosen for the part lacks the technique. Joanna attains instant success and is eventually asked to perform three roles.

Peter, because of his love for Joanna, becomes a surgeon; however, she has no interest in assuming the conventional roles of wife and mother. Therefore, caught in the web of circumstances characteristic of sentimental novels, and through a series of contrived coincidences, Peter ends up in Europe during the war and meets one of his white relatives. Young Meriwether dies in Peter's arms, but not before extracting the promise that Peter will visit the senior Meriwether. By moving beyond hate, Peter not only receives long-awaited recognition from the white Byes but also wins Joanna as his wife.

As evidenced by the many hardships that Maggie undergoes, Fauset suggests that Maggie's aspiration—to transcend one's class through marriage—is the most problematic. Maggie achieves her desired middle-class status not through her marriages but rather through her business acumen. Moreover, by developing a political and racial consciousness and selflessness and traveling to Europe to aid black soldiers, she is reunited with her first love. *There Is Confusion* ends, as do all sentimental novels, on a happy note. While many ideas are introduced in the novel, the theme that dominates is, as critic Carolyn Sylvander puts it, that "surviving the hardships engendered by discrimination places the black person and the race in a position of superiority."

PLUM BUN

Most critics consider Fauset's second novel, *Plum Bun*, to be her best. As in *There Is Confusion*, a middle-class African American family is at the novel's center, but unlike the earlier work, *Plum Bun* centers on one protagonist, Angela. In addition, the novel is structured in five parts, using a nursery rhyme as its epigraph and unifying element:

> To market, to market
> To buy a plum bun;
> Home again, home again,
> Market is done.

In the first section, titled "Home," readers are introduced to the Murray family: Junius and Mattie and their two daughters, Angela and Virginia. This section also provides the background information important to the rest of the novel. Angela and Virginia are exposed early on to their mother's fairy-tale view of marriage. Just as important, they are exposed to her views on color. Although Junius and Virginia are both brown-skinned, Mattie and Angela are light enough to pass—which they often do "for fun." Junius is not opposed to this as long as no principle is being compromised. The result, however, is that Angela grows up seeing her mother on occasion publicly ignore her darker-skinned husband and daughter. When the parents die within two weeks of each other, Angela decides to move to New York in order to further her personal and professional goals.

In the second section, "Market," Angela becomes the art student Angele Mory and is indoctrinated in the worldly ways of courtship. In the third section, titled "Plum Bun," Angele meets Roger Fielding, an affluent white man, whom she dates and eventually hopes to marry. Roger does not propose marriage but rather cohabitation. Angele does not agree, and he eventually ends the relationship, but not before Angele has publicly denied Virginia, who has also moved to New York. In "Home Again," the novel's fourth section, Angele, in search of companionship, admits her love for Anthony Cross, a fellow art student who is also passing. Having resolved never to marry a white woman, Anthony rejects Angele and becomes engaged to Virginia, unaware that Angele and Virginia are sisters.

In the final section, "Market Is Done," Angele decides to focus on her art. She wins a scholarship to study in Paris but forfeits it by revealing that she, too, is black when fellow student Rachel Powell is denied money for her passage because of her race. Angele decides to support her own study in Paris. Before she leaves the United States, she returns "home" to Philadelphia and is reunited with a former admirer, Matthew Henson. Knowing that Virginia is really in love with Matthew, and learning that Matthew loves Virginia, Angele does not interfere. Instead she moves to Paris, seemingly destined to be alone; however, Anthony appears that Christmas Eve, sent with Matthew and Virginia's love. Like *There Is Confusion*, *Plum Bun* has a happy ending.

By including fairy-tale motifs within the marriage plot, Fauset explores the choices and compromises that women make regarding marriage. The novel "without a moral" indeed has one: Adhering to the traditional conceptions of marriage is problematic when race, class, and gender are factors.

The Chinaberry Tree

Fauset's theme of the effects of race, gender, and class as focused within two-parent, multiple-sibling families is abandoned in her third novel. *The Chinaberry Tree* relates the story of two cousins, Laurentine Strange and Melissa Paul, who are both products of illicit relationships. Laurentine is the product of an illicit romantic relationship between a master, Colonel Halloway, and his former slave, Sarah. Accepting the community's opinion that she has "bad blood," Laurentine isolates herself from the community, and rejection from a suitor reinforces her feelings of inadequacy and propels her to further isolation. Melissa, the product of an adulterous relationship between Judy Strange and the married Sylvester Forten, is sent to Red Brook to live with her relatives. She meets and falls in love with Malory Forten, who, unknown to her, is her half brother. The novel explores both women's responses to being innocent victims of fate.

The Chinaberry Tree is not merely Fauset's attempt to reveal that "Negroes are not so vastly different" or that their lives are elements of a play falling together, as stated in the novel's foreword. It is a subtle illustration of women making choices and accepting the consequences: Both Sal and Judy Strange choose forbidden loves. In spite of their "bad blood," as the daughters are seemingly tainted by their mothers' choices, Laurentine and Melissa are able to find true love at the novel's end. What appears to be another example of Fauset's blind acceptance of the values of nineteenth century sentimental fiction is a subtle commentary on women refusing to adhere to the constrictions placed on their lives.

COMEDY, AMERICAN STYLE

Fauset structured her final novel around the elements of drama, with its chapters titled "The Plot," "The Characters," "Teresa's Act," "Oliver's Act," "Phebe's Act," and "Curtain." In this, Fauset's darkest work, she returns to the format of the two-parent family. The novel chronicles the life of Olivia Blanchard Cary, a light-skinned African American who, shaped by two incidents in her childhood, chooses a life of passing. She marries a black doctor, not for love but rather for status, and they have three children. Nonetheless, Olivia's obsession with color consciousness destroys the family. When her oldest child, Teresa, falls in love with the dark-skinned Henry Bates, Olivia intervenes and forces Teresa to marry a Frenchman.

The youngest child, Oliver, suffers the most because of his bronze skin color. Rejected by his mother from birth and often made to play the role of servant or denied in public, he commits suicide. Only Christopher survives intact through his marriage to Phebe Grant. When the novel ends, Olivia has finally achieved her objective: Living alone in France—her husband has divorced her, and her children have abandoned her—she passes as white.

In this, her only novel that does not have a happy ending, Fauset's use of satire is quite evident. One critic, pointing to Fauset's subversion of the Cinderella motif, has noted that neither mother nor daughter is happily married, and both are poor. Another critic has commented on the ironic use of the Snow White motif: Olivia pronounces the bitter truth in her pregnancy with Oliver that he would be "the handsomest and most attractive of us all," and by doing so she unwittingly proclaims that black is beautiful.

Paula C. Barnes

BIBLIOGRAPHY

Calloway, Licia Morrow. "Revising the Victorian Maternal Ideal in Jessie Fauset's *There Is Confusion*." In *Black Family (Dys)function in Novels by Jessie Fauset, Nella Larsen, and Fannie Hurst*. New York: Peter Lang, 2003. Examines *There Is Confusion* with a focus on Fauset's treatment of maternity and her handling of the class pressures on upwardly aspiring black characters.

Harker, Jaime. *America the Middlebrow: Women's Novels, Progressivism, and Middlebrow Authorship Between the Wars*. Amherst: University of Massachusetts Press, 2007. Traces the careers of Fauset and several other women authors who published during the 1920's and 1930's and who viewed fiction as a means of reforming society.

Jones, Sharon L. "Deconstructing the Black Bourgeoisie: Subversions and Diversions in the Fiction of Jessie Fauset." In *Rereading the Harlem Renaissance: Race, Class, and Gender in the Fiction of Jessie Fauset, Zora Neale Hurston, and Dorothy West*. Westport, Conn.: Greenwood Press, 2002. Chapter devoted to Fauset's novels is part of a larger analysis of the works of three African American women writers that demonstrates how their fiction challenges conventional ideas about race, class, and gender oppression.

McDowell, Deborah. "Jessie Fauset." In *Modern American Women Writers*, edited by Lea Baechler and A. Walton Litz. New York: Charles Scribner's Sons, 1991. Presents a general discussion of Fauset's role in the Harlem Renaissance as editor and writer, and analyzes Fauset's four novels to illustrate their "thematic and ironic complexity."

McLendon, Jacquelyn Y. *The Politics of Color in the Fiction of Jessie Fauset and Nella Larsen*. Charlottesville: University of Virginia Press, 1995. Addresses the theme of the "tragic mulatto" in the novels of the two writers. The discussion of Fauset's work focuses on the novels *Plum Bun* and *Comedy, American Style*.

Ransom, Portia Boulware. *Black Love and the Harlem Renaissance (the Novels of Nella Larsen, Jessie Redmon Fauset, and Zora Neale Hurston): An Essay in African American Literary Criticism*. Lewiston, N.Y.: Edwin Mellen Press, 2005. Examines how the three writers use their semiautobiographical fiction to focus on the tensions between black men and women who are trying to define themselves.

Sato, Hiroko. "Under the Harlem Shadow: A Study of Jessie Fauset and Nella Larsen." In *The Harlem Renaissance Remembered*, edited by Arna Bontemps. New York: Dodd, Mead, 1972. While asserting that Fauset "is not a first-rate writer," Sato argues that race is the central concern of the middle-class characters in her novels.

Sylvander, Carolyn. *Jessie Redmon Fauset: Black American Writer*. Troy, N.Y.: Whitston, 1981. Definitive critical biography argues that reading Fauset's novels as compared to her life is too simplistic. Provides analysis of Fauset's work in addition to recounting the details of her life.

Wall, Cheryl. *Women of the Harlem Renaissance*. Bloomington: Indiana University Press, 1995. Presents an excellent discussion of all of Fauset's works. Wall asserts that Fauset achieved distinction as a journalist and essayist instead of as a novelist.

ERNEST J. GAINES

Born: Oscar, Louisiana; January 15, 1933
Also known as: Ernest James Gaines

PRINCIPAL LONG FICTION

Catherine Carmier, 1964
Of Love and Dust, 1967
The Autobiography of Miss Jane Pittman, 1971
In My Father's House, 1978
A Gathering of Old Men, 1983
A Lesson Before Dying, 1993

OTHER LITERARY FORMS

Ernest J. Gaines published a collection of short stories, *Bloodline*, in 1968. One story from that collection, *A Long Day in November*, was published separately in a children's edition in 1971.

ACHIEVEMENTS

Throughout his career, Ernest J. Gaines has been a serious and committed writer of fiction. He has always worked slowly, frustratingly slowly to his admirers, but that is because of his great devotion to and respect for the craft of fiction. His six novels are all set in rural Louisiana, north of Baton Rouge: Gaines, like William Faulkner, has created a single world in which his works are centered. Even though Gaines has written during a time of great racial turmoil and unrest, he has resisted becoming involved in political movements, feeling that he can best serve the cause of art and humanity by devoting himself to perfecting his craft. This does not mean that he has remained detached from political realities. Taken together, his novels cover the period of 1865 to 1980, reflecting the social movements that have affected black Americans during that time. Gaines has said again and again, however, that he is primarily interested in people; certainly it is in his depiction of people that his greatest strength lies. His focus is on the universals of life: love, pride, pity, hatred. He aspires thus not to have an immediate political impact with his writing but to move people emotionally. His supreme achievement in this regard is *The Autobiography of Miss Jane Pittman*. With its publication—and with the highly acclaimed made-for-television film based on the novel—Gaines achieved the recognition he had long deserved.

BIOGRAPHY

From birth until age fifteen, Ernest James Gaines lived in rural Louisiana with his parents. As a boy, he often worked in the plantation fields and spent much of his spare time with his aunt, Miss Augusteen Jefferson. He moved to Vallejo, California, in 1948 to live with his mother and stepfather, and he attended high school and junior college there before serving in the army. After his military service, he earned a B.A. degree at San Francisco State College. On the basis of some stories written while he was a student there, he was awarded the Wallace Stegner Creative Writing Fellowship in 1958 for graduate study at Stanford University.

He was a Guggenheim Fellow in 1971 and won an award from the Black Academy of Arts and Letters in 1972. In 1987 Gaines received a literary award from the American Academy and Institute of Arts and Letters, and in 1993 he was awarded a John D. and Catherine T. MacArthur Foundation fellowship. Also in that year, *A Lesson Before Dying* won the National Book Critics Circle Award. Since 1958 Gaines has lived, impermanently, by his own testimony, in or near San Francisco, feeling that living elsewhere enables him to gain a perspective on his southern material that would be unavailable were he to live in the South full time. By making yearly trips back to Louisiana, where he holds a visiting professorship in creative writing at the University of Southwestern Louisiana in Lafayette, he retains contact with his native region.

ANALYSIS

Before it became fashionable, Ernest J. Gaines was one southern black writer who wrote about his native area. Although he has lived much of his life in California, he has never been able to write adequately about that region. He has tried to write two novels about the West but has failed to finish either of them. Thus, while he has physically left the South, he has never left emotionally. His ties remain with the South, and his works remain rooted there. When he first began reading seriously, Gaines gravitated toward those writers who wrote about the soil and the people who lived close to it, among them William Faulkner, John Steinbeck, Willa Cather, and Ivan Turgenev. He was disappointed to discover that few black writers had dealt with the black rural southern experience. (Richard Wright had begun his career by doing so, and his work weakened as he moved further from the South.) Thus, Gaines began his career with the conscious desire to fill a void. He felt that no one had written fiction about his people.

This fact helps explain why his novels always concentrate on rural settings and on the "folk" who inhabit them. One of the great strengths of his work is voice; the sound of the voice telling the story is central to its meaning. Among his works, *Of Love and Dust*, *The Autobiography of Miss Jane Pittman*, and all the stories in *Bloodline* are told in the first person by rural black characters. The voices of the storytellers, especially Miss Jane's, express the perspective not only of the individual speakers but also in some sense of the entire black community, and it is the community on which Gaines most often focuses his attention.

Louisiana society, especially from a racial perspective, is complicated. Not only blacks and whites live there, but also Creoles and Cajuns. Thus there are competing communities, and some of Gaines's more interesting characters find themselves caught between groups, forced to weigh competing demands in order to devise a course of action.

Several themes recur in the Gaines canon, and together they create the total effect of his work. Generally, he deals with the relationship between past and present and the possibility of change, both individual and social. Using a broad historical canvas in his works, especially in *The Autobiography of Miss Jane Pittman*, Gaines treats the changes in race relations over time, but he is most interested in people, in whether and how they change as individuals. The issue of determinism and free will is therefore a central question in his work. Gaines has been very interested in and influenced by Greek tragedy, and in his fiction, a strain of environmental determinism is evident. In his works prior to and including *The Autobiography of Miss Jane Pittman*, a growing freedom on the part of his black characters can be seen, but the tension between fate and free will always underlies his works.

Some of Gaines's most admirable characters—for example, Marcus in *Of Love and Dust*, and Ned, Joe, and Jimmy in *The Autobiography of Miss Jane Pittman*—have the courage, pride, and dignity to fight for change. At the same time, however, Gaines reveres the old, who, while often resistant to change, embody the strength of the black people. In his work, one frequently finds tension between generations, a conflict between old and young that is reconciled only in the character of Miss Jane Pittman, who even in extreme old age retains the courage to fight for change.

Other recurring tensions and dichotomies are evident in Gaines's novels. Conflict often exists between men and women. Because of slavery, which denied them their manhood, black men feel forced to take extreme actions to attain or assert it, a theme most evident in *Of Love and Dust*, *The Autobiography of Miss Jane Pittman*, *A Gathering of Old Men*, and the stories in *Bloodline*. Women, on the other hand, are often presented in Gaines's fiction as preservers and conservers. Each group embodies a strength, but Gaines suggests that wholeness comes about only when the peculiar strengths of the two sexes are united, again most clearly exemplified in Miss Jane and her relationship with the men in her life.

Among the male characters, a tension exists between fathers and sons. Treated explicitly in Gaines's fourth novel, *In My Father's House*, this theme is implicit throughout the canon. Though young men look to the older generation for models, there are few reliable examples for them to follow, and they find it difficult to take responsibility for their lives and for the lives of their loved ones.

Gaines's characters at their best seek freedom and dignity: Some succeed, and some fail in their attempts to overcome both outer and inner obstacles. Viewed in sequence, Gaines's first three novels move from the almost total bleakness and determinism of *Catherine Carmier* to the triumph of *The Autobiography of Miss Jane Pittman*. *In My Father's House*, however, reflects a falling away of hope in both individual and social terms, perhaps corresponding to the diminution of expectations experienced in America during the late 1970's and early 1980's.

Catherine Carmier

Gaines's first novel, *Catherine Carmier*, based on a work he wrote while an adolescent, has many of the characteristic weaknesses of a first novel and is more interesting for what it anticipates in Gaines's later career than for its intrinsic merits. Though it caused barely a ripple of interest when it was first published, the novel introduces many of the themes that Gaines treats more effectively in his mature fiction. The book is set in the country, near Bayonne, Louisiana, an area depicted as virtually a wasteland. Ownership of much of this region has devolved to the Cajuns, who appear throughout Gaines's novels as Snopes-like vermin, interested in owning the land only to exploit it. Like Faulkner, Gaines sees this kind of person as particularly modern, and the growing power of the Cajuns indicates a weakening of values and a loss of determination to live in right relationship to the land.

Onto the scene comes Jackson Bradley, a young black man born and reared in the area but (like Gaines himself) educated in California. Bradley is a hollow, rootless man, a man who does not know where he belongs. He has found the North and the West empty, with people living hurried, pointless lives, but he sees the South as equally empty. Feeling no link to a meaningful past and no hope for a productive future, Bradley is a deracinated modern man. He has returned to Louisiana to bid final farewell to his Aunt Charlotte, a representative of the older generation, and to her way of life.

While there and while trying to find a meaningful path for himself, Bradley meets and falls in love with Catherine Carmier. She, too, is living a blocked life, and he feels that if they can leave the area, they will be able to make a fulfilling life together. Catherine is the daughter of Raoul Carmier, in many ways the most interesting character in the novel. A Creole, he is caught between the races. Because of his black blood, he is not treated as the equal of whites, but because of his white blood, he considers blacks to be beneath him. He has a near incestuous relationship with Catherine, since after her birth his wife was unfaithful to him and he considers none of their subsequent children his. Feeling close only to Catherine, he forbids her to associate with any men, but especially with black men. A man of great pride and love of the land, Raoul is virtually the only man in the region to resist the encroachment of the Cajuns. His attitude isolates him all the more, which in turn makes him fanatically determined to hold to Catherine.

Despite her love for and loyalty to her father, Catherine senses the dead end her life has become and returns Bradley's love. Though she wants to leave with him, she is paralyzed by her love of her father and by her knowledge of what her leaving would do to him. This conflict climaxes with a brutal fight between Raoul and Bradley over Catherine, a fight that Bradley wins. Catherine, however, returns home to nurse her father. The novel ends ambiguously, with at least a hint that Catherine will return to Bradley, although the thrust of the book militates against that eventuality. Gaines implies that history and caste are a prison, a tomb. No change is possible for the characters because they cannot break out of the cages their lives have become. Catherine will continue living her narrow, unhealthy life, and Bradley will continue searching for something to fill his inner void.

OF LOVE AND DUST

Gaines's second novel, *Of Love and Dust*, was received much more enthusiastically than was *Catherine Carmier*; with it, he began to win the largely positive, respectful reviews that continued with his subsequent work. Like *Catherine Carmier*, *Of Love and Dust* is a story of frustrated love. The setting is the same: rural Louisiana, where the Cajuns are gradually assuming ownership and control of the land. *Of Love and Dust* is a substantial improvement over *Catherine Carmier*, however, in part because it is told in the first person by Jim Kelly, an observer of the central story. In this novel, one can see Gaines working toward the folk voice that became such an integral part of the achievement of *The Autobiography of Miss Jane Pittman*.

The plot of the novel concerns Marcus Payne, a young black man sentenced to prison for murder and then bonded out by a white plantation owner who wants him to work in his fields. Recognizing Marcus's rebelliousness and pride, the owner and his Cajun overseer, Sidney Bonbon, brutally attempt to break his spirit. This only makes Marcus more determined, and in revenge, he decides to seduce Louise, Bonbon's neglected wife. What begins, however, as simply a selfish and egocentric act of revenge on Marcus's part grows into a genuine though grotesque love. When he and Louise decide to run away together, Bonbon discovers them and kills Marcus. Even though he dies, Marcus, by resisting brutalizing circumstances, retains his pride and attempts to prove his manhood and dignity. His attempts begin in a self-centered way, but as his love for Louise grows, he grows in stature in the reader's eyes until he becomes a figure of heroic dimensions.

Through his use of a first-person narrator, Gaines creates a double perspective in the novel, including on the one hand the exploits of Marcus and on the other the black community's reactions to them. The narrator, Jim Kelly, is the straw boss at the plantation, a member of the black community but also accepted and trusted by the whites because of his dependability and his unwillingness to cause any problems. His initial reaction to Marcus—resentment and dislike of him as a troublemaker—represents the reaction of the community at large. The older members of the community never move beyond that attitude because they are committed to the old ways, to submission and accommodation. To his credit, however, Jim's attitude undergoes a transformation. As he observes Marcus, his resentment changes to sympathy and respect, for he comes to see Marcus as an example of black manhood that others would do well to emulate.

Marcus's death gives evidence of the strain of fate and determinism in this novel as well, yet because he dies with his pride and dignity intact, *Of Love and Dust* is more hopeful than *Catherine Carmier*. Gaines indicates that resistance is possible and, through the character of Jim Kelly, that change can occur. Kelly leaves the plantation at the end of the novel, no longer passively accepting what fate brings him but believing that he can act and shape his own life. Though Marcus is an apolitical character, like Jackson Bradley, it is suggested that others will later build on his actions to force social change on the South. *Of Love and Dust* is a major step forward beyond *Catherine Carmier* both artistically and thematically. Through his use of the folk voice, Gaines vivifies his story, and the novel suggests the real possibility of free action by his characters.

The Autobiography of Miss Jane Pittman

Without a doubt, *The Autobiography of Miss Jane Pittman* is Gaines's major contribution to American literature. Except for an introduction written by "the editor," it is told entirely in the first person by Miss Jane and covers approximately one hundred years, from the Civil War to the Civil Rights movement of the 1960's. Basing the novel on stories he heard while he was a child in the company of his aunt, Augusteen Jefferson, and using the format of oral history made popular in recent decades, Gaines created a "folk autobiography" that tells the story of people who are not in the history books. While the work is the story of Miss Jane, she is merely an observer for a substantial portion of its length, and the story becomes that of black Americans from slavery to the present. Gaines's mastery of voice is especially important here, for Miss Jane's voice is the voice of her people.

From the very beginning of the novel, when Miss Jane is determined, even in the face of physical beatings, to keep the name a Union soldier gave her and refuses to be called Ticey, her slave name, to the end of the novel, when she leads her people to Bayonne in a demonstration against segregated facilities, she is courageous and in the best sense of the word "enduring," like Faulkner's Dilsey. In her character and story, many of the dichotomies that run through Gaines's work are unified.

The differing roles of men and women are important elements in the book. Women preserve and sustain—a role symbolized by Miss Jane's longevity. Men, on the other hand, feel the need to assert their manhood in an active way. Three black men are especially important in Miss Jane's life, beginning with Ned, whom she rears from childhood after his mother is killed and who becomes in effect a "son" to her. Like Marcus Payne, Ned is a rebel, but his rebellion is concentrated in the political arena. Returning to Louisiana after the turn of the century, he attempts to lead his people to freedom. Though he is murdered by whites, his legacy and memory are carried on by Miss Jane and the people in the community. Later, in the 1960's, Jimmy Aaron, another young man who tries to encourage his people to effective political action, appears. Again the members of the older generation hang back, fearful of change and danger, but after Jimmy is killed, Jane unites old and young, past and present by her determination to go to Bayonne and carry on Jimmy's work. Thus Marcus's apolitical rebellion in *Of Love and Dust* has been transformed into political action. The third man in Jane's life is Joe Pittman, her husband. A horse-breaker, he is committed to asserting and proving his manhood through his work. Although he too dies, killed by a wild horse he was determined to break, Jane in her understanding and love of him, as well as in her affection for all her men, bridges the gap between man and woman. In her character, the opposites of old and young, past and present, and man and woman are reconciled.

Miss Jane's strength is finally the strength of the past, but it is directed toward the future. When Jimmy returns, he tells the people that he is nothing without their strength, referring not only to their physical numbers but also to the strength of their character as it has been forged by all the hardships they have undergone through history. Even though the people seem weak and fearful, the example of Miss Jane shows that they need not be. They can shake off the chains of bondage and determinism, assert their free spirit through direct action, and effect change. The change has only begun by the conclusion of *The Autobiography of Miss Jane Pittman*, but the pride and dignity of Miss Jane and all those she represents suggest that ultimately they will prevail.

IN MY FATHER'S HOUSE

Gaines's fourth novel, *In My Father's House*, was the first he had written in the third person since *Catherine Carmier*; the effect of its point of view is to distance the reader from the action and characters, creating an ironic perspective. Set during a dreary winter in 1970, in the period of disillusionment following the assassination of Martin Luther King, Jr., the novel suggests that the progress that was implicit in the ending of *The Autobiography of Miss Jane Pittman* was temporary at best, if not downright illusory. The atmosphere of the novel is one of frustration and stagnation.

Both the setting and the protagonist of *In My Father's House* are uncharacteristic for Gaines. Instead of using the rural settings so familiar from his other works, he sets his story in a small town. Rather than focusing on the common people, Gaines chooses as his protagonist Philip Martin, one of the leaders of the black community, a public figure, a minister who is considering running for Congress. A success by practically any measure and pridefully considering himself a *man*, Martin is brought low in the course of the novel. His illegitimate son, Robert X, a ghostlike man, appears and wordlessly accuses him. Robert is evidence that, by abandoning him, his siblings, and their mother many years previously, Martin in effect destroyed their lives. Having been a drinker and gambler, irresponsible, he tries to explain to his son that his earlier weakness was a legacy of slavery. Even though he seems to have surmounted that crippling legacy, his past rises up to haunt him and forces him to face his weakness. Martin wants to effect a reconciliation with his son and thus with his past, but Robert's suicide precludes that. *In My Father's House* makes explicit a concern that was only implicit in Gaines's earlier novels, the relationship between fathers and sons. No communication is possible here, and the failure is illustrative of a more general barrier between the generations. While in the earlier novels the young people led in the struggle for change and the older characters held back, here the situation is reversed. Martin and members of his generation are the leaders, while the young are for the most part sunk in cynicism, apathy, and hopelessness, or devoted to anarchic violence. If the hope of a people is in the young, or in a reconciliation of old and young, hope does not exist in this novel.

A Gathering of Old Men

Hope does exist, however, in Gaines's *A Gathering of Old Men*, for which Gaines returns to his more characteristic rural setting. Here he returns as well to the optimism with which *The Autobiography of Miss Jane Pittman* ends. This time, as at the end of that novel and in *In My Father's House*, it is up to the old among the black community to lead the struggle for change, this time primarily because there are no young men left to lead. All of them have escaped to towns and cities that promise more of a future than does rural Louisiana.

In this small corner of Louisiana, however, as elsewhere in Gaines's fiction, Cajuns are encroaching on the land, replacing men with machines and even threatening to plow up the old graveyard where generations of blacks have been buried. When Beau Boutan, son of the powerful Cajun Fix Boutan, is shot to death in the quarters of Marshall plantation, where Marshall blacks have worked the land since the days of slavery, the old black men who have lived there all of their lives are faced with one last chance to stand up and be men. They stand up for the sake of Matthu, the only one of them who ever stood up before and thus the most logical suspect in the murder. They also stand up because of all the times in their past when they should have stood up but did not. They prove one last time that free action is possible when eighteen or more of them, all in their seventies and eighties, arm themselves with rifles of the same gauge used in the shooting and face down the white sheriff, Mapes, each in his turn claiming to be the killer.

As shut off as the quarters are from the rest of the world, it is easy to forget that the events of the novel take place as recently as the late 1970's. Beau Boutan's brother Gil, however, represents the change that has been taking place in the world outside Marshall. He has achieved gridiron fame at Louisiana State University by working side by side with Cal, a young black man. Youth confronts age when Gil returns home and tries to persuade his father not to ride in revenge against Beau's murderer, as everyone expects him to do. Gil represents the possibility of change from the white perspective. He convinces his father to let the law find and punish Beau's murderer, but he pays a heavy price when his father disowns him. He cannot stop other young Cajuns, led by Luke Will, who are not willing to change but would rather cling to the vigilantism of the old South.

In spite of their dignity and pride, the old men at Marshall risk looking rather silly because after all these years they stand ready for a battle that seems destined never to take place once Fix Boutan decides not to ride on Marshall. Sheriff Mapes taunts them with the knowledge that they have waited too late to take a stand. Ironically, they are ultimately able to maintain their dignity and reveal their growth in freedom by standing up to the one person who has been most valiant in her efforts to help them: Candy Marshall, niece of the landowner. In her effort to protect Matthu, who was largely responsible for rearing her after her parents died, Candy has gone so far as to try to take credit for the murder herself. What she fails to realize is that the days are long past when black men need the protection of a white woman. She is stunned to realize that she too has been living in the past and has been guilty of treating grown black men like children.

The novel does eventually end with a gunfight, because Luke Will and his men refuse to let the murder of a white man by a black one go unavenged. It is fitting that the two men who fall in the battle are Luke Will, the one who was most resistant to change, and Charlie Biggs, the real murderer, who, at fifty, finally proves his manhood by refusing to be beaten by Beau Boutan and then by returning to take the blame for the murder that he has committed. Charlie's body is treated like a sacred relic as each member of the black community, from the oldest to the youngest, touches it, hoping that some of the courage that Charlie found late in life will rub off. Apparently it already has.

With *A Gathering of Old Men*, Gaines returns to first-person narration, but this time the history is told one chapter at a time by various characters involved in or witnessing the action. His original plan was to have the narrator be the white newspaperman Lou Dimes, Candy's boyfriend. He found, however, that there was still much that a black man in Louisiana would not confide to a white man, even a sympathetic one, so he let the people tell their own story, with Dimes narrating an occasional chapter.

A LESSON BEFORE DYING

A Lesson Before Dying, set in Gaines's fictional Bayonne during six months of 1948, reveals the horrors of Jim Crowism in the story of twenty-one-year-old Jefferson, a scarcely literate man-child who works the cane fields of Pichot Plantation. Jefferson hooks up with two criminals who are killed during the robbery of a liquor store, along with the store's white proprietor. Jefferson is left to stand trial before a jury of twelve white men who overlook his naivete despite his lawyer's argument that he is a dumb animal, a "thing" that acts on command, no more deserving of the electric chair than a hog. When this description causes Jefferson to become practically catatonic, his grandmother enlists the local schoolteacher, Grant Wiggins, to help Jefferson gain his manhood before he is put to death. Thus, like *A Gathering of Old Men*, this novel questions the traditional devaluing of black males in the south.

Reluctantly, Wiggins agrees to help Jefferson by encouraging him to speak and to write, visiting him often and giving him a journal in which to record his thoughts. Finally, right before his execution, Jefferson has a breakthrough when he tells Wiggins to thank his students for the pecans they sent him in jail. Wiggins himself becomes the central character as he learns the real lesson of the novel, that all people are connected and responsible for each other. Wiggins comes to terms with his own role in the system that victimizes Jefferson, and the entire community learns from how Jefferson faces his execution. The novel pays a tribute to those who persevere in the face of injustice, and it also puts forward hope for better racial relationships, especially in the character of Paul, the young white jailer who is sympathetic to Jefferson and to Grant Wiggins's attempts to bring forth his humanity.

If *In My Father's House* represents a falling away of hope for human progress and perhaps also a falling away in artistry, one finds once again in *A Gathering of Old Men* and *A*

Lesson Before Dying evidence of the same genuine strengths that Gaines exhibited in *The Autobiography of Miss Jane Pittman*: a mastery of the folk voice, a concern for common people, a reverence for the everyday, a love of the land, and a powerful evocation of the strength, pride, and dignity people can develop by working on and living close to the soil.

Frank W. Shelton
Updated by Rebecca G. Smith

Other major works

short fiction: *Bloodline*, 1968; *A Long Day in November*, 1971.

miscellaneous: *Porch Talk with Ernest Gaines*, 1990; *Mozart and Leadbelly: Stories and Essays*, 2005.

Bibliography

Auger, Philip. *Native Sons in No Man's Land: Rewriting Afro-American Manhood in the Novels of Baldwin, Walker, Wideman, and Gaines*. New York: Garland, 2000. Examines Gaines's use of religious allegory in commenting on and providing role models for manhood in his novels.

Babb, Valerie Melissa. *Ernest Gaines*. Boston: Twayne, 1991. Provides a solid introduction to the author and his works. Clear, critical analysis devotes one chapter to each of Gaines's major works. Includes bibliography and index.

Beavers, Herman. *Wrestling Angels into Song: The Fictions of Ernest J. Gaines and James Alan McPherson*. Philadelphia: University of Pennsylvania Press, 1995. Thoughtful analysis of the literary kinship of Gaines and McPherson with their precursor Ralph Ellison focuses on all three writers' characters' sense of community, storytelling, and self recovery. Begins with a look at their southernness and then examines all three as American writers. Discusses Gaines's work through *A Lesson Before Dying*.

Carmean, Karen. *Ernest J. Gaines: A Critical Companion*. Westport, Conn.: Greenwood Press, 1998. Presents an introductory overview of Gaines's work, with analysis of each of his novels and short-story collections. Includes a thorough bibliography of primary and secondary sources.

Clark, Keith. *Black Manhood in James Baldwin, Ernest J. Gaines, and August Wilson*. Urbana: University of Illinois Press, 2002. Chapter on Gaines's work focuses on the "neo-masculinist literary imagination." The opening chapter of the book outlines the aesthetics of black masculinist protest discourse since 1940, contextualizing the later discussion.

Doyle, Mary Ellen. *Voices from the Quarters: The Fiction of Ernest J. Gaines*. Baton Rouge: Louisiana State University Press, 2002. Examines the ways in which Gaines peoples Louisiana's bayous and cane fields with characters that exemplify their real-life counterparts.

Estes, David E., ed. *Critical Reflections on the Fiction of Ernest J. Gaines.* Athens: University of Georgia Press, 1994. Fourteen essays cover all six novels to 1994 and *Bloodline* as well as film adaptations of Gaines's work, offering detailed explications in addition to broad analyses of pastoralism, humor, race, and gender. Excellent introduction highlights important biographical facts, secondary sources, and literary themes in Gaines's work.

Gaines, Ernest J., Marcia G. Gaudet, and Carl Wooton. *Porch Talk with Ernest Gaines: Conversations on the Writer's Craft.* Baton Rouge: Louisiana State University Press, 1990. Transcription of an intimate interview conducted by colleagues of Gaines offers an insightful look at how the author has transmuted his Louisiana heritage, familial experiences, literary influences, and strong folk tradition into fiction with a distinct voice.

Lowe, John, ed. *Conversations with Ernest Gaines.* Jackson: University Press of Mississippi, 1995. Collection of interviews with Gaines provides information about his life, his themes, and his works. Includes index and chronology of his life.

Simpson, Anne K. *A Gathering of Gaines: The Man and the Writer.* Lafayette: Center for Louisiana Studies, University of Southwestern Louisiana, 1991. Well-documented study offers a biographical sketch, an examination of Gaines's stylistic influences and characteristics, and a critical overview of his fiction. Includes a thorough bibliography.

CHESTER HIMES

Born: Jefferson City, Missouri; July 29, 1909
Died: Moraira, Spain; November 12, 1984
Also known as: Chester Bomar Himes

PRINCIPAL LONG FICTION

If He Hollers Let Him Go, 1945
Lonely Crusade, 1947
Cast the First Stone, 1952 (unexpurgated edition, *Yesterday Will Make You Cry*, 1998)
The Third Generation, 1954
The Primitive, 1955 (unexpurgated edition, *The End of a Primitive*, 1997)
For Love of Imabelle, 1957 (revised as *A Rage in Harlem*, 1965)
Il pluet des coups durs, 1958 (*The Real Cool Killers*, 1959)
Couché dans le pain, 1959 (*The Crazy Kill*, 1959)
Dare-dare, 1959 (*Run Man Run*, 1966)
Tout pour plaire, 1959 (*The Big Gold Dream*, 1960)
Imbroglio negro, 1960 (*All Shot Up*, 1960)
Ne nous énervons pas!, 1961 (*The Heat's On*, 1966; also known as *Come Back Charleston Blue*, 1974)
Pinktoes, 1961
Une affaire de viol, 1963 (*A Case of Rape*, 1980)
Retour en Afrique, 1964 (*Cotton Comes to Harlem*, 1965)
Blind Man with a Pistol, 1969 (also known as *Hot Day, Hot Night*, 1970)
Plan B, 1983 (English translation, 1993)

OTHER LITERARY FORMS

Chester Himes was primarily a writer of long fiction, but near the end of his life he published a revealing two-volume autobiography, which, if not wholly accurate about his life, nevertheless is engaging as a testament of survival of a black artist struggling to make his voice heard. Like many writers of his generation, Himes began publishing short fiction in the many periodicals of the time. As his life and career progressed—and the number of publishers declined—Himes worked less in the field. A posthumous collection of his short fiction was published in 1990. Finally, Himes also turned his hand to dramatic writing, both plays and film scripts, the most accessible of which is "Baby Sister," which was published in his book of miscellaneous writings, *Black on Black: "Baby Sister" and Selected Writings* (1973).

ACHIEVEMENTS

As the title of a biography of Chester Himes suggests, Himes led several lives during the seventy-five years of his troublesome career. He was the youngest son in a rising African American family, who worked his way into the middle class only to fall back again. Himes learned the craft of writing as an inmate in the Ohio correctional system, and after his release from prison he was a writer of angry and violent protest novels, which earned him a reputation as one of the more celebrated black writers in the United States.

Beginning in the mid-1950's, Himes expatriated and became a tangential member of the community of black artists, which included Richard Wright and James Baldwin, who fled American racism to settle in Europe during the period after World War II. In his later years, he wrote a two-volume autobiography and a series of masterful crime novels, the "Harlem domestic" books. The second of the series, *The Real Cool Killers*, won in 1958 the prestigious Grand Prix de la Littérature Policiére for best crime novel published in France. In all of his "lives," Himes struggled to come to grips with the racist American society into which he was born and to realize his place in that society as a black man and as an artist.

From the publication of his first novel, *If He Hollers Let Him Go*, Himes confounded the critics, and they rarely understood his work. Was his fiction too violent or was it merely revealing the realities of American racism? Was Himes sexist or just reflecting the tensions inherent in a community where African American males were desperately searching for a sense of self? Did he compromise his art for the publishing world dominated by white editors when he wrote his Harlem domestic series, or were these hard-hitting yet more mainstream crime novels an extension of his more "artistic" but less popular protest novels? Was his autobiography merely a self-serving complaint against the slights against him or an uncompromising portrait of one black man's struggle for survival?

Perhaps it is because of the contradictions of his life that Himes remains fascinating, and it is through the mixed, often confused, responses to his work that he achieved his measure of importance, not just as a black writer but as an American writer, one who captured something of the truth of America and of its literature.

BIOGRAPHY

Chester Bomar Himes was the youngest of three sons of Joseph Sandy Himes and Estelle Bomar Himes. His father was a teacher of industrial arts and spent the years of Himes's youth as a faculty member at several black institutions predominantly in the South. By the time Himes was in his teens the family had settled in Cleveland, and after his graduation from Glenville High School he entered Ohio State University in the fall of 1926. However, his university career was short-lived, and at the end of the spring quarter, 1927, he was asked to leave because of poor grades and his participation in a speakeasy fight.

Back in Cleveland, Himes slipped into a life on the edges of the city's crime world. After several run-ins with the law he was caught for robbery, convicted, and sentenced to a lengthy term in the Ohio State Penitentiary. For the next seven-and-a-half years Himes

Chester Himes
(Library of Congress)

served time, and in the enforced discipline of prison life he began to write fiction. His first publication, "His Last Day," appeared in *Abbott's Monthly* in November, 1932. Himes was paroled on April 1, 1936, and the next year he married Jean Johnson. After his prison experience Himes worked at a number of menial jobs while continuing to write.

On April 3, 1953, Himes embarked for Europe, and, except for several brief trips to the United States, he remained an exile for the rest of his life. During these years Himes's writing was devoted mainly to his Harlem detective series featuring Grave Digger Jones and Coffin Ed Johnson. Throughout his years in Europe, Himes traveled extensively, finally settling in Alicante, Spain, with his second wife, Leslie Packard. In 1963, Himes suffered a stroke and in his later years experienced various health problems. He died on November 12, 1984, in Moraira, Spain.

ANALYSIS

In his review of *Lonely Crusade*, James Baldwin hit on the central theme of Chester Himes's work: creating individual black characters who were many faceted and reflected the ambivalence of living in an American society full of contradictions and insecurities. Unfortunately, Baldwin's grasp of the essence of Himes's fiction was not shared by all. Many of the reviewers of Himes's early "protest" fiction either criticized the violence of the books, apologized for it, or merely complained about what they saw as his awkwardness of style. Most reviews simply dismissed the books. Some acknowledged that Himes's portrait of American racism was accurate but deplored his lack of any constructive suggestions for its amelioration. Even when Himes received a certain measure of fame through the republication of his detective novels in the United States, the critical notices, with few exceptions, remained slight. After Himes's death, however, this changed. Himes's literary reputation in France undoubtedly affected his reception in the United States.

Himes once believed that in American letters there was room at the top for only one African American writer at a time, and therefore black writers were always competing against one another for that coveted spot. He felt that he always came in second, initially behind Richard Wright and then behind Baldwin. Certainly this is no longer true (if it ever was). The proliferation of novels, drama, and poetry by such authors as Toni Morrison, Ernest J. Gaines, Gloria Naylor, Derek Walcott, Maya Angelou, Alice Walker, and other black writers suggests that whatever constraints Himes felt as an exiled black writer seem to be loosening. Himes is now being accorded a place beside Wright, Baldwin, and Ralph Ellison, the novelists of his generation who opened the doors for African American writers to be accepted as full-fledged American writers, a part of the native grain.

IF HE HOLLERS LET HIM GO

In *If He Hollers Let Him Go* the central character, Bob Jones, is a black Everyman—as his name would suggest—who comes to represent the experience of all black males who find themselves thwarted while trying to live out their dreams. Jones is an African American who has moved to California to work in the defense plants during World War II. Here he experiences American racism in all its ugly insidiousness and spends the five days covered by the novel's narrative trying to escape the oppressions and humiliations society tries to impose on him.

As an articulate man, with a few years of college, Jones is both better educated and more perceptive than the working-class whites he works with in the aircraft plants. When he is elevated to the position of supervisor at work, he brings out the racism of his coworkers, who are jealous of his success. An altercation on the job, tensions with his white girlfriend, and finally the accusation of rape by a woman at work whose overtures he has rejected, convince Jones that his hopes and dreams will not come true even in Los Angeles, where he thought he would be rid of the racist attitudes of his native South. After his arrest a judge strips him of his military deferment, and as the novel ends he is being sent off to join the U.S. Army.

Himes's first published novel provides the basic themes he would pursue not only in his protest books but also in his crime fiction. In the course of the novel Himes explores the issues of race, class, and sexual positioning and demonstrates how Jones, despite his best efforts, remains trapped within a historically determined social role as a black man trying simply to earn a living, gain some personal respect, and find love. At every turn he finds himself prevented from fulfilling the most basic of American rights and aspirations.

THE PRIMITIVE

The narrative of *The Primitive* focuses on writer Jesse Robinson and his relationship with his white girlfriend, Kriss Cummings. Again in this novel Himes uses a contained time scheme, covering only a few days in the lives of his central characters. After a chance meeting with an old acquaintance, Kriss, Jesse experiences a rapidly accelerating series of seriocomic episodes, which propel him to the novel's conclusion: In an alcoholic fog he stabs Kriss to death in her Gramercy Park apartment. The novel alternates between following Kriss's life and Jesse's thoughts as he tries, in vain, to examine his feelings about his relationship with a white woman and what she stands for in his world, as well as his growing sense of himself as a writer trying to come to grips with his experience as an African American living in a racist culture that will give him recognition as neither an artist nor a man.

The Primitive is often described as one of Himes's "confessional" novels, fiction in which he examines themes that had plagued him since the publication of *If He Hollers Let Him Go*: the rejection he felt as a writer and the obsession with white women often experienced by black men. As critics have pointed out, obsession with white women is a constant theme in Himes's writing and represents attraction, repulsion, and, because of the taboo of miscegenation, long a central anxiety of white Americans, the fear of death and social rejection. Rather than merely striking out against white society, Jesse murders Kriss out of self-hatred for his own desires to join that society, moving the murder beyond the blind killing of Bigger Thomas in Wright's *Native Son* (1940). In the end, Jesse, although still a rejected author, discovers that he has the skills of a fine writer who can put into words his feelings about the conditions of his life.

COTTON COMES TO HARLEM

Cotton Comes to Harlem begins in Harlem at a "back to Africa" rally sponsored by the Reverend Deke O'Malley, who is fraudulently bilking his gullible followers. The rally is interrupted by a gang of thieves who steal the raised money and hide it in a bale of cotton, which they lose on their escape. Into this plot come two African American detectives, Grave Digger Jones and Coffin Ed Johnson, two of the toughest police officers in New York. The rest of the novel involves their attempts to recover the loot, expose the fraud, and make amends to the local residents. The ending of the novel provides an ironic twist, as a poor, old man who found the bale does go to Africa to live out the dream promised by the Reverend O'Malley at the novel's opening.

Cotton Comes to Harlem is one a series of crime novels set in New York's Harlem and featuring two African American detectives, a series Himes called his Harlem domestic books. The series began when his French publisher Marcel Duhamel contracted him to write a novel for Gallimard's La Série Noire, a notable series of crime fiction published in France. In these novels, Himes concentrates as much on the social, political, and economic conditions of the people of Harlem as he does on the solving of crimes. As Himes carefully explores the racism inherent in American culture, he chronicles the world of his characters sympathetically, and without becoming didactic he demonstrates the harmful effects of almost four hundred years of oppression and exploitation of African Americans.

Charles L. P. Silet

OTHER MAJOR WORKS

SHORT FICTION: *The Collected Stories of Chester Himes*, 1990.

NONFICTION: *The Quality of Hurt: The Autobiography of Chester Himes, Volume I*, 1972; *My Life of Absurdity: The Autobiography of Chester Himes, Volume II*, 1976; *Conversations with Chester Himes*, 1995 (Michel Fabre and Robert E. Skinner, editors); *Dear Chester, Dear John: Letters Between Chester Himes and John A. Williams* (John A. Williams and Lori Williams, compilers and editors).

MISCELLANEOUS: *Black on Black: "Baby Sister" and Selected Writings*, 1973.

BIBLIOGRAPHY

Fabre, Michael, and Robert Skinner, eds. *Conversations with Chester Himes*. Jackson: University Press of Mississippi, 1995. A collection of interviews in which Himes speaks candidly about his work, the work of other black writers, racial politics in the United States, the African American community in Harlem, and other topics.

Himes, Chester. *Dear Chester, Dear John: Letters Between Chester Himes and John A. Williams*, compiled and edited by John A. Williams and Lori Williams. Detroit, Mich.: Wayne State University Press, 2008. Himes met Williams, a novice African American writer sixteen years his junior, in 1961, and the two became friends who corresponded for almost thirty years. The letters reveal Himes's personality and his experiences as a black writer. Includes an interview with Himes.

Lundquist, James. *Chester Himes*. New York: Frederick Ungar, 1976. An introductory volume to Himes's life and works, with chapters on the war novels, confessional novels, and detective novels. The first chapter, "November, 1928," describes the armed robbery for which Himes was arrested and the subsequent arrest and trial, in detail. Chronology, notes, bibliography of primary and secondary sources, index.

Margolies, Edward. "Race and Sex: The Novels of Chester Himes." In *Native Sons: A Critical Study of Twentieth-Century Negro American Authors*. Philadelphia: J. B. Lippincott, 1968. A discussion of Himes's major novels. The author sees Himes as considerably different than the group of protest writers following Richard Wright and believes that his European sojourn weakened his writings about the United States. Includes a bibliography and an index.

Margolies, Edward, and Michel Fabre. *The Several Lives of Chester Himes*. Jackson: University Press of Mississippi, 1997. This full-length biography of Himes, written by two people who knew him during the last twenty years of his life, is indispensable for information about his life.

Muller, Gilbert. *Chester Himes*. Boston: Twayne, 1989. An excellent introduction to Himes's life and works. Traces the evolution of his writing, describing how he expressed his grotesque, revolutionary view of life for African Americans in the United States in several literary modes, culminating in his detective fiction. Includes chronology, appendix, index, and annotated bibliographies of primary and secondary works.

Sallis, James. *Chester Himes: A Life*. New York: Walker, 2001. Sallis, a novelist and poet, draws on updated information to provide this detailed recounting of the events of Himes's life and how this life related to his writings.

Silet, Charles L. P., ed. *The Critical Response to Chester Himes*. Westport, Conn.: Greenwood Press, 1999. Reviews and essays analyzing Himes's novels, detective fiction, use of the doppelganger, his anti-Semitism, and his hard-boiled detective tradition. Includes bibliography and index.

Skinner, Robert E. *Two Guns from Harlem: The Detective Fiction of Chester Himes*. Bowling Green, Ohio: Bowling Green State University Popular Press, 1989. Skinner's study presents a comprehensive examination of Himes's mystery and detective novels. He describes how Himes's creation of Coffin Ed Johnson and Grave Digger Jones, two African American police officers, led other writers to create hard-boiled ethnic and female detectives.

Walters, Wendy W. "Harlem on My Mind: Exile and Community in Chester Himes's Detective Fiction." In *At Home in Diaspora: Black International Writing*. Minneapolis: University of Minnesota Press, 2005. Walters describes how Himes's sense of homesickness during his self-imposed exile in Paris led him to write detective novels set in Harlem, even though he never lived there. Himes's Harlem is an imaginary home that reflects both his nostalgia for an African American community and a critique of American racism.

ZORA NEALE HURSTON

Born: Notasulga, Alabama; January 7, 1891
Died: Fort Pierce, Florida; January 28, 1960

PRINCIPAL LONG FICTION

Jonah's Gourd Vine, 1934
Their Eyes Were Watching God, 1937
Moses, Man of the Mountain, 1939
Seraph on the Suwanee, 1948

OTHER LITERARY FORMS

In addition to her four novels, Zora Neale Hurston produced two collections of folklore, *Mules and Men* (1935) and *Tell My Horse* (1938), and an autobiography, *Dust Tracks on a Road* (1942). Hurston also published plays, short stories, and essays in anthologies and in magazines as diverse as *Opportunity*, *Journal of Negro History*, *The Saturday Evening Post*, *Journal of American Folklore*, and *American Legion Magazine*. Finally, she wrote several articles and reviews for such newspapers as the *New York Herald Tribune* and the *Pittsburgh Courier*. Hurston's major works were only reissued in the late twentieth century. Some of her essays and stories have also been collected and reprinted. Although the anthologies *I Love Myself When I Am Laughing . . .* (1979) and *The Sanctified Church* (1981) helped to bring her writing back into critical focus, some of her works ceased to be readily available, and her numerous unpublished manuscripts can be seen only at university archives and the Library of Congress.

ACHIEVEMENTS

Zora Neale Hurston was the best and most prolific African American woman writer of the 1930's. Her novels were highly praised. Even so, Hurston never made more than one thousand dollars in royalties on even her most successful works, and when she died in 1960 in Florida, she was nearly penniless and forgotten. Hurston's career testifies to the difficulties of a black woman writing for a mainstream white audience whose appreciation was usually superficial and for a black audience whose responses to her work were, of necessity, politicized.

Hurston achieved recognition at a time when, as Langston Hughes declared, "the Negro was in vogue." The Harlem Renaissance, the black literary and cultural movement of the 1920's, created an interracial audience for her stories and plays. Enthusiasm for her work extended through the 1930's, although that decade also marked the beginning of critical attacks. Hurston did not portray blacks as victims stunted by a racist society. Such a view, she believed, implies that black life is only a defensive reaction to white racism. Black and left-wing critics, however, complained that her unwillingness to represent the

Zora Neale Hurston
(Library of Congress)

oppression of blacks and her focus, instead, on an autonomous, unresentful black folk culture served to perpetuate minstrel stereotypes and thus fueled white racism.

The radical, racial protest literature of Richard Wright, one of Hurston's strongest critics, became the model for black literature in the 1940's, and publishers on the lookout for protest works showed less and less interest in Hurston's manuscripts. Yet, when she did speak out against American racism and imperialism, her work was often censored. Her autobiography, published in 1942, as well as a number of her stories and articles were tailored by editors to please white audiences. Caught between the attacks of black critics and the censorship of the white publishing industry, Hurston floundered, struggling through the 1940's and 1950's to find other subjects. She largely dropped out of public view in the 1950's, though she continued to publish magazine and newspaper articles.

The African American and feminist political and cultural movements of the 1960's and 1970's provided the impetus for Hurston's rediscovery. The publication of Robert Hemenway's excellent book *Zora Neale Hurston: A Literary Biography* (1977) and the reissue of Hurston's novels, her autobiography, and her folklore collections seem to promise the sustained critical recognition Hurston deserves.

BIOGRAPHY

Zora Neale Hurston was born on January 7, 1891, in Alabama. Later, her family lived in the all-black Florida town of Eatonville in an eight-room house with a five-acre garden. Her father, the Reverend John Hurston, mayor of Eatonville for three terms and moderator of the South Florida Baptist Association, wanted to temper his daughter's high spirits, but her intelligent and forceful mother, Lucy Potts Hurston, encouraged her to "jump at de sun." When Hurston was about nine years old, her mother died. That event and her father's rapid remarriage to a woman his daughter did not like prematurely ended Hurston's childhood. In the next few years, she lived only intermittently at home, spending some time at a school in Jacksonville and some time with relatives. Her father withdrew all financial support during this period, forcing her to commence what was to be a lifelong struggle to make her own living.

When Hurston was fourteen years old, she took a job as a wardrobe girl to a repertory company touring the South. Hurston left the troupe in Baltimore eighteen months later and finished high school there at Morgan Academy. She went on to study part-time at Howard University in 1918, taking jobs as a manicurist, a waitress, and a maid in order to support herself. At Howard, her literary talents began to emerge. She was admitted to a campus literary club, formed by Alain Locke, a Howard professor and one of the forces behind the Harlem Renaissance. Locke brought Hurston to the attention of Charles S. Johnson, another key promoter of the Harlem Renaissance. Editor of *Opportunity: A Journal of Negro Life*, he published one of her stories and encouraged her to enter the literary contest sponsored by his magazine.

With several manuscripts but little money, Hurston moved to New York City in 1925, hoping to make a career of her writing. Her success in that year's *Opportunity* contest—she received prizes for a play and a story—won her the patronage of Fanny Hurst and a scholarship to complete her education at Barnard College. She studied anthropology there under Franz Boas, leading a seemingly schizophrenic life in the next two years as an eccentric, iconoclastic artist of the Harlem Renaissance on one hand and a budding, scholarly social scientist on the other.

The common ground linking these seemingly disparate parts of Hurston's life was her interest in black folk culture. Beginning in 1927 and extending through the 1930's, she made several trips to collect black folklore in the South and in the Bahamas, Haiti, and Jamaica. Collecting trips were costly, however, as was the time to write up their results. Charlotte Osgood Mason, a wealthy, domineering white patron to a number of African

American artists, supported some of that work, as did the Association for the Study of Negro Life and History and the Guggenheim Foundation. Hurston also worked intermittently during the 1930's as a drama teacher at Bethune Cookman College in Florida and at North Carolina College, as a drama coach for the WPA Federal Theatre Project in New York, and as an editor for the Federal Writers' Project in Florida.

Mules and Men and several scholarly and popular articles on folklore were the products of Hurston's collecting trips in the late 1920's and early 1930's. In 1938, she published *Tell My Horse*, the result of trips to Haiti and Jamaica to study hoodoo. As a creative writer, Hurston devised other outlets for her folk materials. Her plays, short stories, and three of her novels—*Jonah's Gourd Vine*, *Their Eyes Were Watching God*, and *Moses, Man of the Mountain*—make use of folklore. She also presented folk materials in theatrical revues, but even though the productions were enthusiastically received, she could never generate enough backing to finance commercially successful long-term showings.

Hurston's intense interest in black folklore prevented her from sustaining either of her two marriages. She could not reconcile the competing claims of love and work. She married Herbert Sheen, a medical student, in 1927 but separated from him a few months later. They were divorced in 1931. She married Albert Price III in 1939, and they too parted less than one year later. Other romantic relationships ended for the same reason.

In the 1940's, Hurston lost her enthusiasm for writing about black folk culture. She wrote her autobiography and in 1948 published her last novel, *Seraph on the Suwanee*, a work that turns away from black folk culture entirely. The last decade of her life took a downward turn. Falsely accused of committing sodomy with a young boy, Hurston, depressed, dropped out of public view. Through the 1950's, she lived in Florida, struggling for economic survival. She barely managed to support herself by writing newspaper and magazine articles, many of which expressed her increasing political conservatism, and by working as a maid, a substitute teacher, and a librarian. In 1959, she suffered a stroke. Too ill to nurse herself, she was forced to enter a welfare home. She died there on January 28, 1960.

ANALYSIS

For much of her career, Zora Neale Hurston was dedicated to the presentation of black folk culture. She introduced readers to hoodoo, folktales, lying contests, spirituals, the blues, sermons, children's games, riddles, playing the dozens, and, in general, a highly metaphoric folk idiom. Although she represented black folk culture in several genres, Hurston was drawn to the novel form because it could convey folklore as communal behavior. Hurston knew that much of the unconscious artistry of folklore appears in the gestures and tones in which it is expressed and that it gains much of its meaning in performance. Even *Mules and Men*, the folklore collection she completed just before embarking on her first novel (although it was published after *Jonah's Gourd Vine*), "novelizes" what could have been an anthology of disconnected folk materials. By inventing a narrator who witnesses, even participates in, the performance of folk traditions, she combated the inevitable distortion of an oral culture by its textual documentation.

Hurston's motives for presenting black folklore were, in part, political. She wanted to refute contemporary claims that African Americans lacked a distinct culture of their own. Her novels depict the unconscious creativity of the African American proletariat or folk. They represent community members participating in a highly expressive communication system that taught them to survive racial oppression and, moreover, to respect themselves and their community. At the beginning of Hurston's second novel, for example, the community's members are sitting on porches. "Mules and other brutes had occupied their skins" all day, but now it is night, work is over, and they can talk and feel "powerful and human" again: "They became lords of sounds and lesser things. They passed nations through their mouths. They sat in judgment." By showing the richness and the healthy influence of black folk culture, Hurston hoped not only to defeat racist attitudes but also to encourage racial pride among blacks. Why should African Americans wish to imitate a white bourgeoisie? The "Negro lowest down" had a richer culture.

Hurston also had a psychological motive for presenting black folk culture. She drew the folk materials for her novels from the rural, southern black life she knew as a child and subsequently recorded in folklore-collecting trips in the late 1920's and 1930's. She had fond memories of her childhood in the all-black town of Eatonville, where she did not experience poverty or racism. In her autobiographical writings, she suggests that she did not even know that she was "black" until she left Eatonville. Finally, in Eatonville, she had a close relationship with and a strong advocate in her mother. In representing the rich culture of black rural southerners, she was also evoking a happier personal past.

Although the novel's witnessing narrator provided Hurston with the means to dramatize folklore, she also needed meaningful fictional contexts for its presentation. Her novels are a series of attempts to develop such contexts. Initially, she maintained the southern rural setting for black folk traditions. In her first novel, *Jonah's Gourd Vine*, she re-created Eatonville and neighboring Florida towns. Hurston also loosely re-created her parents' lives with the central characters, John and Lucy Pearson. Though Hurston claimed that an unhappy love affair she had had with a man she met in New York was the catalyst for her second novel, *Their Eyes Were Watching God*, the feeling rather than the details of that affair appear in the novel. The work takes the reader back to Eatonville again and to the porch-sitting storytellers Hurston knew as a child.

MOSES, MAN OF THE MOUNTAIN

With her third novel, *Moses, Man of the Mountain*, however, Hurston turned in a new direction, leaving the Eatonville milieu behind. The novel retells the biblical story of Moses via the folk idiom and traditions of southern rural blacks. Hurston leaves much of the plot of the biblical story intact—Moses does lead the Hebrews out of Egypt—but, for example, she shows Moses to be a great hoodoo doctor as well as a leader and lawgiver. In effect, Hurston simulated the creative processes of folk culture, transforming the story of Moses for modern African Americans just as slaves had adapted biblical stories in spirituals. Hurston may have reenacted an oral and communal process as a solitary writer, but she gave an imaginative rendering of the cultural process all the same.

SERAPH ON THE SUWANEE

Seraph on the Suwanee, Hurston's last novel, marks another dramatic shift in her writing. With this novel, however, she did not create a new context for the representation of folk culture. Rather, she turned away from the effort to present black folklore. *Seraph on the Suwanee* is set in the rural South, but its central characters are white. Hurston apparently wanted to prove that she could write about whites as well as blacks, a desire that surfaced, no doubt, in response to the criticism and disinterest her work increasingly faced in the 1940's. Yet, even when writing of upwardly mobile southern "crackers," Hurston could not entirely leave her previous mission behind. Her white characters, perhaps unintentionally, often use the black folk idiom.

Although Hurston's novels, with the exception of the last, create contexts or develop other strategies for the presentation of folklore, they are not simply showcases for folk traditions; black folk culture defines the novels' themes. The most interesting of these thematic renderings appear in Hurston's first two novels. Hurston knew that black folk culture was composed of brilliant adaptations of African culture to American life. She admired the ingenuity of these adaptations but worried about their preservation. Would a sterile, materialistic white world ultimately absorb blacks, destroying the folk culture they had developed? Her first two novels demonstrate the disturbing influence of white America on black folkways.

JONAH'S GOURD VINE

Jonah's Gourd Vine, Hurston's first novel, portrays the tragic experience of a black preacher caught between black cultural values and the values imposed by his white-influenced church. The novel charts the life of John Pearson, laborer, foreman, and carpenter, who discovers that he has an extraordinary talent for preaching. With his linguistic skills and his wife Lucy's wise counsel, he becomes pastor of the large church Zion Hope and ultimately moderator of a Florida Baptist convention. His sexual promiscuity, however, eventually destroys his marriage and his career.

Though his verbal skills make him a success while his promiscuity ruins him, the novel shows that both his linguistic gifts and his sexual vitality are part of the same cultural heritage. His sexual conduct is pagan and so is his preaching. In praying, according to the narrator, it was as if he "rolled his African drum up to the altar, and called his Congo Gods by Christian names." Both aspects of his cultural heritage speak through him. Indeed, they speak through all members of the African American community, if most intensely through John. A key moment early in the novel, when John crosses over Big Creek, marks the symbolic beginning of his life and shows the double cultural heritage he brings to it. John heads down to the Creek, "singing a new song and stomping the beats." He makes up "some words to go with the drums of the Creek," with the animal noises in the woods, and with the hound dog's cry. He begins to think about the girls living on the other side of Big Creek: "John almost trumpeted exultantly at the new sun. He breathed lustily. He stripped and carried his clothes across, then recrossed and plunged into the swift water and breasted strongly over."

To understand why two expressions of the same heritage have such different effects on John's life, one has to turn to the community to which he belongs. Members of his congregation subscribe to differing views of the spiritual life. The view most often endorsed by the novel emerges from the folk culture. As Larry Neal, one of Hurston's best critics, explains in his introduction to the 1971 reprint of the novel, that view belongs to "a formerly enslaved communal society, non-Christian in background," which does not strictly dichotomize body and soul. The other view comes out of a white culture. It is "more rigid, being a blend of Puritan concepts and the fire-and-brimstone imagery of the white evangelical tradition." That view insists that John, as a preacher, exercise self-restraint. The cultural conflict over spirituality pervades his congregation. While the deacons, whom Hurston often portrays satirically, pressure him to stop preaching, he still has some loyal supporters among his parishioners.

White America's cultural styles and perceptions invade Pearson's community in other ways as well. By means of a kind of preaching competition, the deacons attempt to replace Pearson with the pompous Reverend Felton Cozy, whose preaching style is white. Cozy's style, however, fails to captivate most members of the congregation. Pearson is a great preacher in the folk tradition, moving his congregation to a frenzy with "barbaric thunder-poems." By contrast, Cozy, as one of the parishioners complains, does not give a sermon; he lectures. In an essay Hurston wrote on "The Sanctified Church," she explains this reaction: "The real, singing Negro derides the Negro who adopts the white man's religious ways. . . . They say of that type of preacher, 'Why he don't preach at all. He just lectures.'"

If Pearson triumphs over Cozy, he nevertheless ultimately falls. His sexual conduct destroys his marriage and leads to an unhappy remarriage with one of his mistresses, Hattie Tyson. He is finally forced to stop preaching at Zion Hope. Divorced from Hattie, he moves to another town, where he meets and marries Sally Lovelace, a woman much like Lucy. With her support, he returns to preaching. On a visit to a friend, however, he is tempted by a young prostitute and, to his dismay, succumbs. Although he has wanted to be faithful to his new wife, he will always be a pagan preacher, spirit and flesh. Fleeing back to Sally, he is killed when a train strikes his car.

In its presentation of folklore and its complex representation of cultural conflict, *Jonah's Gourd Vine* is a brilliant first novel, although Hurston does not always make her argument sufficiently clear. The novel lacks a consistent point of view. Though she endorses Pearson's African heritage and ridicules representatives of white cultural views, she also creates an admirable and very sympathetic character in Lucy Pearson, who is ruined by her husband's pagan behavior. Nor did Hurston seem to know how to resolve the cultural conflict she portrayed—hence, the deus ex machina ending. It was not until she wrote her next novel, *Their Eyes Were Watching God*, that Hurston learned to control point of view and presented a solution to the problem of white influences on black culture.

Their Eyes Were Watching God

The life of Janie Crawford, the heroine of *Their Eyes Were Watching God*, is shaped by bourgeois values—white in origin. She finds love and self-identity only by rejecting that life and becoming a wholehearted participant in black folk culture. Her grandmother directs Janie's entrance into adulthood. Born into slavery, the older woman hopes to find protection and materialistic comforts for Janie in a marriage to the property-owning Logan Killicks. Janie, who has grown up in a different generation, does not share her grandmother's values. When she finds she cannot love her husband, she runs off with Jody Stark, who is on his way to Eatonville, where he hopes to become a "big voice," an appropriate phrase for life in a community that highly values verbal ability. Jody becomes that "big voice" as mayor of the town, owner of the general store, and head of the post office. He lives both a bourgeois and a folk life in Eatonville. He constructs a big house—the kind white people have—but he wanders out to the porch of the general store whenever he wants to enjoy the perpetual storytelling that takes place there. Even though Janie has demonstrated a talent for oratory, however, he will not let her join these sessions or participate in the mock funeral for a mule that has become a popular character in the townspeople's stories. "He didn't," the narrator suggests, "want her talking after such trashy people." As Janie tells a friend years later, Jody "classed me off." He does so by silencing her.

For several years, Janie has no voice in the community or in her private life. Her life begins to seem unreal: "She sat and watched the shadow of herself going about tending store and prostrating itself before Jody." One day, after Stark insults her in front of customers in the store, however, she speaks out and, playing the dozens, insults his manhood. The insult causes an irreconcilable break between them.

After Jody's death, Janie is courted by Tea Cake Woods, a laborer with little money. Though many of her neighbors disapprove of the match, Janie marries him. "Dis ain't no business proposition," she tells her friend Pheoby, "and no race after property and titles. Dis is uh love game. Ah done lived Grandma's way, now Ah means tuh live mine." Marriage to Tea Cake lowers her social status but frees her from her submissive female role, from her shadow existence. Refusing to use her money, Tea Cake takes her down to the Everglades, where they become migrant workers. She picks beans with him in the fields, and he helps her prepare their dinners. With Tea Cake, she also enters into the folk culture of the Everglades, and that more than anything else enables her to shed her former submissive identity. Workers show up at their house every night to sing, dance, gamble, and, above all, to talk, like the folks in Eatonville on the front porch of the general store. Janie learns how to tell "big stories" from listening to the others, and she is encouraged to do so.

This happy phase of Janie's life ends tragically as she and Tea Cake attempt to escape a hurricane and the ensuing flood. Tea Cake saves Janie from drowning but, in the process, is bitten by a rabid dog. Sick and crazed, he tries to shoot Janie. She is forced to kill him in self-defense. Not everything she has gained during her relationship with Tea Cake, however, dies with him. The strong self-identity she has achieved while living in the Everglades enables her to withstand the unjust resentment of their black friends as well as her trial for murder in a white court. Most important, she is able to endure her own loss and returns to Eatonville, self-reliant and wise. Tea Cake, she knows, will live on in her thoughts and feelings—and in her words. She tells her story to her friend Pheoby—that storytelling event frames the novel—and allows Pheoby to bring it to the other members of the community. As the story enters the community's oral culture, it will influence it. Indeed, as the novel closes, Janie's story has already affected Pheoby. "Ah done growed ten feet higher from jus' listenin' tuh you," she tells Janie. "Ah ain't satisfied wid mahself no mo'."

In her novels, Hurston did not represent the oppression of blacks because she refused to view African American life as impoverished. If she would not focus on white racism, however, her novels do oppose white culture. In *Their Eyes Were Watching God*, Janie does not find happiness until she gives up a life governed by white values and enters into the verbal ceremonies of black folk culture. Loving celebrations of a separate black folk life were Hurston's effective political weapon; racial pride was one of her great gifts to American literature. "Sometimes, I feel discriminated against," she once told her readers, "but it does not make me angry. It merely astonishes me. How *can* any deny themselves the pleasure of my company? It's beyond me."

Deborah Kaplan

OTHER MAJOR WORKS

SHORT FICTION: *Spunk: The Selected Short Stories of Zora Neale Hurston*, 1985; *The Complete Stories*, 1995.

PLAYS: *Color Struck*, pb. 1926; *The First One*, pb. 1927; *Mule Bone*, pb. 1931 (with Langston Hughes); *Polk County*, pb. 1944.

NONFICTION: *Mules and Men*, 1935; *Tell My Horse*, 1938; *Dust Tracks on a Road*, 1942; *The Sanctified Church*, 1981; *Folklore, Memoirs, and Other Writings*, 1995; *Go Gator and Muddy the Water: Writings*, 1999 (Pamela Bordelon, editor); *Every Tongue Got to Confess: Negro Folk-tales from the Gulf States*, 2001 (Carla Kaplan, editor); *Zora Neale Hurston: A Life in Letters*, 2002 (Kaplan, editor).

MISCELLANEOUS: *I Love Myself When I Am Laughing . . . and Then Again When I Am Looking Mean and Impressive: A Zora Neale Hurston Reader*, 1979 (Alice Walker, editor).

BIBLIOGRAPHY

Boyd, Valerie. *Wrapped in Rainbows: The Life of Zora Neale Hurston*. New York: Scribner, 2002. A comprehensive, meticulously researched account of Hurston the woman and the writer, based in part on information available after the early 1980's. Includes a discussion of the Hurston "resurrection," a list of her published works, a select bibliography, and an index.

Campbell, Josie P. *Student Companion to Zora Neale Hurston*. Westport, Conn.: Greenwood Press, 2001. Designed for students and general readers, this book includes a brief biography, an overview of Hurston's fiction, and separate chapters discussing each of her four novels.

Cooper, Jan. "Zora Neale Hurston Was Always a Southerner Too." In *The Female Tradition in Southern Literature*, edited by Carol S. Manning. Urbana: University of Illinois Press, 1993. Examines the hitherto neglected role that Hurston played in the Southern Renaissance between 1920 and 1950. Argues that Hurston's fiction is informed by a modern southern agrarian sense of community. Suggests that the Southern Renaissance was a "transracial," cross-cultural product of the South.

Cronin, Gloria L., ed. *Critical Essays on Zora Neale Hurston*. New York: G. K. Hall, 1998. A useful collection, featuring contemporary reviews of Hurston's four novels, feminist interpretations and other analyses of her works, and a discussion of Hurston and the Harlem Renaissance. Includes bibliographical references and an index.

Donlon, Jocelyn Hazelwood. "Porches: Stories: Power: Spatial and Racial Intersections in Faulkner and Hurston." *Journal of American Culture* 19 (Winter, 1996): 95-110. Comments on the role of the porch in Faulkner and Hurston's fiction as a transitional space between the public and the private where the individual can negotiate an identity through telling stories.

Glassman, Steve, and Kathryn Lee Siedel, eds. *Zora in Florida*. Orlando: University of Central Florida Press, 1991. This collection of essays by seventeen Hurston scholars explores the overall presence and influence of Florida in and on the works of Hurston. This collection grew out of a Hurston symposium held in Daytona Beach, Florida, in 1989, and includes an excellent introduction to the importance of Florida in the study of Hurston.

Hill, Lynda Marion. *Social Rituals and the Verbal Art of Zora Neale Hurston*. Washington, D.C.: Howard University Press, 1996. Features chapters on Hurston's treatment of everyday life, science and humanism, folklore, color, race, and class. Hill also considers dramatic reenactments of Hurston's writing. Includes notes, bibliography, and an appendix on "characteristics of Negro expression."

Howard, Lillie P. *Zora Neale Hurston*. Boston: Twayne, 1980. A good general introduction to the life and works of Hurston. Contains valuable plot summaries and commentaries on Hurston's works. Supplemented by a chronology and a bibliography.

Hurston, Lucy Anne. *Speak, So You Can Speak Again: The Life of Zora Neale Hurston*.

New York: Doubleday, 2004. A brief biography written by Hurston's niece. Most notable for the inclusion of rare photographs, writings, and other multimedia personal artifacts. Also contains an audio compact disc of Hurston reading and singing.

Lyons, Mary E. *Sorrow's Kitchen: The Life and Folklore of Zora Neale Hurston*. New York: Charles Scribner's Sons, 1990. A straightforward biography of Hurston, written for younger readers. Especially useful for those who need a primer on Hurston's background in all-black Eatonville.

Plant, Deborah G. *Zora Neale Hurston: A Biography of the Spirit*. Westport, Conn.: Praeger, 2007. Portrays Hurston's strength and tenacity of spirit. Her literary achievements, including her novel *Their Eyes Were Watching God*, are also discussed here. This work draws on Hurston's 1942 autobiography *Dust Tracks on the Road* as well as newly discovered sources.

West, Margaret Genevieve. *Zora Neale Hurston and American Literary Culture*. Gainesville: University Press of Florida, 2005. A chronicle of Hurston's literary career, describing how her work was marketed and reviewed during her lifetime and why her writing did not gain popularity until long after her death.

WILLIAM MELVIN KELLEY

Born: Bronx, New York; November 1, 1937

PRINCIPAL LONG FICTION

A Different Drummer, 1962
A Drop of Patience, 1965
Dem, 1967
Dunfords Travels Everywheres, 1970

OTHER LITERARY FORMS

In addition to his novels, for which he is primarily known, William Melvin Kelley is the author of a collection of short stories, *Dancers on the Shore* (1964). Some of these stories were written before his first novel, and almost all introduce characters, themes, and ideas that appear in later works. A 1997 *New Yorker* story, "Carlyle Tries Polygamy: How Many Are Too Many?" reveals that, despite almost thirty years of nearly complete fiction-publication silence, Kelley maintained interest in creatively pursuing some of the personages and ideas that appeared earlier in his short and long fiction. Selections of his fiction mostly appeared in late 1960's and 1970's anthologies of African American writers. He has been a nonfiction and fiction contributor to periodicals such as *Accent*, *Canto*, *Esquire*, *Jazz and Pop*, *Mademoiselle*, *Negro Digest*, *The New Yorker*, *The New York Times Magazine*, *Partisan Review*, *Playboy*, *Quilt*, *River Styx*, *Urbanite*, and *Works in Progress*.

ACHIEVEMENTS

William Melvin Kelley received several awards in the years in which he was actively publishing: the Dana Reed Prize from Harvard University, a Bread Loaf Scholar residency, the John Hay Whitney Foundation Award, the Rosenthal Foundation Award, the Transatlantic Review Award, and a fiction award from the Black Academy of Arts and Letters. These awards confirmed early recognition of Kelley's talent but have little to do with his enduring prominence as the creator of *A Different Drummer*, his first and most accomplished work, which brought him the accolades of such writers as Archibald MacLeish, Thomas Merton, and Frank Tuohy.

As important in its own way as Ralph Ellison's *Invisible Man* (1952), James Baldwin's *Go Tell It on the Mountain* (1953), and William Demby's *Beetlecreek* (1950), *A Different Drummer* broke new ground within the confines of the subject of race in America. Visionary, grounded in myth and American history, it still confounds readers as they try to categorize and label this enduring novel of the civil rights era. Indeed, all Kelley's novels invite readers to consider the simple difference that race makes in America, as well as the complexity of the individual's dilemma and response in respect to this and other aspects of the human condition.

Biography

William Melvin Kelley is the only child of William Melvin Kelley, Sr., and Narcissa Agatha (Garcia) Kelley. His father was a journalist and an editor, for a time, at the *Amsterdam News*. When Kelley was young, the family lived in an Italian American neighborhood in the North Bronx, but later his parents sent him to the Fieldston School, a small, predominantly white, preparatory school in New York, where he became captain of the track team and president of the student council. In 1957, the year of his mother's death, Kelley entered Harvard, intending to study law. By the following year, however, the year of his father's death, he was studying fiction writing with authors John Hawkes and, later, MacLeish. For the rest of his career (which he left unfinished) at Harvard, no other academic subject was relevant to him. Consumed by writing, he said, "I hope only to write fiction until I die, exploring until there is no longer anything to explore . . . [about] the plight of Negroes as individual human beings in America."

In 1962, after the publication of his first novel, Kelley married Karen Isabelle Gibson, a designer, and worked as a writer, photographer, and teacher in New York, France, and the West Indies. He is the father of two children, Jessica and Ciratikaiji. Though he continued to work on a book titled *Days of Our Lives* and occasionally appear in print and in public life, Kelley, in large part, maintained a quiet life.

Analysis

Critics often fix on the interrelatedness of William Melvin Kelley's four novels (and his short stories), and, indeed, though each novel is different in style, setting, characters, and even language, the ideas that spawned them are related and grow from each other. Critic Jill Weyant sees Kelley's work as a saga, in that the

> purpose of writing a serious saga . . . is to depict impressionistically a large, crowded portrait, each individual novel presenting enlarged details of the whole, each complete in itself, yet evoking a more universal picture than is possible in a single volume.

Kelley admits to the possible influence of other great writers of sagas, telling Roy Newquist in an interview,

> Perhaps I'm trying to follow the Faulknerian pattern—although I guess it's really Balzacian when you connect everything. I'd like to be eighty years old and look up at the shelf and see that all of my books are really one big book.

A Different Drummer

A Different Drummer is Kelley's first and finest work, an enduring classic of African American literature. Kelley took his literary inspiration from American writer Henry David Thoreau's resounding celebration of individuality: "If a man does not keep pace with his companions, perhaps it is because he hears a different drummer. Let him step to the music which he hears, however measured or far away." Kelley then adapted this idea to the

William Melvin Kelley
(Library of Congress)

plight of African Americans in a fictional narrative built on a foundation of mythic imagination, American history all the way back to the slave trade, and the racial strife of the 1960's. The black experience of being perceived as different, as a despised people with trenchantly stereotyped racial characteristics, has been anything but positive. It is here, on this ground, that Kelley develops his narrative from two basic questions rooted deeply in the history of American race relations: What would whites do without the black people they so abuse and denigrate, but to whom they are so tied? Also, who might white people be without the prison of their own prejudice?

The novel takes place in the small town of Sutton, in a nameless, imaginary southern state, in June, 1957, when, mysteriously for the white citizens, "all the state's Negro inhabitants departed." The exodus is unconsciously led by the child-sized Tucker Caliban, who, like Rosa Parks (a black woman who refused to relinquish her bus seat to a white man in 1955), simply decided one day that he could no longer comply with the way things had always been in the South. The course of history, or at least his own family history, had to be changed. For four generations the Calibans were defined and limited by their service to the Willsons, and Tucker knows that he cannot reach his full human potential living in the template of the southern racial past. Thus he salts his land, kills his farm animals, axes the grandfather clock that symbolizes all the years of his family's servitude, sets fire to his house, and walks off into the sunset with his pregnant wife and his child. This peaceful, though revolutionary, act of individual initiative and vision is a direct outgrowth of and complement to the rebellion and flight of the massive legendary African whose story begins the novel. This African prince, Tucker's great-grandfather, refused to be enslaved, and it is perhaps his spirit that propels Tucker's quiet self-reliance generations later. Ironically, it is old white Mr. Harper who keeps the memory of the African alive for the white men of Sutton, telling the story on the porch of Thomason's store as often as anyone will listen.

Kelley mixes his multiple points of view between first- and third-person narration, using flashbacks to take his readers inside the heads of the southern whites, not the blacks, who occupy the small southern town of Sutton. The whites who interest Kelley are of two classes. Harry Leland and his young son, Mister Leland, represent the poor-white southerners who wish to break with the past, who wish to know black people as individuals and not as a subjugated mass. The Willsons represent the southern aristocracy, bound by the past and the money they made from slavery, but who are also educated and morally conflicted.

Tucker's opposite, a Harvard-educated black religious leader who comes down from the North to investigate the inspiration behind the exodus, becomes the novel's sacrificial lamb. The ultimately self-seeking Reverend Bennett Bradshaw is superfluous in Sutton; the people have led themselves out of their legacy of bondage and have no need of he who is not one of their own. He becomes flotsam of the most violent of southern white rituals, ironically taking up the cross that the people have left behind.

A Different Drummer is, indeed, as critic David Bradley writes, an "elegant" little book, masterful in its balance of scenes of stunning moment, delivered in the language and points of view of the people most in need of understanding them. Within its covers there is much to understand about the nature of freedom as an individual conviction that must be realized; all social change begins with a human being's belief in his or her own equality, and no lasting social change can happen without it.

A Drop of Patience

With *A Drop of Patience*, Kelley returns to the South, to uncover the life of a blind black boy, Ludlow Washington, who is deposited in an institution and left to exist among the faceless masses that society, and particularly a segregated society, builds institutions to hide. Ludlow cannot walk away from his circumstances, like Tucker Caliban, because he is a child, and blind, so he must transcend in another way. He finds his means of self-expression and his route to finding a place in southern black society in his musical instrument, which is never identified but is clearly some sort of horn with several keys. Extremely talented, Ludlow is released to a black bandleader, who takes him to the small southern city of New Marsails, to play with his group in a local bar. Ludlow is better than the other members of the band, however, and he has to hold his creative compulsion for avant-garde improvisation in check until he is old enough to be free of his contract, which is essentially indenture. Eventually he leaves the South and migrates to the North, becoming a leading jazz musician with his own band and enjoying relative freedom.

Though this is the framework for "one of the finest novels ever written about a jazz musician," according to critic Stanley Crouch, *A Drop of Patience* is not so much a novel about a musician as it is a novel about a blind boy coming to sexual maturity, and a black man who literally cannot see color (and is therefore able to override its coded constraints to discover deeper qualities in people) but who must come to social maturity in a superficial and pervasively race-bound society. It is a society that can drive a sane person mad, and it does this to Ludlow, who must, at bottom, be able to trust his own senses. At novel's end Ludlow chooses a course that will allow him to be a musician and to be a man among people who can see him.

Dem

If *A Drop of Patience* is an enlarged detail of the people who left the imaginary southern state in *A Different Drummer*, then *Dem* is an enlarged detail of the people who are incapable of seeing Ludlow Washington as a human being beyond his racial categorization. *Dem* is the black perspective on American society's "us" and "them" dichotomy, and it makes sense that this novel is both a satire and a comedy. Satire typically employs sarcasm and irony to expose human folly or vice, and comedic writing not only provides an absurd vehicle (lighthearted treatment) to transport an absurd commodity (pervasive race prejudice) but also offers the opportunity to "solve" this immense social problem temporarily with justice and laughter. In short, it provides catharsis.

Mitchell Pierce and his wife, Tam, are upper-middle-class white New Yorkers who are frank stereotypes. They are shallow, insular, and cold, like mannequins or robots—devoid of the redeeming, individual, distinguishing features that human beings possess. Murder cannot move them, and love, to them, is a plot gleaned from soap operas. Tam gets pregnant by both her husband and her maid's black boyfriend and gives birth to twins, one white and one black. The rest of the novel is about Mitchell's ludicrous hunt through Harlem for the father of the black twin, whom he does not recognize when he sees him. For Mitchell, black people are simply a faceless race meant to serve him, and it never occurs to him that the money in his pocket cannot buy them.

DUNFORDS TRAVELS EVERYWHERES

Often dismissed by critics as "experimental," there is no doubt that *Dunfords Travels Everywheres* is a difficult book to read, but its inspiration is, after all, James Joyce's *Finnegans Wake* (1939). Critic Michael Wood notes that like Joyce, Kelley "as a black American and a writer, is caught in the language and culture of an enemy country," and Kelley's two protagonists in this novel, Chig Dunford and Carlyle Bedlow, might be understood to be acting this out. The hallucinatory dream sequences, which connect the separate adventures of these two characters, are their common ground, their realm of unconscious constructions of language with African retentions, characterized by black idiomatic expressions and dialect, phonetic sounds and spellings, puns and exuberant word plays.

The Harvard-educated Chig Dunford, hanging out in an imaginary country in Europe with what amounts to imaginary white friends, blurts out two words that are revelatory. He changes his course and finds himself making a surreal transatlantic journey to America, which is, perhaps, his own "Middle Passage" to a destination of self-realization. By journey's end, he has encountered the Harriet of Ludlow Washington's healing in *A Drop of Patience* as well as his Harlem counterpart, Carlyle Bedlow, who figures prominently in *Dem* and in some of Kelley's short fiction. Further, it might be argued that Chig's voyage to Harlem, to a place where he can be known, is an updated version of Tucker Caliban's journey away from "dem people's" race-based expectations of him.

Cynthia Packard Hill

OTHER MAJOR WORK

SHORT FICTION: *Dancers on the Shore*, 1964.

BIBLIOGRAPHY

Babb, Valerie M. "William Melvin Kelley." In *Afro-American Fiction Writers After 1955*, edited by Thadious M. Davis. Vol. 33 in *Dictionary of Literary Biography*. Detroit, Mich.: Gale Research, 1984. In the absence of book-length secondary sources, this is a good start to learning about Kelley. The bibliography includes critical essays and an interview.

Bradley, David. Foreword to *A Different Drummer*, by William Melvin Kelley. New York: Doubleday, 1989. A carefully researched essay that considers Kelley's first novel in the context of its time and in relation to the novels of William Faulkner, particularly *The Reivers*.

Cataliotti, Robert H. "There Must Be Some People Who Lived for Music: Margaret Walker and William Melvin Kelley." In *The Music in African American Fiction*. New York: Garland, 1995. Cataliotti's examination of how black music and musicians have been represented in African American fiction includes a chapter about Kelley, focusing on his novel *A Drop of Patience*.

Early, Gerald. Introduction to *A Drop of Patience*, by William Melvin Kelley. Hopewell, N.J.: Ecco Press, 1996. With a short overview of the black writers of the 1950's and a brief introduction to the Black Arts movement, Early positions Kelley's "jazz novel" on the cusp, between the two eras and belonging to neither.

Harris-Lopez, Trudier. "Saluting the Land but Not the Imagination: William Melvin Kelley's *A Different Drummer*." In *South of Tradition: Essays on African American Literature*. Athens: University of Georgia Press, 2002. Harris-Lopez's analysis of Kelley's novel is one of twelve essays in which she analyzes twentieth century novels, plays, and other works by African Americans. Includes a bibliography and an index.

Karrer, Wolfgang. "Romance as Epistemological Design: William Melvin Kelley's *A Different Drummer*." In *The Afro-American Novel Since 1960*, edited by Peter Bruck and Wolfgang Karrer. Amsterdam: Gainer, 1982. Karrer considers Kelley's novel of exodus to be romantic rather than realistic, and he positions it among other romantic novels by African American writers.

Ro, Sigmund. *Rage and Celebration: Essays on Contemporary Afro-American Writing*. Atlantic Highlands, N.J.: Humanities Press, 1984. These essays on African American literature focus on Kelley, John Alfred Williams, and James Baldwin.

Sundquist, Eric J. "A Negro-Less World: William Melvin Kelley." In *Strangers in the Land: Blacks, Jews, Post-Holocaust America*. Cambridge, Mass.: Belknap Press, 2005. Sundquist analyzes Kelley's fiction in the context of the how the relationship between African Americans and American Jews has been represented in literature, sociology, entertainment, and historical writing.

Thomas, H. Nigel. "The Bad Nigger Figure in Selected Works of Richard Wright, William Melvin Kelley, and Ernest Gaines." *CLA Journal* 39, no. 2 (December, 1995). A critical examination of how the figure of the "Bad Nigger" has been used by African American writers, particularly Kelley, Richard Wright, and Ernest Gaines.

Wardi, Anissa J. "William Melvin Kelley." In *Contemporary African American Novelists: A Bio-bibliographical Critical Sourcebook*, edited by Emmanuel S. Nelson. Westport, Conn.: Greenwood Press, 1999. The article on Kelley features a brief biography, an analysis of the issues and themes in Kelley's works, a discussion of his critical reception, and bibliographies of primary and secondary sources.

NELLA LARSEN

Born: Chicago, Illinois; April 13, 1891
Died: New York, New York; March 30, 1964
Also known as: Nellie Marion Walker; Allen Semi; Nella Marian Larsen Imes

PRINCIPAL LONG FICTION

Quicksand, 1928
Passing, 1929

OTHER LITERARY FORMS

Although Nella Larsen is known primarily known for her novels, her first foray into writing consisted of two works for children, "Three Scandinavian Games" and "Danish Fun," which were published in 1920 in *The Brownies Book*, a magazine for children published by the National Association for the Advancement of Colored People (NAACP). In addition to a few book reviews, she also published three short stories. The first two, "The Wrong Man" (1926) and "Freedom" (1926), which appeared under the pseudonym Allen Semi (Nella Imes, her married name, in reverse), share a number of plot similarities with her novels, except that the characters in the short stories are not identifiable as African American. In 1930, Larsen became the first African American author to have a work of fiction—her short story "Sanctuary"—published in the prestigious *Forum* magazine. This honor was eclipsed, however, as she was accused of plagiarizing the work. Based on rough drafts Larsen sent to the publishers, they concluded that the similarities were coincidence; nevertheless, "Sanctuary" was Larsen's final published work.

ACHIEVEMENTS

Nella Larson is considered one of the important novelists of the Harlem Renaissance. Her first novel, *Quicksand*, was awarded the Harmon Foundation Bronze Award, and in 1930, following the publication of her novel *Passing*, she became only the fourth black writer to receive a Guggenheim Fellowship.

BIOGRAPHY

Although regarded as one of the most outstanding novelists of the Harlem Renaissance, Nella Larsen has also been described as its mystery woman, having "disappeared" from both literary and historical standpoints. In fact, when she was found dead in her New York City apartment in 1964, no one recognized that an important writer had died; there was only a brief notice in *The New York Times*, which identified her as Nella Larsen Imes, a name recognized by few, as she had divorced three decades earlier. Since the 1970's, however, there has been a burgeoning interest in Larsen, and a number of scholars have attempted to reconstruct her life. As a result, much more has come to be known about her.

Although she listed the year of her birth as 1893, Larsen was born Nellie Marion Walker on April 13, 1891, in Chicago, the daughter of Mary Hansen (or Hanson), a Danish immigrant, and Peter Walker, a black man of Caribbean descent (the Danish West Indies, now the Virgin Islands). Her father died when she was two years old, and her mother remarried, to a man of her own race, and had a second daughter; as a result, Nellie was an outsider in her own family. After leaving to attend the secondary school at Fisk, where she remained for one year, Nellie (now known as Nella) had little contact with her family.

Part of the mystery surrounding Larsen concerns her whereabouts during the period 1908-1912. According to George Hutchinson, one of her biographers, she spent these years, or part of them, in Denmark, as she stated in her 1926 biographical blurb for the publishing company Alfred A. Knopf; nonetheless, it is also thought that she might have spent these years in Chicago. That Larsen was vague regarding these years accounts for the discrepancy between her purported and her actual age.

When Larsen resurfaced, it was in New York City, where she entered the Lincoln School of Nursing, a training program for African Americans. After completing her training, she served as a head nurse for a few months and then accepted a position at Tuskegee Institute in Alabama, where she stayed for one year. Larsen then returned to New York and began to interact with a number of people who were central to the cultural movement that was to become known as the Harlem Renaissance. It was there that she met Elmer Imes, one of the first African Americans to receive a Ph.D. in physics, and they married in 1919. Larsen continued to work as a nurse, but she also began writing and participating in activities at the 135th Street Branch of the New York Public Library. She soon became a volunteer at the library, then a paid assistant, and finally entered library school, where she earned a certificate.

After working for a few years, Larsen took a leave to focus more time on her writing. She published two short stories in 1926, and her first novel, *Quicksand*, appeared in 1928 to literary acclaim. The next year, she published her second novel, *Passing*. When she was awarded a Guggenheim Fellowship in 1930, she traveled to Europe to work on her third novel. The manuscript for that work, titled "Mirage," was not accepted by her publisher; the novel was described as a conventional love triangle. That the same year, Larsen's short story "Sanctuary" was published, and she was accused of plagiarism; in addition, her marriage was in trouble. Larsen returned to the United States and moved to Nashville, Tennessee, where her husband had accepted a teaching position at Fisk University, but she applied for a divorce in 1933. Larsen then returned to New York to continue her career as a writer; she reported working on three other novels, but none was accepted for publication.

When Elmer Imes died in 1941, Larsen was left without the financial support that had provided her the freedom to write. According to Hutchinson, because of the acute shortage of nurses during World War II, Larsen was able to return to her original occupation—as Nella Imes—at Gouverneur Hospital, where she quickly advanced, first to the position of chief nurse and then to night supervisor. When the hospital closed in 1961, Larsen, although of retirement age, became the supervisor of nurses at Metropolitan Hospital. In 1963, she was forced to retire, and six months later was found dead in her apartment. The executor of her estate, a fellow nurse, knew that Larsen had published two novels but had no knowledge of her prominence as a Harlem Renaissance writer; in any case, at the time of Larsen's death, most writers of the Harlem Renaissance were virtually unknown to the public in general. Although much is now known about her life, why Larsen discontinued writing after having being considered the period's "premier novelist" remains a mystery.

ANALYSIS

Nella Larsen was not the most prolific African American novelist of the Harlem Renaissance, but she was considered to be among its most promising. In fact, W. E. B. Du Bois characterized *Quicksand* as the "best piece of fiction that Negro America has produced since the heyday of [Charles Waddell] Chesnutt." Early critics considered Larsen one of the "rear guard" of the Harlem Renaissance, those middle-class writers who were interested in placing the best foot of the race forward, but with the burgeoning interest in African American literature and the rise of African American feminist criticism since the 1970's, Larsen's work has undergone significant reexamination and reevaluation. Her novels are deemed as modernist, particularly in their orientation toward the psychological, their narrative complexity, and their use of symbolism. Characterizing Larsen's fiction are issues of race, gender, and class expressed through themes of identity, marriage, and motherhood. Elements of Larsen's life are also present in her novels.

QUICKSAND

Lines from Langston Hughes's poem "Cross" serve as the opening epigraph to *Quicksand*; however, a number of critics, including Cheryl Wall, have argued that the plight of the mulatto is not the central theme of the novel. *Quicksand* does not meet the conventions of the tragic mulatto story as presented by black or white novelists, as Helga Crane is the product of a white mother and a black father, and her crisis of identity is not so much linked to race as it is to gender—her sexuality—or character. As Arthur P. Davis asserts, it is the cross that Helga carries that is problematic.

Having a spirit of restlessness, Helga is in constant flight. Deciding in Naxos not to marry James Vayle, Helga escapes to Chicago to visit her maternal uncle. Refused refuge by his new wife, she goes to New York, where she interacts with the middle-class society of Harlem. Becoming dissatisfied and feeling out of place, she travels to Denmark to visit her maternal aunt and husband. Viewed as an exotic there, she is first propositioned and then proposed to by a painter, Axel Olsen. Spurning him on the basis of race, she returns to New York, where she again meets Dr. Robert Anderson, the former principal of Naxos. Perhaps misinterpreting a kiss, Helga acknowledges and is prepared to pursue her interest in him although he is now is married. When he apologizes for his action, she becomes distraught and runs out into a drenching rain. She seeks shelter by entering a storefront church, is caught up in the religious fervor, and experiences a conversion. The next day, she marries the visiting minister, the Reverend Mr. Pleasant Green, and the two of them move to rural Alabama. Helga appears satisfied for a while, but her restlessness eventually returns; at the time, she has barely recovered from the birth of her fourth child and is pregnant with the fifth.

Because of Helga's travels, *Quicksand* is informed by the journey motif; the reason for Helga's travels is open to interpretation. Some have suggested that Helga's flight is from her sexual self. Although she was engaged to James Vayle, her flight from Naxos may have been sparked by Dr. Anderson's comment about her being a lady; although other reasons are present, Olsen's proposal triggers her fleeing from Denmark. Marriage is yet another factor. Having rejected promising suitors, black and white, Helga marries one who is (as in Larsen's short-story title) "the wrong man." Helga's restless spirit may be linked to the issue of belonging and lack of family: Her movement from place to place—representing various aspects of both black culture and white culture—is symbolic of her search for home; her inability to abandon her children is the result of her own lack of mothering.

Notably, Helga travels full circle, ending where she began—in the black rural South. Helga, as Lillie P. Howard puts it, spins "round and round in the same spot until she is virtually bogged down inside of herself." The image of spinning echoes the novel's central motif of quicksand, with its corresponding images of suffocation and entrapment. Entrapped in the quagmire of motherhood, Helga finds that physical movement is no longer possible. The quicksand, summarizes Davis, is Helga's "vacillating self."

PASSING

Passing begins with an epigraph from a poem by Harlem Renaissance writer Countée Cullen titled "Heritage," which concludes with the question "What is Africa to me?" As is the case with *Quicksand*, the epigraph may be misleading. According to Deborah McDowell, the lines invite readers to place race at the center of novel; as with *Quicksand*, however, the novel's title better serves to inform a reading of the work.

A number of perspectives on passing for white are suggested in *Passing*. First, as both Irene Redfield and Clare Kendry pass, one socially and the other permanently, the issue of passing as it relates to the tragic mulatto is raised. Again, Larsen revises the stereotype; emphasis in the novel is not on racial pride, and Clare is not in fear that her race will be discovered. According to Jennifer Brody, that fear is Irene's: If Clare returns to the race, this will further jeopardize Irene's fragile marriage.

The various facets of passing are demonstrated not only through the two main characters but also through their childhood friend, Gertrude Martin. In addition to the black woman who passes socially (Irene) and the woman who lives as white (Clare) is the one who passes with her husband's full cognizance (Gertrude). The issue of passing also extends beyond that of individual choice: Irene tries to avert her husband and sons from racial and social issues—she subverts her husband's desire to relocate to the less race-conscious Brazil and does not want him discussing lynching with their son; therefore, it has been argued that she is passing as middle class. Henry Louis Gates, Jr., has commented on the metaphorical dimension of passing in the novel; with Clare's death is suggested the "ironic double sense of 'passing' and 'dying.'"

The notion of passing is not confined to the passer; rather, it affects the passer's entire family. Also present in the novel, thus, are the motifs of motherhood and family. Fearing that their race may be revealed through their children's skin color, Clare and Gertrude each has only one child, and although she is married to a black man, Irene is concerned about the skin coloring of her older son. Unlike Helga Crane of *Quicksand*, who cannot abandon her children, Irene and Clare are both distant mothers, and at least one critic has suggested that Irene passes as a wife and mother. In contrast to *Quicksand*, the father is the dominant parental influence on the major characters, Irene and Clare.

Some scholars have argued that the passing in the novel seems superficial, and consequently they have focused on themes of infidelity, sexuality, and marriage. Because Irene and Clare are in loveless marriages, Clare's increased association with Brian Redfield has led to the suggestion that infidelity is a theme of the novel. Because of the close relationship between the two main characters, who have been described as psychological doubles, some critics have examined the theme of homosexuality; because of the tentativeness of Irene's and Clare's marriages, and Irene's singular focus on security in contrast to Clare's seeming abandon despite her husband's great dislike for Negroes, some have pointed to the centrality of marriage in the novel.

The main characters' closeness provides narrative complexity. Although Clare appears to be the narrative center, the narrative perspective is Irene's; consequently, critics disagree concerning whether Irene or Clare is the protagonist. Interpretation of the ambiguous ending—whether Clare falls, jumps, or is pushed out the sixth-floor window to her death—depends not only on one's determination of which is the main character but also on which theme one views as dominating the novel. Like the ending of *Quicksand*, the ending of *Passing* suggests ambiguity.

Passing continues the themes found in *Quicksand*: the concerns of identity as revealed through race, class, and gender. These concerns, central to Larsen's oeuvre, have in part been responsible for critics' reevaluation of Larsen and for the growing critical opinion that she was one of the chief talents of the Harlem Renaissance and the best black novelist of her generation.

Paula C. Barnes

OTHER MAJOR WORKS

SHORT FICTION: "Freedom," 1926; "The Wrong Man," 1926; "Sanctuary," 1930.

MISCELLANEOUS: *An Intimation of Things Distant: The Collected Fiction of Nella Larsen*, 1992 (also known as *The Complete Fiction of Nella Larsen*, 2001).

Bibliography

Calloway, Licia Morrow. "Elite Rejection of Maternity in Nella Larsen's *Quicksand* and *Passing*." In *Black Family (Dys)function in Novels by Jessie Fauset, Nella Larsen, and Fannie Hurst*. New York: Peter Lang, 2003. Addresses the absence of the maternal influence on the protagonists in both novels as well as the characters' own behavior as mothers.

Davis, Thadious M. *Nella Larsen, Novelist of the Harlem Renaissance: A Life Unveiled*. Baton Rouge: Louisiana State University Press, 1996. First book-length biography of Larsen provides the foundation for subsequent works. Draws on first-person interviews and primary source material.

Hutchinson, George. *In Search of Nella Larsen: A Biography of the Color Line*. Cambridge, Mass.: Belknap Press, 2006. Builds on the two previous Larsen biographies, Davis's (cited above) and Charles R. Larson's *Invisible Darkness: Jean Toomer and Nella Larsen* (1993), and provides additional information uncovered through research into historical documents, particularly regarding Larsen's Copenhagen and final Harlem years.

Larsen, Nella. *Passing*. Edited by Carla Kaplan. New York: W. W. Norton, 2007. In addition to the text of the novel, this edition provides selected reviews and critical essays on the work. Includes a comprehensive bibliography as well as a chronology that correlates the Davis, Larson, and Hutchinson biographies.

Larson, Charles R. Introduction to *Intimation of Things Distant: The Collected Fiction of Nella Larsen*. New York: Anchor Books, 1992. Presents an informative discussion of the similarities between Larsen's life and her fiction.

McDowell, Deborah. Introduction to *Quicksand and Passing*, by Nella Larsen. New Brunswick, N.J.: Rutgers University Press, 1986. Particularly insightful essay focuses on the sexuality of the two novels' protagonists' and thus addresses the approach to black female sexuality taken by a woman writer of the Harlem Renaissance.

HARPER LEE

Born: Monroeville, Alabama; April 28, 1926
Also known as: Nelle Harper Lee

PRINCIPAL LONG FICTION
To Kill a Mockingbird, 1960

OTHER LITERARY FORMS

In addition to the novel that made her famous, Harper Lee wrote for magazines, including *Vogue* and *McCall's*.

ACHIEVEMENTS

Based entirely on her first and only novel, Harper Lee's success has been phenomenal. According to a survey of reading habits conducted in 1991 by the Book-of-the-Month Club and the Library of Congress's Center for the Book, researchers found that her novel *To Kill a Mockingbird* was "most often cited as making a difference in people's lives, second only to the Bible." In 1999, Lee's novel was voted Best Novel of the Century in a poll conducted by *Library Journal*.

In 1961, *To Kill a Mockingbird* won a Pulitzer Prize in fiction, the Brotherhood Award of the National Conference of Christians and Jews, the Alabama Library Association Award, and the British Book Society Award. By 1962 it had become a Literary Guild selection and a Book-of-the-Month Club choice, it had won the Bestsellers' Magazine Paperback of the Year award, and it was featured in the Reader's Digest series of condensed books. In the same year, Lee was given an honorary doctorate by Mount Holyoke College. She received another honorary doctorate, in 1990, from the University of Alabama, and another from the University of Notre Dame, in 2006. In 2007, she was awarded the Presidential Medal of Freedom for her contribution to American literature.

Initially enjoying seventy-three weeks on the national best-seller lists, *To Kill a Mockingbird* has been translated into at least ten languages. A motion-picture adaptation of the novel, starring Gregory Peck, was released in 1962 and won several Academy Awards. President Lyndon B. Johnson appointed Lee to the National Council on the Arts in 1966, on which she served for five years. In 1970, playwright Christopher Sergel published a stage version of the novel titled *Harper Lee's To Kill a Mockingbird: A Full-Length Play*, with Dramatic Publications. The play was professionally performed on both sides of the Atlantic during the 1980's and 1990's.

BIOGRAPHY

The third daughter and youngest child of Amasa Coleman Lee, an attorney and newspaper publisher, and Frances Finch Lee, reportedly a somewhat eccentric pianist, Nelle

Harper Lee grew up in Monroeville, Alabama, where she was born on April 28, 1926. She attended public school there, then went to Huntington College for Women in Montgomery for a year, before transferring to the University of Alabama in 1945. Lee edited the college newspaper, the *Rammer Jammer,* and spent a year as an exchange student at Oxford University.

In 1950, Lee entered law school, no doubt with the intention of following in her father's footsteps. However, after one year she decided to abandon the study of law and go to New York City to pursue a career in writing. Throughout the early 1950's, Lee worked by day as a reservation clerk for Eastern Airlines and British Overseas Airways, living in a cramped apartment with no hot water and writing in her free time. During this period she also made many trips to Monroeville to be with her ailing father, who died in 1962. Happily, Amasa Lee did live long enough to see *To Kill a Mockingbird* become a hugely successful book.

In a short article published in *McCall's* in December, 1961, called "Christmas to Me," Lee recounts how she missed her home and family, contrasting New York City with memories of Monroeville during the Christmas season. However, she made some very close friends in her adopted home, and she spent Christmas with one of these families, who surprised her with a monetary gift. On the accompanying card were the words, "You have one year off from your job to write whatever you please. Merry Christmas." She was overwhelmed, but her benefactors felt that their faith in Lee's ability was well founded.

Lee used this time carefully: A methodical writer, she composed a few pages each day and revised them carefully, completing three short fictional sketches by 1957. After being advised that she must do more to transform this work into a novel, she continued to write for two and a half years, until *To Kill a Mockingbird* went to press in 1960, dedicated to her father and to her older sister, Alice, a partner in the family law firm.

Writer Truman Capote spent a great part of his childhood in Monroeville, staying each summer with relatives whose house was close to the Lees'. The character of Charles Baker Harris, nicknamed Dill, in *To Kill a Mockingbird* is an accurate portrait of the young Capote, who remained close to Lee throughout his life. In the early 1960's, Lee went with Capote to Kansas to help him research his true crime book of nonfiction *In Cold Blood* (1966), which chronicles the murders of the Clutter family in Holcomb, Kansas. Capote dedicated the book to Lee and another lifelong friend, Jack Dunphy. Much of what is known about Lee is revealed in Capote's works and in those written about him by others.

Lee was invited to write the screenplay for the film version of *To Kill a Mockingbird,* but she declined. She was, however, very pleased with screenwriter Horton Foote's script, about which she said, "If the integrity of a film adaptation is measured by the degree to which the novelist's intent is preserved, Mr. Foote's screenplay should be studied as a classic." She was so delighted by Peck's portrayal of Atticus Finch that she honored his performance and resemblance to her father by giving him Amasa Lee's gold pocket watch, which was inscribed "To Gregory from Harper, 1962."

To Kill a Mockingbird has sold millions of copies, but its success did not propel Lee to produce another book. As she told her cousin, Richard Williams, when he questioned her about this, "When you have a hit like that, you can't go anywhere but down." Although known in her hometown as a friendly and jovial woman, Lee consistently refused all interview requests. In 1995, when HarperCollins released the thirty-fifth-anniversary edition of *To Kill a Mockingbird*, Lee declined to write an introduction, stating, "The book still says what it has to say: it has managed to survive the years without preamble." She continued to divide her time between a New York apartment and a modest house in Monroeville, which she shared with her sister, Alice.

Analysis: To Kill a Mockingbird

Although Harper Lee set her novel in a very isolated locale, which she calls Maycomb, in an era when her notion of crossing racial and social boundaries does not always seem imminently attainable, the world of 1960, when *To Kill a Mockingbird* appeared, was radically different. The Civil Rights movement had begun: The U.S. Supreme Court had ruled against school segregation in the 1954 *Brown v. Board of Education* decision, and there had been a successful bus boycott in Montgomery, Alabama, in 1955-1956, which brought activist Martin Luther King, Jr., to public attention. Finally, people who believed in the importance of applying law fairly and breaking racial boundaries (as does her character, Atticus Finch) were being heard.

Most literary critics have written of *To Kill a Mockingbird* in glowing terms. One critic has suggested that Atticus is the symbol of the future, of the "new" South that will arise when it takes into account all human experience, discarding the old romantic notions of an isolated regionalism in favor of a wider Emersonian view of the world.

To Kill a Mockingbird has gained stature over the years, as readers began to think of it as more than merely a skillful depiction of small-town southern life during the 1930's with a coming-of-age theme. Claudia Durst Johnson, who has published two books of analysis on *To Kill a Mockingbird*, suggests that the novel is universally compelling because Lee's overall theme of "threatening boundaries" covers a wide spectrum, from law to social standing, from childhood innocence to racism.

The narrator of the book is Scout (Jean Louise) Finch, who is discussing childhood events with her adult brother, Jem, as the story begins. She then slips effortlessly into the role of the six-year-old tomboy who matures over the three years of the book's action. In the first half of the novel, Scout and Jem, along with their childhood companion, Dill, are fascinated by their mysterious neighbor, Boo (Arthur) Radley. Because no one has seen Boo in many years, the youngsters construct a gothic stereotype of him, imagining him as huge and ugly, a monster who dines on raw squirrels, sports a jagged scar, and has rotten yellowing teeth and bulging eyes. They make plans to lure Boo from his "castle" (in reality the dark, shuttered Radley house), but in the course of their attempts to breach the boundaries of his life, they begin to discover the real Boo, an extremely shy man who has attempted to reach out to the children in a number of ways, and who, in the final chapters of the book, saves their lives.

The second half of the book is principally concerned with the trial of Tom Robinson, a young African American unfairly accused of raping a white woman. Racial tensions in the neighborhood explode; Scout and Jem are shocked to find that not only their peers but also adults they have known their whole lives are harshly critical of their father, Atticus, who provides the legal defense for the innocent man.

Throughout both sections of *To Kill a Mockingbird*, Lee skillfully shows other divisions among people and how these barriers are threatened. Obviously, it is not a matter of race alone that sets societal patterns in this provincial Alabama town. For example, when Atticus's sister, Alexandria, visits the family, she makes it clear that she is displeased by Scout's tomboyish appearance, since she feels a future "southern belle" should be interested in more ladylike clothing and more feminine behavior. Furthermore, as Jem tells Scout later, there is a strict caste system in Maycomb, with each group threatened by any possible abridgments of the social order. As Jem suggests, there are the "old" families—the gentry, who are usually educated, frequently professional, but, given the era, often cash-poor. On the next level down are the "poor but proud" people, such as the Cunninghams. They are country folk who pay their bills with crops and adamantly refuse all charity. Beneath them is the group commonly called "poor white trash," amply represented by Bob Ewell, "the only man ever fired by the WPA for laziness," and his pitiful daughter, Mayella, the alleged victim of the rape. At the lowest rung of the social ladder are African Americans, although many are clearly superior to some of the poor white trash, who have only their skin color as their badge of superiority. They are represented by Robinson, the accused rapist, and Calpurnia, the housekeeper for the motherless Finch family.

In addition to the clearly defined social castes, there are deviants, such as Dolphus Raymond, a white man involved in a long relationship with a black woman. He pretends to be an alcoholic to "give himself an excuse with the community" for his lifestyle. There is Mrs. Henry Lafayette Dubose, a member of the upper class who became a morphine addict, whose one desire is to overcome her habit before her death. Also featured is Miss Maudie, the friendly neighbor who seems to represent, along with Atticus, the best hope for change in the community.

Lee uses many symbols in the book, none more pervasive than the mockingbird of the title. The bird is characterized as an innocent singer who lives only to give pleasure to others. Early in the novel, when Atticus gives Jem and Scout air rifles, he makes it clear that it would be a sin to harm a mockingbird, a theme reiterated by Miss Maudie. Two of the main characters are subtly equated with the birds: Boo Radley and Tom Robinson, both innocents "caged for crimes they never committed." Atticus himself is a symbol of conscience. Unlike his sister, he is a nonconformist, an atypical southerner, a thoughtful, bookish man at odds with his environment. He constantly tells his children that they can understand other people only by walking in their shoes. He is mindful of majority opinion but asserts, "The one thing that doesn't abide by majority rule is a person's conscience."

Sometimes, of course, violent action is necessary to alter boundaries. This is foreshadowed early in the novel when Atticus finds it necessary to shoot a rabid dog. However, later, when he faces the mob from Old Sarum, who are intent on lynching Robinson, he simply sits in front of the jail, ostensibly reading a newspaper. Atticus seems very calm, upset only by the appearance of the children and Jem's refusal to take Dill and Scout home, not by the men who threaten violence. After Scout recognizes Cunningham and mentions Walter, his son, as her school friend, the group leaves. Braxton Underwood, owner of the *Maycomb Tribune*, leans out of his window above the office holding a double-barreled shotgun, saying, "I had you covered all the time, Atticus," suggesting that there may well be occasions in which force is appropriate.

Tried before a jury of white men, in an echo of the 1931 Scottsboro Nine case, which convicted nine innocent black youth of raping two white women, Robinson is found guilty in spite of proof that he could not have committed the crime. Yet even here there is a bit of hope for change to come, because the jury does not reach a quick decision, deliberating for three hours in a case involving the strongest taboo in the South, a black man sexually assaulting a white woman. Robinson, however, does not believe that Atticus's legal appeals will save him, and again violence erupts when he is shot and killed while trying to escape from the prison exercise yard.

There was some criticism of the melodramatic ending of the novel, in which Ewell attacks the Finch children, who are in costume returning from a school Halloween pageant. Jem's arm is broken in the scuffle, and Scout is saved from the attacker by Boo Radley, who kills Ewell with his own knife. However, in addition to providing closure for the plot, Lee uses this ending to confirm her view of Atticus and his moral character. Initially, when Sheriff Heck Tate comes to the Finch home to learn the details of the evening's happenings, Atticus mistakenly assumes that Jem has killed Ewell while defending Scout. Tate tries to reassure Atticus, saying, "Bob Ewell fell on his knife. He killed himself." Atticus believes that the sheriff is suggesting a cover-up for Jem, which he refuses, saying, "I can't live one way in town and another way in my home." Finally he realizes that it was Boo Radley who had stabbed Ewell with a kitchen knife, not Jem. Atticus then agrees out of kindness to the reclusive Boo to go along with the sheriff's version of the death. When he tells Scout that Sheriff Tate was right, she says, "Well, [telling the truth would] be sort of like shootin' a mockingbird, wouldn't it?"

Edythe M. McGovern

BIBLIOGRAPHY

Bloom, Harold, ed. *Harper Lee's "To Kill a Mockingbird."* New York: Chelsea House, 2007. Part of the Bloom's Modern Critical Interpretations series, this volume includes a number of critical essays concerning the novel. Essays explore the issues of romantic regionalism, Harper Lee's tragic vision, the female voice in the novel, and the novel's "destabilization of heterosexuality." Includes an introduction by Bloom, a chronology, a bibliography, and an index.

Johnson, Claudia Durst. *To Kill a Mockingbird: Threatening Boundaries*. New York: Twayne, 1994. An analysis of the novel, placing the book within the historical context of southern racism and the Civil Rights movement of the late 1950's. Johnson also discusses the book's critical reception and its place in American literature.

_______. *Understanding "To Kill a Mockingbird": A Student Casebook to Issues, Sources, and Historic Documents*. Westport, Conn.: Greenwood Press, 1994. A reference source for students and other readers. Includes an analysis of unifying themes in the book and primary documents related to racism in the United States, the Scottsboro trials in the 1930's, and the Civil Rights movement of the 1950's and 1960's.

Mancini, Candice, ed. *Racism in Harper Lee's "To Kill a Mockingbird."* Detroit, Mich.: Greenhaven Press, 2008. Designed for middle school and high school students, this book examines racism as it relates to the novel's author, characters, and situations. Includes a brief biography of Lee and a time line of her life, a bibliography, an index, and illustrations.

Moates, Marianne M. *A Bridge of Childhood: Truman Capote's Southern Years*. New York: Holt, 1989. This biography about Capote's early years discusses his friendship with Lee and why he was used as the basis for the character Dill in *To Kill a Mockingbird*. Recounts childhood episodes that Lee used in her novel.

O'Neill, Terry, ed. *Readings on "To Kill a Mockingbird."* San Diego, Calif.: Greenhaven Press, 2000. Designed for high school students, this book contains essays analyzing the novel's literary techniques, critical reception, social issues, and the character of Atticus Finch. It also includes a brief biography of Lee, a summary of the novel's plot and characters, and a bibliography.

Petry, Alice Hall. *On Harper Lee: Essays and Reflections*. Knoxville: University of Tennessee Press, 2007. A collection of essays, the majority of which provide analyses of *To Kill a Mockingbird*. Includes discussions of the book's religious vision, humor, and humanity, and of the South African response to the book. The final essay addresses Harper's literary status as a "one hit wonder."

Remler, Nancy Lawson, and Hugh Lawson. "Situating Atticus in the Zone: A Lawyer and His Daughter Read Harper Lee's *To Kill a Mockingbird*." In *Literature and Law*, edited by Michael J. Meyer. Amsterdam: Rodopi, 2004. This collection examines legal issues in selected works of literature. Remler and Lawson's chapter focuses on the treatment of the law and the legal system in Lee's novel.

Shields, Carol. *Mockingbird: A Portrait of Harper Lee*. New York: Henry Holt, 2006. Shields's biography recounts the events that led Lee to write *To Kill a Mockingbird*, as well as her decision to shun the spotlight after its publication.

CLAUDE MCKAY

Born: Sunny Ville, Jamaica; September 15, 1889
Died: Chicago, Illinois; May 22, 1948
Also known as: Festus Claudius McKay; Eli Edwards; Hugh Hope

PRINCIPAL LONG FICTION

Home to Harlem, 1928
Banjo: A Story Without a Plot, 1929
Banana Bottom, 1933

OTHER LITERARY FORMS

Claude McKay's literary career started when he began writing poetry at an early age in his native Jamaica. In 1917, he published two poems in *Seven Arts* under the pen name Eli Edwards. Later in New York, when he was coeditor of the magazine *The Liberator*, he published one of his most famous poems, "If We Must Die" (1919), as well as essays and articles. A collection of McKay's short stories as well as a nonfiction volume were published in Russian in the early 1920's; English translations of these works did not appear until the late 1970's. *Gingertown*, a collection of short stories, was published in 1932, and McKay also wrote two autobiographical books: *A Long Way from Home* (1937) and *Harlem: Negro Metropolis* (1940). His poems have been published in several collections. A memoir of his youth, *My Green Hills of Jamaica*, was not published until 1979, when it appeared with some of his short fiction in *My Green Hills of Jamaica, and Five Jamaican Short Stories*.

ACHIEVEMENTS

Claude McKay was always considered a talented writer, and for a time during his youth and early adulthood, his literary output brought him fame and popularity. In 1912, when he was only twenty-three years old, the Jamaican Institute of Arts and Sciences in Kingston awarded him a gold medal for his poetry published that year in two volumes, *Songs of Jamaica* and *Constab Ballads*. In 1922, as a representative of the American Workers Party, he attended the Third Communist International Conference in Moscow, Russia, and had the singular honor of addressing the assemblage. In 1928 he won the Harmon Gold Award for Literature, presented by the National Association for the Advancement of Colored People (NAACP), for his novel *Home to Harlem*. In 1937, when his memoir *A Long Way from Home* was published, he was the recipient of the James Weldon Johnson Literary Award.

BIOGRAPHY

Festus Claudius McKay was born to Hannah Ann Elizabeth McKay (née Edwards) and Thomas McKay, peasant farmers and landowners of Clarendon Parish, Jamaica. He was educated by his schoolteacher brother, Uriah Theodore, studying, among other things, British and classical literature. Encouraged in his early attempts to write poetry, by 1912 McKay had published two volumes of poetry, *Songs of Jamaica* and *Constab Ballads*. They were written in the dialect of Jamaica's folk culture and were based on peasant life and his experiences working for a brief time in 1911 as a policeman.

In 1912, McKay went to the United States to attend college, starting at Tuskegee Institute in Alabama but transferring to Kansas State College. After a year in Kansas, however, he dropped out and went to New York City, where he worked at various jobs, including that of railroad dining-car waiter. He married his childhood sweetheart, Imelda Lewars, in 1914, but she returned to Jamaica to have their daughter, who was named Ruth Hope, and McKay reportedly never saw his daughter. He and his wife divorced after only about a year of marriage.

He continued to write poetry, sometimes using the pseudonym Eli Edwards. He was also becoming more seriously involved with radical political and literary figures such as Hubert H. Harrison and Cyril V. Briggs, two West Indian writers with socialist and communist leanings, and Max and Crystal Eastman, siblings who were prominent in socialist activities. McKay's association with the Eastmans, who were editors of the radical journal *The Liberator*, led to the publication of his most famous poem, "If We Must Die," in the journal's July, 1919, issue.

McKay's fame from the popularity of "If We Must Die" led to many different opportunities for the writer. He got the chance in 1920 to travel to England, where he wrote articles, often under the name Hugh Hope, for the Socialist periodical *Worker's Dreadnought*. Later, in 1922, he went to Russia to attend a Communist congress. He was still writing poetry and published four volumes by 1922 as well as a series of articles that appeared in *The Liberator* and in the Soviet press.

For ten years, McKay traveled throughout Europe and North Africa, spending brief periods in Germany and Spain and more significant time in Paris and southern France, where he wrote his first novel, "Color Scheme"; unable to find a publisher for the work, he burned it. His second novel, *Home to Harlem*, not only found a publisher in 1928 but also received considerable acclaim. He next wrote *Banjo*, which was published in 1929. By 1932, McKay had moved to Tangier, Morocco, where he wrote several short stories that were published in a collection titled *Gingertown*. His last novel, *Banana Bottom*, was published in 1933. Neither of his last two novels was a commercial success, and when he returned to the United States in 1934, McKay was not only financially destitute but also sick, having contracted syphilis. Ever the writer, he continued writing, but only his articles were published with any consistency; they appeared in such periodicals as *The Catholic Worker* and *Interracial Review*.

McKay spent some time mostly unemployed, ill, and lonely, having been rescued by his friend Max Eastman from a federal government "welfare camp" in 1934, where he participated in the Federal Writers' Project. His autobiographical *A Long Way from Home* was published in New York in 1936, and by 1944 he had become an American citizen and joined the Catholic Church. He completed the memoir *My Green Hills of Jamaica*, which was not published until 1979.

McKay suffered from hypertension and edema in 1942, and in 1943 he had a stroke. A heart attack at age fifty-eight, on May 22, 1948, caused his death, and he was buried in Queens, New York.

Analysis

Claude McKay said about his writing, "I must write what I feel, what I know, what I think, what I have seen, what is true"; he also wrote, "Art is not a means of escape but a way to confront the world and expose the true nature of the human spirit." Having this philosophy and the personal experiences of an exiled Jamaican living first in the United States and then in Europe and North Africa, he found race, class, colonialism, communism, and capitalism to be themes that captured and held his attention throughout most of his career. That he was living during chaotic times—those of World War I and the Great Depression, when the influence of radical movements such as Black Nationalism was growing and spreading—only contributed to his ongoing interest in finding a distinctive black identity to complement his pride in his African heritage.

McKay was certainly a man of contradictions. In his search for his own distinctive identity and place in the world, he experienced various lifestyles and even philosophies, searching for one with which he could feel comfortable. He tried homosexuality even as he tried marriage. He tried Soviet communism, which did not appeal to him and was ultimately disillusioning. The leaders of the Black Nationalist movement did not meet his expectations. He abandoned even atheism and agnosticism finally, as he embraced Roman Catholicism at last.

McKay developed a prose writing style that included the beautiful imagery he had shown in his poetry, especially in his descriptions of the physical attributes of African American characters and of the sights and sites of the New York neighborhood of Harlem. He created natural and unforced dialogue for his characters and "brutally honest" narrative. Although by the standards of the early twenty-first century his style might be considered stilted, his works were ahead of their time in their realism. Some critics consider McKay to be the "first and most militant voice of the Harlem Renaissance."

He used picaresque elements in his novels, which show the working-class lives of African Americans in the 1920's. Because he tried to portray these lives in a realistic, even naturalistic manner, some critics at the time of their publication condemned what they saw as a "blatant focus on sex, drugs, alcohol and . . . prostitution." McKay's position, however, was that he was presenting black life not only as he lived it but also as he observed it, both in Harlem and, later, in France. He was not surprised that the black intelligentsia, so clamorously represented by Alain Locke and W. E. B. Du Bois, did not like his portrayal. McKay believed that his mission was to show life as he saw it, not as one might wish it to be. Through themes of dislocation, marginality, alienation, and disillusionment, he created stories about characters who were living in the midst of irreconcilable cultural clashes between two societies, one black, the other white.

HOME TO HARLEM

Home to Harlem, McKay's most widely read novel, is the story of Jake, a black soldier who has gone absent without leave from his unit during World War I and returned to his home in Harlem. He almost immediately picks up a young woman in a cabaret and spends the night with her. The next morning, when he discovers that she has gone, leaving behind his last fifty dollars that he had given her and a sweet note, he is dismayed to realize he has no way to find her again. The rest of the story follows Jake as he encounters other women and finds work to support his various ways of entertaining himself in the many "metropolitan fleshpots" of Harlem. It ends happily with Jake once more finding the sweet girl he first met on his return to Harlem.

This novel has been described as "luxuriating" in the "sounds, sights, smells, language, and rhythms" of the African American community. Although Jake is the ostensible "hero" of the story, Harlem is actually the main character. Harlem comes to life with McKay's realistic depictions of cabarets, rent parties, and the poolrooms where his characters spend their days and nights. A character named Ray, thought by some critics to be the personification of McKay himself, provides insight into the many aspects of life among the working poor, whom he describes as "simple, earth-loving animals without aspiration." Such views, of course, added to criticisms at the time of publication that the novel only reinforced the negative stereotypes of black people that black leaders condemned. Nevertheless, either because of its depiction of African American life as mostly low life or in spite of that depiction, *Home to Harlem* was the first novel by a black writer to find a place on American best-seller lists.

BANJO

Banjo is a somewhat didactic episodic novel set in Marseilles, France, on the docks—an area with which McKay was familiar, having spent time there during his sojourn in southern France. Its black characters have drifted to Marseilles from many other parts of the world, and McKay's somewhat sentimentalized depictions of them as honest, natural, and even pure are similar to the depictions of Mexican and Spanish peasants as well as American "Okies" found in the writings of John Steinbeck and Ernest Hemingway. McKay's characters are vagabonds who have strayed to Marseilles from West and East Africa, from the West Indies, and from the southern and northern parts of the United States. They congregate in Marseilles on the beaches or at their work on the docks, where they engage in lengthy and occasionally far-fetched discourses on the issues that interested McKay.

The main character, Lincoln Agrippa Daily, is called "Banjo" because he plays the instrument. One of his friends, Goosey, a black racist who hates white people, derides his affinity for the instrument, which he sees as a symbol of slavery; Goosey argues that black people should not play the banjo because of its long connection with the degrading tradition of the minstrel show. Banjo contends that he plays the instrument because he likes its sharp, loud sound, which reminds him of what "American Negro" life is like. His character shows how a black man seeks the true meaning of human existence in a white society that excludes him.

A character probably patterned after McKay is Ray, a writer from the Caribbean who is in Marseilles after leaving New York City. Through him, McKay expounds many of his own views about Black Nationalism as an outgrowth of universal racial subordination. All the characters in *Banjo*, who are blacks from all over the world, discuss such issues as well as pan-Africanism, exposing those concerns significant to black men who wander the world searching for a home away from the homes from which they are exiled. The novel continues McKay's preoccupation with race and class and the influence that capitalism, communism, and colonialism have on them. *Banjo* reportedly had an impact on some of the pioneers of the negritude literary movement, such as Aimé Césaire in the French West Indies and Léopold Senghor in French West Africa.

BANANA BOTTOM

Of McKay's three novels, *Banana Bottom* is generally considered his consummate achievement. Continuing his enduring theme of the black person's quest for a cultural identity in a white world, it tells the story of Bita Plant, a Jamaican girl educated in England by white missionaries. Bita returns after seven years to Banana Bottom, her native Jamaican village, to find her English-culture education at odds with her cultural heritage. Once home, where she is exposed to her more natural culture, with its festivals and West Indian superstitions, she embraces her roots and rejects what McKay portrays as a "colonial cultural ideology."

Banana Bottom is considered McKay's "mellowest" novel, rich in a lyrical style and in humor and melodrama. It shows that the peasant's own culture is to be preferred to the artificiality of an imposed Western culture.

Jane L. Ball

OTHER MAJOR WORKS

SHORT FICTION: *Sudom lincha: Rasskazy o zhizni negrov v severnoi Amerike*, 1925 (*Trial by Lynching: Stories About Negro Life in America*, 1977); *Gingertown*, 1932.

POETRY: *Constab Ballads*, 1912; *Songs of Jamaica*, 1912; *Spring in New Hampshire, and Other Poems*, 1920; *Harlem Shadows*, 1922; *Selected Poems of Claude McKay*, 1953; *Complete Poems*, 2004.

NONFICTION: *Negry v Amerike*, 1923 (*The Negroes in America*, 1979); *A Long Way from Home*, 1937; *Harlem: Negro Metropolis*, 1940.

MISCELLANEOUS: *The Passion of Claude McKay: Selected Poetry and Prose, 1912-1948*, 1973 (Wayne F. Cooper, editor; contains social and literary criticism, letters, prose, fiction, and poetry); *My Green Hills of Jamaica, and Five Jamaican Short Stories*, 1979.

Bibliography

Cooper, Wayne F. *Claude McKay: Rebel Sojourner in the Harlem Renaissance—A Biography*. Baton Rouge: Louisiana State University Press, 1987. Describes McKay's life and career, providing insight into his complex personality. Discusses his social criticism as well as his poetry and his fiction.

Giles, James R. *Claude McKay*. Boston: Twayne, 1976. Critical study of McKay's fiction provides a good introduction to his work.

Gosciak, Josh. *The Shadowed Country: Claude McKay and the Romance of the Victorians*. New Brunswick, N.J.: Rutgers University Press, 2006. Examines McKay's contributions to literature beyond the Harlem Renaissance, with a focus on the context of his poetry and fiction within the late Victorian and early modern periods.

Hathaway, Heather. *Caribbean Waves: Relocating Claude McKay and Paule Marshall*. Bloomington: Indiana University Press, 1999. Explores the influence of McKay's and Marshall's immigrant status on the works of these two Caribbean authors. Presents analyses of their works that focus on issues of cultural dislocation.

Holcomb, Gary Edward. *Claude Mckay, Code Name Sasha: Queer Black Marxism and the Harlem Renaissance*. Gainesville: University Press of Florida, 2007. Discusses in depth McKay's novels *Home to Harlem* and *Banjo*, as wall as his unpublished work "Romance in Marseilles."

_______. "Diaspora Cruises: Queer Black Proletarianism in Claude McKay's *A Long Way from Home*." *Modern Fiction Studies* 49, no. 4 (Winter, 2003): 714-745. Presents discussion of McKay's role in the Harlem Renaissance, the black diaspora, Black Nationalism, and the black/white gay subculture of the era.

Maiwald, Michael. "Race, Capitalism, and the Third Sex Ideal: Claude McKay's *Home to Harlem* and the Legacy of Edward Carpenter." *Modern Fiction Studies* 48, no. 4 (Winter, 2002): 825-857. Discusses how *Home to Harlem* was influenced by Edward Carpenter's theories on sexuality, socialism, and gender.

Ramesh, Kotti Sree, and Kandula Nirupa Rani. *Claude McKay: The Literary Identity from Jamaica to Harlem and Beyond*. Jefferson, N.C.: McFarland, 2006. Explores McKay's life and writings with a focus on the author's cross-cultural experiences.

TERRY MCMILLAN

Born: Port Huron, Michigan; October 18, 1951

PRINCIPAL LONG FICTION

Mama, 1987
Disappearing Acts, 1989
Waiting to Exhale, 1992
How Stella Got Her Groove Back, 1996
A Day Late and a Dollar Short, 2001
The Interruption of Everything, 2005

OTHER LITERARY FORMS

Although she dabbled in poetry in her earliest attempts at writing, Terry McMillan's first publication was a short story, "The End," published in *Yardbird Reader* in 1976. Another short story, "Ma'Dear," originally published in *Callaloo*, is included in *Breaking Ice: An Anthology of Contemporary African-American Fiction*, which McMillan edited in 1990. McMillan has also collaborated on screenplays based on her novels, and in 2006 she published a collection of tips for high school students, *It's OK If You're Clueless: And Twenty-three More Tips for the College Bound*. She has also written articles for periodicals such as *Ebony* magazine.

ACHIEVEMENTS

Terry McMillan has achieved considerable commercial success with her novels, three of which have been adapted into films. The film version of her novel *Waiting to Exhale*, which sold nearly four million copies and stayed on the *New York Times* best-seller list for months, was released in 1995; McMillan collaborated with Ronald Bass on the screenplay. The film adaptation of *How Stella Got Her Groove Back*, also written by McMillan and Bass, was released in 1998, and the adaptation of *Disappearing Acts* was made for cable television network HBO in 2000.

McMillan won the first *Essence* magazine college writing contest in 1974. In 1986 she received a New York Foundation of the Arts Fellowship and the Doubleday/Columbia University Literary Fellowship. She was a three-time fellow at the Yaddo Artist Colony and the MacDowell Colony. Her book *Mama* received the American Book Award from the Before Columbus Foundation in 1987. In 2008, the Essence Literary Awards presented McMillan with its Lifetime Achievement Award.

BIOGRAPHY

Terry McMillan was born on October 18, 1951, in Port Huron, Michigan, to Madeline Washington Tillman, a domestic and auto factory worker, and Edward Lewis McMillan, a blue-collar worker. Her father suffered from tuberculosis and was in a sanitarium during his daughter's early years. The family included four other children, three girls and a boy. When McMillan was thirteen years old, her parents divorced, so she was essentially raised by her mother, a single parent.

McMillan's interest in writing began when, at age sixteen, she worked at a library and became an avid reader of such authors as Henry David Thoreau, Nathaniel Hawthorne, Charlotte and Emily Brontë, and Thomas Mann. When she discovered works by African American writer James Baldwin, she realized that black people could be authors, too. At age seventeen, she moved to Los Angeles and enrolled in an African American literature class at Los Angeles City College. There she studied the works of Zora Neale Hurston, Richard Wright, Jean Toomer, and, most significant, Ann Petry; Petry's novel *The Street* (1946), which depicts a black heroine's existence in a harsh urban environment, had an impact on McMillan's earliest writing.

McMillan's first efforts at writing were in poetry, and when she was in college, some of her poems were published in campus newspapers. Her formal education included courses in journalism taken at the University of California at Berkeley. Then, when McMillan met black novelist and critic Ishmael Reed at a writing workshop at Berkeley, he encouraged her in her writing, and eventually Reed published her first short story, "The End," in 1976.

After McMillan completed her undergraduate studies with a bachelor of science degree from Berkeley in 1979, she moved to New York City. She enrolled at Columbia University to pursue a master of fine arts degree, joined the Harlem Writers Guild, and attended artists' colonies in upstate New York and in New Hampshire. At the urging and encouragement of other members of the Harlem Writers Guild, she expanded one of her short stories into the novel *Mama*, which was published in 1987.

Mama received little promotion from the publishing company, so McMillan undertook the promotion herself, writing more than three thousand letters to all the black organizations she could think of, including chain and independent bookstores and colleges. She offered to do readings and book signings and ultimately received enough favorable responses to develop a publicity tour. As a consequence, the first printing of *Mama* book sold quickly, and McMillan's successful efforts made an impression on her publisher, making her next book an easier sell.

Her personal life went through several shifts. She developed a drug and alcohol addiction but overcame it in 1981. In 1984 she gave birth to a son she named Solomon; McMillan's relationship with the child's father, Leonard Welch, ended soon after Solomon's birth. Later, Welch would take McMillan to court in a defamation suit, claiming that the main male character in her second novel, *Disappearing Acts*, was based on him and was disparaging and embarrassing. In the end, however, the court ruled in McMillan's favor. A second relationship, this time her marriage to Jonathan Plummer, also ended in divorce and legal conflict.

In addition to writing and promoting her books, McMillan has held various teaching positions. From 1987 to 1990 she taught creative writing at the University of Wyoming in Laramie, and from 1990 to 1992, she was a tenured associate professor at the University of Arizona at Tucson.

ANALYSIS

Terry McMillan's novels depict African American women whose lives are filled with personal crises, romantic entanglements, and conflicts as they aspire to upward mobility and professional success. The stories, written with honesty and humor and featuring engaging, interesting characters, chronicle the friendships between women and relationships between men and women. Considered autobiographical in tone, McMillan's novels explore African American urban family life in an episodic format, using an "earthy" vernacular that some critics have found distracting but that McMillan defends as accurate. She contends that the amount of profanity her characters use reflects the way women of her era actually talk—and she is quick to comment that male writers are rarely chastised for the language they use, suggesting the existence of a double standard.

In regard to style, McMillan has expressed her belief that every sentence does not have to be perfect, that in fact her first draft is usually the "most honest." She does not worry about how pretty her writing sounds or how lilting the imagery is, because most readers, she asserts, do not care about that sort of thing anyway. She believes that it is the people in the story who count; the human element and emotional responses are what make for interesting writing. Apparently, the critics' opinions about some of her work have not been shared by McMillan's fans, as most of her books have been commercial successes.

The themes of McMillan's novels reflect what critics consider to be the author's greater interest in material wealth and conspicuous consumption than in such unresolved issues as racial discrimination and women's rights. Most critics agree, however, that her stories cross the lines of race and sex to reveal universal lessons of life and love, and that their engaging narratives, appealing characters, and insights into the contemporary African American experience are a valuable contribution to popular literature. McMillan's upbeat novels about today's black women are in fact a new literary genre.

Because her novels have strong, feisty black heroines, McMillan is often compared favorably to such black writers as Zora Neale Hurston and Alice Walker. However flattering such comparisons may be, McMillan has stated her belief that African American women of her generation look at life differently from those earlier writers. Her heroines are intelligent, attractive, often unattached, often professionally successful middle-class black women who have strong, empowering relationships with each other and close ties with family. They also are often in disastrous relationships with the men in their lives.

MAMA

The protagonist of *Mama* is Mildred Peacock, a twenty-seven-year-old mother of five who tries to hold things together when her abusive husband, Crooks, leaves her to deal with her own alcoholism and the bills that are piling up. To support her family, Mildred holds rent parties and takes all kinds of menial jobs, even working for a while as a prostitute. As her life sinks deeper and deeper into a morass of unpaid bills and increasing depression, she tries to escape more and more through alcohol. Finally, however, with her oldest daughter's support, she begins to turn things around, even deciding to go to a community college to improve herself and her lot.

Mama has been praised for its realistic detail and powerful characterizations, particularly of Mildred. Although it sometimes lacks focus and a clear point of view, this first novel clearly showed McMillan to be a writer with promise.

DISAPPEARING ACTS

The story of *Disappearing Acts* is told in alternating first-person monologues by the two main characters: Zora Banks is a music teacher who aspires to be a singer, and her lover, Franklin Swift, is a sometime construction worker. Theirs is a tumultuous relationship filled with passion, expectations, and disappointments. When Zora bears Franklin's child, she assumes full responsibility for raising the boy. At story's end, she has made it clear that she intends to leave Franklin behind and return to her family to raise her son.

Critics have described some of the writing in *Disappearing Acts* as wooden and have argued that occasionally McMillan states the obvious, but they have praised the dialogue as often lively and even explosive between the characters. The novel has been described as funny, earthy, and intensely realistic.

WAITING TO EXHALE

Waiting to Exhale may be McMillan's best-known work. The four women protagonists, all successful, independent black women in their late thirties, have a strong camaraderie based on their deep friendships with one another as well as on their disappointing relationships with men. They get together often to share their thoughts and feelings, revealing the pitfalls in their professional lives and the shortcomings of the men they meet and try to cultivate but usually discard. Because they so often find the black men they meet "sorry" and lacking for various reasons, some critics have accused McMillan of "bashing" African American men in general. The women in the story, however, never seem to give up on the notion of finding "Mr. Right," and even though the novel ends with two of the women still without significant others, two do find good men. The main point of the work, however, is that regardless of their success or failure in romance, the women are strong in their friendship and in their mutual support.

Spending months on the *New York Times* best-seller list, *Waiting to Exhale* resonated with African American readers in ways not seen since Alice Walker's *The Color Purple* (1982). It had sold about four million copies by the year 2000.

How Stella Got Her Groove Back

After McMillan took a vacation in Jamaica during which she met and fell in love with a young man about twenty years her junior, she wrote *How Stella Got Her Groove Back*, a novel more autobiographical than any of her previous ones. The main character, Stella Payne, is in her forties (as was McMillan at the time she was writing) and has gone to Jamaica on vacation in an attempt to "get her groove back"—to regain her zest for life. In Jamaica she meets Winston Shakespeare, a young man who charms her with his good looks and his directness and honesty. She is hesitant in her attraction to him because of the difference in their ages, but after a while she comes to believe that her hesitation is based not on her feelings but rather on what she thinks society expects of her. Throwing reservations about their relationship to the wind, she does the unorthodox and takes Shakespeare back to her home in California to live with her and her son. She loses her job as a security analyst and has to live for a while on her savings, but her main concerns arise from her ongoing questioning of her relationship with a man nearly half her age.

How Stella Got Her Groove Back was written in less than a month. It is written in a style similar to stream of consciousness, with free-flowing sentences and paragraphs and little punctuation. McMillan wanted the style to reflect the main character's desire to be free from slavish regard for what other people believe or think. Some critics have described the book as no better than a run-of-the-mill romance novel, but with a first printing of eight hundred thousand copies and the sale of film rights, it was clearly a huge commercial success.

The Interruption of Everything

The Interruption of Everything is the story of Marilyn Grimes, who, at forty-four years old, finds herself heading toward menopause and an unexpected, unwanted pregnancy. Already the mother of three grown children, she is also dealing with a live-in mother-in-law, Arthurine, who has an old pet dog named Snuffy. Marilyn's husband, Leon, is a hardworking man, but Marilyn suspects that he is handling a midlife crisis by having an affair. On top of these problems, her own mother, Lovey, seems to be slipping into dementia, and Marilyn's sister, Joy, a drug addict, is not raising her two children properly.

Marilyn has McMillan's trademark "best girlfriends" to listen to her complaints and concerns. There is also the man in her life, who, like many of McMillan's male characters, leaves a lot to be desired. Told with the author's usual irreverence, this is a story of a woman who must face and deal with her midlife dilemmas with little help from others. The result is a touching and often hilarious look at the way a contemporary woman manages the issues she faces when she reaches her forties.

Jane L. Ball

Other major works

SCREENPLAYS: *Waiting to Exhale*, 1995 (adaptation of her novel; with Ronald Bass); *How Stella Got Her Groove Back*, 1998 (adaptation of her novel; with Bass).

NONFICTION: *The Writer as Publicist*, 1993 (with Marcia Biederman and Gary Aspenberg); *It's OK If You're Clueless: And Twenty-three More Tips for the College Bound*, 2006.

EDITED TEXT: *Breaking Ice: An Anthology of Contemporary African-American Fiction*, 1990.

BIBLIOGRAPHY

Ellerby, Janet M. "Deposing the Man of the House: Terry McMillan Rewrites the Family." *MELUS* 22, no. 2 (Summer, 1997): 105-117. Uses McMillan's novels *Mama*, *Disappearing Acts*, and *Waiting to Exhale* as a basis for a discussion of how black families differ from white families. Addresses how McMillan's work contributes to an understanding of the evolving black family.

Fish, Bruce, and Becky D. Fish. *Terry McMillan*. Philadelphia: Chelsea House, 2002. Biography aimed at young readers provides informative discussion of McMillan's life and career. Includes photographs.

McMillan, Terry. "Author Spotlight: Terry McMillan." *Ebony*, July, 2005. McMillan focuses on discussion of her novel *The Interruption of Everything*.

_______. "Terry McMillan: The Novelist Explores African Americans from the Point of View of a New Generation." Interview by Wendy Smith. *Publishers Weekly*, May 11, 1992. McMillan reveals details of her early exposure to writing and of her experiences with publishers as a first-time novelist. Includes some discussion of her first three novels.

Patrick, Diane. *Terry McMillan: The Unauthorized Biography*. New York: St. Martin's Press, 1999. Emphasizes McMillan's achievement in rising from humble beginnings to become a best-selling author and argues that her success has changed the publishing industry's approach to works by black authors.

Richards, Paulette. *Terry McMillan: A Critical Companion*. Westport, Conn.: Greenwood Press, 1999. Presents analyses of McMillan's novels that place them within their cultural and literary contexts.

TONI MORRISON

Born: Lorain, Ohio; February 18, 1931
Also known as: Chloe Anthony Wofford

PRINCIPAL LONG FICTION

The Bluest Eye, 1970
Sula, 1973
Song of Solomon, 1977
Tar Baby, 1981
Beloved, 1987
Jazz, 1992
Paradise, 1998
Love, 2003
A Mercy, 2008

OTHER LITERARY FORMS

Although primarily a novelist, Toni Morrison has published some short fiction, a few works of nonfiction, some edited volumes, and some children's books. Among her edited volumes are *The Black Book: Three Hundred Years of African American Life* (1974), a collection of documents and articles on African American history compiled by Middleton Harris, and a collection of Toni Cade Bambara's writings titled *Deep Sightings and Rescue Missions: Fiction, Essays, and Conversations* (1996). Among Morrison's notable nonfiction works are many essays, such as "The Site of Memory," published in *Inventing the Truth: The Art and Craft of Memoir*, edited by William Zinsser (1987), and "Unspeakable Things Unspoken: The Afro-American Presence in American Literature," which first appeared in the winter, 1989, issue of the *Michigan Quarterly Review*. She has also published the nonfiction works *Remember: The Journey to School Integration* (2004) and *What Moves at the Margin: Selected Nonfiction* (2008).

With her son, Slade Morrison, she has produced several children's books in a series titled Who's Got Game?; titles in the series include *The Ant or the Grasshopper?* (2003) and *The Lion or the Mouse?* (2003). Morrison's first play, *Dreaming Emmett* (pr. 1986), was commissioned by the New York State Writers Institute of the State University of New York. *Honey and Rue*, a musical piece with lyrics by Toni Morrison and music by André Previn, was commissioned by Carnegie Hall for soprano Kathleen Battle and premiered in 1992.

ACHIEVEMENTS

Toni Morrison is widely regarded as one of the most significant African American novelists to have emerged in the 1970's. Her novel *Sula* was nominated for the National Book Award in 1975, and in 1977, *Song of Solomon* won the National Book Critics Circle

Award. The former was a Book-of-the-Month Club alternate and the latter, a main selection. In 1988, *Beloved* was awarded the Pulitzer Prize, and in 1993, Morrison became the first black woman to be honored with the Nobel Prize in Literature.

Morrison's fiction, especially *Song of Solomon*, has been compared to Ralph Ellison's *Invisible Man* (1952) for its mixture of the literal and the fantastic, the real and the surreal. Morrison has been praised for her use of language and for the sense of voice that emerges not only in her dialogue but also in the movement of her narratives. Morrison's novels are also remarkable for their sense of place, for the detailed, coherent physical worlds she creates. Finally, her fiction is noteworthy for its depiction of the deep psychic realities of women's experience.

BIOGRAPHY

Toni Morrison was born Chloe Anthony Wofford, the second of four children. Morrison's father was a shipyard welder. When she was in the first grade, she was the only black student in her class and the only child who was already able to read. Her early literary influences include Leo Tolstoy, Gustave Flaubert, and Jane Austen. Later, as a student at Howard University, Morrison toured the South with the Howard University Players. She married Harold Morrison in 1958; they had two children before divorcing in 1964.

Morrison received her B.A. in English and minored in classics. She taught at the State University of New York at Purchase as a professor of English in 1971-1972 and was the Albert Schweitzer Chair in the Humanities at State University of New York at Albany from 1984 to 1989. From 1989 until she retired in 2006, Morrison was Robert F. Goheen Professor in the Council of the Humanities at Princeton University. During her career, she has also served as trustee of the National Humanities Center and as cochair of the Schomberg Commission for the Preservation of Black Culture. She is a member of the American Academy and Institute of Arts and Letters, the National Council on the Arts, the Authors Guild, and the Authors League of America. In addition to her writing, Morrison has become a popular public lecturer, focusing on African American literature.

ANALYSIS

In all of her fiction, Toni Morrison explores the conflict between society and the individual. She shows how the individual who defies social pressures can forge a self by drawing on the resources of the natural world, on a sense of continuity within the family and within the history of a people, and on dreams and other unaccountable sources of psychic power. Many of her works also confront some sort of sexual depravity that has become a controlling influence on the lives of the characters.

THE BLUEST EYE

In *The Bluest Eye*, Morrison shows how society inflicts on its members an inappropriate standard of beauty and worth, a standard that mandates that to be loved one must meet the absolute "white" standard of blond hair and blue eyes. Morrison's narrator says that two of the most destructive ideas in history are the idea of romantic love (canceling both lust and caring) and the idea of an absolute, univocal standard of beauty.

In the novel, the most extreme victim of these destructive ideas is Pecola, a young African American girl who finds refuge in madness after she has been thoroughly convinced of her own ugliness (confirmed when she is raped by her own father, Cholly). Mrs. Breedlove, Pecola's mother, is another victim who gets her idea of an unvarying standard of beauty from romantic motion pictures that glorify white film stars. When she realizes the impassable gap between that ideal and her physical self (she has a deformed foot and two missing teeth), she also gives up any hope of maintaining a relationship with Cholly, her husband, except one of complete antagonism and opposition. Mrs. Breedlove even comes to prefer the little white girl she takes care of at work to her own daughter, Pecola, whom she has always perceived as ugly.

The ideal of unattainable physical beauty is reinforced by the sugary, unattainable world of the family depicted in school readers—of Mother and Father and Dick and Jane and their middle-class, suburban existence. The contrast between that false standard of life and the reality lived by the African American children in the novel makes them ashamed of their reality, of the physical intimacy of families in which the children have seen their fathers naked.

Although Pecola is thoroughly victimized, Freida and Claudia MacTeer, schoolmates of Pecola, do survive with some integrity and richness. Freida seems to accept Shirley Temple as the ideal of cuteness, but her sister Claudia, a center of consciousness in the novel, responds with anger and defiance, dismembering the hard, cold, smirking baby dolls she receives at Christmas. What Claudia really desires at Christmas is simply an experience of family closeness in the kitchen, an experience of flowers, fruit, and music, of security.

Claudia's anger at the white baby dolls springs from a conviction of her own reality and her own worth. In defense of her own individuality, Claudia rejects Shirley Temple and "Meringue Pie," the "high yellow" princess, Maureen Peal. It is that defense of her own reality that makes Claudia sympathize with Pecola and try to defend her, even to the point of sacrificing Freida's money and her own.

Claudia is especially puzzled and regretful that nobody says "poor baby" to the raped Pecola, that nobody wants to welcome her unborn baby into the world. It would be only natural, "human nature," it seems, for people to sympathize with a victim and rejoice at the creation of a human life. Instead, the springs of human sympathy have been dammed up by social disapproval. Suffering from the self-hatred they have absorbed from the society around them, the members of the black community maintain inflexible social standards and achieve respectability by looking down on Pecola. The two MacTeer sisters appeal to nature to help Pecola and her unborn baby, but nature fails them just as prayer did: No marigolds sprout and grow that year. The earth is unyielding. The baby is stillborn. Eventually, even the two girls become distanced from Pecola, whose only friend is an imaginary one, a part of herself who can see the blue eyes she was promised. Pecola functions as a scapegoat for the society around her, and Claudia's sympathy later grows into an understanding of how the members of the black community used Pecola to protect themselves from scorn and insult. What finally flowers in Claudia is insight and a more conscious respect for her own reality.

SULA

Sula also explores the oppressive nature of white society toward African Americans, evident in the very name of the "Bottom," a hillside community that had its origin in the duplicitous white treatment of an emancipated black slave who was promised fertile "bottom land" along with his freedom. In a bitterly ironic twist, the whites take over the hillside again when they want suburban houses that will catch the breeze. In taking back the Bottom, they destroy a place, a community with its own identity. In turn, the black community, corrupted by white society, rejects Sula for her experimenting with her life, for trying to live free like a man instead of accepting the restrictions of the traditional female role.

Sula provokes the reader to question socially accepted concepts of good and evil. As Sula is dying, she asks her girlhood friend Nel, "How do you know that you were the good one?" Although considered morally loose and a witch by the townspeople, the unconventional Sula cannot believe herself to be an inferior individual. Contrasting the traditional role of mother and churchwoman that Nel has embraced, Sula's individuality is refreshing and intriguing. Despite her death, Sula maintains an independence that ultimately stands in proud opposition to the established network of relationships that exists within conventional society.

The novel shows that the Bottom society encompasses both good and evil. The people are accustomed to suffering and enduring evil. In varying degrees, they accept Eva's murder of her drug-addict son, Plum, and Hannah's seduction of their husbands, one after another. The community, nevertheless, cannot encompass Sula, a woman who thinks for herself without conforming to their sensibilities. They have to turn her into a witch, so that they can mobilize themselves against her "evil" and cherish their goodness. Without the witch, their goodness grows faint again. Like Pecola, Sula is made a scapegoat.

Growing up in the Bottom, Sula creates an identity for herself, first from the reality of physical experience. When she sees her mother, Hannah, burning up in front of her eyes, she feels curiosity. Her curiosity is as honest as Hannah's admission that she loves her daughter Sula the way any mother would, but that she does not like her. Hearing her mother reject her individuality, Sula concludes that she has no one to count on except herself.

In forging a self, Sula also draws on sexual experience as a means of feeling both joy and sadness and as a means of feeling her own power. Sula does not substitute a romantic dream for the reality of that physical experience. She does finally desire a widening of that sexual experience into a continuing relationship with Ajax, but the role of nurturing and possession is fatal to her. Ajax leaves, and Sula sickens and dies.

A closeness to the elemental processes of nature gives a depth to the lives of the Bottom-dwellers, although nature does not act with benevolence or even with consistency. Plum and Hannah, two of Eva's children, die by fire, one sacrificed by Eva and one ignited by capricious accident. Chicken Little and several of those who follow Shadrack on National Suicide Day drown because acts of play go wrong and inexplicably lead to their destruction. Sula's supposed identity as a witch is connected to the plague of robins that coincides with her return to the Bottom. The people of the Bottom live within nature and try to make some sense of it, even though their constructions are strained and self-serving.

On one level, Sula refuses any connection with history and family continuity. Her grandmother Eva says that Sula should get a man and make babies, but Sula says that she would rather make herself. On the other hand, Sula is a descendant of the independent women Eva and Hannah, both of whom did what they had to do. It is at least rumored that Eva let her leg be cut off by a train so that she could get insurance money to take care of her three children when BoyBoy, her husband, abandoned her. When her husband died, Hannah needed "manlove," and she got it from her neighbors' husbands, despite community disapproval. In their mold, Sula is independent enough to threaten Eva with fire and to assert her own right to live, even if her grandmother does not like Sula's way of living.

To flourish, Morrison suggests, conventional society needs an opposite pole. A richness comes from the opposition and the balance—from the difference—and an acceptance of that difference would make scapegoats unnecessary. The world of the Bottom becomes poorer when Sula dies.

SONG OF SOLOMON

In *Song of Solomon*, Morrison again traces the making of a self. The novel is a departure for Morrison in that the protagonist is not female but a young man, Milkman Dead. Milkman grows up in a comfortable, insulated, middle-class African American family, the grandson of a doctor on his mother's side and the son of a businessman, whose father owned his own farm. Son of a doting mother, Milkman is breast-fed a long time, the reason for his nickname, and is sent to school in velvet knickers. Guitar Baines, a Southside black, becomes Milkman's friend and an ally against the other children's teasing.

As the novel progresses, and as Milkman discovers the reality of his family and friends as separate people with their own griefs and torments, Milkman comes to feel that everyone wants him dead. (Ironically, Milkman's last name actually is "Dead," the result of a drunken clerk's error when Milkman's grandfather was registering with the Freedmen's Bureau.) Milkman learns that his mere existence is extraordinary, as even before his birth, his father tried to kill him. Milkman survived that threat through the intercession of his mother and, especially, of his aunt, Pilate, a woman with no navel. After having been conjured by Pilate into making love to his wife again, years after he had turned against her, Macon Dead wanted the resulting baby aborted. Ruth, the baby's mother, out of fear of her husband, took measures to bring about an abortion, but Pilate intervened again and helped Ruth to find the courage to save the child and bear him.

In the present action of the novel, Hagar, Milkman's cousin, his first love and his first lover, pursues him month after month with whatever weapon she can find to kill him. Hagar wants Milkman's living life, not his dead life, but Milkman has rejected her, out of boredom and out of fear that he will be maneuvered into marrying her. At this point, he does not want to be tied down—he wants freedom and escape.

Hagar, like Pecola of *The Bluest Eye*, feels unlovely and unloved, rejected because Milkman does not like her black, curly hair. Pilate says that Milkman cannot *not* love her hair without *not* loving himself because it is the same hair that grows from his own body. Hagar is another victim of an absolutely univocal standard of beauty, and she is a character who needs a supporting society, a chorus of aunts and cousins and sisters to surround her with advice and protection. Instead, she has only Pilate and Reba, grandmother and mother, two women so strong and independent that they do not understand her weakness. Unhinged by Milkman's rejection of her, Hagar chases Milkman with various weapons, is repeatedly disarmed, and finally dies in total discouragement.

Trying to find out about his family's past, Milkman travels to Virginia, to Shalimar, a black town, where the men in the general store challenge him to fight, and one attacks him with a knife. Milkman does not understand why these people want his life, but they think he has insulted and denied their masculinity with his powerful northern money and his brusque treatment of them, by not asking their names and not offering his own.

The most serious threat to Milkman's life, however, turns out to be Guitar, Milkman's friend and spiritual brother. When Guitar tries to kill Milkman, he is betraying the reality of their friendship for the idea of revenge against whites and compensation for the personal deprivation he has suffered. Guitar thinks that Milkman has a cache of gold that he is not sharing with him, so he decides to kill him. Guitar rationalizes his decision by saying that the money is for the cause, for the work of the Seven Days, a group of seven black men sworn to avenge the deaths of innocent blacks at the hands of the whites.

Milkman's being alive at all, then, is a triumph, a victory that he slowly comes to appreciate after coming out of his comfortable shell of self-involvement. Unwillingly, Milkman comes to know the suffering and grief of his mother and father and even his sisters Magdalene and Corinthians. The decisive experience in his self-making, however, is the quest for Pilate's gold on which his father sets him. In the first stage, the men are convinced that Pilate's gold hangs in a green sack from the ceiling of her house, and Guitar and Milkman attempt to steal it. The two friends succeed in taking the sack because the women in the house are simply puzzled, wondering why the men want a sack that is really full of old bones. In leaving the house, however, the two men are arrested, and Pilate must rescue them and the bones by doing an Aunt Jemima act for the white policemen. Milkman's father, Macon, is convinced that the gold still exists somewhere, and Milkman sets out to find it by going back to Pennsylvania, where Macon and Pilate grew up, and later to Virginia, where the previous generation lived.

Milkman's making of a self includes many of the archetypal adventures of the heroes of legend and myth. Like other heroes of legend, Milkman limps, with one leg shorter than the other, a mark of his specialness. Like Oedipus's parents, his parents try to kill him early in his life. There is a wise old lady who gives him help and advice. He goes on a quest for a treasure, and he hopes for gold and the hand of a beautiful princess. He solves a puzzle or riddle to achieve his quest and confirm his identity. He has a transcendent experience and reaches heights of prowess (he can fly). When his people turn against him, he gives his life for them.

Like Sula, too, Milkman creates a self from the reality of physical experience, the processes of nature, a connection to history and family continuity, and springs of human possibility through myth, dreams, legends, and other sources of psychic power. Milkman reaches an understanding of physical experience and the processes of nature in a struggle against the physical environment. As a rich city boy, Milkman was insulated from nature, but in his trip south to try to get the gold, he overcomes a series of physical obstacles to reach the cave where Macon and Pilate in their youth encountered white people and gold. Milkman gets there only after falling into the river and climbing up twenty feet of rock, splitting his shoes and the clothes that mark him as a city man. During the trip, Milkman loses his possessions—trunk, clothes, and whiskey—and he makes it on his own, in a place where his father's name and father's money do not protect him. Milkman succeeds in finding Circe, who years ago sheltered Pilate and Macon when their father was killed, and he reaches the cave, where there is no longer any gold.

Milkman also encounters nature as an obstacle to be overcome when, after the knife fight in Shalimar, he is invited to go on a coon hunt into the woods with the older men of Shalimar. Again, Milkman undergoes a test, having to move through the woods in the dark, having to show the courage and physical endurance necessary to be one of the hunters. Milkman also experiences the music of the hunt, the communication between the men and the dogs, the language before language, of a time when people were so close to their physical reality that they were in harmony with all creatures.

Milkman also creates himself in searching for his origins. In searching for his fathers, he discovers himself; like Telemachus of Greek mythology and James Joyce's Stephen Dedalus, Milkman must find the reality of his fathers to know his own potential. Milkman's original pursuit of the gold seems to be an impulse he gets from his father, the man of business, and even from his father's father, who was a lover of property. The quest, however, changes as Milkman pursues it, finding the thread of his family's history. Stopping in Pennsylvania, Milkman hears the stories of the men who knew his father and grandfather and who rejoice in their successes. The story of the Dead family dramatizes the dream and the failure of that dream for blacks in America. When the older Macon

Dead was killed by white men for his flourishing farm, the possibilities of his neighbors were narrowed and their lives scarred. Seeing his father and grandfather through their former neighbors' eyes helps Milkman to understand better the pride that Macon had when he said that his father had let Macon work side by side with him and trusted him to share in his achievements.

In Shalimar, Milkman also learns about his great-grandfather by piecing together the memories of people there and by deciphering a children's game and song, a song about Solomon and Rynah that seems to be interspersed with nonsense words. Milkman matches this song to a song that he had heard Pilate sing about Sugarman. He solves the riddle of the song, and he even figures out what the ghost of Pilate's father meant when he said, "Sing," and when he told Pilate to go get the bones. Finally, he discovers that his grandmother was an American Indian, Singing Bird, and that his great-grandfather, Solomon, was one of the legendary flying Africans, the father of twenty-one sons, a slave who one day flew back to Africa. His grandfather Jake had fallen through the branches of a tree when Solomon dropped him, trying to take his last baby son back with him. Learning about that magic enables Milkman himself to fly when he surrenders to the air and lets himself be upheld.

Milkman creates a self so that he can share it and even sacrifice it for a friend. With Pilate, Milkman buries the bones of Jake, his grandfather, on Solomon's Leap. Guitar, who has continued to stalk Milkman, shoots and kills Pilate, but Milkman, saying to Guitar, "Do you want my life? Take it if it is any good to you," leaps into the air and flies. Guitar is free to kill his friend, but Milkman soars. The ending of the novel shows the transcendence of the spirit, as the hero achieves his destiny. The satisfaction of the ending, which also soars into legend, comes from the triumph of the human spirit, the triumph that even death cannot destroy. *Song of Solomon* is a beautiful, serious, funny novel that moves beyond the social to the mythic.

Tar Baby

Tar Baby explores three kinds of relationships: the relationships between blacks and whites; the relationships within families, especially between parents and children; and the relationships between African American men and women. In the epigraph to the novel, Saint Paul reproaches the Corinthians for allowing contentions to exist among their ranks; the quotation serves to foreshadow the discord that abounds in the novel's relationships.

In *Tar Baby*, Morrison depicts not a self-contained black society but an onstage interaction between blacks and whites. The novel juxtaposes two families, a white family of masters and a black family of servants. The white family includes a retired candy maker, Valerian Street, and his wife, Margaret, once the "Principal Beauty of Maine," who is now in her fifties. The couple's only son, Michael, lives abroad; his arrival for Christmas is expected and denied by various characters. The black family consists of Sydney Childs, who is Valerian's valet and butler, and Sydney's wife, Ondine, who serves as cook and housekeeper. They are childless, but their orphan niece, Jadine, plays the role of their daughter. (Valerian has acted as Jadine's patron, paying for her education at the Sorbonne.)

The pivotal character in the novel, who enters and changes the balance of power and the habitual responses of the families, is a black man who rises out of the sea. His true name is Son, although he has gone by several aliases. The veneer of politeness and familiarity between the characters is shaken by Son's abrupt appearance. Uncomfortable racial and personal assumptions are put into words and cannot be retracted. The Principal Beauty is convinced that Son has come to rape her: What else would a black man want? (Jadine is convinced that if Son wants to rape anyone, it is she, not Margaret.) Sydney finds Son a threat to his respectability as a Philadelphia black, because when Son appears, the white people lump all blacks together. Ondine seems less threatened, but most of her energy goes into her running battle with the Principal Beauty. Jadine is apprehensive at Son's wild appearance, and later she is affronted by his direct sexual approach. Only Valerian welcomes Son. He sees Son as a vision of his absent son, Michael, and he invites him to sit down at the dining table and be a guest.

Son's coming is the catalyst that causes timeworn relationships to explode when Michael does not come for Christmas. His failure to appear leads to the revelation that the Principal Beauty abused her son as a child, pricking him with pins and burning him with cigarettes. Ondine, the black woman, finally hurls this accusation at Margaret, the white, and makes explicit what the two women have known mutually since the beginning. Valerian, who has been haunted by the memory of Michael as a lonely child who would hide under the sink and sing to himself, is hit with a reality much harsher than he has known or admitted.

Structured as it is in terms of families, the whole novel revolves around family responsibilities, especially between parents and children. Michael Street does not come home for Christmas, but the abuse he suffered as a child seems to justify his absence. Thus, the undutiful mother Margaret has thrown the whole family off balance. In the black family, later in the novel, attention is drawn to the undutiful daughter Jadine, although it seems implied that she has learned this undutifulness, partly at least, from whites, wanting her individual success to be separate from family ties and responsibilities. This undutifulness also springs from a question of identity. In Paris, even before she comes to Valerian's island, Jadine feels affronted by a beautiful, proud, contemptuous African woman in yellow who buys three eggs and carries them on her head. She is herself and embodies her tradition consummately, exhibiting balance and physical grace that symbolize spiritual poise. Jadine feels diminished and threatened by the African woman, who spits at her. The scorn sends Jadine back to her family, Sydney and Ondine.

Jadine is similarly disturbed by her dream of the women with breasts, the mothers, who reproach her for not joining that chain of mothers and daughters who become mothers with daughters. Although Jadine herself is an orphan, reared by Ondine and Sydney and owing much to their care, she refuses to take the self-sacrificing role of the woman who cares for her family. Jadine wants money and the power it brings in the white world. Eventually she wants to run her own business, perhaps a boutique. Also, she may choose a white husband, like the man who bought her a seductive sealskin coat.

Jadine is the Tar Baby of the novel, and Son is Br'er Rabbit from the Uncle Remus stories. As the Tar Baby, Jadine acts as a possible trap for Son set by his enemies, white society. Jadine, who has absorbed many white values, wants money and success. Son wants something purer, something associated with nature (he is associated with the sea and the beauty of the savannahs) and with family tradition. Nature, direct physical experience, and family traditions that are integral to personal identity are all important values in Son's existence. Son has a home—the completely black town of Eloe—and there he abides by the ideas of respectability held by his father and his aunt Rosa. (He asks Jadine to sleep at Aunt Rosa's, apart from him, and he comes to her secretly only when she threatens to leave if he does not.) To amuse herself in the traditional town, in which she is uncomfortable, Jadine takes photographs of the people and steals their souls, stealing their individual beauty and grace. In the photographs, they seem graceless, poor, and stupid, even to Son, who usually sees them with loving eyes.

Individually, Son and Jadine love each other, but they seem unable to find a world in which they can both thrive. Son is an undaunted lover, however, unwilling to let Jadine go, even when she flees from him. Son tries to return to Isle de Chevaliers, Valerian's island, to get news of Jadine, but the only way he can get there seems to be through the help of Thérèse, a half-blind, fifty-year-old black woman who says that her breasts still give milk. Thérèse takes him by boat to the island of the horsemen. Son has said that he cannot give up Jadine, but Thérèse tells him to join the fabled black horsemen who see with the mind. At the end of the novel, Son is running toward his destiny, whether that be Jadine and some way to make her part of his world or the black horsemen who ride free through the hills. Readers do not know what Son's fate is to be; they only know that Son is running toward it, just as Br'er Rabbit ran from his enemy Br'er Fox and from the Tar Baby. Like Milkman Dead at the end of *Song of Solomon*, Son leaps into mythic possibility; like Br'er Rabbit, Son, the black man, is a figure with the power to survive.

BELOVED

In editing *The Black Book*, a collection of African American historical memorabilia, Toni Morrison discovered an article that would serve as the foundation of her fifth novel. *Beloved* is based on a true account of a runaway slave mother who, rather than allowing her children to be taken back into slavery, murders three of the four. As the novel begins, Sethe's sons, Buglar and Howard, have already run away, while Denver, the youngest child, has survived the murder attempt and still lives with her mother in a house beset by the spirit of her murdered sister, Beloved. Morrison deliberately disorients the reader as she delves into the "interior life" of slavery, creating an experience similar to that of slavery as the narrative breaks apart, shifts, and confounds.

The house at 124 Bluestone Road is personified as a tormented being when Beloved returns, emerging from a lake, fully clothed, the same age she would have been had she survived the infanticide. What the spirit wants initially is unclear. Morrison uses metaphorical imagery with tremendous skill, such as in her description of Sethe's back, a relief map of scars from savage beatings, as resembling the branches of a chokecherry tree. When Paul D, a former slave whom Sethe once knew, moves in, Beloved wreaks havoc. The spirit behaves like an enraged toddler, but the damage she does is that of a full-grown woman. As the ghost continues to threaten her mother and sister, the characters' thoughts intertwine until the reader cannot be certain which character is which.

JAZZ

Morrison intended *Jazz*, another novel inspired by a news article, to follow *Beloved* as the second of a trilogy, although the narrative does not pick up where *Beloved* ends. Joe Trace, a married man and cosmetics salesman, shoots his teenage lover, Dorcas, at a party. She dies refusing to reveal his name. At her funeral, Violet, Joe's wife, a hairdresser, defaces the girl's corpse. Set in 1926, *Jazz* begins after Violet has cut the dead girl's face, twenty years after she and Joe arrived in Harlem from the South, where they scraped out a living as sharecroppers. After Dorcas's funeral, Violet returns home and releases her caged parrot, the only creature in her life who says "I love you" anymore.

The deep, unrealized passion for human contact that Morrison depicts in *Beloved* takes root in *Jazz*, but it too becomes messy, dangerous, and out of control. Violet's mind unravels, and, strangely, she turns to Alice Manfred, Dorcas's aunt, for comfort. The theme of mother loss, profound and frustrated, also continues in *Jazz*: Dorcas's mother burns to death in an intentionally set fire; Violet's mother throws herself down a well because of her despair over not providing for her children. Years later, Violet longs so achingly for a child that she considers stealing one. It is only at the end of *Jazz*, when Violet and Joe reconcile and Violet buys a sick parrot that she nurses back to health by playing jazz for it, that there is some hope of a lasting human connection.

PARADISE

Paradise, Morrison's seventh novel, like her previous two, was inspired by a little-known event in African American history, this time the post-Civil War westward migration of former slaves set on establishing their own all-black utopias. The all-black town in the book is named Ruby. Shifting back and forth across a century of time, *Paradise* begins in 1976, when a group of Ruby's settlers' male descendants attack a mansion-turned-convent of women, convinced that the town's survival is threatened by the women's eschewing of male companionship and their questionable pasts.

The story of Ruby's establishment is related: The town is founded as a response not only to white racism but also to other African Americans who turned away would-be settlers in other towns for having skin that was "too black." Twin brothers Deacon and Steward, the town's elders, are deeply committed to keeping Ruby as pristine and trouble-free as possible. Together, they symbolize Ruby's twin identity and conscience.

Initially, Ruby has no crime and therefore needs no police. There is no hunger; those who have resources assist those in need. However, the town's total isolation from the outside world proves to be its undoing as the rebellion of the 1960's youth movement seeps into Ruby. A ragtag group of women, most escaping either abusive relationships or the responsibilities of motherhood, settle outside Ruby. Among others, there is Consolata, the maternal leader; Seneca, abandoned as a child by her teenage mother; and Pallas, a white woman fleeing her wealthy but negligent parents. The violent confrontation between the men of Ruby and the self-exiled women is brought on, in part, by the black men's anger at women who have willfully chosen a life without men.

Love

In *Love*, Morrison deconstructs familial relationships in an African American community that has been strongly influenced by the presence of Bill Cosey, a wealthy black man who owned a resort hotel that catered to both blacks and whites during the years just before and during the Civil Rights movement of the 1960's. Christine, Cosey's granddaughter, and Heed are the main characters; as old women, they have an intense hatred for each other. Their animosity seems to be based on Heed's marriage to Cosey—Heed was an uneducated, poverty-stricken eleven-year-old child when she was sold into marriage with Cosey. Until late in the novel, readers are led to believe that, with the marriage, Heed usurped Christine's place in her grandfather's affections.

As in many of Morrison's novels, a shifting narrative perspective provides insight into the characters, in this case the women and the man around whose life theirs seemingly revolved. Monologues from L, the spirit for whom the novel is named, provide what seem to be the most strongly objective point of view on the women's past. L is able to understand what motivates Christine, the granddaughter who was thrown aside by her best friend's marriage to her grandfather, as well as the confusion and insecurity of Heed, the child tied to a fifty-two-year-old man. Additionally, L provides insight into May, Christine's mother and Bill Cosey's daughter-in-law.

Sandler and Vida Gibbons are minor characters whose memories of Cosey provide more insight into the depraved man who had such a strong hold over the community. Though introduced early, Sandler reveals his true connection to Cosey only a little at a time. Sandler reminisces about fishing trips with Cosey but neglects to reveal that those fishing trips included sexual escapades. Heed and Christine both add their own flashbacks to the narrative, clarifying that their adult hatred of each other stems more from the devastation that Heed and Cosey's marriage wrought on both than from a problem between the girls. Intertwined with the stories of the other characters is the story of Romen, the Gibbonses' grandson, and Junior Viviane, a troubled young woman who answers Heed's advertisement for a companion. Junior's ravenous hunger for food, shelter, and sex reflect Bill Cosey in many ways.

Bill Cosey seems to be the central axis around which all of the women's lives revolve. His sexual appetite is seemingly boundless. He is well known for his affairs with women during and between his marriages, including a relationship with his daughter-in-law, but a darker side emerges as readers recognize that his marriage to an eleven-year-old child is just the tip of his depravity. There is also the suggestion that he has molested his granddaughter and had homosexual relations not only with Sandler Gibbons but also with rich and influential white men in the community. Cosey's significance is primarily as an agent of separation and of unity. His depraved sexual behavior started a rift between the girls that his marriage to Heed increased. Each lost her best friend as a result of fear that the other would see the manner in which Cosey's depravity had shadowed her own soul. Though the story is really about Christine and Heed, Cosey unifies the characters in complicated ways that leave readers wondering whether he was good or bad.

Kate Begnal; Nika Hoffman
Updated by Theresa L. Stowell

OTHER MAJOR WORKS

PLAY: *Dreaming Emmett*, pr. 1986.

NONFICTION: *Playing in the Dark: Whiteness and the Literary Imagination*, 1992; *Conversations with Toni Morrison*, 1994 (Danille Taylor-Guthrie, editor); *Remember: The Journey to School Integration*, 2004; *What Moves at the Margin: Selected Nonfiction*, 2008 (Carolyn C. Denard, editor).

CHILDREN'S LITERATURE: *The Big Box*, 1999 (with Slade Morrison); *The Book of Mean People*, 2002 (with Slade Morrison); *The Ant or the Grasshopper?*, 2003 (with Slade Morrison); *The Lion or the Mouse?*, 2003 (with Slade Morrison); *Poppy or the Snake?*, 2003 (with Slade Morrison); *The Mirror or the Glass?*, 2004 (with Slade Morrison).

EDITED TEXTS: *To Die for the People: The Writings of Huey P. Newton*, 1972; *The Black Book: Three Hundred Years of African American Life*, 1974; *Race-ing Justice, Engendering Power: Essays on Anita Hill, Clarence Thomas, and the Construction of Social Reality*, 1992; *Deep Sightings and Rescue Missions: Fiction, Essays, and Conversations*, 1996 (of Toni Cade Bambara's writings); *Birth of a Nation'hood: Gaze, Script, and Spectacle in the O. J. Simpson Case*, 1997 (with Claudia Brodsky Lacour).

BIBLIOGRAPHY

Bloom, Harold, ed. *Toni Morrison*. New York: Chelsea House, 1990. Provides a fine selection of critical essays on Morrison's works, with an excellent introduction by Bloom and an extensive bibliography.

Conner, Marc C., ed. *The Aesthetics of Toni Morrison: Speaking the Unspeakable*. Jackson: University Press of Mississippi, 2000. Collection of essays concentrates on the imagery and stylistics of Morrison's writings and her ability to convey the "unspeakable" aspects of African American experience.

Decker, James M. "Toni Morrison's Sula and Subjective Ideology." In *Ideology.* New York: Palgrave Macmillan, 2004. Scholarly work provides a close reading of *Sula* from an ideological viewpoint.

Denard, Carolyn C., ed. *Toni Morrison: Conversations.* Jackson: University Press of Mississippi, 2008. Collection of previously published interviews with Morrison covers topics such as her early life, her teaching philosophy, and her perspectives on American society, American literature, and her own work, including the evolution of her writing style.

Fultz, Lucille P. *Toni Morrison: Playing with Difference.* Urbana: University of Illinois Press, 2003. Examines Morrison's approach to differences (for example, black and white, male and female, wealth and poverty) in her intricate narratives.

Furman, Jan, ed. *Toni Morrison's "Song of Solomon."* New York: Oxford University Press, 2003. Collection of essays presents the major critical responses to Morrison's novel; intended as a starting point for students first encountering the book.

Harris, Trudier. *Fiction and Folklore: The Novels of Toni Morrison.* Knoxville: University of Tennessee Press, 1991. Examines the use of African and African American myth and folklore in Morrison's novels through *Beloved*, with a focus on the archetypes and antiheroes that pervade the stories. An important scholarly guide to understanding the subtext of Morrison's work.

O'Reilly, Andrea. *Toni Morrison and Motherhood: A Politics of the Heart.* Albany: State University of New York Press, 2004. Discusses the ways in which Morrison depicts mothers and motherhood in her works. Considers Morrison's connection between mothering and racism, sexism, and culture.

Otten, Terry. *The Crime of Innocence in the Fiction of Toni Morrison.* Columbia: University of Missouri Press, 1989. Groundbreaking study of Morrison's first five novels explores the mythic substance in the writings by tracing the motif of the biblical Fall. Provides insightful readings and unflagging attention to the historical and literary backdrop.

Tully, Justine, ed. *The Cambridge Companion to Toni Morrison.* New York: Cambridge University Press, 2007. Collection of essays offers an excellent introduction to and ex amination of Morrison's whole body of work. Covers all aspects of her writings, from narrative sequences to themes to political philosophy. Includes a chronology and critical guide for further reading.

GLORIA NAYLOR

Born: New York, New York; January 25, 1950

PRINCIPAL LONG FICTION

The Women of Brewster Place: A Novel in Seven Stories, 1982
Linden Hills, 1985
Mama Day, 1988
Bailey's Café, 1992
The Men of Brewster Place, 1998
1996, 2005

OTHER LITERARY FORMS

In 1986, Gloria Naylor wrote a column, *Hers*, for *The New York Times*. She is also the writer of a number of screenplays, short stories, and articles for various periodicals. She is known primarily, however, for her novels.

ACHIEVEMENTS

Enjoying both critical and popular acclaim, Gloria Naylor's work has reached a wide audience. *The Women of Brewster Place* won the 1983 American Book Award for best first novel and was later made into a television miniseries. Naylor's other awards include a National Endowment for the Arts Fellowship in 1985 and a Guggenheim Fellowship in 1988.

Surveying the range of African American life in the United States, from poor ghetto to affluent suburb to southern offshore island, Naylor's work examines questions of black identity and, in particular, celebrates black women. In the face of enormous problems and frequent victimization, black women are shown coping through their sense of community and their special powers. Male readers might find less to cheer about in Naylor's early works, as she writes from a feminist perspective. Later works, however, recognize the plight of black males, acknowledging their struggles and celebrating their achievements. Though Naylor's focus is the black experience, her depictions of courage, community, and cultural identity have universal appeal.

BIOGRAPHY

The oldest child of parents who had migrated from Mississippi, Gloria Naylor was born and reared in New York City, her parents having left the South the year before her birth. An avid reader as a child, Naylor seemed to have inherited her passion for reading from her mother, a woman who would go to great lengths to purchase books to which she was denied access in Mississippi libraries because blacks were not allowed inside. The year Naylor graduated from high school, Martin Luther King, Jr., was assassinated, and the shock of this event caused Naylor to delay her college education. She chose instead to become a missionary for the Jehovah's Witnesses in New York, North Carolina, and Florida. She eventually found missionary life too strict, but her zeal apparently carried over into her later feminism. Although her writings are not religious, a fundamentalist pattern of thinking pervades them. She tends to separate her characters into the sheep and the goats (the latter mostly men), the saved and the damned, with one whole book, *Linden Hills*, being modeled on Dante's *Inferno* (c. 1320).

In high school Naylor read widely in the nineteenth century British novelists, but later in a creative writing course at Brooklyn College she came across the book that influenced her most—*The Bluest Eye* (1970), by the black American novelist Toni Morrison. The example of Morrison inspired Naylor to write fiction and to focus on the lives of black women, who Naylor felt were underrepresented (if not ignored) in American literature. Naylor began work on *The Women of Brewster Place*, which was published the year after her graduation from Brooklyn College with a bachelor of arts degree in English. By that time, Naylor was studying on a fellowship at Yale University, from which she received a master of arts degree in African American studies in 1983.

Naylor's background and literary achievements won for her numerous invitations for lectureships or other appointments in academia. She held visiting posts at George Washington University, the University of Pennsylvania, Princeton, New York University, Boston University, Brandeis, and Cornell. Diverse in her pursuits, Naylor wrote a stage adaptation of *Bailey's Café*. She founded One Way Productions, an independent film company, and became involved in a literacy program in the Bronx. She settled in Brooklyn, New York.

Analysis

White people do not appear often and are not featured in the work of Gloria Naylor, yet their presence can be felt like a white background noise, or like the boulevard traffic on the other side of the wall from Brewster Place. White culture is simply another fact of life, like a nearby nuclear reactor or toxic waste dump, and the effects of racism and discrimination are omnipresent in Naylor's work. Against these stifling effects her characters live their lives and try to define their sense of black identity, from the ghetto dwellers of Brewster Place to the social climbers of Linden Hills to the denizens of Willow Springs, a pristine southern island relatively untouched by slavery and segregation.

Naylor writes about these settings and characters in a romantic mode that sometimes verges on the melodramatic or gothic. The influence of her earlier reading—such authors as Charlotte Brontë and Emily Brontë, Charles Dickens, William Faulkner, and Morrison—is apparent. The settings have heavy but obvious symbolic meanings, some derived from literary references: Brewster Place is a dead-end street, Linden Hills is a modern version of Dante's Hell, and Willow Springs recalls the magical isle of William Shakespeare's *The Tempest* (1611). The weather and numerous details also carry symbolic freight, almost as much as they do for such an emblematic writer as Nathaniel Hawthorne. In addition to literary influences, the symbolism seems to draw on Hollywood, particularly Hollywood's gothic genre, horror films; for example, in *Linden Hills* the character Norman Anderson suffers from attacks of "the pinks"—imaginary blobs of pink slime—while the rich undertaker Luther Nedeed locks his wife and child away in the basement.

These two examples also show, in an exaggerated fashion, how Naylor's characters fit into the Romantic mode. Her characters tend to go to extremes, to be emotional and obsessive, or to have a single trait or commit a single act that determines their whole life course. While rather one-dimensional and melodramatic, they nevertheless linger in the memory. Such is the case with Luther Nedeed, who represents Satan in *Linden Hills*, and with the old conjure woman Miranda "Mama" Day, who represents Satan's usual opposition in the scheme of things.

In Naylor, this scheme of things illustrates how she has transferred her former missionary fervor, along with the framework of religious thought, to her feminism. Luther Nedeed's behavior is only the most sensational example of men's cruelty to women in Naylor's work; he has a large following. On the other hand, the mystical ability of Mama Day, the Prospero of women's rights, to command the forces of nature and the spirit world is only the most sensational example of women's special powers in Naylor's thinking. Even the women of Brewster Place demonstrate these powers through their mutual love and support, enabling them to triumph over devastating personal tragedies and demeaning circumstances.

Naylor's men are another story: If not outright demons or headed that way, they seem to lack some vital force. Even the best men are fatally flawed—they are subject to the pinks, are addicted to wine, or have weak hearts. Failing at key moments, they are useful only as sacrifices to the feminine mystique. A prime example is the engineer George Andrews of *Mama Day*, who, for all his masculine rationality and New York smarts, does not know how to handle (significantly) a brooding hen. A close reading of Naylor's works reveals the men's victimization, along with the women's; however, Naylor is concerned with the women in her earlier novels. Naylor's later works indicate that she has expanded her vision to include men.

THE WOMEN OF BREWSTER PLACE

Naylor began fulfilling her commitment to make black women more prominent in American fiction with *The Women of Brewster Place: A Novel in Seven Stories*. The seven stories, featuring seven women, can be read separately, but they are connected by their setting of Brewster Place and by characters who appear, or are mentioned, in more than one story. The women arrive on the dead-end street by different routes that exhibit the variety of lives of black women, but on Brewster Place they unite into a community.

The middle-aged bastion of Brewster Street is Mattie Michael, who over the course of her life was betrayed by each of the three men she loved—her seducer, her father, and her son. She mothers Lucielia Louise Turner (whose grandmother once sheltered Mattie) when Ciel's abusive boyfriend destroys her life. In addition, Mattie welcomes her close friend Etta Mae Johnson, who also once gave Mattie refuge. Etta Mae is a fading beauty who has used men all of her life but is now herself used by a sleazy preacher for a one-night stand. The other women featured are the young unwed Cora Lee, a baby factory; Kiswana Browne, an aspiring social reformer who hails from the affluent suburb of Linden Hills; and Lorraine and Theresa, two lesbians seeking privacy for their love.

Few men are in evidence on Brewster Place, and these few inspire little confidence. C. C. Baker and his youth gang lurk about the alleyway and, in the novel's brutal climax, rape Lorraine. The crazed Lorraine in turn kills the wino Ben, the old janitor who earlier had befriended her. Naylor acknowledges the plight of the men, however. In her description of the gang members, she says,

> Born with the appendages of power, circumcised by a guillotine, and baptized with the steam of a million nonreflective mirrors, these young men wouldn't be called upon to thrust a bayonet into an Asian farmer, target a torpedo, scatter their iron seed from a B-52 into the wound of the earth, point a finger to move a nation, or stick a pole into the moon—and they knew it. They only had that three-hundred-foot alley to serve them as stateroom, armored tank, and executioner's chamber.

As these scenes suggest, Brewster Place is located in a ghetto plagued by social ills. The women must face these on a daily basis in addition to their personal tragedies and dislocations. Instead of being overcome by their sufferings, however, the women find within themselves a common fate and a basis for community. They gain strength and hope from their mutual caring and support. In addition to their informal support system, they form a block association to address larger problems. The ability of women to unite in such a community inspires admiration for their courage and their special powers.

Linden Hills

The community feelings of Brewster Place, from which the women gain a positive sense of identity, somehow make the ghetto's problems seem less awesome, paradoxically, than those of Linden Hills, an affluent suburb. If Brewster Place is a ghetto, Linden Hills is a hell. Naylor underlines this metaphor by deliberately modeling *Linden Hills* after Dante Alighieri's *Inferno*. Linden Hills is not a group of hills, but only a V-shaped area on a hillside intersected by eight streets. As one travels down the hill, the residents become richer but lower on the moral scale. Lester and Willie, two young unemployed poets who perform odd jobs for Christmas money (they are the modern counterparts of Vergil and Dante), take the reader on a guided tour.

Lester's sister Roxanne deems black Africans in Zimbabwe unready for independence; one young executive, Maxwell Smyth, encourages another, Xavier Donnell, no longer to consider Roxanne as a prospective corporate bride; and Dr. Daniel Braithwaite has written the authorized twelve-volume history of Linden Hills without making a single moral judgment. Other sellouts are more personal: The young lawyer Winston Alcott leaves his gay lover to marry, and Chester Parker is eager to bury his dead wife in order to remarry.

Significantly, Linden Hills is ruled by men. The archfiend is Luther Nedeed, the local undertaker and real estate tycoon who occupies the lowest point in Linden Hills. Speaking against a low-income housing project planned for an adjacent poor black neighborhood, Nedeed urges outraged Linden Hills property owners to make common cause with the racist Wayne County Citizens Alliance. Most damning of all, however, is that Nedeed disowns his own wife and child and imprisons them in an old basement morgue; the child starves, but the wife climbs up to confront the archfiend on Christmas Eve.

MAMA DAY

It is clear that, while examining problems of middle-class black identity in *Linden Hills*, Naylor has not overlooked the plight of black women. In *Mama Day*, Naylor returns to a more celebratory mood on both subjects. The setting of *Mama Day* is a unique black American culture presided over by a woman with even more unique powers.

The coastal island of Willow Springs, located off South Carolina and Georgia but belonging to no state, has been largely bypassed by the tides of American history, particularly racism. The island was originally owned by a white person, Bascombe Wade, who also owned slaves. Bascombe married Sapphira, one of his slaves, and they had seven sons. In 1823, Bascombe freed his other slaves and deeded the island to them, his sons, and their respective descendants in perpetuity (the land cannot be sold, only inherited). Bascombe was more or less assimilated, and a black culture grew up on the island that was closely tied to the land, to the culture's beginnings, and to African roots. In other words, Willow Springs is definitely a mythical island—a tiny but free black state flourishing unnoticed under the nose of the Confederacy. Naylor underlines the island's mythic qualities by drawing parallels between it and the magical isle of *The Tempest*.

If Prospero presides over Shakespeare's island, then Prospero's daughter, Miranda "Mama" Day (actually a great-granddaughter of the Wades), presides over Willow Springs. Known and respected locally as an old conjure woman, Mama Day is a repository and embodiment of the culture's wisdom. In particular, she is versed in herbs and other natural phenomena, but she also speaks with the island's spirits. Mama Day uses her powers to heal and aid new life, but other island people who have similar powers are not so benevolent. One such person is Ruby, who stirs her knowledge with hoodoo to kill any woman who might take her man.

Unhappily, Mama Day's grandniece, Cocoa, down from New York on a visit with her husband, George, arouses Ruby's jealousy. By pretending to be friendly, Ruby is able to give Cocoa a deadly nightshade rinse, scalp massage, and hairdo. Just as a big hurricane hits the island, Cocoa begins to feel the effects of the poison. George, an engineer, native

New Yorker, and football fan, works frantically to save Cocoa, but he is overmatched. With his urbanized, masculine rationality, he cannot conceive of what he is up against or how to oppose it. Suffering from exhaustion and a weak heart, he is eventually killed in an encounter with a brooding hen.

Meanwhile, Mama Day has been working her powers. She confronts Ruby in a conjuring match, good magic versus bad magic, just as in Mali's oral epic tradition of the thirteenth century ruler Sundjata and in other traditions of modern Africa. Ruby is destroyed by lightning strikes, and Cocoa is saved. It is too late for George the doubter, however, who learns about the mystical powers of women the hard way.

BAILEY'S CAFÉ

In each of Naylor's first three novels, clear links to the work that follow it are evident. The character Kiswana Browne in *The Women of Brewster Place* serves as the connection to *Linden Hills*, having moved from that bourgeois community to Brewster Place to stay in touch with the struggles of her people. Willa Prescott Nedeed, the imprisoned wife in *Linden Hills*, points the way to *Mama Day*, since she is grandniece to Mama Day and first cousin to Cocoa. It is George, Cocoa's husband, who provides the link to *Bailey's Café*, Naylor's fourth novel.

In perhaps her most ambitious work yet, Naylor moves her readers from the magical island of Willow Springs to an equally intriguing site, for Bailey's Café is both nowhere and everywhere. It is sitting at the edge of the world yet is found in every town. As the café's proprietor, Bailey (though that is not his real name), tells readers,

> Even though this planet is round, there are just too many spots where you can find yourself hanging onto the edge . . . and unless there's some place, some space, to take a breather for a while, the edge of the world—frightening as it is—could be the end of the world.

Bailey's Café offers that breather, though some who enter the front door decide not to take it, instead going right through the café out the back door and dropping off into the void.

Like the inhabitants of Brewster Place, the customers in Bailey's Café are marginalized people. Their lives have taken them beyond the poverty and hard times of their urban sisters and brothers to the very edge of despair. However, for the women who people this extraordinary novel, Bailey's is simply a place to get directions to Eve's boardinghouse. Sweet Esther, abused to the point that she will receive visitors only in the dark; Peaches, whose effect on men drives her to mutilate her face with a can opener; Jesse, whose loss of marriage, child, and good name lead her to female lovers and heroin; and the pregnant virgin Mariam, ostracized from her village and bearing the effects of female circumcision—all find at Eve's a haven for their battered souls.

Throughout the individual stories of these women, Naylor uses unifying imagery: flower imagery, since each woman is associated with a particular bloom; musical imagery, jazz mostly, though the chords of the broken lives suggest the blues; and religious imagery, figuring heavily in Eve and her garden, but most noticeably in the virgin birth at the end of the novel. This birth is where the connection to *Mama Day* is made clear. Explaining the circumstances of his birth to Cocoa, George told of being left as an infant outside Bailey's Café by his mother, who was later found drowned. The last few pages of *Bailey's Café* reveal George as the drowned Mariam's child, recursively pointing back to *Mama Day*.

Similar to Naylor's other novels in its concentration on the diverse lives of black people, *Bailey's Café* nonetheless marks a shift for Naylor. This shift is evident in her inclusion of Mariam, from Ethiopia, who broadens the depiction of the black experience by encompassing an African one. Mariam is also Jewish, a fact that links her to the Jewish shopkeeper, Gabriel, in the novel. The coming together of the characters in celebration of the baby's birth—a celebration that intermixes different cultural and religious beliefs—brings a multicultural component to the novel absent in Naylor's other works.

Another notable change is Naylor's foregrounding of male characters. Bailey himself, the novel's narrator, is an example. His running commentary on the customers who find themselves in his establishment, his knowledge of Negro Leagues Baseball, and his narration of his courtship of his wife, Nadine, make him a central and engaging figure throughout the book. Another example is Miss Maples, the cross-dressing male housekeeper at Eve's boardinghouse. His rather lengthy individual story is included with those of the women; it points to Naylor's intention to portray a different kind of male identity as well as her desire to cultivate a different relationship with her male characters. This shift links *Bailey's Café* to *The Men of Brewster Place*, Naylor's fifth novel.

THE MEN OF BREWSTER PLACE

Naylor's return to Brewster Place gives readers the opportunity to revisit the male characters introduced in the first book (generally portrayed negatively) and see them in a different light. No longer assuming background roles, they are up front, giving an account of their actions in the first book. In *The Women of Brewster Place*, Mattie's son Basil skipped town while awaiting sentencing, causing his mother to lose the property she had put up for his bail. Here Basil does return, check in hand, to repay his mother for her loss; however, she is dead, and his unfulfilled desire to make amends leads him into a detrimental relationship and a prison sentence. Eugene, absent from his daughter's funeral in the first book, is in fact on site. His grief compels him to undergo a harsh punishment, one that has much to do with the fact that he could never tell Ciel that he is gay. C. C. Baker, responsible for the vicious gang rape of Lorraine, executes another heinous crime in this book but gives the reader insight into his tragic character. When he squeezes the trigger to kill his brother, he does so with eyes closed, thanking God "for giving him the courage to do it. The courage to be a man."

In *The Men of Brewster Place*, Naylor seems to be acknowledging that there is after all more than one side to a story and that she is ready to let the whole story be known. Passages from the first book provide continuity between the two works, as does the resurrected voice of Ben, the janitor killed by Lorraine. Reminiscent of the character Bailey in *Bailey's Café*, Ben is both character and narrator.

However, Naylor brings some new voices to Brewster Place when she introduces Brother Jerome and Greasy. These characters link together the lives of the men living in Brewster Place. Brother Jerome is a retarded child with an ability to play the piano that speaks of genius. The blues that pour from his fingers speak to the lives of each man, rendering their conditions tangible. Greasy makes his brief but memorable appearance in the story called "The Barbershop," leaving the men to carry the burden of his self-inflicted demise. Naylor's portrayals of these two characters are perhaps the most moving of the book. These characterizations, along with the complexity of all the male characters, point to a Naylor who is taking a broader view. She had prefaced *The Women of Brewster Place* with a poem by Langston Hughes that asked the question, "What happens to a dream deferred?" In *The Men of Brewster Place*, she seems ready to acknowledge that deferred dreams are not only the province of women.

Harold Branam
Updated by Jacquelyn Benton

Other major works

NONFICTION: *Conversations with Gloria Naylor*, 2004 (Maxine Lavon Montgomery, editor).

EDITED TEXT: *Children of the Night: The Best Short Stories by Black Writers, 1967 to the Present*, 1995.

Bibliography

Braxton, Joanne M., and Andrée Nicola McLaughlin, eds. *Wild Women in the Whirlwind: Afro-American Culture and the Contemporary Literary Renaissance*. New Brunswick, N.J.: Rutgers University Press, 1990. This wide-ranging collection of critical articles brings the cultural history of black women's writing to the 1980's. Barbara Smith's article "The Truth That Never Hurts: Black Lesbians in Fiction in the 1980's" discusses the section of *The Women of Brewster Place* entitled "The Two," but other articles also bear indirectly on Naylor's important themes.

Felton, Sharon, and Michelle C. Loris, eds. *The Critical Response to Gloria Naylor*. Westport, Conn.: Greenwood Press, 1997. A collection of essays analyzing four of Naylor's novels—*The Women of Brewster Place*, *Linden Hills*, *Mama Day*, and *Bailey's Café*—from a wide variety of perspectives.

Fowler, Virginia C. *Gloria Naylor: In Search of Sanctuary*. New York: Twayne, 1996. Fowler analyzes Naylor's first four novels; she also explains how Jehovah's Witnesses, of which Naylor was a member until she was twenty-five years old, and Naylor's feminism have influenced her fiction. Includes an interview that Fowler conducted with Naylor, a bibliography, and a chronology of Naylor's life.

Gates, Henry Louis, Jr., and K. Anthony Appiah, eds. *Gloria Naylor: Critical Perspectives Past and Present*. New York: Amistad, 1993. Focuses on Naylor's first four novels, with reviews of each book and essays analyzing her work. Two of the essays examine the role of William Shakespeare and of black sisterhood in Naylor's novels.

Kelley, Margot Anne, ed. *Gloria Naylor's Early Novels*. Gainesville: University Press of Florida, 1999. A collection of essays analyzing Naylor's first four novels, with several essays examining her work from a feminist perspective. Includes bibliographical references and an index.

Montgomery, Maxine Lavon. "Authority, Multivocality, and the New World Order in Gloria Naylor's *Bailey's Café*." *African American Review* 29, no. 1 (Spring, 1995): 27. Montgomery discusses *Bailey's Café* as a woman-centered work that draws on black art forms and biblical allusions. Though she fails to recognize the true identity of Mariam's child (George of *Mama Day*), Montgomery otherwise provides a valid reading of *Bailey's Café*, commenting on the "more mature voice" with which Naylor addresses the concerns of her earlier novels.

_______, ed. *Conversations with Gloria Naylor.* Jackson: University Press of Mississippi, 2004. A compilation of previously conducted interviews and conversations with Naylor, in which Naylor addresses a wide range of topics. Includes Naylor's conversations with writers Toni Morrison and Nikki Giovanni.

Puhr, Kathleen M. "Healers in Gloria Naylor's Fiction." *Twentieth Century Literature* 40, no. 4 (Winter, 1994). Puhr discusses the healing powers of Naylor's female characters, principally Mattie Michael (*The Women of Brewster Place*), Willa Nedeed (*Linden Hills*), and Miranda (*Mama Day*), as well as Naylor's healing places, particularly the café and Eve's garden in *Bailey's Café*. She also discusses Naylor's works in terms of African American ancestry, generational conflicts, and broken dreams.

Stave, Shirley A., ed. *Gloria Naylor: Strategy and Technique, Magic and Myth*. Newark: University of Delaware Press, 2001. A collection of essays focusing on *Mama Day* and *Bailey's Café*. Stave argues that Naylor deserves an elevated position in the American literary canon.

Whitt, Margaret Earley. *Understanding Gloria Naylor.* Columbia: University of South Carolina Press, 1998. A thoughtful examination of Naylor's novels, through *The Men of Brewster Place*, that discusses major themes, symbolism, character development, Naylor's critical reputation, and her literary influences.

Wilson, Charles E., Jr. *Gloria Naylor: A Critical Companion*. Westport, Conn.: Greenwood Press, 2001. An analysis of Naylor's first five novels, with a separate chapter devoted to an examination of each book. The first chapter chronicles the events of Naylor's life, including information obtained in an interview conducted for this book, while another chapter establishes Naylor's place within African American literature.

ISHMAEL REED

Born: Chattanooga, Tennessee; February 22, 1938
Also known as: Ishmael Scott Reed; Emmett Coleman

PRINCIPAL LONG FICTION

The Free-Lance Pallbearers, 1967
Yellow Back Radio Broke-Down, 1969
Mumbo Jumbo, 1972
The Last Days of Louisiana Red, 1974
Flight to Canada, 1976
The Terrible Twos, 1982
Reckless Eyeballing, 1986
The Terrible Threes, 1989
Japanese by Spring, 1993

OTHER LITERARY FORMS

Ishmael Reed may be best known as a satiric novelist, but he also gained a reputation as a respected poet, essayist, and editor. His poetry collections, which include *Catechism of D Neoamerican Hoodoo Church* (1970), *Conjure: Selected Poems, 1963-1970* (1972), *Chattanooga* (1973), *A Secretary to the Spirits* (1977), and *New and Collected Poems* (1988), established him as a major African American poet, and his poetry has been included in several important anthologies. In well-received collections of essays, including *Shrovetide in Old New Orleans* (1978), *God Made Alaska for the Indians* (1982), and *Writin' Is Fightin'* (1988), Reed forcefully presented his aesthetic and political theories.

Reed also proved to be an important editor and publisher. *Nineteen Necromancers from Now* (1970) was a breakthrough anthology for several unknown black writers. *Yardbird Lives!* (1978), which Reed edited with novelist Al Young, includes essays, fiction, and graphics from the pages of the *Yardbird Reader*, an innovative periodical that published the work of minority writers and artists. Reed's most ambitious editing project resulted in *Calafia: The California Poetry* (1979), an effort to gather together the forgotten minority poetry of California's past.

ACHIEVEMENTS

Ishmael Reed earned a place in the first rank of contemporary African American authors, but such recognition did not come immediately. Most established reviewers ignored Reed's first novel, *The Free-Lance Pallbearers*, and many of the reviews that were written dismissed the novel as offensive, childish, or self-absorbed. Although *Yellow Back Radio Broke-Down* was even less traditional than its predecessor, it received much more critical attention and became the center of considerable debate. Some reviewers attacked the novel as overly clever, bitter, or obscure, but many praised its imaginative satire and technical innovation. Moreover, the controversy over *Yellow Back Radio Broke-Down* stirred new interest in *The Free-Lance Pallbearers*. Reed's increasing acceptance as a major African American author was demonstrated when his third novel, *Mumbo Jumbo*, was reviewed on the front page of *The New York Times Review of Books*. Both *Mumbo Jumbo* and *Conjure*, a poetry collection published in the same year, were nominated for the National Book Award.

Subsequent novels maintained Reed's position in American letters. In 1975, his *The Last Days of Louisiana Red* received the Rosenthal Foundation Award, and some reviewers viewed *Flight to Canada* as Reed's best novel. Yet his work proved consistently controversial. His novels have, for example, been called sexist, a critical accusation that is fueled by comparison of Reed's novels with the contemporary powerful fiction written by African American women such as Alice Walker and Toni Morrison. The charge of sexism is further encouraged by Reed's satiric attack on feminists in *Reckless Eyeballing*. Reed has also been called a reactionary by some critics because of his uncomplimentary portrayals of black revolutionaries. His fiction has been translated into three languages, and his poetry is included in *Poetry of the Negro*, *New Black Poetry*, *The Norton Anthology of Poetry*, and other anthologies. In 1998, Reed was awarded the MacArthur "genius" fellowship, a fitting recognition for a writer who consciously attempted to redefine American and African American literature.

BIOGRAPHY

The jacket notes to *Chattanooga* glibly recount the life of Ishmael Reed with the following: "born in Chattanooga, Tennessee, grew up in Buffalo, New York, learned to write in New York City and wised up in Berkeley, California." Each residence played a crucial role in his development.

Reed was given the name Emmett Coleman at birth. He was born to Henry Lenoir and Thelma Coleman, but before he was two years old, his mother remarried, this time to auto worker Bennie Reed. When the young Reed was four years old, his mother moved the family to Buffalo, New York, where she found factory work. Reed graduated from Buffalo's East High School in 1956 and began to attend Millard Fillmore College, the night division of the University of Buffalo, supporting himself by working in the Buffalo public library. A satiric short story, "Something Pure," which portrayed Christ's return as an advertising man, brought Reed the praise of an English professor and encouraged him to enroll in day classes. Reed attended the University of Buffalo until 1960, when he withdrew because of money problems and the social pressures that his financial situation created.

Reed married Priscilla Rose Thompson and moved into the notorious Talbert Mall projects. The two years he spent there provided him with a painful but valuable experience of urban poverty and dependence. His daughter, Timothy Bret Reed, was born there. During his last years in Buffalo, Reed wrote for the *Empire Star Weekly*, moderated a controversial radio program for station WVFO, and acted in several local stage productions.

From 1962 to 1967, Reed lived in New York City. As well as being involved with the Civil Rights movement and the Black Power movement, Reed served as editor of *Advance*, a weekly published in Newark, New Jersey. His work on *Advance* was admired by Walter Bowart, and together they founded the *East Village Other*, one of the first and most successful underground newspapers. An early indication of Reed's commitment to encouraging the work of minority artists was his organization in 1965 of the American Festival of Negro Art.

In 1967, Reed moved to Berkeley, California, and began teaching at the University of California, Berkeley. In 1970, he and his first wife divorced (after years of separation), and he married Carla Blank. In 1971, with Al Young, Reed founded Yardbird Publishing Company, which from 1971 to 1976 produced the *Yardbird Reader*, an innovative journal of ethnic writing and graphics. The Reed, Cannon, and Johnson Communications Company, which later became Ishmael Reed Books, was founded in 1973 and has published the work of William Demby, Bill Gunn, Mei Mei Bressenburge, and other ethnic writers. In 1976, Reed and Victor Cruz began the Before Columbus Foundation. Reed's daughter, Tennessee, was born in 1977.

Reed was denied tenure in the English Department at Berkeley, but he continued to serve as a lecturer at there. He also taught at Yale, Harvard, Columbia, Dartmouth, and a number of other colleges and universities. In 1995, he was awarded an honorary doctorate in letters from the State University of New York at Buffalo.

Reed made important contributions as a poet, novelist, essayist, playwright, and as an editor and publisher. He stated that he considers himself a global writer, and his success at writing poetry in the African language of Yoruba and his study of Japanese language and culture for his novel *Japanese by Spring* support this assertion. He also extended his literary range to include plays, such as *The Preacher and the Rapper* (published in 1997), and jazz albums, such as *Conjure I* (1983) and *Conjure II* (1989), and he even completed a libretto and served as the executive producer for a paid-television soap opera called *Personal Problems* (1981).

In the early 1990's, Reed was best known for his controversial essays on such issues as the beating of Rodney King by Los Angeles Police Department officers, the criminal and civil trials of O. J. Simpson, and the hearings on U.S. Supreme Court nominee Clarence Thomas. Some of these essays were collected in *Airing Dirty Laundry* (1993). However, Reed's most important contribution to American letters may well be his work as an editor and publisher for other ethnic writers. In all of his publishing ventures, Reed tries to expose readers to the work of Asian Americans, African Americans, Chicanos, and Native Americans in an effort to help build a truly representative and pluralistic national literature.

Analysis

Ishmael Reed is consciously a part of the African American literary tradition that extends back to the first-person slave narratives, and the central purpose of his novels is to define a means of expressing the complexity of the African American experience in a manner distinct from the dominant literary tradition. Until the middle of the twentieth century, African American fiction, although enriched by the lyricism of Jean Toomer and Zora Neale Hurston, concentrated on realistic portrayals of black life and employed familiar narrative structures. This tendency toward social realism peaked with Richard Wright's *Native Son* (1940) and *Black Boy* (1945), but it was continued into the late twentieth century by authors such as James Baldwin. Reed belongs to a divergent tradition, inspired by Ralph Ellison's *Invisible Man* (1952), a countertradition that includes the work of Leon Forrest, Ernest J. Gaines, James Alan McPherson, Toni Morrison, and Alice Walker.

Believing that the means of expression is as important as the matter, Reed argues that the special qualities of the African American experience cannot be adequately communicated through traditional literary forms. Like Amiri Baraka, Reed believes that African American authors must "be estranged from the dominant culture," but Reed also wants to avoid being stifled by a similarly restrictive countertradition. In *Shrovetide in Old New Orleans*, Reed says that his art and criticism try to combat "the consciousness barrier erected by an alliance of Eastern-backed black pseudo-nationalists and white mundanists." Thus, Reed works against the stylistic limitations of the African American literary tradition as much as he works with them. Henry Louis Gates, Jr., compared Reed's fictional modifications of African American literary traditions to the African American folk custom of "signifying," maintaining that Reed's novels present an ongoing process of "rhetorical self-definition."

Although Reed's novels are primarily efforts to define an appropriate African American aesthetic, his fiction vividly portrays the particular social condition of black Americans. In his foreword to Elizabeth and Thomas Settle's *Ishmael Reed: A Primary and Secondary Bibliography* (1982), Reed expresses his bitterness over persistent racism and argues that the personal experience of racism that informs his art makes his work inaccessible and threatening to many readers:

> I am a member of a class which has been cast to the bottom of the American caste system, and from those depths I write a vision which is still strange, often frightening, "peculiar" and "odd" to some, "ill-considered" and unwelcome to many.

Indeed, "Ishmael" seems to be an ironically appropriate name for this author of violent and darkly humorous attacks on American institutions and attitudes, for the sharpness and breadth of his satire sometimes make him appear to be a person whose hand is turned against all others. His novels portray corrupt power brokers and their black and white sycophants operating in a dehumanized and materialistic society characterized by its prefabricated and ethnocentric culture. Yet Reed's novels are not hopeless explications of injustice, for against the forces of repression and conformity he sets gifted individuals who escape the limitations of their sterile culture by courageously penetrating the illusions that bind them. Moreover, in contrast to many white authors who are engaged in parallel metafictive experiments, Reed voices a confident belief that "print and words are not dead at all."

Reed's narrative technique combines the improvisational qualities of jazz with a documentary impulse to accumulate references and allusions. In his composite narratives, historical and fictional characters coexist in a fluid, anachronistic time. In an effort to translate the vitality and spontaneity of the oral, folk tradition into a literature that can form the basis for an alternative culture, Reed mixes colloquialisms and erudition in novels that are syncretized from a series of subtexts. The literary equivalent of scat singing, his stories-within-stories parody literary formulas and challenge the traditional limits of fiction.

Reed claims that his novels constitute "an art form with its own laws," but he does not mean to imply that his work is private, for these "laws" are founded on a careful but imaginative reinterpretation of the historical and mythological past. The lengthy bibliography appended to *Mumbo Jumbo* satirizes the documentary impulse of social realist authors, but it also underscores Reed's belief that his mature work demands scholarly research to be decoded. This artistic process of reinterpretation often requires the services of an interlocutor, a character who explicitly explains the events of the narrative in terms of the mythological past. Reed's novels describe a vision of an Osirian/Dionysian consciousness, a sensuous humanism that he presents as an appropriate cultural alternative for nonwhite Americans. His imaginative reconstructions of the American West, the Harlem Renaissance, the American Civil War, and contemporary U.S. politics, interwoven with ancient myths, non-European folk customs, and the formulas of popular culture, are liberating heresies meant to free readers from the intellectual domination of the Judeo-Christian tradition.

THE FREE-LANCE PALLBEARERS

Reed's first novel, *The Free-Lance Pallbearers*, takes place in a futuristic America called HARRY SAM: "A big not-to-be-believed out-of-sight, sometimes referred to as O-BOP-SHE-BANG or KLANG-A-LANG-A-DING-DONG." This crumbling and corrupt world is tyrannized by Sam himself, a vulgar fat man who lives in Sam's Motel on Sam's Island in the middle of the lethally polluted Black Bay that borders HARRY SAM. Sam, doomed by some terrifying gastrointestinal disorder, spends all of his time on the toilet, his filth pouring into the bay from several large statues of Rutherford B. Hayes.

The bulk of the novel, although framed and periodically informed by a jiving narrative voice, is narrated by Bukka Doopeyduk in a restrained, proper English that identifies his passive faith in the establishment. Doopeyduk is a dedicated adherent to the Nazarene Code, an orderly in a psychiatric hospital, a student at Harry Sam College, and a hapless victim. His comically futile efforts to play by the rules are defeated by the cynics, who manipulate the unjust system to their own advantage. In the end, Doopeyduk is disillusioned: He leads a successful attack on Sam's Island, uncovers the conspiracy that protects Sam's cannibalism, briefly dreams of becoming the black Sam, and is finally crucified.

The Free-Lance Pallbearers is a parody of the African American tradition of first-person, confessional narratives, a book the narrator describes as "growing up in soulsville first of three installments—or what it means to be a backstage darky." Reed's novel challenges the viability of this African American version of the bildungsroman, in which a young protagonist undergoes a painful initiation into the darkness of the white world, a formula exemplified by Wright's *Black Boy* and Baldwin's *Go Tell It on the Mountain* (1953). In fact, the novel suggests that African American authors' use of this European form is as disabling as Doopeyduk's adherence to the dictates of the Nazarene Code.

The Free-Lance Pallbearers is an unrestrained attack on U.S. politics. HARRY SAM, alternately referred to as "Nowhere" or "Now Here," is a dualistic vision of a United States that celebrates vacuous contemporaneity. The novel, an inversion of the Horatio Alger myth in the manner of Nathanael West, mercilessly displays American racism, but its focus is the corruptive potential of power. Sam is a grotesque version of Lyndon B. Johnson, famous for his bathroom interviews, and Sam's cannibalistic taste for children is an attack on Johnson's Vietnam policy. With *The Free-Lance Pallbearers*, Reed destroys the presumptions of his society, but it is not until his later novels that he attempts to construct an alternative.

YELLOW BACK RADIO BROKE-DOWN

Yellow Back Radio Broke-Down is set in a fantastic version of the Wild West of popular literature. Reed's protagonist, the Loop Garoo Kid, is a proponent of artistic freedom and an accomplished Voodoo *houngan* who is in marked contrast to the continually victimized Doopeyduk. Armed with supernatural "connaissance" and aided by a white python and the hip, helicopter-flying Chief Showcase, the Kid battles the forces of realistic mimesis and political corruption. His villainous opponent is Drag Gibson, a degenerate cattle baron given to murdering his wives, who is called upon by the citizens of Yellow Back Radio to crush their rebellious children's effort "to create [their] own fictions."

Although *Yellow Back Radio Broke-Down* satirizes Americans' eagerness to suspend civil rights in response to student protests against the Vietnam War, its focus is literature, specifically the dialogue between realism and modernism. The Loop Garoo Kid matches Reed's description of the African American artist in *Nineteen Necromancers from Now*: "a conjurer who works JuJu upon his oppressors; a witch doctor who frees his fellow victims from the psychic attack launched by demons." Through the Loop Garoo Kid, Reed takes a stand for imagination, intelligence, and fantasy against rhetoric, violence, and sentimentality. This theme is made explicit in a debate with Bo Shmo, a "neo-social realist" who maintains that "all art must be for the end of liberating the masses," for the Kid says that a novel "can be anything it wants to be, a vaudeville show, the six o'clock news, the mumblings of wild men saddled by demons."

Reed exhibits his antirealist theory of fiction in *Yellow Back Radio Broke-Down* through his free use of time, characters, and language. The novel ranges from the eighteenth century to the present, combining historical events and cowboy myths with modern technology and cultural detritus. Reed's primary characters are comically exaggerated racial types: Drag Gibson represents the whites' depraved materialism, Chief Showcase represents the American Indians' spirituality, and the Loop Garoo Kid represents the African Americans' artistic soul. Reed explains the novel's title by suggesting that his book is the "dismantling of a genre done in an oral way like radio." "Yellow back" refers to the popular dime novels; "radio" refers to the novel's oral, discontinuous form; and a "broke-down" is a dismantling. Thus, Reed's first two novels assault America in an attempt to "dismantle" its cultural structure.

MUMBO JUMBO

In *Mumbo Jumbo*, Reed expands on the neo-hoodooism of the Loop Garoo Kid in order to create and define an African American aesthetic based on Voodoo, Egyptian mythology, and improvisational musical forms, an aesthetic to challenge the Judeo-Christian tradition, rationalism, and technology.

Set in Harlem during the 1920's, *Mumbo Jumbo* is a tragicomical analysis of the Harlem Renaissance's failure to sustain its artistic promise. Reed's protagonist is PaPa LaBas, an aging hoodoo detective and cultural diagnostician. LaBas's name, meaning "over there" in French, reveals that his purpose is to reconnect African Americans with their cultural heritage by reunifying the Text of Jes Grew, literally the Egyptian Book of Thoth. Reed takes the phrase Jes Grew from Harriet Beecher Stowe's Topsy and James Weldon Johnson's description of African American music's unascribed development, but in the novel, Jes Grew is a contagion, connected with the improvisational spirit of ragtime and jazz, that begins to spread across America in the 1920's. Jes Grew is an irrational force that threatens to overwhelm the dominant, repressive traditions of established culture. LaBas's efforts to unify and direct this unpredictable force are opposed by the Wallflower Order of the Knights Templar, an organization dedicated to neutralizing the power of Jes Grew in order to protect its privileged status. LaBas fails to reunify the text, a parallel to the dissipation of the Harlem Renaissance's artistic potential, but the failure is seen as temporary; the novel's indeterminate conclusion looks forward hopefully to a time when these artistic energies can be reignited.

The novel's title is double-edged. "Mumbo jumbo" is a racist, colonialist phrase used to describe the misunderstood customs and language of dark-skinned people, an approximation of some critics' description of Reed's unorthodox fictional method. Yet "mumbo jumbo" also refers to the power of imagination, the cultural alternative that can free African Americans. A text of and about texts, *Mumbo Jumbo* combines the formulas of detective fiction with the documentary paraphernalia of scholarship: footnotes, illustrations, and a bibliography. Thus, in the disclosure scene required of any good detective story, LaBas, acting the part of interlocutor, provides a lengthy and erudite explication of the development of Jes Grew that begins with a reinterpretation of the myth of Osiris. The parodic scholarship of *Mumbo Jumbo* undercuts the assumed primacy of the European tradition and implicitly argues that African American artists should attempt to discover their distinct cultural heritage.

THE LAST DAYS OF LOUISIANA RED

In *The Last Days of Louisiana Red*, LaBas returns as Reed's protagonist, but the novel abandons the parodic scholarship and high stylization of *Mumbo Jumbo*. Although LaBas again functions as a connection with a non-European tradition of history and myth, *The Last Days of Louisiana Red* is more traditionally structured than its predecessor. In the novel, LaBas solves the murder of Ed Yellings, the founder of the Solid Gumbo Works. Yellings's business is dedicated to combating the effects of Louisiana Red, literally a popular hot sauce but figuratively an evil state of mind that divides African Americans. Yelling's gumbo, like Reed's fiction, is a mixture of disparate elements, and it has a powerful curative effect. In fact, LaBas discovers that Yellings is murdered when he gets close to developing a gumbo that will cure heroin addiction.

In *The Last Days of Louisiana Red*, Reed is examining the self-destructive forces that divide the African American community so that its members fight one another "while above their heads . . . billionaires flew in custom-made jet planes." Reed shows how individuals' avarice leads them to conspire with the establishment, and he suggests that some of the most vocal and militant leaders are motivated by their egotistical need for power rather than by true concern for oppressed people. Set in Berkeley, *The Last Days of Louisiana Red* attacks the credibility of the black revolutionary movements that sprang up in the late 1960's and early 1970's.

FLIGHT TO CANADA

Flight to Canada, Reed's fifth novel, is set in an imaginatively redrawn Civil War South, and it describes the relationship between Arthur Swille, a tremendously wealthy Virginia planter who practices necrophilia, and an assortment of sociologically stereotyped slaves. The novel is presented as the slave narrative of Uncle Robin, the most loyal of Swille's possessions. Uncle Robin repeatedly tells Swille that the plantation is his idea of heaven, and he assures his master that he does not believe that Canada exists. Raven Quickskill, "the first one of Swille's slaves to read, the first to write, and the first to run away," is the author of Uncle Robin's story.

Like much of Reed's work, *Flight to Canada* is about the liberating power of art, but in *Flight to Canada*, Reed concentrates on the question of authorial control. All the characters struggle to maintain control of their stories. After escaping from the plantation,

Quickskill writes a poem, "Flight to Canada," and his comical verse denunciation of Swille completes his liberation. In complaining of Quickskill's betrayal to Abraham Lincoln, Swille laments that his former bookkeeper uses literacy "like that old Voodoo." In a final assertion of authorial control and the power of the pen, Uncle Robin refuses to sell his story to Harriet Beecher Stowe, gives the rights to Quickskill, rewrites Swille's will, and inherits the plantation.

THE TERRIBLE TWOS

In *The Terrible Twos*, Reed uses a contemporary setting to attack Ronald Reagan's administration and the exploitative nature of the U.S. economic system. In the novel, President Dean Clift, a former model, is a mindless figurehead manipulated by an oil cartel that has supplanted the real Santa Claus. Nance Saturday, another of Reed's African American detectives, sets out to discover Saint Nicholas's place of exile. The novel's title suggests that, in its second century, the United States is acting as selfishly and irrationally as the proverbial two-year-old. The central theme is the manner in which a few avaricious people seek vast wealth at the expense of the majority of Americans.

RECKLESS EYEBALLING

Reckless Eyeballing takes place in the 1980's, and Reed employs a string of comically distorted characters to present the idea that the American literary environment is dominated by New York women and Jews. Although *Reckless Eyeballing* has been called sexist and anti-Semitic by some, Reed's target is a cultural establishment that creates and strengthens racial stereotypes, in particular the view of African American men as savage rapists. To make his point, however, he lampoons feminists, using the character Tremonisha Smarts, a female African American author who has written a novel of violence against women. Reed's satire probably is intended to remind readers of Alice Walker's *The Color Purple* (1982).

Because the novel's central subject is art and the limitations that society places on an artist, it is appropriate that Reed once again employs the technique of a story-within-a-story. Ian Ball, an unsuccessful African American playwright, is the novel's protagonist. In the novel, Ball tries to succeed by shamelessly placating the feminists in power. He writes "Reckless Eyeballing," a play in which a lynched man is posthumously tried for "raping" a woman with lecherous stares, but Ball, who often seems to speak for Reed, maintains his private, chauvinistic views throughout.

THE TERRIBLE THREES

The Terrible Threes, a sequel to *The Terrible Twos*, continues Reed's satiric attack on the contemporary capitalist system, which, he argues, puts the greatest economic burden on the least privileged. (Reed also was planning a third book in the series, *The Terrible Fours*.) In the first book, there appears a character named Black Peter—an assistant to St.

Nicholas in European legend. This Black Peter is an impostor, however, a Rastafarian who studied and appropriated the legend for himself. In *The Terrible Threes*, the true Black Peter emerges to battle the false Peter but is distracted from his mission by the need to do good deeds. Black Peter becomes wildly popular because of these deeds, but a jealous St. Nick and concerned toy companies find a way to put Santa Claus back on top. Capitalism wins again.

JAPANESE BY SPRING

Japanese by Spring is postmodern satire. Like much of Reed's imaginative work, the book mixes fictional characters with "fictionalized" ones. Reed himself is a character in the book, with his own name. The protagonist of *Japanese by Spring* is Benjamin "Chappie" Puttbutt, a teacher of English and literature at Oakland's Jack London College. Chappie dabbled in activist politics in the mid-1960's, but his only concern in the 1990's is receiving tenure and the perks that accompany it. He will put up with virtually anything, including racist insults from students, to avoid hurting his chances at tenure. As in many of Reed's books, Chappie is passive in the face of power at the beginning of his story. He is a middle-class black conservative, but only because the climate at Jack London demands it. Chappie is a chameleon who always matches his behavior to the ideology of his environment. However, when he is denied tenure and is about to be replaced by a feminist poet who is more flash than substance, Chappie's hidden anger begins to surface.

Chappie also has been studying Japanese with a tutor named Dr. Yamato. This proves fortuitous when the Japanese buy Jack London and Dr. Yamato becomes the college president. Chappie suddenly finds himself in a position of power and gloats over those who denied him tenure. He soon finds, however, that his new bosses are the same as the old ones. Dr. Yamato is a tyrant and is eventually arrested by a group that includes Chappie's father, a two-star Air Force general. Dr. Yamato is released, though, and a surprised Chappie learns that there is an "invisible government" that truly controls the United States. Chappie has pierced some of his illusions, but there are others that he never penetrates, such as his blindness to his own opportunism.

The novel's conclusion moves away from Chappie's point of view to that of a fictionalized Ishmael Reed. This Reed skewers political correctness but also shows that the people who complain the most about it are often its greatest purveyors. Reed also lampoons American xenophobia, particularly toward Japan, but he does so in a balanced manner that does not gloss over Japanese faults. Ultimately, though, Reed uses *Japanese by Spring* as he used other novels before, to explore art and politics and the contradictions of America and race.

Carl Brucker
Updated by Charles A. Gramlich

Other major works

poetry: *Catechism of D Neoamerican Hoodoo Church*, 1970; *Conjure: Selected Poems, 1963-1970*, 1972; *Chattanooga*, 1973; *A Secretary to the Spirits*, 1977; *Cab Calloway Stands In for the Moon*, 1986; *New and Collected Poems*, 1988; *New and Collected Poems, 1964-2006*, 2006.

nonfiction: *Shrovetide in Old New Orleans*, 1978; *God Made Alaska for the Indians*, 1982; *Writin' Is Fightin': Thirty-seven Years of Boxing on Paper*, 1988; *Airing Dirty Laundry*, 1993; *Conversations with Ishmael Reed*, 1995; *Another Day at the Front: Dispatches from the Race War*, 2002 (essays); *Blues City: A Walk in Oakland*, 2003; *Mixing It Up: Taking on the Media Bullies and Other Reflections*, 2008.

edited texts: *Nineteen Necromancers from Now*, 1970; *Yardbird Lives!*, 1978 (with Al Young); *Calafia: The California Poetry*, 1979 (with Young and Shawn Hsu Wong); *The Before Columbus Foundation Fiction Anthology: Selections from the American Book Awards, 1980-1990*, 1992 (with Kathryn Trueblood and Wong); *MultiAmerica: Essays on Cultural Wars and Cultural Peace*, 1997; *From Totems to Hip-Hop*, 2003.

miscellaneous: *The Reed Reader*, 2000.

Bibliography

Boyer, Jay. *Ishmael Reed*. Boise, Idaho: Boise State University Press, 1993. A brief, fifty-two-page overview of Reed's life and works. Includes a bibliography. One of the volumes in the Western Writers series.

Dick, Bruce Allen, and Amritjit Singh, eds. *Conversations with Ishmael Reed*. Jackson: University Press of Mississippi, 1995. A compilation of twenty-six interviews with the author that were conducted from 1968 until 1995. Includes one self-interview and a chronology of significant events in Reed's life.

Dick, Bruce Allen, and Pavel Zemliansky, eds. *The Critical Response to Ishmael Reed*. Westport, Conn.: Greenwood Press, 1999. Discusses Reed's novels in chronological order. Contains book reviews, essays, an interview in which Reed discusses works in progress, a chronology of his life, and bibliographical information.

Fox, Robert Elliot. *Conscientious Sorcerers: The Black Post-Modern Fiction of LeRoi Jones/Amiri Baraka, Ishmael Reed, and Samuel R. Delaney*. New York: Greenwood Press, 1987. A comparison of works by three African American writers who emerged in the 1960's. Fox situates Reed within both the tradition of black fiction and the self-conscious style of contemporary postmodernist fiction.

Gates, Henry Louis, Jr. *The Signifying Monkey: A Theory of Afro-American Literary Criticism*. New York: Oxford University Press, 1988. The section on Reed examines his fiction, especially the novel *Mumbo Jumbo*, as an extension of the tendency of black English to play deliberately with language.

McGee, Patrick. *Ishmael Reed and the Ends of Race*. New York: St. Martin's Press, 1997. McGee looks at Reed's refusal to meet expectations associated traditionally with African American writers, and he examines Reed's use of satire and his antagonism toward political correctness.

Mvuyekure, Pierre-Damien. *The "Dark Heathenism" of the American Novelist Ishmael Reed: African Voodoo as American Literary Hoodoo*. Lewiston, N.Y.: Edwin Mellen Press, 2007. Mvuyeukure defines Reed's nine novels as postcolonial writings characterized by "neohoodoism," an aesthetic derived from African voodoo. He demonstrates how Reed transforms the English language and debates about colonialism into discourses about self-empowerment and self-representation, reconnecting African Americans with Africa.

_______, ed. *A Casebook Study of Ishmael Reed's "Yellow Back Radio Broke-Down."* Chicago: Center for Book Culture, 2003. A collection of four essays that analyze Reed's novel from several perspectives, including that of African voodoo and American jazz.

Weisenburger, Steven. *Fables of Subversion: Satire and the American Novel, 1930-1980*. Athens: University of Georgia Press, 1995. A discussion of Reed's use of encyclopedic Menippean satire in his novel *Mumbo Jumbo* is included in this study of satire in thirty postmodern American novels.

HARRIET BEECHER STOWE

Born: Litchfield, Connecticut; June 14, 1811
Died: Hartford, Connecticut; July 1, 1896
Also known as: Harriet Elizabeth Beecher; Catharine Stowe

PRINCIPAL LONG FICTION

Uncle Tom's Cabin: Or, Life Among the Lowly, 1851-1852 (serial); 1852 (book)
Dred: A Tale of the Great Dismal Swamp, 1856
The Minister's Wooing, 1859
Agnes of Sorrento, 1862
The Pearl of Orr's Island, 1862
Oldtown Folks, 1869
My Wife and I, 1871
Pink and White Tyranny, 1871
We and Our Neighbors, 1875
Poganuc People, 1878

OTHER LITERARY FORMS

In 1843, Harriet Beecher Stowe (stoh) gathered a number of her sketches and stories into a volume called *The Mayflower: Or, Sketches of Scenes and Characters of the Descendants of the Pilgrims* (1843). For forty years thereafter, she published short fiction and miscellaneous essays in magazines. In *A Key to Uncle Tom's Cabin* (1853), she assembled a mass of sources and analogues for the characters and incidents of her most famous novel. Her 1869 *Atlantic Monthly* article "The True Story of Lady Byron's Life" and a subsequent elaboration, *Lady Byron Vindicated* (1870), caused a sensation at the time. She also published a geography for children (1833, her earliest publication, issued under her sister Catharine's name), poems, travel books, collections of biographical sketches, and a number of other children's books.

Stowe's stories and sketches remain readable. Her best collection, *Sam Lawson's Oldtown Fireside Stories* (1872), differs from the novel *Oldtown Folks* mainly in that it has little in the way of plot. Selections from Stowe's frequently long and chatty letters can be found in the *Life of Harriet Beecher Stowe* (1889), written by her son, Charles Edward Stowe, and in more recent biographies, but hundreds of her letters remain unpublished and scattered in various archives.

ACHIEVEMENTS

Known primarily today for her antislavery novel *Uncle Tom's Cabin*, Harriet Beecher Stowe also interpreted the life of her native New England in a series of novels, stories, and sketches. Along with Ralph Waldo Emerson and Oliver Wendell Holmes, she contributed

Harriet Beecher Stowe
(Library of Congress)

to the first issue of *The Atlantic Monthly* (November, 1857) and for many years thereafter contributed frequently to that Boston-based magazine. As an alert and intelligent member of a famous family of Protestant ministers, she understood the Puritan conscience and outlook as well as anyone in her time, and as a shrewd observer of the commonplace, she deftly registered Yankee habits of mind and speech. All of her novels feature authentic New England characters; after *Uncle Tom's Cabin* and *Dred*, she turned to settings that included all six New England states. Despite a contradictory idealizing tendency, she pioneered in realism.

One of the first American writers to apply a talent for dialect and local color to the purposes of serious narrative, Stowe exerted a strong influence on Sarah Orne Jewett, Mary Wilkins Freeman, and other regionalists of the later nineteenth century. Without a doubt, however, her greatest achievement was the novel that, beginning as an intended short serial in a Washington antislavery weekly, the *National Era*, forced the American reading public to realize for the first time not only that slavery was a national problem but also that slaves were people with hopes and aspirations as legitimate as their own. Critics as diverse as Henry Wadsworth Longfellow, Heinrich Heine, William Dean Howells, and Leo Tolstoy in the nineteenth century, and Edmund Wilson and Anthony Burgess in the twentieth, have used superlatives to praise *Uncle Tom's Cabin*.

Biography

Harriet Beecher Stowe was born Harriet Elizabeth Beecher on June 14, 1811, the seventh child of Lyman and Roxana Beecher. By this time her father's fame as a preacher had spread well beyond the Congregational Church of Litchfield, Connecticut. All seven Beecher sons who lived to maturity became ministers, one becoming more famous than his father. Harriet, after attending Litchfield Academy, a well-regarded school, was sent to the Hartford Female Seminary, which was founded by her sister, Catharine—in some respects the substitute mother whom Harriet needed after Roxana died in 1816 but did not discover in the second Mrs. Beecher. In later years, Harriet would consistently idealize motherhood. When Catharine's fiancé, a brilliant young man but one who had not experienced any perceptible religious conversion, died in 1822, the eleven-year-old Harriet felt the tragedy. In 1827, the shy, melancholy girl became a teacher in her sister's school.

In 1832, Lyman Beecher accepted the presidency of Lane Seminary in Cincinnati, Ohio, and soon Catharine and Harriet had established another school there. Four years later, Harriet married a widower named Calvin Stowe, a Lane professor. In the years that followed, she had seven children. She also became familiar with slavery, as practiced just across the Ohio River in Kentucky; with the abolitionist movement, which boasted several notable champions in Cincinnati, including the future chief justice of the United States, Salmon P. Chase; and with the Underground Railroad. As a way of supplementing her husband's small income, she also contributed to local and religious periodicals.

Not until the Stowes moved to Brunswick, Maine, in 1850, however, did she think of writing about slavery. Then, urged by her brother, Henry, by then a prominent minister in Brooklyn, New York, and by other family members in the wake of the U.S. Congress's enactment of the Fugitive Slave Act and spurred by a vision she experienced at a church service, she began to construct *Uncle Tom's Cabin*. Even as a weekly serial in the *National Era*, it attracted much attention, and its publication in 1852 as a book made Stowe an instant celebrity. After that year, from her new base in Andover, Massachusetts, where her husband taught, she twice visited Europe; met Harriet Martineau, John Ruskin, the Brownings, and Lady Byron, among others; and saw the scope of her fame increase even further.

Stowe wrote another slavery novel, *Dred*, and then turned her literary attention to New England. The drowning of her son, Henry, a Dartmouth student, in the summer of 1857, marred for her the successes of these years. In the fall of 1862, infuriated by the lack of British support for the North in the American Civil War and skeptical that President Abraham Lincoln would fulfill his promise to issue a proclamation of emancipation, Stowe visited Lincoln, who is reported to have greeted her with the words, "So this is the little lady who made this big war." She left Washington, D.C., satisfied that the president would keep his word.

Following Calvin Stowe's retirement from Andover, the family moved to Hartford, the winters usually being spent in northern Florida. Two of the most sensational scandals of the post-Civil War era involved Stowe, the first arising when she published an imprudent and detailed account of Lord Byron's sins as revealed to her some years earlier by the now deceased widow of the poet, the second being an adultery suit brought against her brother, Henry, in which Stowe characteristically defended him to the hilt. The Byron affair in particular turned many people against her, although her books continued to be commercial successes throughout the 1870's. The most severe personal abuse ever directed at a respectable nineteenth century woman bothered Stowe far less than another personal tragedy: the alcoholism and eventual disappearance of her son, Fred, in San Francisco, California, in 1870.

In the last twenty-three years of her life, Stowe became the central attraction of the Hartford neighborhood known as Nook Farm, also the home of Charles Dudley Warner and Mark Twain, the latter moving there in part because of its Beecher connections. Her circle of friends included Annie Fields, wife of *The Atlantic Monthly* publisher; George Eliot, with whom she corresponded; and Holmes, always a staunch supporter. In her final years, her mind wandered at times, but she was still writing lucid letters two years before her death on July 1, 1896, at the age of eighty-five.

ANALYSIS

In 1869, after finishing her sixth novel, *Oldtown Folks*, Harriet Beecher Stowe began a correspondence with Eliot by sending her a copy of the novel. Although an international celebrity, Stowe wanted the approval of this younger and less famous woman who had contributed notably to a movement—literary realism—just beginning to be critically recognized. Like Stowe, Eliot came from a deeply religious background and had formed a union with an unromantic and bookish, but supportive, man. Unlike the American novelist, Eliot had rejected religion for rationalism and Romanticism for realism. Had Calvin Stowe's first wife not died, it would have been unthinkable for Harriet Beecher to live with him as Eliot did with George Henry Lewes. In life, the former Miss Beecher cheerfully married the unexciting scholar; in *The Minister's Wooing*, she would not permit her heroine Mary Scudder to marry her scholarly suitor (as Eliot's Dorothea Brooke in *Middlemarch*, 1871-1872, was permitted to marry hers, Dr. Casaubon).

Stowe's hope, in a measure fulfilled, that Eliot would like *Oldtown Folks* may be taken as signifying her desire to be recognized as a realist, even though her own realism was strongly tinged with the Romanticism Eliot had come to despise. The young Harriet Beecher had probably learned something from John Bunyan's *The Pilgrim's Progress* (1678, 1684), but most of her other reading—*The Arabian Nights' Entertainments*, Cotton

Mather's *Magnalia Christi Americana* (1702), and the works of Sir Walter Scott and Lord Byron—had little to teach an incipient realist. Nor did American literature in the 1830's, when she began to write, furnish any likely models. As a result, the reader finds in her works a mingling of realist and Romantic elements.

Stowe's settings, particularly the New England ones, ring true. She understood her cultural roots, and she proved able to recollect childhood impressions almost photographically. She possessed a keen ear for dialect and a sharp eye for the idiosyncrasies of people she scarcely seemed to have noticed until they turned up in her writing. She used the novel to probe urgent social issues such as slavery and women's rights. Although she liked nature and worked hard at describing it accurately, she disdained her native region's characteristic transcendental interpretations of it. She displayed the realist's aversion to mystery, mysticism, and the making of history into legend.

The Romantic tendencies of Stowe's fiction stand out against its realistic background. Her heroines are invariably saintly, as are certain of her black male characters such as Uncle Tom and, in *Dred*, Uncle Tiff. Her recalcitrant heroes often undergo rather unconvincing conversions. Occasionally, she introduces a mythic, larger-than-life character such as Dred. In common with most of the generation of American realists who followed her, she never renounced the heroic but sought to demonstrate its presence among humble and common people. Her heroes differ from those of Twain, Howells, and Henry James, however, in drawing their strength from a firm Christian commitment: Stowe's piety has been something of an impediment to her modern readers.

The looseness of plotting about which Stowe's critics have complained so much derives in large measure from her inability to develop convincing central characters in most of her novels. Four of her last five novels have plural nouns—words such as "neighbors" and "folks" and "people"—in their titles, but even *Uncle Tom's Cabin* is not about Uncle Tom in the sense that Charles Dickens's *David Copperfield* (1849-1850, serial; 1850, book) or Gustave Flaubert's *Madame Bovary* (1857) is about its title character. In fact, Stowe changed the title of *Dred* for a time to *Nina Gordon*, a more central character but one who dies many chapters from the end. *My Wife and I* and *Oldtown Folks* are narrated by relatively colorless central characters.

One of Stowe's most persistent and indeed remarkable narrative traits also works against her realism on occasions. As she confides at the beginning of chapter 44 of *Dred*, "There's no study in human nature more interesting than the aspects of the same subject in the points of view of different characters." That she periodically allowed this interest to distract her from the task at hand is clear. Although she experimented with different points of view—omniscient, first-person, dramatic, and circulating (the last primarily through the use of the epistolary method)—she worked before the time when novelists such as Joseph Conrad, James Joyce, and William Faulkner developed techniques capable of sustaining this kind of interest. It should be pointed out that Stowe uses the expression "points of view" in the sense of "opinions," and she is more likely to present the conflict of opinions through conversations than through living, breathing embodiments of motivating ideas.

It is as a realist before her time that Stowe is most profitably considered. Even where her realism does not serve a socially critical purpose, as it does in *Uncle Tom's Cabin* and *My Wife and I*, she makes her readers aware of the texture, the complexity, of social life—particularly the conflicts, tensions, and joys of New England community life. Understanding how people grow from their geographic, social, religious, and intellectual roots, she is able to convey the reality of isolated Maine coastal villages and the jaunty postwar Manhattan of aspiring journalists. In her best work, she depicts evil not as the product of Mephistophelean schemers or motiveless brutes but of high-minded people incapacitated by a crucial weakness, such as the irresolute Augustine St. Clare of *Uncle Tom's Cabin*, the temporizing Judge Clayton of *Dred*, and the imperceptive Dr. Hopkins of *The Minister's Wooing*.

UNCLE TOM'S CABIN

Uncle Tom's Cabin: Or, Life Among the Lowly, remains one of the most controversial of novels. Extravagantly admired and bitterly detested in the 1850's, it still arouses extreme reactions more than one-and-a-half centuries later. An early barrage of challenges to its authenticity led Stowe to work furiously at the assembling of *A Key to Uncle Tom's Cabin* the next year. In 262 closely printed, double-columned pages, she impressively documented horrors that verified "the truth of the work." This book unfortunately encouraged the development of an essentially nonliterary mass of criticism, with the result that the novel early gained the reputation of a brilliant piece of propaganda—even President Lincoln supposedly accepting the Civil War as its legacy—but unworthy of serious consideration on artistic grounds.

It did not help the novel's cause that the inevitable later reaction against this enormously popular story coincided with the effort, spearheaded by James, to establish the novel as a form of art rather than as a mere popular entertainment. A writer who strove too single-mindedly for mere verifiability did not merit consideration as an artist. In the same year that *Uncle Tom's Cabin* began appearing serially, Nathaniel Hawthorne—James's chief example of the American artist—prefaced his *The House of the Seven Gables* (1851) with a firm declaration of its imaginary basis, which contrasted sharply with his attempt to provide a "historical" one for *The Scarlet Letter* one year earlier. Hawthorne's star as a writer of fiction gradually rose: Stowe's sank. Like "Old Ironsides," the vigorous youthful poem of Stowe's staunch friend of later years, *Uncle Tom's Cabin* was relegated to the status of a work that made things happen—important historically but damned by that very fact to the region of the second-rate.

In *A Key to Uncle Tom's Cabin*, Stowe herself called *Uncle Tom's Cabin* "a very inadequate representation of slavery," but her excuse is significant: "Slavery, in some of its workings, is too dreadful for the purposes of art." She was acknowledging a problem that would continue to bedevil realists for most of the rest of the century. The most prominent spokesperson for realism, Howells, agreed with her, and until the 1890's, realists would generally exclude things considered "too dreadful." As late as 1891, Thomas Hardy induced mass revulsion by allowing his heroine to be raped in *Tess of the D'Urbervilles* (1891) while referring to her in his subtitle as "a pure woman."

Stowe sandwiched the story of Uncle Tom, the meek Christian capable of turning the other cheek even to the sadistic Simon Legree, between the resolute George and Eliza Harris's escape from slavery and the Harris family's fortuitous reunion at the end of the novel. If the plot is untidy and contrived, a number of the individual characters and episodes have remained among the most memorable in fiction. The famous scene in which Eliza crosses the Ohio River ice in early spring is "true" not because the feat had been accomplished (although Stowe knew it had) but because she makes the reader feel Eliza's desperation, the absolute necessity of the attempt, and the likelihood that a person who grew up in her hard school would develop the resources to succeed.

The meeting between Miss Ophelia and Topsy illustrates Stowe's talent for dramatizing the confrontation of stubborn viewpoints. Sold down the river by his first owner, Tom has rescued the angelic daughter of Augustine St. Clare and has been installed to the St. Clare household. Miss Ophelia, a Vermont cousin of St. Clare, has been brought south to take care of Eva, whose mother is languidly incompetent. St. Clare despises slavery but feels powerless to resist it; Ophelia's intransigent New England conscience will not permit her to acquiesce in it. After listening to a considerable amount of her antislavery rhetoric, St. Clare gives his cousin a little black girl rescued from alcoholic parents. Ophelia is revolted by Topsy, so utterly different from the golden, cherubic Eva. Topsy, shrewd and skeptical beyond her years, embodies the insidiousness of slavery itself. Neither was premeditated but simply "grow'd" and now must somehow be dealt with as found. Ophelia must find room in her heart for the little "black spider" or lose face with her cousin. Her struggle with Topsy—and with her own physical aversion—is fierce and richly comical, and its successful outcome believable.

For the modern reader, the death scenes in the novel are more of a problem. Little Eva's protracted illness and beatific death exactly pleased the taste of Stowe's time. Today, her father's senseless and sudden death as a result of his attempt to mediate a tavern brawl seems more like real life—or would if Stowe had not permitted St. Clare to linger long enough to undergo a deathbed religious conversion. Modern reaction to Stowe's climactic scene is complicated by the hostility of writers such as James Baldwin to the character of Uncle Tom, who, in dying at the hands of Legree's henchmen, wins their souls in the process. Whether or not the conversion of Sambo and Quimbo convinces today's reader, Tom's character has been firmly established, and he dies in precisely the spirit the reader expects.

Far less satisfactory is the subsequent escape of two of Legree's slaves from his clutches. Stowe did nothing beforehand to induce belief in a brutal master who could melt into helpless impassivity at the sight of a lock of his dead mother's hair. Finding it expedient to make Legree superstitious, she established this side of his character belatedly and ineptly, and she failed to understand that her conception of the power of motherhood was not universally shared.

In short, the reader's admiration is interrupted by idealistic and sentimental material that does not support Stowe's goal of depicting life as it was. Nor is this inconsistency surprising. No American had ever written such a novel: realistic in impulse and directed at a current social problem of the greatest magnitude. She had no models and could not, like Twain after her, draw on experiences as Missourian, journalist, Western traveler, and—before he wrote his greatest books—neighbor of Stowe and reader of her work.

Like Twain and Howells after her, Stowe did not banish Romanticism from her novels, but her commitment to realism is clear. Thirty years before Twain's accomplishments with dialect in *Adventures of Huckleberry Finn* (1884), and nearly two decades before Bret Harte popularized the concept of local color, Stowe used dialects—not with perfect consistency but not for the conventional purpose of humor either. For the first time in major American fiction, dialect served the purpose of generating a credible environment for a serious narrative. In the process, she changed the perceptions of hundreds of thousands of readers forever.

Within a year, the book had made Stowe internationally known. When, after several years of minor literary activity, she returned to the subject of slavery, events were unfolding that led inexorably to war. Her brother, Henry, was outraging North and South alike by holding his own mock slave auction in his Brooklyn church. John Brown was launching his personal civil war in Kansas. In the chamber of the U.S. Senate, abolitionist Charles Sumner was nearly beaten to death by a southern colleague. Stowe herself had been busy with antislavery petitions and appeals.

DRED

From this context emerged *Dred*, a more somber novel. As it opens, Nina Gordon has returned to her North Carolina plantation from New York upon the death of her father. She has dallied with several suitors but has sense enough to prefer Edward Clayton, an idealistic young lawyer from another part of her native state. After successfully prosecuting a white man who had hired and then physically abused Nina's domestic slave Milly, Clayton's ambition to counteract such abuses legally is checked when an appeals judge—a man of undoubted probity and, ironically, Clayton's own father—reverses the earlier decision on the grounds that no slave has any rights under state law. Meanwhile, Nina's attempt at benign management of her plantation is set back by the appearance of her wastrel brother Tom, who especially enjoys tormenting her able quadroon steward Harry. Although bearing a strong resemblance to George Harris of *Uncle Tom's Cabin*, Harry is different in two important ways. First, Stowe develops the frustration of this educated and sensitive man much more thoroughly. Second, Harry is, unknown to Nina, the Gordon children's half brother.

When Nina dies in a cholera epidemic, Tom asserts control over the plantation, and Clayton returns home with the resolve to press for changes in a legal code that permits a man to own and mistreat his own brother. Harry is driven to rebel and flee into the nearby swamp, where he falls under the influence of Dred, whom the author styles after the son of the famous black rebel Denmark Vesey, but who resembles even more closely that other noted rebel, Nat Turner.

What happens next exemplifies Stowe's familiarity with the clergy and her talent for controversy. Invited by his uncle to a Presbyterian ministers' conference, Clayton seeks there the moral support for legal reform. Even though he finds one minister passionately committed to rights for slaves, the majority of the brethren turn out to be complacent trimmers, and Clayton learns that he can expect no help in that quarter. Stowe strategically places the conference between two scenes of desperation, both of which illustrate the social system's assault on the family. In the former, Uncle Tiff, the black guardian of two white children whose father is a shiftless squatter on the Gordon plantation, vows to preserve them from the corrupting influence of their slatternly stepmother and takes them to Dred's hidden fastness in the swamp. In the latter, another quadroon Gordon offshoot, Cora, confesses in court to the murder of her own two children to "save" them, as she puts it, from being sold away.

In the swamp, Tiff and the children are succored by Dred, who is one of Stowe's most bizarre creations: half Robin Hood, half self-appointed executioner for the Lord. Too mythic a hero for a realistic novel, Dred unfortunately develops quickly into a very tedious one too, ranting interminably in his guise of Old Testament prophet. Even he is no match, however, for the committed Christian Milly, although she can accomplish no more than the postponement of his planned revenge against the hated whites. When Tom Gordon organizes a party to ransack the swamp for Dred and Harry, the former is killed, and Harry and his wife, along with Tiff and his young charges, escape to the North. In an obviously Pyrrhic victory, Clayton, baffled by his neighbors in his attempt to educate the slaves on his own estate, takes them off to Canada, where they continue to work for him in their freedom.

Tiff is another saintly domestic slave, but he has no power to reclaim any Sambo or Quimbo from degradation. There are no spectacular personal conversions in *Dred* and no hope of any social one. Milly, who has had to endure the loss by death or sale of all her numerous children, seems to win a legal victory over a cruel master and a moral one over the vindictive fugitive Dred, but both turn out to be illusory. Not only the fugitive blacks but also Clayton the hero must leave the country. If *Uncle Tom's Cabin* stands as a warning to a divided society, *Dred* is a prophecy of disintegration.

The Minister's Wooing

Stowe's next two novels have much in common. Both *The Minister's Wooing* and *The Pearl of Orr's Island* are anchored in New England coastal communities, and both put

Yankee manners and speech on display. Each novel boasts a saintly heroine who effects the conversion of a dashing young man with a strong affinity for the sea. Although the former novel paints Newport, Rhode Island, less colorfully than the latter does coastal Maine, *The Minister's Wooing* is a more carefully constructed novel that analyzes New England character more profoundly.

More than any other Stowe novel, *The Minister's Wooing* focuses on its principals: Samuel Hopkins, Congregationalist minister of Newport, and Mary Scudder, daughter of Hopkins's widowed landlady. In several respects, the minister is the historical Dr. Hopkins, learned protégé of the great Jonathan Edwards, eminent theologian in his own right and vigorous opponent of slavery in a town consecrated to the slave trade. In the 1780's, when the novel is set, however, the real Hopkins was in his sixties and had a wife and eight children; Stowe makes him middle-aged and a bachelor. Another celebrity of the time plays a significant role: Aaron Burr in the years before he became senator, vice president, and killer of Alexander Hamilton in a duel. Burr is depicted as a charming, unscrupulous seducer of women—a distortion of the historical Burr, no doubt, but one based on his reputation.

Stowe's motive for involving these men in her story of pious young Mary Scudder is utterly serious. As friend and student of Edwards, Hopkins represents the stern, uncompromising Puritan past. As Edwards's worldly and skeptical grandson, Burr stands for the repudiation of the past. Mary's choice is not—what would be easy for her—between Hopkins and Burr but between Hopkins and her young lover James Marvyn, who resembles Burr only in his impatience with the hard and incomprehensible doctrines of his forebears. James has grown up with Mary but has gravitated to the sea, and he is not quite engaged to her when he is reported lost in a shipwreck. Mrs. Scudder thereafter nudges Mary toward a union with the unexciting minister, himself an admirer of the young lady's ardent—if for his taste too sunny—Christianity.

Stowe neatly balances the claims of Hopkins's exacting Old Testament theology and Mary's simpler faith in the loving kindness of Jesus. In comforting the lost James's mother, long appalled by the minister's remorseless logic and now driven to near psychosis by her son's supposed death, Mary's cheerful faith receives its first test. She also befriends an aristocratic young Frenchwoman—Burr's intended victim—and learns of the world of adulterous intrigue. As in her previous novels, Stowe introduces a black servant who has looked on life long and maintained a practical Christianity that is proof against all temptation to despair. Having been freed by her master, Mr. Marvyn, under the minister's influence, Candace works freely for the Marvyns and venerates Dr. Hopkins, not failing, however, to draw Mrs. Marvyn gently from "the fathomless mystery of sin and sorrow" to the "deeper mystery of God's love." Meanwhile, Mary's faith deepens, Stowe probably raising more than a few Protestant eyebrows by likening her explicitly to the Virgin Mary, who "kept all things and pondered them in her heart."

In real life, Catharine Beecher's beloved did not survive his shipwreck, and Stowe's elder sister agonized long over the possibility of his having died unregenerate. In life, Henry Stowe did not miraculously escape drowning. James Marvyn, on the other hand, after a considerable interval in which he inexplicably fails to notify either Mary or his family of his survival, returns a week before Mary's scheduled wedding with the minister. After having promised herself to Hopkins, Mary will not of course renege, so it falls to Miss Prissy, her dressmaker and friend, to approach the formidable theologian with the fact—which he is incapable of divining—that James is Mary's true love. Miss Prissy is one of Stowe's well-conceived realistic characters; an incurable gossip and a hypocrite in her professed admiration for the minister's sermons, she is nevertheless willing to assume the unpleasant initiative on behalf of her friend. Apprised of the true situation, the minister releases Mary and promptly marries her to Marvyn.

As she had in her first *Atlantic Monthly* short story, Stowe depicts in this novel the psychology of bereavement; what she refuses to present is not death itself but the possibility of a good-hearted lad dying unregenerate. She demonstrates how the rigorous faith of a Hopkins can be a barrier, even a poison, to the unstable, but of the efficacy of Christianity to restore lost lambs, she can conceive no doubt. Even the heterodox Burr nearly succumbs to Mary's entreaties to reform. Stowe's less saintly believers, such as Miss Prissy, and her magnanimous skeptics, like Augustine St. Clare of *Uncle Tom's Cabin*, are more credible. As for Hopkins, willing to jeopardize his church financially and socially by his insistence that the most influential of his parishioners renounce his connections with the slave trade, his final renunciation of Mary is quite consistent with his previous rock-ribbed selflessness.

OLDTOWN FOLKS

Oldtown Folks, at which Stowe worked in the postwar years and published whole in 1869—for she refused to serialize it in the usual way—repeats many of the concerns of *The Minister's Wooing* and even reintroduces Jonathan Edwards's grandson, here known as Ellery Davenport. Longer, more varied, and much more rambling, this novel contains a considerable amount of Stowe's best writing. In the preface, her narrator, Horace Holyoke, vows to "interpret to the world the New England life and character of the early republic." Today, no one would choose a loose, leisurely narrative to achieve such an ambition, and perhaps no one but Stowe would have attempted it in the 1860's. It is no coincidence that *Oldtown Folks* attracted the attention of Perry Miller, the distinguished twentieth century interpreter of the New England tradition.

The Minister's Wooing had been a theological novel in which no one had very much fun. As if to redress the deficiency, Stowe widens her focus, invests this work with more of the engaging minor characters of *The Pearl of Orr's Island*, and shows her villagers enjoying themselves. Her twenty-seventh chapter, "How We Kept Thanksgiving at Oldtown," which has become an anthology piece in recent years, argues that Oldtown (based on her husband's hometown of Natick, Massachusetts) has fun precisely because the inhabitants take human life seriously enough "to believe they can do much with it." Sam Lawson—Stowe's most famous character outside *Uncle Tom's Cabin*—far from exemplifying the protestant work ethic, is the town idler, universally valued for his skill at "lubricating" with his humorous anecdotes and relaxed manner the "incessant steampower in Yankee life." By contrast, the character most devoted to work, Miss Asphyxia Smith, is easily the most hateful character in the book.

Sam also serves the tenuous plot interest by coming upon two of its three principals (narrator Horace Holyoke is the other) in an abandoned house to which they had fled from Miss Asphyxia's clutches, for, like Uncle Tiff's young charges in *Dred*, Harry and Tina Percival have been successively deserted by their scalawag father and subjected to the slow death of their mother. Tina, who is adopted by Mehitabel Rossiter, a woman of no physical beauty but much strength of character and intellect, grows into a beautiful and kindhearted but willful woman—exactly the type favored by the unprincipled Davenport. Harry grows up as Horace's companion in the nearby Holyoke household.

Tina, not knowing that Davenport numbers among his previous victims Ellen Rossiter, Mehitabel's younger sister, marries him, and it appears that Stowe will not permit her protagonist the usual eleventh-hour rescue. Tina endures ten years with the erratic Davenport, generously adopting his daughter by Ellen Rossiter, but then, in a switch on the Burr story, Davenport is killed in a duel. Two years (but only three paragraphs) later, Tina and Horace marry and settle in Boston. At the end of the novel, the Horace Holyokes are discovered back in Oldtown visiting its most durable inhabitant, Sam Lawson.

Any synopsis leaves untouched the merits of *Oldtown Folks*: the interplay of its varied and vital minor characters and the development of its seduction theme. Of the former, Miss Asphyxia, "a great threshing-machine of a woman"; Horace's peppery grandmother, "a valiant old soul, who fearlessly took any bull in life by the horns, and was ready to shake him into decorum"; and Lawson, half nuisance, half good neighbor, are only three of the most memorable. As seducer, Davenport takes advantage of several factors: the intransigence of Calvinism in its death throes, embodied in brilliant but outdated theorizers such as this novel's version of Hopkins, Dr. Stern; the Calvinist legacy of neurosis, skepticism, and rebellion (Miss Rossiter, Tina, and Davenport himself); and the ineffectuality of well-intentioned observers such as Horace and Harry. Thwarted by orthodoxy, which has become a cruel instrument in the hands of its conservative defenders, and averse to the rationalism that played such a large part in the creation of the new republic, the Oldtowners are easily taken in by Davenport, who has turned the passion and intellectual energy inherited from Edwards and the rest of his Puritan forebears to the service of selfish and worldly ends.

MY WIFE AND I *and* WE AND OUR NEIGHBORS

In *My Wife and I* and its sequel, *We and Our Neighbors*, Stowe turns to contemporary Manhattan life, a frivolous and even more worldly existence dotted nevertheless by young men and women of impulses Stowe characterizes as Christian but that may strike today's reader as more generally humanitarian. The full spectrum of views on women's rights is on display, including a conviction, expressed by a young woman struggling for the opportunity to study medicine, that "marriage ought never to be entered on as a means of support." The main business of the two novels, however, is to educate Harry Henderson for marriage and thus to provide a base of operations for his wife, who dedicates herself to neighborliness and charitable offices. Stowe retains her observant eye and spicy descriptive powers, but her narrator cannot "interpret" the Gilded Age as Horace Holyoke in *Oldtown Folks* could interpret post-Revolutionary New England.

POGANUC PEOPLE

Pink and White Tyranny, the story of a man who married and must endure a selfish and demanding woman, must rank, along with the earlier *Agnes of Sorrento*, among Stowe's weakest books. Finally, in *Poganuc People*, she returns to the milieu of *The Minister's Wooing*, *The Pearl of Orr's Island*, and her Oldtown books.

Poganuc is the Litchfield of her childhood and Dolly Cushing her closet approximation to an autobiographical heroine. The principal conflict is not between the old religion and the new worldliness but between entrenched Congregationalism and upstart Episcopalianism. The novel begins and ends at Christmas, when the liturgical and social differences between the two denominations stand out most sharply. Like Maggie Tulliver in Eliot's *The Mill on the Floss* (1860), Dolly is precocious, sensitive, and consequently often uncomfortable, but instead of developing the crises of her heroine's maturation, as does Eliot, Stowe whisks her off to a fashionable Boston marriage with a successful merchant, after which the author makes a final survey of the Poganuc people going about their business under the immemorial elms of the village.

Stowe seldom brought her psychological insights to bear on the development of her main characters, with the result that the less important ones invariably seem more convincing. Whether because her most productive years antedated the time of the realist novel and particularly the psychological novel, or because she felt too strongly the nineteenth century prohibition against a woman exploring the conflicts and repressions of her own life, Stowe left unwritten what might have constituted her richest vein of realism. She never wrote a novel expressing what it felt like to be a vocationless Harriet Beecher approaching womanhood or a Harriet Beecher Stowe struggling with sickness, poverty, and the multitudinous demands of husband and children. The woman who wrote of domesticity in her time avoided calling attention to its tensions, exactions, and restrictions. Whatever else family life meant to Stowe, it helped prepare her to do what no American novelist had done before: write powerfully and feelingly about slavery.

Robert P. Ellis

OTHER MAJOR WORKS

SHORT FICTION: *The Mayflower: Or, Sketches of Scenes and Characters of the Descendants of the Pilgrims*, 1843; *Sam Lawson's Oldtown Fireside Stories*, 1872.

POETRY: *Religious Poems*, 1867.

NONFICTION: *A Key to Uncle Tom's Cabin*, 1853; *Sunny Memories of Foreign Lands*, 1854; *Lady Byron Vindicated*, 1870; *Palmetto Leaves*, 1873.

CHILDREN'S LITERATURE: *First Geography for Children*, 1833 (as Catharine Stowe).

MISCELLANEOUS: *The Oxford Harriet Beecher Stowe Reader*, 1999 (Joan D. Hedrick, editor).

BIBLIOGRAPHY

Ammons, Elizabeth, ed. *Critical Essays on Harriet Beecher Stowe*. Boston: G. K. Hall, 1980. This useful collection contains essays on Stowe by literary critics and feminist scholars. Dorothy Berkson's essay "Millennial Politics and the Feminine Fiction of Harriet Beecher Stowe" is particularly good.

Boydston, Jeanne, Mary Kelley, and Anne Margolis. *The Limits of Sisterhood: The Beecher Sisters on Women's Rights and Woman's Sphere*. Chapel Hill: University of North Carolina Press, 1988. A superb study of Stowe and her sisters, Catharine and Isabella. Brief but insightful essays address each woman as an individual and as a sister. Primary documents are appended to each chapter, providing excellent resources. Illustrations, careful documentation, and a detailed index make this an invaluable text.

Donovan, Josephine. *"Uncle Tom's Cabin": Evil, Affliction, and Redemptive Love*. Boston: Twayne, 1991. Places *Uncle Tom's Cabin* in literary and historical context. As her subtitle suggests, Donovan views Stowe's masterpiece as a book about evil and its redemption, taking it more or less at face value and reading it with the approach she believes Stowe intended—which has a decidedly feminist bent.

Hedrick, Joan D. *Harriet Beecher Stowe: A Life*. New York: Oxford University Press, 1994. Stowe's family kept a tight rein on her literary remains, and the only previous attempt at a full-scale independent biography, Forrest Wilson's *Crusader in Crinoline* (1941), is now very much out of date. Hedrick's book makes use of new materials, including letters and diaries, and takes fresh approaches to Stowe occasioned by the Civil Rights and women's movements.

Lang, Amy Schrager. *Prophetic Woman: Anne Hutchinson and the Problem of Dissent in the Literature of New England*. Berkeley: University of California Press, 1987. An excellent feminist study, focusing on *Uncle Tom's Cabin* and Stowe's role in the history of Puritan suppression of women who achieve public notice. Stowe's novel constitutes a culmination in this process and presents a model of women as moral superiors who represent the possibility of a future without slavery.

Riss, Arthur. *Race, Slavery, and Liberalism in Nineteenth-Century American Literature*. New York: Cambridge University Press, 2006. In his analysis of Stowe and two other writers who were involved in antebellum debates about slavery, Riss maintains that the proposition that "all men are created equal" can be an argument both for and against race-based slavery.

Robbins, Sarah. *The Cambridge Introduction to Harriet Beecher Stowe.* New York: Cambridge University Press, 2007. A concise introduction, designed to familiarize students and other readers with Stowe's work. Contains biographical information and analysis of Stowe's writings; discusses her life and work within the context of nineteenth century American literature, womanhood, racial politics, religion, and class identity. The final chapter surveys critical reception to her works in both the nineteenth and twentieth centuries.

Sundquist, Eric J., ed. *New Essays on "Uncle Tom's Cabin."* New York: Cambridge University Press, 1986. A collection of essays on Stowe's most famous novel. The introduction discusses changing literary theories as they relate to *Uncle Tom's Cabin.* The six diverse contributions by notable scholars include analyses of genre and gender issues. A selected bibliography also notes additional criticism.

Tompkins, Jane. *Sensational Designs: The Cultural Work of American Fiction, 1790-1860.* New York: Oxford University Press, 1985. Tompkins addresses *Uncle Tom's Cabin* from the perspective of "the politics of literary history." Nineteenth century popular domestic novels represent attempts to reorganize culture from a woman's perspective, and Stowe's novel is representative of "America's religion of domesticity" as empowerment of women. An excellent and influential study.

Weinstein, Cindy. *The Cambridge Companion to Harriet Beecher Stowe.* New York: Cambridge University Press, 2004. Collection of essays examining Stowe's works and literary influence, including analyses of *Uncle Tom's Cabin* and *The Pearl of Orr's Island* and discussions of race, regionalism, the law, and the American reform tradition.

ALICE WALKER

Born: Eatonton, Georgia; February 9, 1944
Also known as: Alice Malsenior Walker

Principal long fiction

The Third Life of Grange Copeland, 1970
Meridian, 1976
The Color Purple, 1982
The Temple of My Familiar, 1989
Possessing the Secret of Joy, 1992
By the Light of My Father's Smile, 1998
Now Is the Time to Open Your Heart, 2004

Other literary forms

Alice Walker has published many volumes of short fiction, poetry, and essays in addition to her novels, as well as several children's books. Walker was an early editor at *Ms.* magazine, in which many of her essays first appeared. Her interest in the then little-known writer Zora Neale Hurston led her to take a pilgrimage to Florida to place a tombstone on Hurston's unmarked grave and to her editing of *I Love Myself When I Am Laughing . . . and Then Again When I Am Looking Mean and Impressive: A Zora Neale Hurston Reader* (1979); she also provided an introduction to Robert Hemenway's *Zora Neale Hurston: A Literary Biography* (1977). In her collection of essays titled *We Are the Ones We Have Been Waiting For: Light in a Time of Darkness* (2006), Walker advocates an appreciation for the times in which we live, when social, political, and environmental progress is needed and can be made.

Achievements

Alice Walker's literary reputation is based primarily on her fiction, although her second book of poetry, *Revolutionary Petunias, and Other Poems* (1973), received the Lillian Smith Award and a nomination for a National Book Award. Her first short-story collection, *In Love and Trouble: Stories of Black Women* (1973), won the Rosenthal Award of the National Institute of Arts and Letters. In addition, Walker has been the recipient of a Charles Merrill writing fellowship, an award for fiction from the National Endowment for the Arts, and a Guggenheim Fellowship. She has also been a Bread Loaf Scholar and a fellow at the Radcliffe Institute. Walker's books have been translated into more than twenty-four languages.

Her first novel, *The Third Life of Grange Copeland*, was widely and enthusiastically reviewed in publications as varied as *The New Yorker*, *The New Republic*, and *The New York Times Book Review*, although journals aimed primarily at a black readership were often silent on the work or critical of its violence and graphic depiction of rural black life.

With the publication of *Meridian*, Walker's second novel, her work as a poet, novelist, essayist, editor, teacher, scholar, and political activist came together. *Meridian* was universally praised in scholarly journals, literary magazines, popular magazines, and black-oriented journals. Some critics, mainly black male reviewers, objected again to the honest, straightforward portrayals of black life in the South and to Walker's growing feminism, which they saw as being in conflict with her commitment to her race. Walker's third novel, *The Color Purple*, was widely acclaimed. Feminist and *Ms.* editor Gloria Steinem wrote that this novel "could be the kind of popular and literary event that transforms an intense reputation into a national one," and Peter Prescott's review in *Newsweek* began by saying, "I want to say at once that *The Color Purple* is an American novel of permanent importance." These accolades were substantiated when Walker received both the American Book Award and the 1983 Pulitzer Prize for fiction.

The Temple of My Familiar has been compared to Thomas Pynchon's *Gravity's Rainbow* (1973) in its revision of Western history as it has traditionally been understood and in Walker's use of various techniques such as oral storytelling, letters, and journals. This novel has also been criticized for what some have seen as its sentimental and clichéd language, however. Critics have appreciated *Possessing the Secret of Joy* for Walker's willingness to expose and critique the African practice of female circumcision, which Westerners find abhorrent. Some critics argue, however, that the novel is written from an ethnocentric viewpoint and does not consider the practice within the context of African culture. Reactions to *By the Light of My Father's Smile* have been widely varied, with some critics praising Walker's treatment of issues of sexuality, particularly the need for fathers to understand their daughters as sexual beings, and others asserting that Walker let her own political agenda steer the novel's plot and style. Similarly, while Walker's prose style in *Now Is the Time to Open Your Heart* has been described as fluent and evocative, the novel has also been criticized for a heavy-handed New Age spirituality.

Biography

Alice Malsenior Walker was born in Eatonton, Georgia, on February 9, 1944, the last of eight children of Willie Lee and Minnie Lou Grant Walker, sharecroppers in rural Georgia. Her relationship with her father, at first strong and valuable, became strained as she became involved in the civil rights and feminist movements. A moving depiction of her estrangement from her father occurs in her essay "My Father's Country Is the Poor," which appeared in *The New York Times* in 1977. For Walker, a loving and healthy mother-daughter relationship has endured over the years. An account of that relationship is central to her essays "In Search of Our Mothers' Gardens" and "Lulls—A Native Daughter Returns to the Black South" and in Mary Helen Washington's article "Her Mother's Gifts," in which Walker acknowledges that she often writes with her mother's voice—"Just as you have certain physical characteristics of your mother . . . when you're compelled to write her stories, it's because you recognize and prize those qualities of her in yourself."

One of the central events in Walker's childhood was a BB gun accident that left her, at age eight, blind in one eye. Scar tissue from that wound, both physical and psychological, seems to have left her with a compensating acuteness of vision, despite the conviction that she was permanently disfigured. Walker was affected enough by the accident to say in a 1974 interview with John O'Brien, "I have always been a solitary person, and since I was eight years old (and the recipient of a disfiguring scar, since corrected, somewhat), I have daydreamed—not of fairy-tales—but of falling on swords, of putting guns to my heart or head, and of slashing my wrists with a razor." Walker's partial blindness allowed her to attend Spelman College in Atlanta on a scholarship for the handicapped, following her graduation from Butler-Baker High School in 1961. She left Spelman after two years—which included summer trips to the Soviet Union and to Africa as part of a group called Experiment in International Living—for Sarah Lawrence College, from which she graduated in 1965.

Walker's political activity governed her movements during the years immediately following her college graduation: She spent the summer of 1965 in the Soviet Union and also worked for civil rights in Liberty County, Georgia. The next year she was a caseworker for New York City's Department of Social Services, and then a voter-registration worker in Mississippi. In 1967, she married Melvyn Leventhal, a civil rights lawyer, and moved to Jackson, Mississippi, where she continued her civil rights work, lived in the heart of the South as part of an interracial couple, and taught at Jackson State University, while continuing to write stories, poems, and essays. Walker's daughter, Rebecca Grant, was born in 1969. Walker taught at Tougaloo College in Mississippi for a year before returning to the East, where she was a lecturer in writing and literature at Wellesley College, an editor at *Ms.* magazine, and an instructor at the University of Massachusetts at Boston. By 1977, she had divorced her husband, accepted a position as associate professor of English at Yale University, and written six books, before moving to San Francisco in 1978 and writing a books of poems, *Good Night, Willie Lee, I'll See You in the Morning* (1979) and editing *I Love Myself When I Am Laughing . . . and Then Again When I Am Looking Mean and Impressive*, a collection of writings on Zora Neale Hurston, in the same year. These were followed by *You Can't Keep a Good Woman Down* (1981), a book of short stories.

After her 1982 novel *The Color Purple* won critical acclaim, Walker and her family shared the success with Eatonton. Walker's sister established The Color Purple Educational Scholarship Fund, and Walker adopted three elementary schools to help provide needed supplies for students who maintained above-average grades. Walker continued her activities in political forums as well, working for civil rights and protesting against nuclear weapons. She became a devoted and vocal objector to the practice of female genital mutilation ("female circumcision") in Africa, through public speaking and through her novel *Possessing the Secret of Joy* and her nonfiction book *Warrior Marks: Female Genital Mutilation and the Sexual Blinding of Women* (1993), which focus on the horrors and scars of this practice.

Walker also used her success to help other female writers. She advocated for classes in women's literature and helped promote the works of neglected female and black writers. In 1984, she began her own publishing company, Wild Trees Press. In 1994, Walker changed her name to Alice Tallulah-Kate Walker, and in 1997, the Alice Walker Literary Society was chartered at Spelman College. In 2007, Walker agreed to place her personal and literary archive at Emory University.

ANALYSIS

The story of Alice Walker's childhood scar provides the most basic metaphor of her novels: the idea that radical change is possible even under the worst conditions. Although she was never able to regain the sight in one eye, Walker's disfigurement was considerably lessened:

> I used to pray every night that I would wake up and somehow it would be gone. I couldn't look at people directly because I thought I was ugly. . . . Then when I was fourteen, I visited my brother Bill [who] took me to a hospital where they removed most of the scar tissue—and I was a *changed person*. I promptly went home, scooped up the best-looking guy, and by the time I graduated from high school, I was valedictorian, voted "Most Popular," and crowned queen!

The idea that change and personal triumph are possible despite the odds is central to all of Walker's writing. Her work focuses directly or indirectly on the ways of survival adopted by black women, usually in the South, and is presented in a prose style characterized by a distinctive combination of lyricism and unflinching realism. Walker's women attempt not merely to survive, but to survive completely with some sense of stability, despite the constant thread of family violence, physical and mental abuse, and a lack of responsibility on the part of the men in their lives. Walker is simultaneously a feminist and a supporter of civil rights, not only for African Americans but also for oppressed minorities everywhere.

Walker's vision was shaped in part by a work from the first flowering of black writing in America: Jean Toomer's *Cane* (1923). She said in 1974 about Toomer's book that "it has been reverberating in me to an astonishing degree. *I love it passionately*; could not possibly exist without it." Like *Cane*, the first part of which centers mainly on women in the South, Walker's novels are made up of nearly equal parts of poetry, portraiture, and drama, broken up into a series of sections and subsections. Other important literary influences on Walker include Zora Neale Hurston, from whom she inherited a love of black folklore; Flannery O'Connor, who wrote of southern violence and grotesqueries from her home in Milledgeville, Georgia, less than ten miles from Walker's childhood home; and Albert Camus, whose existentialism speaks to the struggle for survival and dignity in which Walker's characters are engaged.

Walker herself has defined her "preoccupations" as a novelist: "The survival, the survival *whole* of my people. But beyond that I am committed to exploring the oppressions, the insanities, the loyalties, and the triumphs of black women." *The Third Life of Grange Copeland*, on the surface a novel about the cycle of rage and violence torturing the lives of a father and his son, is as much about the recipients of that rage—the women and children whose lives are directly affected. Although the novel is unremitting in its picture of desperate poverty's legacy of hatred, hopelessness, and cruelty, it concludes optimistically with Ruth Copeland's hope for a release from sorrow through the redemption promised by the early days of the Civil Rights movement and by the knowledge and love inherited at the sacrificial death of her grandfather. These threads of political awareness and spirituality run throughout Walker's work.

THE THIRD LIFE OF GRANGE COPELAND

Writing in 1973, Walker observed that her first novel, *The Third Life of Grange Copeland*, "though sometimes humorous and celebrative of life, is a grave book in which the characters see the world as almost entirely menacing." This dark view of life is common to Grange Copeland, the patriarch of a family farming on shares in rural Georgia, his son Brownfield, and the wives and daughters of both men. For all these characters, the world is menacing because of the socioeconomic position they occupy at the bottom of the scale of the sharecropping system. Father and son menace each other in this novel because they are in turn menaced by rage born out of the frustration of the system. Although the white people of the book are nearly always vague, nameless, and impersonal, they and the system they represent have the ability to render both Grange and Brownfield powerless.

It is not accidental that these characters' names have agricultural connotations. "Grange" suggests a late nineteenth century association of farmers, a feudal farm and grain storage building, and a combination of graze and range, while "Brownfield" and "Copeland" are self-explanatory—for the inability to cope with the land is what leads both male characters along virtually parallel paths. For the father, the mere appearance of the white farm boss's truck is enough to turn his face "into a unnaturally bland mask, curious and unsettling to see." The appearance of the truck causes the son to be "filled with terror of this man who could, by his presence alone, turn his father into something that might as well have been a pebble or a post or a piece of dirt." Although Grange is, in this same image, literally a piece of land, he eventually returns to the South and learns to live self-sufficiently, farming a section of soil he tricked his second wife into giving to him. Brownfield, in contrast, is never able to escape from the sharecropping system, although he sees that, like his father, he is "destined to be no more than overseer, on the white man's plantation, of his own children." Brownfield is able to live obliviously on a farm in Georgia, content to blame all his problems on others. The poor rural black workers of this novel are themselves little more than a crop, rotated from farm to farm, producing a harvest of shame and hunger, cruelty and violence.

Unlike the men of the novel, the women are menaced by both blacks and whites, by both the agricultural system and the "strange fruit" it produces. Margaret, Grange's first wife, is both physically and mentally degraded by her husband and then sexually exploited by a white truck driver, resulting in her second pregnancy. Unable to cope with this situation, Grange deserts his family, after which his wife poisons both her child and herself. Following his father's pattern, Brownfield marries and begins to work the land, but after "a year when endless sunup to sundown work on fifty rich bottom acres of cotton land and a good crop brought them two diseased shoats for winter meat." he too begins to abuse his wife.

Although Brownfield's wife, Mem, is a schoolteacher intelligent enough to try to break the cycle of raising others people's crops, her brief rebellion against her husband's malevolent beatings and mental tortures is a failure: He is able to subjugate her through repeated pregnancies that sap her rebellion as they turn her once rich and strong body into a virtual wasteland of emaciation. Because her body, which represents the land of the South, is still able to produce children despite its depleted condition, Brownfield is enraged enough to murder her in retaliation for her physical shape: "He had murdered his wife because she had become skinny and had not, with much irritation to him, reverted, even when well-fed, to her former plumpness. . . . Plumpness and freedom from the land, from cows and skinniness, went all together in his mind." Despite his irrational abuse of her, Mem is not ashamed "of being black though, no matter what he said. . . . Color was something the ground did to the flowers, and that was an end to it."

What the ground did to these generations of southern black people is the subject of Walker's novel—the whole lurid history of violence, hatred, and guilt that she chronicles in this story of one family's griefs. By the book's end, Brownfield Copeland has murdered his wife and an unnamed albino baby, while Grange Copeland has murdered his son Brownfield—first spiritually, then physically—and indirectly has killed his first wife and her infant.

Walker's characters are allegorical representations of the classic modes of survival historically adopted by black Americans in dealing with their oppression. Brownfield identifies with whites by daydreaming of himself on a southern plantation, sipping mint juleps, and then by bargaining for his freedom with the sexual favors of black women. Both of Grange's wives attempt to be true to the white stereotype of black women as promiscuous sexual beings, free of any moral restraints. Brownfield's wife, Mem, attempts the passive resistance advocated by Martin Luther King, Jr., but she is destroyed by what her husband calls "her weakness . . . forgiveness, a stupid belief that kindness can convert the enemy." Brownfield's daughter, Daphne, who calls herself the Copeland Family Secret Keeper, tries the strategy of inventing a falsely romantic history of the past, of the good old days when her father was kind, echoing those historical revisionists who try to argue that slavery was not that bad. Brownfield's other daughters try to stay away from their father altogether, regarding him "as a human devil" of whom they were afraid "in a more distant, impersonal way. He was like bad weather, a toothache, daily bad news."

Each of the title character's three lives (at home in the South as a sharecropper married to Margaret; in the North as a hustler of alcohol, drugs, and women; and finally back in the South as a farmer married to Josie and rearing his granddaughter Ruth) parallels a traditional survival strategy, which Grange summarizes as follows: "The white folks hated me and I hated myself until I started hating them in return and loving myself. Then I tried just loving me, and then you, and *ignoring* them much as I could." To put it another way, Grange tries at first to adapt to the system by believing what whites say about blacks; then he turns to the classic escape of the runaway slave—heading North to freedom; finally, he tries the technique of praising black life while ignoring whites altogether. A large part of the novel's devastation is caused by the repeated use of these techniques, not against whites, but against other members of the Copeland family. Only Ruth, the granddaughter through whom Grange seeks redemption, is able to deal with whites in an intelligent, balanced, nondestructive yet independent way. She has learned from her grandfather, and from her family history, that pure hatred becomes self-hatred, and violence begets self-violence; she therefore becomes the novel's symbol of the new black woman, ready to assume her place in black history as a courageous worker in the Civil Rights movement, which the rest of her family has been groping to discover.

MERIDIAN

Walker's second novel, *Meridian*, picks up chronologically and thematically at the point where her first novel ends. *Meridian* describes the struggles of a young black woman, Meridian Hill, about the same age as Ruth Copeland, who comes to an awareness of power and feminism during the Civil Rights movement, and whose whole life's meaning is centered in the cycles of guilt, violence, hope, and change characteristic of that dramatic time. Thematically, *Meridian* picks up the first novel's theme of self-sacrificial murder as a way out of desperate political oppression in the form of the constant question that drives Meridian Hill: "Will you kill for the Revolution?" Meridian's lifelong attempt to answer that question affirmatively (as her college friends so easily do) while remaining true to her sense of responsibility to the past, her sense of ethics, and her sense of guilt of having given to her mother the child of her teenage pregnancy constitutes the section of the novel titled "Meridian."

The second third of the novel, "Truman Held," is named for the major male character in the narrative. The third major section of the novel, "Ending," looks back at the turmoil of the Civil Rights movement from the perspective of the 1970's. Long after others have given up intellectual arguments about the morality of killing for revolution, Meridian is still debating the question, still actively involved in voter registration, political activism, and civil rights organization, as though the movement had never lost momentum. Worrying that her actions, now seen as eccentric rather than revolutionary, will cause her "to be left, listening to the old music, beside the highway," Meridian achieves release and atonement through the realization that her role will be to "come forward and sing from memory songs they will need once more to hear. For it is the song of the people, transformed by the experiences of each generation, that holds them together."

In 1978, Walker described *Meridian* as "a book 'about' the Civil Rights movement, feminism, socialism, the shakiness of revolutionaries and the radicalization of saints." Her word "about" is exact, for all of these topics revolve not chronologically but thematically around a central point—the protagonist, Meridian Hill. In some ways, Meridian *is* a saint; by the book's end she has sustained her belief in the Civil Rights movement without losing faith in feminism and socialism, despite family pressures, guilt, literally paralyzing self-doubts, the history of the movement, and the sexism of many of its leaders. In contrast, Truman Held represents those males who were reported to have said that "the only position for a woman in the movement is prone."

Although Truman Held is Meridian's initial teacher in the movement, she eventually leaves him behind because of his inability to sustain his initial revolutionary fervor and because of his misogyny. Unlike Brownfield Copeland, Truman argues that women are of less value than they should be, not because of skinniness, but because "black women let themselves go . . . they are so fat." Later in the novel, Truman marries a white civil rights worker whose rape by another black man produces disgust in him, as much at his wife as at his friend. When Truman seeks Meridian out in a series of small southern hamlets where she continues to persuade black people to register to vote and to struggle for civil rights, he tells her that the movement is ended and that he grieves in a different way than she. Meridian answers, "I know how you grieve by running away. By pretending you were never there." Like Grange Copeland, Truman Held refuses to take responsibility for his own problems, preferring to run away to the North.

Meridian's sacrificial dedication to the movement becomes a model for atonement and release, words that once formed the working title of the book. *Meridian* could also have been called "The Third Life of Meridian Hill" because of similarities between Meridian's life and Grange Copeland's. Meridian leads three lives: as an uneducated child in rural Georgia who follows the traditional pattern of early pregnancy and aimless marriage, as a college student actively participating in political demonstrations, and as an eccentric agitator—a performer, she calls herself—unaware that the movement has ended. Like Grange Copeland in another sense, Meridian Hill is solid proof of the ability of any human to change dramatically by sheer will and desire.

Meridian is always different from her friends, who, filled with angry rhetoric, ask her repeatedly if she is willing to kill for the revolution, the same question that Grange asked himself when he lived in the North. This question haunts Meridian, because she does not know if she can or if she should kill, and because it reminds her of a similar request, posed in a similar way by her mother: "Say it now, Meridian, and be saved. All He asks is that we acknowledge Him as our Master. Say you believe in Him . . . don't go against your heart." In neither case is Meridian able to answer yes without going against her heart. Unlike her college friends and Truman Held, who see the movement only in terms of future gains for themselves, Meridian is involved with militancy because of her past: "But what none of them seemed to understand was that she felt herself to be, not holding on to something from the past, but *held* by something in the past."

Part of the past's hold on her is the sense of guilt she feels about her relationships with her parents. Although her father taught her the nature of the oppression of minorities through his knowledge of American Indians, her strongest source of guilt comes from her mother, who argues, like Brownfield Copeland, that the responsibility for all problems stems from outside oneself: "The answer to everything," said Meridian's mother, "is we live in America and we're not rich." Meridian's strongest sense of past guilt comes from the knowledge she gains when she becomes pregnant: "It was for stealing her mother's serenity, for shattering her mother's emerging self, that Meridian felt guilty from the very first, though she was unable to understand how this could possibly be her fault."

Meridian takes the form of a series of nonchronological sections, some consisting of only a paragraph, some four or five pages long, that circle around the events of Meridian's life. The writing is clear, powerful, violent, lyrical, and often symbolic. Spelman College, for example, is here called Saxon College. The large magnolia tree in the center of the campus, described with specific folkloric detail, is destroyed by angry students during a demonstration: "Though Meridian begged them to dismantle the president's house instead, in a fury of confusion and frustration they worked all night, and chopped and sawed down, level to the ground, that mighty, ancient, sheltering music tree." This tree (named The Sojourner, perhaps for Sojourner Truth) expands symbolically to suggest both the senseless destruction of black ghettos by blacks during the turmoil of the 1960's and Meridian Hill herself, who receives a photograph years later of The Sojourner, now "a gigantic tree stump" with "a tiny branch, no larger than a finger, growing out of one side." That picture, suggesting as it does the rebirth of hope despite despair, also evokes the last vision of Meridian expressed by the now-shamed Truman Held: "He would never see 'his' Meridian again. The new part had grown out of the old, though, and that was reassuring. This part of her, new, sure and ready, even eager, for the world, he knew he must meet again and recognize for its true value at some future time."

THE COLOR PURPLE

Like Walker's first two novels, *The Color Purple* is unusual in style: It presents the author's familiar and yet fresh themes—survival and redemption—in epistolary form. Most of the novel's letters are written by Celie, an uneducated, unloved black woman living in rural Georgia in the 1920's; Celie's letters are written in what Walker calls "black folk English," a language of wit, strength, and natural humor. Ashamed of having been raped by her stepfather, a man whom Celie thinks at the time is her father, she begins to send letters to God, in the way that children send letters to Santa Claus, because her rapist told her to tell nobody but God. Although her early letters tell of rape, degradation, and pain, of her stepfather's getting rid of the two children born of his cruelty, the tone is nevertheless captivating, ironic, and even humorous. Soon the despair turns into acceptance, then into understanding, anger, rebellion, and finally triumph and loving forgiveness as the fourteen-year-old Celie continues to write until she reaches an audience, some thirty years later. Like the author, who began writing at the age of eight and has turned her childhood experiences in rural Georgia into novels of violence, hatred, understanding, love, and profound hope for the future, Celie is a writer, a listener, a thinker, and a promoter of Walker's constant theme: "Love redeems, meanness kills."

Like Meridian Hill, Celie compares herself to a tree. After her stepfather's repeated rapes, Celie is sold into a virtual state of slavery to a man who beats her, a man she does not know, love, or talk to, a man she can never call anything but Mr. ——, an ironic throwback to a convention of the eighteenth century English epistolary novel. Celie tries to endure by withholding all emotion: "I make myself wood. I say to myself, Celie, you a tree. That's how come I know trees fear man." Like The Sojourner, or like the kudzu vine of the deep South that thrives despite repeated attempts to beat it back, Celie continues to express her fears and hopes in a series of letters written in a form of black English that is anything but wooden. The contrast between the richly eccentric prose of Celie's letters and the educated yet often lifeless sentences of her sister Nettie's return letters supports Walker's statement that "writing *The Color Purple* was writing in my first language." The language of the letters is at first awkward, but it is never difficult to follow. As Celie grows in experience, in contact with the outside world, and in confidence, her writing gradually becomes more sophisticated and more like standard written English, but it never loses its originality of rhythm and phrase.

Based on Walker's great-grandmother, a slave who was raped at age twelve by her owner, Celie works her way from ignorance about her body and her living situation all the way through to an awakening of her self-worth as well as to an understanding of the existence of God, the relations between men and women, and the power of forgiveness in uniting family and friends. Much of this transformation is brought about through the magic of a blues singer named Shug Avery, who guides Celie in understanding sexuality, men, and religion without causing her to lose her own fresh insights, naïve though they are.

The letters that make up the novel are something like the missives that the protagonist of Saul Bellow's novel *Herzog* (1964) writes but never sends, in that they are often addressed to God and written in an ironic but not self-conscious manner. Because of the combination of dark humor and despair, the letters also evoke memories of the desperate letters from the physically and spiritually maimed addressed to the hero of Nathanael West's *Miss Lonelyhearts* (1933). Although Celie is unlettered in a traditional sense, her ability to carry the complicated plot forward and to continue to write—first without an earthly audience, and then to her sister, whom she has not seen for more than twenty years—testifies to the human potential for self-transformation.

Discussing Celie's attempts to confirm her existence by writing to someone she is not certain exists, Gloria Steinem says, "Clearly, the author is telling us something about the origin of Gods: about when we need to invent them and when we don't." In a sense, Shug Avery becomes a god for Celie because of her ability to control the evil in the world and her power to change the sordid conditions of Celie's life. Early in the book, when Celie is worrying about survival, about rape, incest, beatings, and the murder of her children, her only source of hope is the name "Shug Avery," a name with a magical power to control her husband. Not even aware that Shug is a person, Celie writes, "I ast our new mammy bout Shug Avery. What it is?" Finding a picture of Shug, Celie transfers her prayers to what is at that point only an image: "I see her there in furs. Her face rouge. Her hair like somethin tail. She grinning with her foot up on somebody motocar. Her eyes serious tho. Sad some. . . . An all night long I stare at it. An now when I dream, I dream of Shug Avery. She be dress to kill, whirling an laughing." Shug Avery becomes a god to Celie not only because she is pictured in the first photograph Celie has ever seen but also because she is dressed in a style that shows a sense of pride and freedom.

Once Celie's sister's letters begin to appear, mailed from Africa, where Nettie is a missionary, the ironic connection between the primitive animism of the Africans and Celie's equally primitive reaction to Shug's picture becomes clear. Although Nettie has crossed the ocean to minister to a tribe of primitive people, her own sister is living in inhuman conditions in Georgia: ignorance, disease, sexism, lack of control of the environment, and the ever-increasing march of white people. When Shug explains her own animistic religious beliefs—which include the notion that God is not a he or a she but an it (just as Celie once thought Shug Avery was an it)—Celie is converted to a pantheistic worship that makes her early identification with trees seem less naïve.

When the narrator of Herman Melville's "Bartleby the Scrivener" (1853) tries to explain Bartleby's withdrawal from life, he thinks of the dead-letter office in which the scrivener was rumored to have worked and says, "On errands of life, these letters speed to death." In contrast, Celie's and Nettie's letters, ostensibly written to people long thought to be dead, speed across the ocean on errands of life, where they grow to sustain not only the sisters in the book but also all those lucky enough to read them. As the author says of *The Color Purple*, "It's my happiest book . . . I had to do all the other writing to get to this point." For the reader who has gotten to this point in Walker's career by reading all of her other books, there is no question that Walker's name could be substituted for Celie's in the author's statement about her most recent novel: "Let's hope people can hear Celie's voice. There are so many people like Celie who make it, who come out of nothing. People who triumph."

POSSESSING THE SECRET OF JOY

The novels *By the Light of My Father's Smile* and *Possessing the Secret of Joy* share strong characters whose sexual identities suffer because of the need of the individuals to conform to the societies in which they live. Only through death can Tashi and Mad Dog become complete and escape the male-dominated world and its restrictions.

Walker combines fact and fiction in *Possessing the Secret of Joy* to illustrate the effects that female genital mutilation has on the women who are subjected to the procedure. The main character, Tashi, an African tribal woman, willingly undergoes the traditional ritual of genital mutilation because of her desire to conform to her culture and feel complete. The procedure, however, leaves her physically and mentally scarred. Tashi realizes that she has been destroyed emotionally and made to feel as if she were something other than her true self. After her mutilation, she marries Adam Johnson and moves to the United States. She is renamed Evelyn Johnson, and the shift of her chapter headings from "Tashi" to "Evelyn" demonstrates the conflict within her as she struggles to find her true identity. That conflict leads her to madness.

Tashi strives to understand her insanity and to interpret her recurring nightmares of a tower. With the help of her therapists, Mzee and Raye, and the members of her family, Tashi realizes the reasons for her insanity and gradually becomes stronger and able to face her nightmares and what they represent. The story is related through the eyes of all the main characters, a technique that provides insight into the effects that Tashi has on those around her. Through its main characters—Tashi, Olivia, and Adam—*Possessing the Secret of Joy* is connected to, but is not a sequel to, Walker's previous novels *The Color Purple* and *The Temple of My Familiar*.

By the Light of My Father's Smile

Walker's sixth novel, *By the Light of My Father's Smile*, follows the Johnson family on a journey through life and to rebirth through death. Magdalena, referred to as Mad Dog, discovers her sensuality and its connection with her spirituality while living with her parents in Mexico, where the parents are pretending to be missionaries in order to do an anthropological study of the Mundo people. Magdalena is acutely aware of her emotions and sensuality, and she is severely beaten by her father when he discovers her sexual activity.

Magdalena's sister Susannah, shadowed by Magdalena's anger and frustration, is awakened to her true desires by her friend Irene, who is able to survive and accept life on her own terms despite the restrictions placed on her by her society. Susannah realizes that her unhappiness is the result of having been "sucked into the black cloth" and hypocrisy of the world. All of the members of the Johnson family suffer through life searching for true love and happiness, which they find only in death. The story moves between the spiritual world and the physical world as the father watches his two daughters come to terms with their anger and their true spirits. As characters pass into the spiritual world, they are enlightened to their failings in the physical world and make amends with those they have injured. Only when acceptance of each soul is obtained can the four family members cross the river and live in eternity.

NOW IS THE TIME TO OPEN YOUR HEART

In *Now Is the Time to Open Your Heart*, Walker continues her theme of sexual and spiritual exploration. The novel opens with Kate Talkingtree, a fifty-seven-year-old African American woman, meditating in a group, in a large hall surrounded by redwood trees. When the group's teacher begins to speak, Kate notices his southern European appearance and notes the description on the program that shows he has had a privileged upbringing among "educated and cultured people"; he has studied and lived in Europe and has been a "prominent professor at one of the country's most famous universities." As Kate looks around the circle, she notices that others in it have what she considers the same air of entitlement and that she is the only person of color there; for Kate, this makes what the teacher has said about "hot" revolutions in such countries as Africa and Cuba being less successful than the "cool" one introduced by Buddha twenty-five hundred years ago seem disingenuous. Unable to meditate from this point on and then awakening from a dream in which she has found an anaconda in her freezer and feels the need to kill it before it thaws, Kate decides that she must have a different kind of spiritual adventure.

As her lover, Yolo, watches her leave, Kate departs for a rafting expedition on the Colorado River with other women who are also seeking spiritual enlightenment. Although the pitching and plunging of the boat makes Kate ill, the nurturing and care that she receives from the other women contribute to a cleansing process as Kate remembers failed relationships, including the husband who became physically abusive when she suggested that they spend time apart and the opportunistic woman she married, who, it turned out, only wanted Kate for what she could get from her financially. At the same time Kate is having her spiritual retreat, Yolo is on his own quest, vacationing in Hawaii, where he encounters on the beach the body of a young man who has died from an overdose of crystal methamphetamine. Yolo meets the man's mother, Alma, who explains that the drug has taken over the island.

Meanwhile, Kate listens to the stories of other women on the rafting expedition, including Lalika, who explains that she has been "incested" from the time she was able to crawl and was raped and beaten by patrolmen in the prison where she was incarcerated after murdering a man who raped her. Through the guidance of leaders Armando and Anunu, Kate begins to discover her own spiritual strength. When Kate and Yolo return from their adventures—Kate having healed her own wounds by communing with others among the walking wounded, and Yolo having helped a grieving mother heal as well as learning about the destructiveness of colonialism to indigenous Hawaiian culture—they realize that they are each other's spiritual partners and invite those they met on their journeys to their nontraditional wedding.

Timothy Dow Adams; Mary A. Blackmon
Updated by Holly L. Norton

OTHER MAJOR WORKS

SHORT FICTION: *In Love and Trouble: Stories of Black Women*, 1973; *You Can't Keep a Good Woman Down*, 1981; *The Complete Stories*, 1994; *Alice Walker Banned*, 1996 (stories and commentary).

POETRY: *Once: Poems*, 1968; *Five Poems*, 1972; *Revolutionary Petunias, and Other Poems*, 1973; *Good Night, Willie Lee, I'll See You in the Morning: Poems*, 1979; *Horses Make a Landscape Look More Beautiful*, 1984; *Her Blue Body Everything We Know: Earthling Poems, 1965-1990 Complete*, 1991; *Absolute Trust in the Goodness of the Earth: New Poems*, 2003; *A Poem Traveled Down My Arm: Poems and Drawings*, 2003.

NONFICTION: *In Search of Our Mothers' Gardens: Womanist Prose*, 1983; *Living by the Word: Selected Writings, 1973-1987*, 1988; *Warrior Marks: Female Genital Mutilation and the Sexual Blinding of Women*, 1993 (with Pratibha Parmar); *The Same River Twice: Honoring the Difficult*, 1996; *Anything We Love Can Be Saved: A Writer's Activism*, 1997; *The Way Forward Is with a Broken Heart*, 2000; *Sent by Earth: A Message from the Grandmother Spirit After the Attacks on the World Trade Center and Pentagon*, 2001; *We Are the Ones We Have Been Waiting For: Light in a Time of Darkness*, 2006.

CHILDREN'S LITERATURE: *Langston Hughes: American Poet*, 1974; *To Hell with Dying*, 1988; *Finding the Green Stone*, 1991; *There Is a Flower at the Tip of My Nose Smelling Me*, 2006; *Why War Is Never a Good Idea*, 2007.

EDITED TEXT: *I Love Myself When I Am Laughing . . . and Then Again When I Am Looking Mean and Impressive: A Zora Neale Hurston Reader*, 1979.

BIBLIOGRAPHY

Bates, Gerri. *Alice Walker: A Critical Companion*. Westport, Conn.: Greenwood Press, 2005. Well-crafted work presents biographical material and also discusses Walker's major works, tracing the themes of her novels to events in her life.

Bloom, Harold, ed. *Alice Walker*. New York: Chelsea House, 1989. Collection of important critical essays, arranged chronologically, examines Walker's fiction, poetry, and essays from a variety of perspectives. Provides useful discussions of her first three novels and assessments of her social and political views in connection with her works and those of other African American female authors. Includes an informative editor's introduction and a chronology of Walker's life.

_______. *Alice Walker's "The Color Purple."* Philadelphia: Chelsea House, 2000. Collection of essays by such eminent critics as Henry Louis Gates, Jr., and bell hooks examines the themes and techniques in Walker's most popular and critically acclaimed novel.

Bloxham, Laura J. "Alice [Malsenior] Walker." In *Contemporary Fiction Writers of the South*, edited by Joseph M. Flora and Robert Bain. Westport, Conn.: Greenwood Press, 1993. Provides a general introduction to Walker's "womanist" themes of the oppression of black women and change through affirmation of self. Also presents a brief summary and critique of previous criticism of Walker's work.

Dieke, Ikenna, ed. *Critical Essays on Alice Walker.* New York: Greenwood Press, 1999. Collection of essays pays particular attention to Walker's poetry and to her developing ecofeminism.

Dixon, Henry O. *Male Protagonists in Four Novels of Alice Walker: Destruction and Development in Interpersonal Relationships.* Lewiston, N.Y.: Edwin Mellen Press, 2007. Examines the roles that male characters play in four of Walker's early novels: *The Third Life of Grange Copeland*, *Meridian*, *The Color Purple*, and *The Temple of My Familiar.*

Gates, Henry Louis, Jr., and K. A. Appiah, eds. *Alice Walker: Critical Perspectives Past and Present.* New York: Amistad, 1993. Collection presents reviews of Walker's first five novels and critical analyses of several of her works of short and long fiction. Also includes two interviews with Walker, a chronology of her works, and an extensive bibliography of essays and texts.

Lauret, Maria. *Alice Walker.* New York: St. Martin's Press, 2000. Offers provocative discussion of Walker's ideas on politics, race, feminism, and literary theory. Of special interest is the exploration of Walker's literary debt to Zora Neale Hurston, Virginia Woolf, and even blues singer Bessie Smith.

Montelaro, Janet J. *Producing a Womanist Text: The Maternal as Signifier in Alice Walker's "The Color Purple."* Victoria, B.C.: English Literary Studies, University of Victoria, 1996. Examines the themes of feminism and motherhood in Walker's novel.

Wade-Gayles, Gloria. "Black, Southern, Womanist: The Genius of Alice Walker." In *Southern Women Writers: The New Generation*, edited by Tonette Bond Inge. Tuscaloosa: University of Alabama Press, 1990. Provides an excellent, thorough introduction to Walker's life and literary career. Emphasizes Walker's voice as a black, southern woman throughout her works and argues that Walker's commitment is to the spiritual wholeness of her people.

White, Evelyn C. *Alice Walker: A Life.* New York: W. W. Norton, 2004. Comprehensive biography chronicles the events of Walker's life. Draws on interviews with Walker, her family members, and her friends.

COLSON WHITEHEAD

Born: New York, New York; 1969
Also known as: Arch Colson Chipp Whitehead

PRINCIPAL LONG FICTION

The Intuitionist, 1999
John Henry Days, 2001
Apex Hides the Hurt, 2006
Sag Harbor, 2009

OTHER LITERARY FORMS

Although Colson Whitehead is primarily a novelist, he has also published the collection of essays *The Colossus of New York: A City in Thirteen Parts* (2003), a work that makes clear the importance of place and surroundings for him. Working as a journalist and as a critic of books, music, and television has enabled Whitehead to develop the keen sense of language and its nuances that plays a significant role in his fiction. He has published articles in a wide variety of publications, including *The New York Times*, *Salon*, *Spin*, *New York Magazine*, *Harper's*, and *Granta*.

ACHIEVEMENTS

Colson Whitehead was heralded as a talented writer from the publication of his first novel. *The Intuitionist* received the New Voices Award presented by the Quality Paperback Book Club and was a finalist in the competition for the Hemingway Foundation/PEN Award. Whitehead was from this first endeavor opening the way for a new type of novel that defies classification. *The Intuitionist* can be read as an allegory, as a detective novel, or even as a comedic tale. His next novel, *John Henry Days*, further broke the boundaries of the traditional novel with its multilevel structure, its satire, and its probing look at historical and contemporary racism. The work received the Young Lions Award and was a finalist for both the National Book Critics Circle Award and the Pulitzer Prize. Whitehead's ability to create fiction that goes beyond the traditional norms of the genre earned him a MacArthur Fellowship in 2002. His work continues the tradition of the intellectual black novel, which is part of the canon of African American literature.

BIOGRAPHY

Arch Colson Chipp Whitehead was born in Manhattan in New York City in 1969; he grew up in the Fort Greene neighborhood in Brooklyn. He attended Trinity School and Harvard University, and after graduating from Harvard in 1991, he began a career in journalism as a pop-culture critic for *The Village Voice*. At first he wrote about books and music; later, he became the newspaper's television columnist.

Whitehead first decided he wanted to be a writer of fiction when he was a child and began reading Stephen King's books. While in college, he discovered the works of more authors who increased his desire to write, including the fiction of Thomas Pynchon and Ishmael Reed. In 1999, Whitehead published his first novel, *The Intuitionist*. His second novel, *John Henry Days*, followed in 2001. His next publication was the collection of essays *The Colossus of New York*, which appeared in 2003. In this nonfiction work composed of personal memories, vignettes, and meditations, Whitehead captures all of the varied and often contradictory qualities of New York City. In 2006, he returned to fiction with the publication of another novel, *Apex Hides the Hurt*. His fourth novel, *Sag Harbor*, published in 2009, is a semiautobiographical story. Whitehead is a fellow at the Cullman Center for Scholars and Writers.

Analysis

Colson Whitehead writes novels that break the traditional rules of fiction writing. His works defy classification into the standard categories. In *The Intuitionist*, the inclusion of features of the detective story add to the intrigue of the novel, but at the same time the work satirizes the detective story. The novel is really neither satire nor detective fiction per se. The setting of *The Intuitionist* is anachronistic: The city in which the fiction takes place is futuristic in the technology depicted and in the focus of the inhabitants on verticality; in this world, elevators are the cornerstone of society. Ethically and morally, however, the inhabitants of the city resemble people living in a city in the United States in the mid-twentieth century.

In *John Henry Days*, Whitehead experiments even more with the novel form. He exercises his privilege as author to take the narrative where he wishes, ignoring any traditional formula. The work includes many digressions and interpolated stories as Whitehead presents events without regard for chronological order. There is a shooting in the novel that Whitehead recounts very early in the work and then again near the end—and neither time does he reveal who was killed. The novel ends without closure; rather, the reader is left to finish the story.

The Intuitionist

The Intuitionist is a combination of allegory, detective novel, futuristic novel, and social satire that addresses prejudice and racial discrimination. The story is set in a large metropolitan city in the middle of the twentieth century. The society is highly advanced technologically and totally devoted to a cult of elevators. Progress is linked to verticality and its improvement, and modernization and success are equated with upward mobility. Everyone reads *Lift*, a weekly magazine that informs the public about what is happening in the elevator industry. Other aspects of the society contrast sharply with its technologically advanced status, however. Political corruption, exploitation, and racial prejudice govern everyday life. Technologically the society is futuristic, but morally it remains locked in a

1940's or 1950's mentality. Using elements of the detective story of the mid-twentieth century—such as mobsters, abandoned warehouses, and late-night assignations—Whitehead gives the story an ambiance of believability.

The Intuitionist recounts the trials of Lila Mae Watson, an African American elevator inspector. She works for the Department of Elevator Inspectors, which, in this verticality obsessed society, is one of the most powerful departments, possibly the most powerful, in the metropolis. All elevator inspectors adhere to one of two different approaches to elevator inspection: An elevator inspector is either an Empiricist or an Intuitionist. An Empiricist inspects an elevator by getting into the elevator shaft and checking the mechanism to see if it meets the specifications. An Intuitionist, in contrast, evaluates the condition of an elevator by listening and by feeling the mechanism's vibrations, becoming one with the elevator. The department is heavily staffed by Empiricists, and Lila Mae is an Intuitionist. Lila Mae's life is a constant ordeal, as she is marginalized by her race, her sex, and her adherence to Intuitionist theory.

In spite of her exclusion, Lila Mae has an impressive record as an inspector and is assigned to inspect the elevators in the Fanny Briggs Memorial Building. A short time after she has inspected the elevators there, one of the elevators crashes. This is a catastrophe for her, given that it could mean the end of her career, and she becomes determined to find out what happened. The Elevator Guild is in the process of electing a new guild chair; the two candidates are Frank Chancre, an Empiricist, and Orville Lever, an Intuitionist. Lila Mae becomes convinced that Chancre, who is known to have connections to a mob boss, has had the elevator sabotaged.

Whitehead complicates his narrative by adding another intrigue: Suddenly papers from the research of the late James Fulton, father of Intuitionism, start showing up with Lila Mae's name on them. Fulton had been researching a black box, the perfect next-generation elevator. Lila Mae decides that she must find the blueprints for the black box and at the same time exonerate herself in regard to the crash. Whitehead turns his narrative into a detective novel as he relates Lila Mae's search, which involves deceptions, false leads, and mob enforcers, and an ambiance of danger invades the narrative. After he has led the reader as well as Lila Mae down a number of false trails, Whitehead concludes the story in a totally unexpected way. The elevator was not sabotaged, it just did a free fall, as elevators sometimes do. Arbo Elevators believed that Lila Mae had Fulton's papers on the black box, and the company wanted them to avoid bankruptcy. Whitehead then adds a section on Fulton's thoughts during his last working days and concludes the novel with Lila Mae, who has become obsessed with completing Fulton's research, alone in a small room working to create the perfect elevator.

In *The Intuitionist* Whitehead uses the metaphor of verticality to delineate African Americans' difficulty in being upwardly mobile in a racially prejudiced society. He develops this theme through the characters of Lila Mae and James Fulton. Lila Mae's father was an elevator operator in a department store where no African Americans were allowed, with the exception of those who worked there. Lila Mae is determined to achieve upward mobility through her own efforts. She puts up with living in a converted janitor's closet at the elevator inspectors' academy, and nothing—not the ransacking of her apartment, her kidnapping by Chancre's thugs, or her deception by Fulton's false nephew—deters her from her goal. Lila Mae is determined to succeed in spite of a system that puts every obstacle in her way.

James Fulton, a light-skinned African American, had been able to achieve upward mobility because of his ability to pass for white. He had become a respected researcher in verticality, in upward mobility in elevators, but throughout his life he knew that the discovery of his true racial identity would have destroyed his career and denied him acceptance in society. Consequently, infuriated and seeking revenge, he played a joke on everyone by creating the concept of the black box. The perfect elevator that was to transform the city's landscape was not real—it was simply a trick that the clever Fulton played to get back at the prejudiced closed society in which he lived.

JOHN HENRY DAYS

John Henry Days incorporates allegory, comedy, pathos, satire, and social realism while at the same time elucidating the dilemma of keeping history and myth alive in a mechanized, materialistic world of consumerism. The novel is set in 1996 during John Henry Days—a festival honoring the American folk legend—in Talcott, West Virginia. At the same time, the post office in Talcott is issuing a new commemorative stamp featuring John Henry—part of a series honoring other American folk legends as well, such as Paul Bunyan and Pecos Pete. J. Sutter, an African American who is very aware of being a member of a racial minority group, is a junketeer who is trying to set a record for having attended the most consecutive events. Pamela, an African American whose deceased father left a large collection of John Henry memorabilia, is at the Talcott festivities because the town wants to buy her father's collection. Other characters include Albert Miggs, a stamp collector; Lucien Joyce, the owner of a publicity agency that has a list of reporters (including Sutter) ready to cover such events; and Sutter's cronies Dave, Frenchie, Tiny, and One Eye.

The apparent narrative is a sprawling account of the days of the John Henry celebration, which are typical of such small-town festivals. Sutter's motel is just adequate; the food, except for the prime rib, is scarcely exciting; the talent is local. The actor Ben Vereen was scheduled to attend the celebration, but he was taken ill at the last minute. Neither Pamela nor the junketeers are really pleased to be there. Pamela has a purpose beyond the town's interest in her father's collection—she has actually come to bury her father's ashes in the neglected cemetery where John Henry is buried. The junketeers are there for the free food and drink and whatever else they can get for free and because they are on the list—and, of course, Sutter is there because he is going for the record. Miggs is there because he collects railroad stamps, and he wants the new John Henry stamp for his collection.

The real narrative of this novel is found in the digressions, however—in the interpolated stories and the long conversations of the junketeers. In these parts of the book, Whitehead examines a number of concepts and issues. One of the major themes of the novel is consumerism, with a focus on how advertising controls people's lives. Sutter and the other junketeers make their living by going from one publicity event to another and writing about the events for various publications. Lucien Joyce, whose agency employs them, has a reputation for being willing to publicize any event, no matter how trivial, for the right amount of money. The junketeers glory in all the free things they get: food, liquor, motel rooms, and sometimes articles that are being publicized. Receipts are everything; turned in, they produce reimbursement. The John Henry Days celebration is cluttered with John Henry merchandise. Whitehead depicts an America obsessed with material things and the desire to get as much as possible for free.

The legend of John Henry—the railroad steel-driving man who died with a hammer in his hand, competing against a steel-driving machine—as well as a chapter on Pamela's temporary job for an Internet company and the junketeers' lifestyle, especially Sutter's, elucidate the enslavement and dehumanization of people, first by the forces of industrialization and then by those of the digital information age. In chapters about John Henry, Whitehead depicts how John Henry trades his enslavement in the cotton fields for a comparable slavery, driving steel, laying track for the railroad, and buying at the company store.

Sutter and the other junketeer journalists go where the events are. Just as John Henry exists to drive steel, Sutter and the others exist to follow the event circuit. When Sutter enters the Big Bend Tunnel with Pamela, he is enticed but also frightened by the fact that the tunnel cuts him off from the digital information world. Whitehead emphasizes the total lack of interaction among the temporary workers at Pamela's workplace as well as their lack of individuality: All have exactly the same items with which to work, and all make no attempt to personalize their workstations. Whitehead portrays these characters as functions of their work environment. The characters are closed, hiding their inner selves, hiding what Sutter is afraid might be released in the Big Bend Tunnel.

In both the main narrative of *John Henry Days* and in the digressions, Whitehead illustrates the difficulty of being a dark-skinned individual in a racially prejudiced society. John Henry was a black man, yet he is the folk hero of a prejudiced white population. Pamela and Sutter are the only two African Americans at the John Henry Days opening banquet. Sutter is there because he is a journalist who will publicize the event; Pamela is there because she has her father's collection—both characters have something the town wants. The novel ends with Sutter trying to decide if he will leave early with Pamela or stay for the banquet. A shooting takes place, but the outcome is unclear: Has Sutter been killed? Whitehead gives clues, but the reader must decide whether the clues are false.

Shawncey Webb

OTHER MAJOR WORK

NONFICTION: *The Colossus of New York: A City in Thirteen Parts*, 2003.

BIBLIOGRAPHY

Bell, Bernard W. *The Contemporary African American Novel: Its Roots and Modern Literary Branches*. Amherst: University of Massachusetts Press, 2004. Discusses Whitehead's work and the work of other African American writers as seeking experimentation in the novel and abandoning the traditions and roots of the African American novel.

Liggins, Saundra. "The Urban Gothic Vision of Colson Whitehead's *The Intuitionist* (1999)." *African American Review* 40, no. 2 (2006): 359-370. Places the novel in the gothic tradition based on its setting and the "horror" created by the allegorical treatment of the black struggle for upward mobility.

Porter, Everette. "Writing Home." *Black Issues Book Review*, May/June, 2002. Offers discussion of Whitehead's obsession with place and its influence on his novels.

Russell, Alison. "Recalibrating the Past: *The Intuitionist*." *Critique* 49, no. 1 (2007): 46-60. Describes *The Intuitionist* as an anti-detective novel and discusses textual authority in regard to race, identity, and history.

Whitehead, Colson, and Walter Mosley. "Eavesdropping." Interview. *Book*, May, 2001. In conversation with author Mosley, Whitehead discusses his goals in writing, the difficulties he encountered in publishing *The Intuitionist*, and his sense of himself as a black writer.

JOHN EDGAR WIDEMAN

Born: Washington, D.C.; June 14, 1941

PRINCIPAL LONG FICTION

A Glance Away, 1967
Hurry Home, 1970
The Lynchers, 1973
Hiding Place, 1981
Sent for You Yesterday, 1983
The Homewood Trilogy, 1985 (includes *Damballah*, *Hiding Place*, and *Sent for You Yesterday*)
Reuben, 1987
Philadelphia Fire, 1990
The Cattle Killing, 1996
Two Cities, 1998
Fanon, 2008

OTHER LITERARY FORMS

An intensely lyrical novelist, John Edgar Wideman has also published numerous short stories based on family members, friends, and neighbors from his childhood community of Homewood, a long-standing all-black subdivision of Pittsburgh, Pennsylvania. Twelve of these pieces are presented as letters in his critically acclaimed collection *Damballah* (1981), which has also been published with two of his novels as *The Homewood Trilogy*. Wideman's autobiographical *Brothers and Keepers* (1984) blends facts with fictionalized characters and incidents as the author scrutinizes his own relationship to his brother, Robert Wideman, imprisoned for life in Pennsylvania's Western State Penitentiary. *Fever* (1989), a collection of twelve stories, combines themes of family and community with those of displacement, estrangement, and cultural loss. Uncollected poetry, reviews, and essays on black American literature by Wideman abound in the foremost scholarly journals and literary digests.

ACHIEVEMENTS

When he emerged upon the literary scene in the late 1960's, John Edgar Wideman stood out from his peers as a black American writer who did not address exclusively themes of racial conflict and militant nationalism. He concentrated instead on individual psychological struggles that transcend color lines. His earliest novels having been enthusiastically received; he was lauded as a successor to William Faulkner.

After being asked to teach African American literature and essentially having to "teach himself" the field, Wideman began to centralize racial themes overtly in his writing, most radically with the publication of *The Lynchers*, which begins with a chronology of more than one hundred historically documented lynchings. His primary critical acclaim, however, came with the publications of the Homewood series, engendered by the death of his grandmother, Freeda French, in 1973. *Sent for You Yesterday*, the final work of the Homewood Trilogy, received the 1984 Faulkner Award for Fiction from PEN, the International Association of Poets, Playwrights, Editors, Essayists, and Novelists. Wideman was the first author ever to receive two PEN/Faulkner Awards; he was honored with the second for *Philadelphia Fire*. In addition, he was awarded the Lannan Literary Fellowship for Fiction in 1991 and a MacArthur Foundation Award (a "genius grant") in 1993.

In spite of favorable reviews of his fiction, some critics have accused Wideman of indulging in an unconventional style at the expense of theme. More often than not, however, his experimentation extends meaning by illustrating the impact of the past in addition to the inextricable bonds among generations. His autobiographical *Brothers and Keepers*, which displays some of his innovative techniques, earned a National Book Critics Circle Award nomination. In 1998, Wideman won the prestigious Rea Award, sponsored by the Dungannon Foundation and established to honor a short-story author "for literary power, originality, and influence on the genre." Wideman's critical accolades have been profuse, but it is his range of style, continual formalistic innovation, and his powerful prose that warrant his consideration as one of the best American writers of his generation.

BIOGRAPHY

Born in Washington, D.C., on June 14, 1941, John Edgar Wideman initially aspired to be a professional basketball player. Consequently, he served as both a Benjamin Franklin Scholar at the University of Pennsylvania and captain of the school's championship basketball team. A member of Phi Beta Kappa, he was graduated from the University of Pennsylvania in 1963 with a B.A. in English. Promptly selected as only the second black Rhodes Scholar in history, he received his B.Ph. degree from Oxford University in 1966, specializing as a Thouron Fellow in the eighteenth century novel. He then spent one year as a Kent Fellow at the University of Iowa Writers' Workshop, subsequently returning to lecture at his alma mater, Pennsylvania. While writing and teaching literature at the University of Wyoming, he endured the conviction of his oldest son Jacob, on charges of fatally stabbing another youth during a camping trip in Arizona. This tragedy recalls the imprisonment of his brother Robert for involvement in a robbery and killing. His daughter Jamila, having inherited her father's basketball prowess, garnered a position playing in the Women's National Basketball Association (WNBA) professional league. In 1986 Wideman became professor of English at the University of Massachusetts, Amherst. Since the 1980's he has frequently contributed articles and review essays to *The New York Times Book Review* and to popular magazines such as *TV Guide*, *Life*, and *Esquire*.

Analysis

The recurring thematic emphasis in John Edgar Wideman's novels is on the way history, both collective and personal, and the stories that arise from that history shape notions of reality. From gay college professors to ghetto junkies, Wideman's characters are often uncomfortable with their places in history and unsure that they even understand those few traditions that they do observe. Therefore, they shuttle between the imaginary and the real in order to rediscover the past, revive it, or at least preserve whatever parts they do recall. Despite Wideman's literary beginnings in the racially turbulent 1960's, when blacks in America articulated their estrangement from Africa, his white as well as black characters crave the rootedness that distinguishes those who have come to terms with their backgrounds. Shifting from the anonymous northern cities of his first three novels to the clearly delineated Homewood of *Hiding Place* and *Sent for You Yesterday*, Wideman nevertheless consistently indicates that ignorance of heritage results in isolation and psychological turmoil. The same observation is later applied to Philadelphia, specifically Osage Avenue.

Wideman forgoes strictly chronological plot development, adopting instead an intricate experimental style consisting of stream-of-consciousness narrative, long interior monologues, dream sequences, surrealistic descriptions, and abrupt shifts in time, diction, and points of view. Beginning each novel almost exclusively in medias res, he employs a technique influenced by the works of T. S. Eliot, James Joyce, and Jean Toomer, yet indisputably original. In *The Lynchers*, for example, he illustrates the traditionally victimized status of black Americans with a preface that cites more than one hundred documented lynchings. Reeling between their own ravaged communities and impenetrable white ones, the black protagonists of his first two novels, *A Glance Away* and *Hurry Home*, occupy a jumbled landscape where blues clubs coexist with biblical icons. Similarly, in *Hiding Place* and *Sent for You Yesterday*, Wideman retells the stories of his ancestors until a shack or a cape acquires the same expressive quality as a cross. As the author himself explains, "You can call it experimentation, or you can call it ringing the changes. . . . value spontaneity, flexibility, a unique response to a given situation. . . . Getting too close to the edge but then recovering like the heroes of the Saturday matinee serials. That's excitement."

A Glance Away

Dedicated to "Homes," Wideman's first novel, *A Glance Away*, creates thematic excitement with its treatment of two drifting men coming to terms with their pasts. After a year spent at a rehabilitation center for drug addicts, Eddie Lawson, a disillusioned young black man, returns to his listless, decaying urban neighborhood. Rather than celebrating, however, he spends his gloomy homecoming confronting the goblins that drove him to the brink in the first place: his mother Martha Lawson's idealization of his dead older brother, his girlfriend Alice Smalls's rejection of him for sleeping with a white woman, and his own self-disgust over abandoning a secure postal job for menial, marginal employment.

Dejected and defeated by nightfall, he drags himself to grimy Harry's Place in order to cloak his memories in a narcotic haze. There, he is reconciled by his albino friend Brother Smalls with another outcast named Robert Thurley, a white college professor struggling with his own record of divorce, alcoholism, and homosexuality. Though discrepancies between wealth and power divide the two homeless men, each manages to urge the other to maintain his faith in people despite his guilt-ridden history.

A Glance Away generated much favorable critical response in particular for Wideman's depiction of the alienated Thurley. In trying to disavow his personal past, this connoisseur of food and art embraces a surfeit of creeds and cultures. "In religion an aesthetic Catholic, in politics a passive Communist, in sex a resigned anarchist," he surrounds himself with treasures from both East and West and indulges in a smorgasbord of the globe's delicacies. Yet as a real measure of the displacement that these extravagances so futilely conceal, he quotes lines from T. S. Eliot's "The Love Song of J. Alfred Prufrock" (1917), in which a similarly solitary speaker searches for intimacy in a world bereft of its cultural moorings.

Emphasizing his protagonists' self-absorption and the estrangement of their family members and friends, Wideman abandons strictly chronological plot development in favor of lengthy interior monologues. Conversations tend to be short; more likely than not they are interrupted by unspoken flashbacks and asides. Using speech to measure isolation, the author portrays both Eddie and Thurley as incapable of communicating adequately. Eddie, for example, becomes tongue-tied around a group of southern travelers, shuddering in his bus seat instead of warning them as he wishes for the reality of the northern mecca that they seek. Similarly, despite the empowering qualities of a gulp of Southern Comfort, Thurley delivers a lecture on Sophocles' *Oedipus Tyrannus* (c. 429 B.C.E.) fraught with "futility and detachment, . . . introspection and blindness." In one brilliant play on this speechlessness, both men suddenly converse as if they were actors on a stage. This abrupt emphasis on what is spoken—to the exclusion of private thoughts—stresses each person's imprisonment within him- or herself. Flowing from a weaker artist's pen, *A Glance Away* would have become a mere exercise in allusive technique and stream-of-consciousness style. On the contrary, it reads with the effortless ease of a masterfully crafted lyrical poem. Key to its success is Wideman's careful alliance of form and content, not to mention his insightful treatment of a rootlessness that transcends the barriers of race.

HURRY HOME

The same compact length as the novel that precedes it, *Hurry Home* similarly focuses on the theme of rootlessness. Its ambitious protagonist, the honors graduate Cecil Otis Braithwaite, is in many ways an upscale Eddie Lawson with a wife and an advanced degree. After slaving through law school, supporting himself with a meager scholarship and his earnings as a janitor, Cecil has lost his aspirations and his love for his girlfriend, Esther

Brown. In search of something more, he escapes from his wedding bed to Europe, where he roams indiscriminately for three years among its brothels as well as its art galleries. In the tradition of Robert Thurley of *A Glance Away*, two white men as displaced as Cecil attempt to guide him: Charles Webb, belatedly in search of an illegitimate son, and Albert, a mercenary in Webb's employ who has also abandoned a wife. Too lost to save themselves, however, this pair can offer no enduring words of solace to Cecil.

Hurry Home is more sophisticated than *A Glance Away* in its treatment of the isolation theme. It suggests, for example, that the upwardly mobile Cecil is not merely disturbed by his personal past; he is estranged as well from his African and European cultures of origin. On the other hand, nowhere does *Hurry Home* convey the hope that pervades its predecessor. Cecil travels more extensively than does Eddie to reclaim his past, yet he gains no key to it to speak of. Confronting his European heritage merely confirms his status as "a stranger in all . . . tongues." He flees to the African continent by boat, "satisfied to be forever possessed," only to be forever rebuffed from a past that "melts like a wax casing as I am nearer . . . the flame." When he returns at last to his Washington, D.C., tenement, the fruitlessness of his journey is underscored. There, he finds all the same as when he first entered following his miserable nuptials. Symbolically limning his rootlessness, he switches vocations, abandoning the tradition-steeped protocol of the bar for the faddish repertoire of a hairdresser. Thus, "hurry home," the catchphrase for his odyssey, is an ironic one. Cecil really can claim no place where a heritage nurtures and sustains him, no history that he can truly call his own.

Hurry Home displays a masterful style commensurate with that of the later Homewood novels. In addition to a more controlled stream-of-consciousness technique, recurring Christian symbols, icons of Renaissance art, and fragments from Moorish legend powerfully indicate Cecil's fractured lineage. This second novel being a more refined paradigm than the first, Wideman seemed next inclined to break new ground, to address intently the racial polarization that had unsettled American society by the early 1970's, producing that period's most influential published works.

The Lynchers

Distinguished from the previous two novels by its bawdy humor and portrayal of a professional black woman, *The Lynchers* is set in the generic northeastern slum, pockmarked by the self-inflicted wounds of the 1960's, that has become a Wideman trademark. Central to the action are four frustrated black men: Willie "Littleman" Hall, an unemployed dwarf; Leonard Saunders, a ruthless hustler turned repressed postal clerk; Thomas Wilkerson, a plodding fifth-grade schoolteacher; and Graham Rice, an introspective janitor with a persecution complex. Disenchanted with the superficial changes that the Civil Rights movement has wrought—the "job here or a public office there, . . . one or two black faces floating to the top"—these four conclude that violence is the only means to effect a lasting alteration of the white power structure. With Littleman as the ringleader and mastermind, they plan to flex the latent power of the black community and turn the tables on their oppressors by kidnapping and lynching a white policeman.

The plot falls apart, however, once Littleman is badly beaten by the authorities for delivering a militant speech at Woodrow Wilson Junior High School. Suspicion, distrust, and doubt override the remaining conspirators so that they foil themselves instead of their "white butcher pig" enemy. Thus, in a perverse way the weapons of the executioner do revert to black hands. Lynching becomes a symbol of frustration turned inward, of despairing hearts made so taut in their efforts to beat more freely that they burst.

Unlike *A Glance Away* and *Hurry Home*, *The Lynchers* is a total immersion into blackness. Perhaps the critics wanted another black/white character dichotomy, for their assessments of this novel were at best mixed. Nevertheless, Wideman again displays strong gifts of characterization without diminishing the theme's universal appeal. A continuation of his preoccupation with rootlessness, *The Lynchers* showcases men who feel acutely that they belong nowhere. Wilkerson, for example, is the Cecil type, the black professional who is alienated from his working-class roots, condescended to by whites possessing similar educational backgrounds, and unwelcome in the clubs and restaurants that they patronize. Saunders, like Eddie, is a marginally good citizen, at once attracted to and repelled by "the life" of conning and thieving. In an intricate new twist to this scenario, Wideman depicts the older generation as a group as anchorless as the young. For example, Wilkerson's father, a drunk and a philanderer, stabs a longtime friend to death.

In its familiar inner-city setting and cast of alienated men (a passing reference is even made to Cecil Braithwaite as Littleman's lawyer), *The Lynchers* recalls Wideman's preceding works. In its use of a symbol generated exclusively from the black experience, it acts as a transition between these two novels and Wideman's fourth and fifth endeavors. No longer primarily gleaning symbols from Christianity and the European classics, here Wideman unifies his montage of dialogues with "the hawk," a symbol indigenous to the men's own harsh environment. This frigid, anthropomorphic wind that lashes the streets indicates the blacks' powerlessness and the hollow bravado of their ill-fated intrigue. They cannot even abduct the police officer without using one of their own people, his black girlfriend, Sissie, as a pawn.

HIDING PLACE

After an eight-year interval during which he researched black American literature and culture, Wideman applied folk sources more fully than ever before in *Hiding Place*, one of the three works of fiction that make up the Homewood Trilogy. Challenged to enlarge his black readership without limiting the universal relevance of his themes, he chose to emphasize one black family based largely on his own Homewood clan. In this novel's swift, uncomplicated plot, Tommy Lawson, a tough, wisecracking youth from the black neighborhood of Homewood, is running from the police for his involvement in a robbery and killing. He seeks refuge among the weedy plots and garbage piles of desolate Bruston

Hill, a once-fertile area to which his ancestor Sybela Owens fled from the South and slavery with Charlie Bell, her white owner's recalcitrant son. In the lone residence at the crest of the Hill, a rotting wooden shack sardonically known as "that doghouse," the reclusive "Mother" Bess Owens reluctantly offers her sister's great-grandson a temporary haven. After Tommy regains the courage to elude the authorities eager to convict him for a murder that he did not commit, Bess reaffirms her ties to her kin and ends her self-imposed isolation. Not knowing whether Tommy is dead, has escaped, or has been captured, she burns her shack and prepares to reenter Homewood to retell Tommy's tragic story so that another like it might never happen again.

Though Bess does not leave her longtime home until the novel's final chapter, *Hiding Place* is as much the story of her isolation from family as it is one of Tommy's. Just as Tommy has shirked his responsibilities as a husband, father, and son, Bess has turned her back on the younger generations of kin whose ways are alien to her. Widowed and childless, she has retreated into an archaic lifestyle, shunning the twentieth century amenities of electricity and phones, in order to avoid intimacy with others. Physically rooting herself among Bruston Hill's ruins, she has been running from the present in her mind by focusing her thoughts on the past, especially the deaths of loved ones that have occurred. Only when she becomes involved in Tommy's affairs does she rekindle her commitment to the family.

In *Hiding Place*, Wideman's style dramatically differs from those of the canonized white writers who were his early models. With a method many reviewers have compared to jazz, his characters unfold the histories of five generations of Lawsons and Frenches. Bess herself repeats certain key events in the family history several times; one of her favorites is the one in which Mary Hollinger revives her cousin Freeda French's stillborn baby by plunging it into the snow. Yet like a jazz improvisation, where instruments alternately play solo and play together, she retells the tale each time in a different way, varying her approach to it with different bits of superstition, mysticism, and folklore. Even Wideman's Clement, an inarticulate orphan similar to Benjy Compson in William Faulkner's *The Sound and the Fury* (1929), bears the unique stamp of the black American experience. As the author himself avows, Clement's assimilation into Homewood reflects the nature of the black community as a tolerant extended family.

Its legacy of songs, tales, and superstitions notwithstanding, the Homewood that finally draws Bess back is a model of urban blight, a "bombed out" no-man's-land of "pieces of buildings standing here and there and fire scars and places ripped and kicked down and cars stripped and dead at the curb." This dying landscape, and in a similar way Bess's ramshackle Bruston Hill homestead, proclaims the present descendants' dissociation from their ancestors and one another. In *Sent for You Yesterday*, the final installment of the Homewood Trilogy and the 1984 PEN/Faulkner Award winner for outstanding fiction, this undercurrent becomes the novel's predominant theme. Carl French and his lover Lucy Tate relate the stories of a Homewood gone by to the latest generation of listeners, as if the recovery of the past is integral for the entire community's survival and solidarity.

SENT FOR YOU YESTERDAY

Sent for You Yesterday cannot be divided easily into main story and subplots. All the episodes in it are major in scope and significance. The most memorable ones include the saga of the piano player Albert Wilkes, who slept with a white woman and murdered a white policeman; the tragedy of Samantha, whose college education could not shield her from grief and madness; and the bittersweet adventures of the resilient Brother Tate, an albino and best friend of Carl who communicates only with gestures and scat sounds. Retold by Carl's nephew Doot, a former Homewood resident modeled largely after Wideman himself, each tale conveys a lesson to a younger generation. More than mere exempla, however, the stories emphasize the cyclic nature of the human condition: Each generation rises to further, alter, and often reenact the accomplishments of its predecessors. Thus, Uncle Carl's street in Homewood becomes to Doot "a narrow, cobbled alley *teeming* with life. Like a wooden-walled ship in the middle of the city, like the ark on which Noah packed two of everything and prayed for land." This determination to survive that the ark imagery calls to mind impels Carl and Lucy to share Homewood's history. By remembering past lives, by preserving traditions, they ensure their own enduring places in the memories of their heirs.

REUBEN

Traditions preserved and memories presented from black America's African past form the backbeat of *Reuben*, Wideman's next novel of community and interracial struggle. From a rusting trailer that his clients describe as part office, part altar to the gods, the dwarf Reuben serves the poor of Homewood in need of a lawyer, a psychologist, a warrior, or a priest. Like West African *griots* or oral scribes, who commit to unerring memory genealogies, triumphs, faults, and names, Reuben relies on a mix of law and bureaucratic legerdemain that he has heard from his own employers and remembered. Like an obliging ancestral spirit shuttling prayers from this world to the next, Reuben negotiates pacts between the ghetto's bombed-out streets and the oak, plush, and marble interiors of City Hall. As he prescribes legal strategies and bestows grandfatherly advice, he also steers his clients to confront and abandon the views that have overturned their lives. When words and contracts alone will not do, Reuben rustles deep within collective memory and knots a charm: "A rag, a bone, a hank of hair. Ancient grains of rice." Reuben transforms garbage into power, excrement into nourishment, gristle into life. He preaches reincarnation and the nature of things dead to rise again, and he catalyzes his clients to seek similar transformations in themselves.

Infused with magic and spiritualism, *Reuben* also is illustrated by the ravaged images of the inner city. Wideman likens ghetto buildings to the rat-infested holds of slave ships and the people in those buildings to roles of both predator and prey. Much of the Homewood population resembles a coffle of freshly branded slaves, slaves who are bound by laws instead of chains, by the welfare system or underworld crime instead of a plantation economy. Others are human versions of rats—snitching, beating, starving, stealing, and otherwise pestering their neighbors with an eat-or-be-eaten mentality. "There were historical precedents, parallels," Reuben understands. "Indian scouts leading long-hairs to the hiding places of their red brethren. FBI informers, double agents, infiltrators of the sixties. An unsubtle variation of divide and conquer." In this bleak landscape, the game of divide and conquer has changed little since enslavement.

PHILADELPHIA FIRE

Philadelphia Fire, *The Cattle Killing*, and *Two Cities* are framed within a geographic shift from Pittsburgh to Philadelphia. In keeping with Wideman's fluid notion of history and myth as mutually interlocking categories of representation, *Philadelphia Fire* recasts the 1985 police bombing of the building occupied by the radical MOVE organization. John Africa, MOVE's leader, is represented as Reverend King, who is described as "a nouveau Rousseau." King leads a rebellion against the infringement on African American individual and communal rights couched in the guises of "urbanization" and "integration" by espousing an ideology that embraces a return to nature and a rejection of modern material values. Elsewhere, Wideman asserts that "the craziness of MOVE is their sanity; they were saying no to the system . . . it makes perfect sense. So the myth of integration is analogous to the prophecy of the cattle killing."

THE CATTLE KILLING

This prophecy serves as the guiding metaphor for the novel *The Cattle Killing*, and it refers to the lies told to the African Xhosa people in order to make them believe that to combat European oppression they must kill their cattle. The cattle are their life force, and their destruction leads to the near annihilation of Xhosa culture. The people die as their cattle die, struck down because they believed the lie of the prophecy: "The cattle are the people. The people are the cattle." Wideman subtly extends this metaphor to consider the problem of intraracial crime ravaging American inner cities and connects contemporary circumstances with the diseased and disintegrating conditions surrounding the yellow fever outbreak of eighteenth century Philadelphia.

In all three instances—in Africa, in Philadelphia, in black urbania—there is a potential for annihilation because of an epidemic fueled by hysteria, exacerbated by racist ideology and carried out by those who believe the "lie" and perpetrate their self-destruction. The narrator of *Cattle Killing*, Isaiah, called "Eye," is an obvious recasting of the biblical figure who prophesies the downfall of the nation of Israel. He is a prophet who warns of false prophecies—in this case, the lie of integration, which is intricately entwined with modernization and its attenuating conspicuous consumption, the theme foregrounded in *Philadelphia Fire*. This text's distinction from *Philadelphia Fire*, however, lies in the vision of hope with which readers are left; *The Cattle Killing* is also a love story.

TWO CITIES

The Cattle Killing and the following novel, *Two Cities*, mark a thematic shift for Wideman. Though harkening back to the theme of love (a kind of communal love) inherent in the Homewood Trilogy, the novels transcend that representation, exploring the healing potential of intimate, spiritual love. *Two Cities*, which links Philadelphia and Pittsburgh, Cassina Way and Osage Avenue, explores the difficulty of loving in troubled times. It overwhelmingly endorses the embracing of love, not merely physical love but also self-love, love of community, and love of life, as the only viable means of refusing and subverting the lies that have threatened to destroy the African American community.

From the beginning of his extensive literary career, critics have often compared Wideman's prose to the experimental fictions of the eighteenth century English writer Laurence Sterne. The sociable Sterne had befriended Ignatius Sancho, a gregarious former slave, a prodigious correspondent, and host of one of London's most popular salons. Sancho admired Sterne's mock humility and imitated his wit and playful style. In turn, Sterne admired the double entendre, self-scrutiny, and flair for detail in the letters of his African friend.

In Wideman's novels, the voices of the African Sancho and the Englishman Sterne converge. These works present black America from the perspectives of the enslaved and the descendants of the enslaved as well as from the vantage point of those whites who served as either tormentors and oppressors or benefactors and friends. These works warn of the potholes where our elders slipped before, and they expose the reader to the vistas that people often fail to notice and enjoy. They achieve Wideman's goal of "expanding our notions of reality, creating hard, crisp edges you can't swallow without a gulp."

Barbara A. McCaskill
Updated by Heather Russell Andrade

OTHER MAJOR WORKS

SHORT FICTION: *Damballah*, 1981; *Fever: Twelve Stories*, 1989; *All Stories Are True*, 1992; *The Stories of John Edgar Wideman*, 1992; *God's Gym*, 2005.

NONFICTION: *Brothers and Keepers*, 1984; *Fatheralong: A Meditation on Fathers and Sons, Race and Society*, 1994; *Conversations with John Edgar Wideman*, 1998 (Bonnie TuSmith, editor); *Hoop Roots*, 2001; *The Island: Martinique*, 2003.

EDITED TEXTS: *My Soul Has Grown Deep: Classics of Early African-American Literature*, 2001; *Twenty: The Best of the Drue Heinz Literature Prize*, 2001.

BIBLIOGRAPHY

Auger, Philip. *Native Sons in No Man's Land: Rewriting Afro-American Manhood in the Novels of Baldwin, Walker, Wideman, and Gaines*. New York: Garland, 2000. Analyzes the representation of masculinity in Wideman's works.

Bell, Bernard W. *The Afro-American Novel and Its Tradition*. Amherst: University of

Massachusetts Press, 1987. Provides a short but incisive overview of Wideman's evolving concerns as an African American as well as a postmodernist innovator. Also notes Wideman's evocative uses of history as an imaginative paradigm and identifies as his major theme "the conflict between [his protagonists'] ascribed and achieved identities as black men."

Coleman, James W. *Blackness and Modernism: The Literary Career of John Edgar Wideman*. Jackson: University Press of Mississippi, 1990. Discusses all of Wideman's novels through 1989 and includes an interview with the author. Supplemented with a brief bibliography of critical sources.

Dubey, Madhu. "Literature and Urban Crisis: John Edgar Wideman's *Philadelphia Fire*." *African American Review* 32 (Winter, 1998): 579-595. Examines *Philadelphia Fire* in relation to the novel's implicit critique of urban renewal and its attenuating glorification of consumption and excess, legitimation of law and order, and the resulting dispossession, displacement, and segregation of the city's inhabitants.

Mbalia, Doreatha D. *John Edgar Wideman: Reclaiming the African Personality*. Selinsgrove, Pa.: Susquehanna University Press, 1995. Discusses, among other topics, Wideman's narrative technique. Includes bibliography and index.

Rushdy, Ashraf. "Fraternal Blues: John Edgar Wideman's Homewood Trilogy." *Contemporary Literature* 32, no. 3 (Fall, 1991): 312-345. Begins by suggesting that the narrator of the trilogy utilizes three modes of narrating that are depicted in the three texts, respectively: letters, stories, and the blues. Argues that the narrative voice gains an understanding of self when it finds a "blues voice."

TuSmith, Bonnie, ed. *Conversations with John Edgar Wideman*. Jackson: University Press of Mississippi, 1998. Collection of interviews with Wideman covers a wide range of topics, including the sources of Wideman's fiction, his perspectives on race in the United States, his philosophical thought, and his writing technique.

TuSmith, Bonnie, and Keith E. Byerman, eds. *Critical Essays on John Edgar Wideman*. Knoxville: University of Tennessee Press, 2006. Collection of essays covers all of Wideman's major works and addresses such topics as the cultural context of his fiction, his writing style, and his use of personal narrative. Includes bibliography and index.

Wideman, John Edgar. *Hoop Roots*. Boston: Houghton Mifflin, 2001. Wideman reflects on his enduring relationship to the game of basketball, a sport that has played a pivotal role in his personal life and appears frequently in his fiction.

_______. "John Edgar Wideman." Interview by Kay Bonetti. In *Conversations with American Novelists*, edited by Kay Bonetti, Greg Michaelson, Speer Morgan, Jo Sapp, and Sam Stowers. Columbia: University of Missouri Press, 1997. Wideman discusses the oral tales told to him by his aunt, which he developed into the stories in the Homewood Trilogy. Also addresses the politics of writing in the United States, the risks that writers have to take to write truthfully about themselves and those they love, and his fiction's concern with brotherhood and sisterhood.

JOHN A. WILLIAMS

Born: Jackson, Mississippi; December 5, 1925
Also known as: John Alfred Williams; J. Dennis Gregory

PRINCIPAL LONG FICTION

The Angry Ones, 1960 (also known as *One for New York*)
Night Song, 1961
Journey out of Anger, 1963
Sissie, 1963
The Man Who Cried I Am, 1967
Sons of Darkness, Sons of Light: A Novel of Some Probability, 1969
Captain Blackman, 1972
Mothersill and the Foxes, 1975
The Junior Bachelor Society, 1976
!Click Song, 1982
The Berhama Account, 1985
Jacob's Ladder, 1987
Clifford's Blues, 1998

OTHER LITERARY FORMS

Known primarily as a novelist but also as a short-story writer, John A. Williams has produced an extraordinary number of nonfiction pieces, many of them journalistic. He was among the first African Americans of his generation to write a fact book about Africa, *Africa: Her History, Lands, and People* (1962). His treatment of 1960's social issues can be found in *The Protectors: The Heroic Story of the Narcotics Agents, Citizens, and Officials in Their Unending, Unsung Battles Against Organized Crime in America and Abroad* (1964) and in *This Is My Country Too* (1965), which documents Williams's travels throughout the United States in 1963-1964, from articles serialized in *Holiday* magazine.

A controversial work, *The King God Didn't Save: Reflections on the Life and Death of Martin Luther King, Jr.* (1970) is a critical look at civil rights leader Martin Luther King, Jr.'s public and private life, and *The Most Native of Sons: A Biography of Richard Wright* (1970) treats the life of the famed black novelist Richard Wright. A comprehensive compilation of articles, some autobiographical, was published in *Flashbacks: A Twenty-Year Diary of Article Writing* (1973). Williams has also produced an award-winning book of poetry, *Safari West* (1998), the play *Last Flight from Ambo Ber* (pr. 1981), dealing with the Falashas in Ethiopia, and the libretto for the opera *Vanqui* (pr. 1999).

John A. Williams
(Library of Congress)

ACHIEVEMENTS

One of the most prolific and influential writers of his era, John A. Williams infuses his works with self-exploration, reflecting the collective social experience of African Americans. He has lectured widely, contributed extensively to anthologies, and edited numerous collections, such as *The Angry Black* (1962), *Beyond the Angry Black* (1966), *Amistad I* (1970), *Amistad II* (1971), *Yardbird No. 2* (1978), *The McGraw-Hill Introduction to Literature* (1985), *Way B(l)ack Then and Now: A Street Guide to African Americans in Paris* (1992), and *Bridges: Literature Across Cultures* (1994). In the 1970's, he was a contributing editor for such publications as *American Journal* and *Politicks*, and in the 1980's he served in a similar capacity for the distinguished, groundbreaking publication *Journal of African Civilizations*.

Williams has been the recipient of numerous awards, beginning with his recognition in 1962 by the National Institute of Arts and Letters. His other honors and achievements include the Richard Wright-Jacques Roumain Award (1973), the National Endowment for the Arts Award (1977), the Lindback Award for Distinguished Teaching, Rutgers University (1982), the American Book Award for *!Click Song* (1983), the New Jersey Literary

Hall of Fame Michael Award (1987), the American Book Award for *Safari West* (1998), and induction into the National Literary Hall of Fame (1998).

BIOGRAPHY

John Alfred Williams was born near Jackson, Mississippi, in Hinds County, to Ola and John Henry Williams. Williams's mother, whose African name means "Keeper of the Beautiful House" or "He Who Wants to Be Chief," had been born in Mississippi; his father's roots were in Syracuse, New York, where the couple met. When Williams was six months old, he returned with his mother to Syracuse. The family resided in the multiethnic Fifteenth Ward, and Williams attended Washington Irving Elementary, Madison Junior High, and Central High School. He joined the U.S. Navy in 1943 and served in the Pacific. After discharge in 1946 and his return to Syracuse, he completed his secondary education, followed by a brief term at Morris Brown College in Atlanta and then enrollment at Syracuse University, where he studied creative writing.

In 1947, Williams married Carolyn Clopton, with whom he had two sons, Gregory and Dennis. In 1950, Williams earned his bachelor of arts degree and continued at Syracuse to pursue graduate study. During this period, he worked at a variety of jobs—foundry work, social work, public relations, insurance, radio and television—while developing as a journalist. Following the failure of his marriage in 1952 and a brief stay in California in 1954, he was determined to become a professional writer. In 1946, he had contributed pieces to the Syracuse newspaper, the *Progressive Herald*, continuing through 1955 as a reporter for the *Chicago Defender*, the *Pittsburgh Courier*, the *Los Angeles Tribune*, and *The Village Voice*.

After moving to New York in 1954, Williams worked for a vanity publisher, Comet Press, in 1955-1956 and at Abelard-Schuman in 1957-1958. In 1958, Williams was director of information for the American Committee on Africa, a reporter for *Jet* magazine, and a stringer for the Associated Negro Press. Based in Barcelona for a period, he was employed in 1959 by WOV Radio in New York; his first published novel, *The Angry Ones*, appeared in 1960.

Though Williams was nominated in 1962 for the Prix de Rome by the American Academy of Arts and Letters, his name was withdrawn for reasons that Williams attributed to his upcoming interracial marriage. In 1963, he contributed an article to *Ebony* magazine and began writing for *Holiday*, and in 1964 he was an Africa correspondent for *Newsweek*. In 1965, he married Lorrain Isaac, with whom he had a son, Adam. Williams began his career in higher education in 1968, teaching at the College of the Virgin Islands and the City College of New York. He held positions at the University of California, Santa Barbara; University of Hawaii; Boston University; New York University; University of Houston; and Bard College. From 1979 to 1994, he taught at Rutgers while continuing his literary activities. Following the publication of *Safari West* in 1998, his long-awaited novel *Clifford's Blues* (1998) was published; it was his first novel in twelve years.

ANALYSIS

John A. Williams's novels draw on personal experience, though they are not strictly autobiographical; they reflect the racial issues facing American society, especially during the civil rights period. Williams writes in the clear, readable prose of a journalist; his plot structures mix linear time with flashback passages to achieve a seamless continuity. His characters have been writers, jazz musicians, black mothers, and military veterans, and his themes have addressed the hardships of the black writer, the expatriate in Europe, black family life, interracial relationships, and political conspiracy. The presentation of jazz is a frequent element, and New York City is a repeated setting, though Williams has also depicted the Caribbean and Africa.

THE ANGRY ONES

Williams's initial novel is a first-person narrative drawing on autobiographical elements. Like Williams, Stephen Hill, the African American main character, is a World War II veteran, who works for a vanity press in New York. Early in the novel, Williams refers to African and Native American origins and jazz contexts. The novel is principally about Steve's relationships with his employer, coworkers, and friends. One of Steve's closest associates is Linton Mason, a white former college mate and editor at McGraw-Hill. The novel uses Lint's success in publishing to indicate the racial divide, sexual jealousy, and the benefits of being white in racist America. Another theme is the search for a meaningful relationship, the choice between interracial and intraracial love. The causes of black anger are linked to Steve's frustrating attempts to rise within the company run by Rollie Culver and, generally, the treatment of black men in New York's publishing world, symbolized by the suicide of Steve's black friend, Obie Roberts. The novel presents racism through the day-to-day experiences of the main character.

NIGHT SONG

Set in Greenwich Village, New York, in the 1950's, *Night Song* is a jazz novel that mirrors the life of famed alto saxophonist Charlie Parker through the portrayal of Eagle (Richie Stokes), a drug-addicted musician who retains the capabilities of jazz performance despite his debilitation. Eagle befriends the alcoholic David Hillary, an out-of-work white college professor employed in the jazz café run by Keel Robinson, a former black preacher and Harvard graduate involved in an interracial relationship with Della. Each of the characters is fractured, most notably Eagle, whose alcoholism and addiction are implicitly the result of the racist treatment of the black artist. Williams portrays David as a savior and betrayer of Eagle; David's "healing" is the ironic result of his association with Eagle, Keel, and Della.

SISSIE

Titled for the mother of two principal characters, Iris and Ralph, *Sissie* is divided into four parts. Through memories, the novel presents the stories of Iris, Ralph, and Sissie

Joplin, with Sissie's history revealed in parts 3 and 4, resulting in a Joplin family saga. Iris's story—her failed marriage, her career in Europe, and her relationship with the jazz musician called Time—is the first extended flashback. Ralph's recollections—his experiences in the service, his struggle as a writer in New York—are presented through psychoanalysis, a device that reveals racial issues from the viewpoint of a white psychologist, a symbol of societal norms. Sissie Joplin, a matriarchal figure, has an affair that threatens the stability of her marriage, which undergoes numerous challenges, such as the difficulty of surviving economic hard times and the struggle to find personal fulfillment through love. Sissie is ultimately the catalyst for Ralph and Iris's recognition of their family's conflicted yet sustaining experiences.

The Man Who Cried I Am

Williams's best-received and perhaps most influential work, *The Man Who Cried I Am* revolves around Max Reddick, an African American writer reunited in Amsterdam with his Dutch former wife, Margrit. Williams presents, within a twenty-four-hour time period, the downward spiral of Reddick, a Chester Himes figure, who is suffering from colon cancer. Through flashbacks, Reddick's recollections of a thirty-year past present the social experience of black Americans through the civil rights era. The novel portrays Reddick's association with Harry Ames, a character based on black novelist Richard Wright, who has uncovered the King Alfred Plan, a plot to place America's black population in concentration camps. Other characters in the novel also resemble actual black writers or political figures, such as Marion Dawes, a James Baldwin type; Paul Durrell, a Martin Luther King, Jr., replica; and Minister Q, a Malcolm X parallel. Furthermore, Williams develops African characters, such as Jaja Enzkwu, who reveals the King Alfred Plan to Harry Ames. The involvement of the Central Intelligence Agency (CIA) in Reddick's death points to an international conspiracy against black people, demonstrating Williams's tragic vision of global race relations.

Captain Blackman

An exploration of black contributions in American wars, this novel employs a narrative strategy in which time is fluid. At the outset, Captain Blackman, a soldier in the Vietnam War who teaches his troops the history of black Americans in the military, is wounded and trapped by the Viet Cong. His hallucinations are used to develop scenes in various American wars, from the American Revolution through Vietnam. In these settings, Blackman experiences battle and the racial circumstances affecting black troops. The novel mixes fictional characterizations with historical fact, as in the reference to the Battle of Bunker Hill in the American Revolution. Williams portrays a possible nuclear Armageddon in which black people become the forces of control, though the reversal of power from black to white is itself part of the dream visions of Blackman.

!CLICK SONG

Considered by Williams at the time to be the novel in which he achieved the most effective coalescence of his literary intentions, *!Click Song*, titled after a vocal sound found in the Xhosa language of South Africa, parallels two writers, one black, the other white and Jewish. Using flashbacks, manipulating linear time, the narrative develops the literary careers of Cato Douglass and Paul Cummings. Divided into three sections, "Beginnings," "Middle," and "Endings," *!Click Song* uses the first-person narrator, Cato, as a representation of the journey of the black American writer. Beginning with the funeral of Paul, who committed suicide, the novel returns to the undergraduate experiences of the two veterans pursuing creative writing, circumstances that suggest the author's biography. Parallels to Williams's life are inescapable, especially in the treatment of Cato's career. However, Williams goes beyond mere autobiography by using Cato to symbolize the black artist who resists cultural falsehood, as in the closing section in which Cato in the 1960's offers a countertext to the withholding of information about black culture by major museums.

JACOB'S LADDER

Jacob's Ladder explores the predicament of an African American military attaché, Jacob Henry (Jake), caught in the turmoil of American destabilizing efforts in Pandemi, a fictitious West African country, where he had spent part of his youth as the son of a black American missionary. Resembling Liberia, Pandemi is ruled by Chuma Fasseke, Jake's childhood friend. The government of Chuma Fasseke has replaced that of the Franklins, a family descended from nineteenth century repatriated African Americans. The novel also offers a parallel to Nigeria in the portrayal of Taiwo Shaguri, the head of state of Temian. Containing elements of an espionage thriller, *Jacob's Ladder* proposes that an African country can attain nuclear capabilities. Williams humanizes Jake and Fasseke, creating a work deeper than clandestine intrigue. The final sections describe the fall of Fasseke and the takeover of the nuclear power plant by his opposition, assisted by the CIA. The epilogue uses the ironic device of the press release to show the perspective of the international press.

Joseph McLaren

OTHER MAJOR WORKS

PLAYS: *Last Flight from Ambo Ber*, pr. 1981; *Vanqui*, pr. 1999 (libretto).

POETRY: *Safari West*, 1998.

NONFICTION: *Africa: Her History, Lands, and People*, 1962; *The Protectors: The Heroic Story of the Narcotics Agents, Citizens, and Officials in Their Unending, Unsung Battles Against Organized Crime in America and Abroad*, 1964 (as J. Dennis Gregory with Harry J. Anslinger); *This Is My Country Too*, 1965; *The King God Didn't Save: Reflections on the Life and Death of Martin Luther King, Jr.*, 1970; *The Most Native of Sons: A Biography of Richard Wright*, 1970; *Flashbacks: A Twenty-Year Diary of Article Writing*,

1973; *Minorities in the City*, 1975; *If I Stop I'll Die: The Comedy and Tragedy of Richard Pryor*, 1991 (with Dennis A. Williams); *Way B(l)ack Then and Now: A Street Guide to African Americans in Paris*, 1992 (with Michel Fabre); *Dear Chester, Dear John: Letters Between Chester Himes and John A. Williams*, 2008 (John A. Williams and Lori Williams, editors).

EDITED TEXTS: *The Angry Black*, 1962; *Beyond the Angry Black*, 1966; *Amistad I*, 1970 (with Charles F. Harris); *Amistad II*, 1971 (with Harris); *The McGraw-Hill Introduction to Literature*, 1985 (with Gilbert H. Muller); *Bridges: Literature Across Cultures*, 1994 (with Muller, author).

BIBLIOGRAPHY

Bryant, Jerry H. "John A. Williams and the Realist's Dilemma." In *Victims and Heroes: Racial Violence in the African American Novel*. Amherst: University of Massachusetts Press, 1997. This analysis of Williams's novels is included in a study of how violence is depicted in African American literature from slave narratives through the late twentieth century.

Campbell, James. "The Man Who Came and Cried: John A. Williams." In *Syncopations: Beats, New Yorkers, and Writers in the Dark*. Berkeley: University of California Press, 2008. Campbell, a columnist for *The Times Literary Supplement*, has compiled a collection of his profiles and essays about writers, including Williams, who wrote after the 1950's.

Cash, Earl A. *John A. Williams: The Evolution of a Black Writer.* New York: Third Press, 1975. This text is the first book-length study of Williams's works, covering the novels through *Captain Blackman* and his nonfiction. Includes a bibliography and an index.

Gayle, Addison, Jr. *The Way of the New World: The Black Novel in America*. Garden City, N.Y.: Doubleday, 1975. Gayle addresses the shift from protest to history in Williams's novels *The Man Who Cried I Am* and *Captain Blackman*.

Muller, Gilbert H. *John A. Williams*. Boston: Twayne, 1984. This introductory overview provides a comprehensive treatment of Williams's life and the themes of his work through *!Click Song*. Includes biographical information, a chronology, a bibliography, and an index.

Nadel, Alan. "My Country Too: Time, Place, and African American Identity in the Work of John Williams." In *Containment Culture: American Narrative, Postmodernism, and the Atomic Age*. Durham, N.C.: Duke University Press, 1995. Nadel's study of "cultural narratives of containment" written during the Cold War includes a chapter on Williams's work, namely *The Man Who Cried I Am*, *Captain Blackman*, and *Sissie*.

Ramsey, Priscilla R. "John A. Williams: The Black American Narrative and the City." In *The City in African-American Literature*, edited by Yoshinobu Hakutani and Robert Butler. Madison, N.J.: Fairleigh Dickinson University Press, 1995. Ramsey provides an overview of selected Williams novels, focusing on their urban realities.

Ro, Sigmund. "Toward the Post-Protest Novel: The Fiction of John A. Williams." In *Rage and Celebration: Essays on Contemporary Afro-American Writing*. Atlantic Highlands, N.J.: Humanities Press, 1984. Ro argues that Williams's novels develop from protest fiction to novelistic treatments of 1960's racial issues.

Tal, Kali. "'That Just Kills Me.'" *Social Text* 20 (Summer, 2002): 65-92. Discusses *Sons of Darkness, Sons of Light* in a study of militant black futurist novels. For advanced students.

RICHARD WRIGHT

Born: Roxie, Mississippi; September 4, 1908
Died: Paris, France; November 28, 1960
Also known as: Richard Nathaniel Wright

PRINCIPAL LONG FICTION

Native Son, 1940
The Outsider, 1953
Savage Holiday, 1954
The Long Dream, 1958
Lawd Today, 1963
A Father's Law, 2008

OTHER LITERARY FORMS

In addition to his novels, Richard Wright published collections of essays and short stories and two autobiographical volumes. Two collections of short fiction, the early *Uncle Tom's Children* (1938) and the posthumously collected *Eight Men* (1961), represent some of Wright's finest writing. Wright himself felt that the characters in *Uncle Tom's Children* were too easily pitied and that they elicited from readers a sympathy that was unlike the tough intellectual judgment he desired. Wright later wrote that his creation of Bigger Thomas in *Native Son* was an attempt to stiffen that portrayal so that readers could not leniently dismiss his characters with simple compassion, but would have to accept them as free, fully human adults whose actions require assessment. Nevertheless, the stories of *Uncle Tom's Children* are carefully written, and the characters, though sometimes defeated, embody the kind of independence and intractability that Wright valued in his fiction.

Two stories from *Eight Men* reveal the themes to which Wright gave sustained development in his novels. In "The Man Who Was Almos' a Man," the main character learns that power means freedom, and although he first bungles his attempt to shoot a gun, his symbol of power, he lies to his family, keeps the gun, and at the conclusion of the story leaves home to grow into manhood elsewhere. In "The Man Who Lived Underground," the main character, nameless at first, is accused of a crime he did not commit. Fleeing underground to the sewers of the city, he becomes a voyeur of life, seen now from a new perspective. The values that served him badly aboveground do not serve him at all below. By the end of the story, he has come to understand that all men are guilty; his name is revealed, and with his new values, he ascends once more to accept responsibility for the crime. Since all men are guilty, it is less important to him that the crime is not his own than that he acknowledge freely that he shares in human guilt.

Even more important than these two collections is the first volume of Wright's autobi-

Richard Wright
(Library of Congress)

ography, *Black Boy: A Record of Childhood and Youth* (1945), which opens up a world of experience to the reader. It traces the first seventeen years of Wright's life—from his birth in Mississippi and the desertion of the family by his father through years of displacement as he travels from one relative to another with his ill mother and religious grandmother. The early years find Wright, like his later protagonists, an outsider, cut off from family, from friends, from culture. He is as out of place among blacks as among whites, baffled by those blacks who play the roles whites expect of them, himself unable to dissimulate his feelings and thoughts. Although the work is nonfiction, it is united by powerful metaphors: fire, hunger, and blindness. Wright's inner fire is mirrored throughout the work by actual fires; indeed, his first act is to set afire the curtains in his home. His physical hunger, a constant companion, is an image of his hunger for knowledge and connection, and his two jobs in optical factories suggest the blindness of society, a blindness given further representation in *Native Son*.

What Wright learns in *Black Boy* is the power of words. His early life is marked by physical violence: He witnesses murders and beatings, but it is the violence of words that offers liberation from his suffocating environment. Whether it is the profanity with which he shocks his grandmother, the literalness with which he takes his father's words, or the crude expressions with which he taunts Jewish shopkeepers, he discovers that words have a power that makes him an equal to those around him. When he feels unequal, as in his early school experiences, he is speechless. The culmination of this theme occurs when Wright acquires a library card and discovers through his readings of the works of American social critics of the early part of the twentieth century, such as H. L. Mencken and Sinclair Lewis, that he is not alone in his feelings and that there are others who share his alienation and discontent.

When Wright finally sees his father many years after his desertion, his hatred dissolves: He realizes that his father, trapped by his surroundings, with neither a cultural past nor an individual future, speaks a language different from his own, holds different thoughts, and is truly a victim and therefore not worthy even of his hatred. Wright's characters must never be victims, for as such they hold no interest. At the end of the book, he goes north, first to Memphis and, when that fails, north again to Chicago, pursuing the dream, having now the power of words to articulate it and to define himself.

The record of Wright's years in Chicago is found in the posthumously published second autobiographical volume, *American Hunger* (written in 1944, published in 1977). Largely a record of his involvement and later disillusionment with the Communist Party, this book is interesting for its view of a later, mature Wright who is still struggling with institutions that would limit his freedom.

ACHIEVEMENTS

In his best work, Richard Wright gives American literature its strongest statement of the existential theme of alienated people defining themselves. Wright's use of the black American as archetypal outsider gives his work a double edge. On one hand, no American writer so carefully illuminates the black experience in America: The ambivalence of black feeling, the hypocrisies of the dominant culture, and the tension between them find concrete and original manifestation in Wright's work, a manifestation at once revealing and terrifying. It is not only in his revelation of black life, however, that Wright's power lies, for as much as his writing is social and political, it is also personal and philosophical. The story of alienated people is a universal one; because the concrete experiences of the outsider are so vividly rendered in Wright's fiction, his books have an immediate accessibility. Because they also reveal deeper patterns, they have further claims to attention. Much of Wright's later fiction seems self-conscious and studied, but it cannot diminish the greatness of his finest work.

BIOGRAPHY

Born in Mississippi of sharecropper parents, Richard Nathaniel Wright had a lonely and troubled childhood. His father deserted the family early, and after his mother suffered a stroke, Wright was forced at a young age to work to help support the family, which moved frequently from one relative to another. His portrayal of his mother is of a stern but loving parent, unable to contend with the stronger personality of his extremely religious grandmother. Wright's grandmother believed that all fiction was "the devil's lies"; her chief goal was to force Wright into a religious conversion, a goal in which she was singularly unsuccessful.

Wright's direct connection to family members who had been slaves came through both sets of grandparents. Richard Wilson, his mother's father, had been a slave in the cotton fields and had fled slavery to serve in the Civil War. His anger against whites carried throughout his life and was fueled by the government's refusal to offer disability assistance. This bitter figure was a strong influence on Wright's own angst. Less influential to Wright's ideology was his paternal grandfather, Nathaniel Wright, who had been a slave, a Civil War soldier, and a sharecropper in the post-Civil War south.

Wright moved from school to school, attempting to make friends and make his talents known. Though both tasks were difficult, he became valedictorian of his class. Even this accomplishment was spoiled when the principal insisted that Wright read a speech that the principal himself had written, and Wright refused. An uncle told Richard, "They're going to break you," and society, both black and white, seemed intent on doing so. Wright was determined to resist, not to be claimed by his environment as he felt so many blacks around him were.

Wright left Mississippi for Memphis, Tennessee, had little luck there, and—with money stolen from the film theater where he worked—moved to Chicago. When others stole, Wright disapproved—not for moral reasons, but because he felt stealing did not change the fundamental relationship of a person to his environment. When it offered a chance to change that environment, Wright accepted it.

In Chicago, Wright became involved with others who viewed the country as he did, first in a federal theater project and then with the Communist John Reed Club, which supported his writing until Wright's goals differed from their own. In 1937, he moved to New York City to become the editor of the *Daily Worker.* A year later, he published his first important work, *Uncle Tom's Children*, after which he won a Guggenheim Fellowship, which provided him with the time and funds to write *Native Son*. The novel was published to great acclaim and was followed by a second major work, *Black Boy.* Although his writing career was a success, Wright was arguing more frequently with the Communist party, with which he finally broke in 1944, and was becoming less optimistic about the hope of racial progress in the United States.

In 1946, Wright moved to France, where he spent the rest of his life. Although he wrote a great deal there, nothing in his later work, with the possible exception of *The Outsider,* approaches the strength of *Native Son* and *Black Boy.* The existentialism that was always implicit in his work became the dominant theme, but—displaced from his native environment—Wright never again found a convincing dramatic situation in which to work out his preoccupations.

Wright died in France of a heart attack on November 28, 1960. After his death, several more of his works were published, including the novels *Lawd Today* and, much later, *A Father's Law.*

Analysis

Richard Wright's best work is the story of one man's struggle to define himself and by so doing make himself free and responsible, fully human, a character worthy not of pity but of admiration and horror simultaneously. Typically, the character is an outsider, and Wright uses blackness as a representation of that alienation, though his characters are never as interested in defining their blackness as in defining their humanity. Although many characters in Wright's works are outsiders without being aware of their condition, Wright is never interested in them except as foils. Many of them avoid confronting themselves by fleeing to dreams; religion and liquor are two avoidance mechanisms for Wright's characters, narcotics that blind them to their surrounding world, to what they are and what they might be.

Even Wright's main characters must not think about that world too often: To let it touch them is to risk insanity or violence, and so his characters strive to keep the fire within in check, to keep the physical hunger satisfied. Thus, all of Wright's protagonists are initially trapped by desire and by fear—fear of what might happen to them, what they may do, if they risk venturing outside the confines of black life in America—and the desire to do so. The life outside may be glimpsed in films; Bigger Thomas, for example, goes to a film and watches contrasting and artificial views of black and white society. Yet as untruthful as both views are, they remind Bigger of a reality beyond his present situation. Desire is often symbolized by flight; Bigger, like other Wright characters, dreams of flying above the world, unchained from its limitations.

Most of Wright's stories and novels examine what happens when the protagonist's fear is mastered for a moment when desires are met. The manifestation of desire in Wright is almost always through violence (and it is here, perhaps, that he is most pessimistic, for other, more positive, manifestations of desire, such as love, can come only later, after the protagonists have violently acted out their longings). Violence is central to Wright's fiction, for as important as sex may be to his characters, power is much more so, and power is often achieved through violence; in Wright's world, beatings and murders are frequent acts—central and occasionally creative.

Once the character has acted, he finds himself trapped again in a new set of oppositions, for in acting, he has left the old sureties behind, has made himself free, and has begun to define and create himself. With that new freedom comes a new awareness of responsibility. He is without excuses, and that awareness is as terrifying as—though more liberating than—the fears he has previously known. Although Wright does not always elaborate on what may follow, the characters open up new possibilities for themselves. If one may create oneself by violence, perhaps, Wright sometimes suggests, there are other, less destructive ways as well.

Some of Wright's novels end on this note of optimism, the characters tragically happy: tragic because they have committed violent and repulsive acts, but happy because for the first time they have *chosen* to commit them; they have freed themselves from their constraints, and the future, however short it may be, lies open. Others end simply with tragedy, the destruction achieving no purpose, the characters attaining no illumination.

LAWD TODAY

Lawd Today, written before *Native Son* but not published until after Wright's death, tells the story of Jake Jackson from his awakening on the morning of February 12, 1936, to that day's violent conclusion. Jackson is Wright's most inarticulate protagonist: He has a banal life, undefined dreams, and a vague sense of discontent that he is unable to explain. Violent and prejudiced, he speaks in clichés, a language as meaningless as his life.

The book incorporates a montage of radio broadcasts, newspaper articles, and religious and political pamphlets into the narration of Jake's day. Divided into three sections, *Lawd Today* opens with Jake's dream of running up an endless staircase after a disappearing voice. That dream gives way to the reality of his life: hunger, anger, and recrimination. Tricked by Jake into an abortion for which Jake still owes five hundred dollars and now claiming to have a tumor that will cost another five hundred dollars to remove, Jake's wife represents his entrapment. In the first section, "Commonplace," Jake reveals his brutish and trivial character: his anger at his wife, a jealousy and resentment that lead him to bait her so he can hit her, a mock battle straightening his hair, and a meeting with friends who work with him at the post office. As they play bridge to pass the time until work, Wright presents without comment their stupid, cliché-ridden conversation.

The second section, "Squirrel Cage," shows the men at work. They are all alienated in meaningless, routine jobs, but Jake's position is the most desperate, for his wife has been to see his boss, and he is now threatened with the loss of his job. Falling deeper into debt by borrowing more money and making mistakes on the job, Jake is trapped by his work—despite his own protestations, as a self-proclaimed Republican and capitalist, that work is liberating. This section, too, ends with a long, rambling, and banal conversation among the men at work.

In the concluding section, "Rat's Alley," the men go to a brothel for a good time on some of Jake's borrowed money. There, Jake is robbed and then beaten for his threats of revenge. Finally, Jake stumbles homeward, his day nearing an end. The February weather, pleasant when the book began, has turned bad. All of Jake's frustration and anger finally erupt; he beats his wife, whom he finds kneeling asleep by the bed in an attitude of prayer. As they struggle, he throws objects through the window. She grabs a shard of broken glass and slashes him three times. The book ends with Jake lying in a drunken stupor, bleeding, while his wife is on her knees, also bleeding, praying for death. Outside, the wind blows mercilessly.

Although some of the experimentalism of *Lawd Today* seems artificial, and although the protagonist is too limited to sustain the reader's interest, this early work is powerful and economical. The situation, if not the character, is typical of Wright's work, and the reader understands Jake's violent frustration. *Lawd Today* has its flaws, but it foreshadows the strengths of Wright's best work and in its own right is a daring and fascinating novel.

NATIVE SON

Along with *Black Boy*, *Native Son* is one of Wright's finest achievements: a brilliant portrayal of, as Wright put it, the way the environment provides the instrumentalities through which one expresses oneself and the way that self becomes whole despite the environment's conspiring to keep it divided. The book parallels Theodore Dreiser's *An American Tragedy* (1925): Both are three-part novels in which there is a murder, in part accidental, in part willed; an attempted flight; and a long concluding trial, in both cases somewhat anticlimactic. Both novels are concerned with the interplay of environment and heredity, of fate and accident, and both have protagonists who rebel against the world that would hold them back.

In the first part of *Native Son*, Bigger Thomas is a black man cut off from family and peers. Superficially like his friends, he is in fact possessed of a different consciousness. To think about that consciousness is for him to risk insanity or violence, so Bigger endeavors to keep his fears and uncertainty at a preconscious level. On the day of the first section, however, he is required by the welfare agency to apply for a job as a menial at the home of the rich Dalton family. Mr. Dalton is a ghetto landlord who soothes his conscience by donating sums of money for recreational purposes. That it is a minuscule part of the money he is deriving from blacks is an irony he overlooks. Mrs. Dalton is blind, a fact that is necessary to the plot as well as being symbolic. Their daughter, Mary, is a member of the Communist Party, and from the moment she sees Bigger, who wants nothing more than to be left alone, she begins to enlist his support.

The first evening, Bigger is to drive Mary to a university class. In reality, she is going with Jan Erlone, her Communist boyfriend, to a party meeting. Afterward, they insist that Bigger take them to a bar in the black part of town. Jan and Mary are at this point satirized, for their attitudes toward blacks are as limited and stereotyped as any in the novel. Bigger does not want to be seen by his friends with whites, but that fact does not occur to Mary. After much drinking, Bigger must carry the drunken Mary to her bedroom. He puts her to bed, stands over her, attracted to the woman he sees. The door opens and Mrs. Dalton enters. When Mary makes drunken noises, Bigger becomes frightened that Mrs. Dalton will come close enough to discover him, so he puts a pillow over Mary's face to quiet her. By the time Mrs. Dalton leaves, Mary is dead.

Wright wanted to make Bigger a character it would be impossible to pity, and what follows is extremely grisly. Bigger tries to put Mary's body in the furnace and saws off her head to make her fit. However accidental Mary's death may appear to the reader, Bigger himself does not regard it as such. He has, he thinks, many times wanted to kill whites without ever having the opportunity to do so. This time there was the act without the desire, but rather than seeing himself as the victim of a chance occurrence, Bigger prefers to unite the earlier desire with the present act, to make himself whole by accepting responsibility for the killing. Indeed, he not only accepts the act but also determines to capitalize on it by sending a ransom note. Later, accused of raping Mary as well, an act he considered but did not commit, he reverses the process, accepting responsibility for this, too, even though here there was desire but no act. His only sign of conscience is that he cannot bring himself to shake the ashes in the furnace; this guilt is not redemptive, but his undoing, for, in an implausible scene in the Dalton basement, the room fills with smoke, the murder is revealed to newspaper reporters gathered there, and Bigger is forced to flee.

He runs with his girlfriend, Bessie Mears. She, like Bigger, has a hunger for sensation, which has initially attracted him to her. Now, however, as they flee together, she becomes a threat and a burden; huddled with her in an abandoned tenement, Bigger wants only to be rid of her. He picks up a brick and smashes her face, then dumps her body down an air shaft. His only regret is not that he has killed her, but that he has forgotten to remove their money from her body.

The rest of the plot moves quickly: Bigger is soon arrested, the trial is turned into a political farce, and Bigger is convicted and sentenced to death. In the last part of the novel, after Bigger's arrest, the implications of the action are developed, largely through Bigger's relations to other characters. Some of the characters are worthy only of contempt, particularly the district attorney, who, in an attempt at reelection, is turning the trial into political capital. Bigger's mother relies on religion. In a scene in the jail cell, she falls on her knees in apology before Mrs. Dalton and urges Bigger to pray, but toughness is Bigger's code. He is embarrassed by his mother's self-abasement, and although he agrees to pray simply to end his discomfort, his attitude toward religion is shown when he throws away a cross a minister has given him and throws a cup of coffee in a priest's face. In his view, they want only to avoid the world and to force him to accept guilt without responsibility.

Bigger learns from two characters. The first is Boris Max, the lawyer the Communist Party provides. Max listens to Bigger, and for the first time in his life, Bigger exposes his ideas and feelings to another human. Max's plea to the court is that, just as Bigger must accept responsibility for what he has done, so must the society around him understand its responsibility for what Bigger has become and, if the court chooses to execute Bigger, understand the consequences that must flow from that action. He does not argue—nor does Wright believe—that Bigger is a victim of injustice. There is no injustice, because that would presume a world in which Bigger could hope for justice, and such a world does not exist; more important, Bigger is not a victim, for he has chosen his own fate. Max argues rather that all men are entitled to happiness. Like all of Wright's protagonists, Bigger has earlier been torn between the poles of dread and ecstasy. His ecstasy, his happiness, comes from the meaningfulness he creates in his existence, a product of self-realization. Unhappily for Bigger, he realizes himself through murder: It was, he feels, his highest creative act.

If Max articulates the intellectual presentation of Wright's beliefs about Bigger, it is Jan, Mary's lover, who is its dramatic representation. He visits Bigger in his cell and, having at last understood the futility and paucity of his own stereotypes, admits to Bigger that he too shares in the responsibility for what has happened. He, too, addresses Bigger as a human being, but from the unique position of being the one who is alive to remind Bigger of the consequences of his actions, for Bigger learns that Jan has suffered loss through what he has done and that, while Bigger has created himself, he has also destroyed another.

Native Son ends with the failure of Max's appeals on Bigger's behalf. He comes to the cell to confront Bigger before his execution, and the novel closes with Bigger Thomas smiling at Max as the prison door clangs shut. He will die happy because he will die fulfilled, having, however terribly, created a self. *Native Son* is Wright's most powerful work, because his theme, universal in nature, is given its fullest and most evocative embodiment. In the characterization of Bigger, alienated man at his least abstract and most genuine, of Bigger's exactly rendered mind and milieu, and of Bigger's working out of his destiny, *Native Son* is Wright's masterpiece.

Unlike many highly acclaimed books of the 1940's, *Native Son* and *Black Boy* have not become dated. They offer a lacerating challenge to contemporary readers and writers—a challenge to share the relentless integrity of Wright's vision.

THE OUTSIDER

Wright's next novel, *The Outsider*, written in France and published thirteen years after *Native Son*, suffers from a surfeit of internal explanation and a failure to provide a setting as rich as that of *Native Son*. Still, its portrayal of Cross Damon and his struggle to define himself, while too self-conscious, adds new dimensions to Wright's myth.

As the novel opens, Damon is trapped by his life. His job with the post office is unfulfilling, his wife is threatening, and his underage mistress is pregnant. He "desires desire," but there is no way for that desire to be completed. "A man creates himself," he has told his wife, but the self Damon has created is a nightmare. He broods, his brooding as close as he comes to religion. Another underground man, Damon gets his chance for new life on the subway. Thought dead after his identification papers are found near the mangled body of another, Damon gets a chance to create himself anew. He must invent, he thinks, not only his future, but also a past to fit with his present; this new opportunity brings with it a different and more potent sense of dread.

From the beginning of this new life, Damon is remarkably successful at the mechanics of creating a past. He easily obtains a birth certificate and a draft card. At a deeper level, however, he traps himself as surely as he has been trapped in his old life, so that his new one becomes a continuous act of bad faith. Even before he leaves Chicago, he hides in a brothel where he encounters a coworker who recognizes him. Damon murders the man and throws his body out a window. The pattern of violence, so typical of Wright's characters, begins in earnest for Damon.

Taking a train to New York, Cross meets two people who will influence his new life, a black waiter who introduces him to the world of Communist politics in New York City, and Ely Houston, the district attorney, who is the most articulate person in the novel and the only one fully to understand Damon. Houston asks Damon why, when all blacks are outsiders, so few seem conscious of this fact. Wright suggests that being human is too much to be borne by people, that the struggle to define oneself is too difficult; the novel is a testament to that suggestion.

The Communist Party members, too, are outsiders, and there is nothing unified about their company. Each one that Damon meets is playing god, hoping to protect and extend his personal power. Their awareness of their motives varies, but they are a threat to Damon, and the action of the book is propelled by a series of murders: Damon himself wants to act like a god. Near the end of the book, Houston comes to understand that Damon is the killer, but—rather than indicting and punishing him legally—Houston allows him to go free, alone with his knowledge of what he is. Damon is horrified by his fate, but he is robbed of even that when he is killed by two Communist Party members who fear him.

The Outsider is both an extension and a modification of Wright's earlier views; it is far more pessimistic than *Native Son*, and the influence of the French existentialists is more pervasive. Like earlier Wright heroes, Damon is engaged in defining the world and himself. "The moment we act 'as if' it's true, then it's true," he thinks, because each person, in the absence of a god, is able to create the world and its truth. From Fyodor Dostoevski, Wright again borrows the notion of underground man and the idea that without a god, all is permitted. Yet as each man plays god, as each becomes criminal, policeman, judge, and executioner, there are no longer limits. People desire everything, and desire is described as a floating demon. People are jealous gods here—the worlds they create are petty, their jealousy destructive. Cross Damon is loved in the novel, but that love, unlike the love in *Native Son*, which is held up as potentially meaningful, is here without promise. Although he creates himself and his world in *The Outsider*, all that is made is violent and brutal, a world without redemption even in the act of self-realization.

At the end of the novel, Cross Damon dies, not with Bigger Thomas's smile, but with the knowledge that alone, people are nothing. Searching in his last moments of freedom for a clean, well-lighted place in which to rest before he confronts the world again, Cross finds only death. Before he dies, he admits his final act of bad faith: He has thought that he could create a world and be different from other men, that he could remain innocent. Like Joseph Conrad's Kurtz in *Heart of Darkness* (1902), Damon dies realizing the futility of that hope; having looked into his own heart of darkness, he dies with the word "horror" on his lips.

It is Wright's bleakest conclusion, the book his most relentless examination of the consequences of his own philosophy. If *The Outsider* lacks the narrative drive of *Native Son*, it remains a strongly conceived and troubling piece of fiction.

THE LONG DREAM

The Long Dream, despite some effective scenes, is one of Wright's weakest novels. The story of Rex "Fishbelly" Tucker's growing up and coming to terms with his environment is a pale repetition of earlier themes. The first section describes Tucker's youth. His father, an undertaker, is the richest black man in town, but his money comes also from a brothel he runs on the side. Tucker admires his father's success while detesting his obsequiousness with whites. When, however, Fishbelly is arrested, he twice faints at the white world's threats. Having presented himself as a victim, he becomes one. Walking home after his father has arranged his freedom, Fishbelly sees an injured dog, which he puts out of its misery. Fishbelly then comes upon a white man who is pinned to the ground with a car door on his body. When the white man calls out to Fishbelly, using the term "nigger," Fishbelly walks on, leaving the man to die.

In the second section, Fishbelly finds a woman, but she and forty-one others are burned to death in a fire at the bar. The rest of the novel is an unconvincing story of the police who want the return of the cancelled checks that Fishbelly's father has used to pay them off, the police's arranged murder of the father, the subsequent framing and imprisoning of Fishbelly for rape, and Fishbelly's keeping the checks for his future use. All of this is seriously contrived. At the end, Fishbelly is on a plane leaving for France, where his childhood friends are stationed in the army, which they describe as exciting. He is talking to an Italian whose father has come to America and found a dream, where Fishbelly himself has known only a nightmare. France, he dreams, will offer him what America has not.

In Fishbelly's attempt to understand himself and his environment, he is a typical Wright protagonist. He is weaker than Wright's usual characters, however, and that shallowness, coupled with an implausible plot, prevents the novel from being entirely successful.

A FATHER'S LAW

Julia Wright, Richard Wright's daughter, had *A Father's Law*, his last unfinished novel, published on the one hundredth anniversary of his birth. Along with providing intriguing insight into a partial biographical critique, Julia Wright's introduction to the novel shares her touching memory of finding the manuscript in the months after Wright's death.

The novel is a study in the ironies present in the law that Ruddy Turner must enforce, both as a police officer and as a father. The story begins with Ruddy's promotion from police captain in an African American neighborhood in Chicago to the position of police chief in an affluent white area of the city. The police commissioner hopes to stir up the complacent citizens of Brentwood Park against the crime that runs rampant in the area. As soon as Ruddy assumes his new office, he is confronted with a portion of that crime—five unsolved murders. In the midst of work challenges, Ruddy also faces concerns at home. His relationship with his academically brilliant son, Tommy, is conflicted. He cannot understand either Tommy's ways of thinking or his motivations. Tommy's educational interest in the psychological motivations behind acts of crime further separates the father and son. While Tommy questions why people do not commit crimes, his father questions why they do. Ruddy's lack of comprehension of his son's reasoning and actions leads him to suspect his own son in the murders. The novel's end leaves Ruddy wrestling with his son's very public confession, a confession that undermines the father's law in every way.

The question of guilt is a central focus of the novel. Ruddy, Tommy, and Tommy's former fiancé, Marie, are all engulfed in guilt. Marie, who has been diagnosed with hereditary congenital syphilis, has been jilted by Tommy. She is blameless, yet she is isolated, and it is her guilt that serves as the psychological driving force behind Tommy's guilt—both literally and figuratively. Further, the lack of ability even to acknowledge, let alone feel, guilt is the problem with Brentwood Park, the scene of both men's downfall. Ruddy's own youthful decision to become a law enforcer in an effort to assuage his feelings of guilt ironically turns back on him with his suspicions of his son and Tommy's subsequent confession to the crimes.

Like Wright's other novels, this novel also deals with isolation. Ruddy is isolated from his friends and fellow officers as he worries that his son is a murderer. Marie is isolated from her parents, her lover, and all other human contact when she is diagnosed with an illness that brings moral condescension. Tommy is isolated from his father and his fiancé. While Ruddy's isolation is partially self-inflicted because he does not want others to know of his doubts about his own child, Marie is isolated as a result of other people's choices. She is truly the innocent victim.

A Father's Law is a brilliant reflection on the meaning of law, the motivations of people, the way guilt works in our lives, and the isolation of human beings. Even in its incomplete state, this deeply psychological piece is further evidence of Wright's genius.

Howard Faulkner
Updated by Theresa L. Stowell

OTHER MAJOR WORKS

SHORT FICTION: *Uncle Tom's Children: Four Novellas*, 1938 (expanded as *Uncle Tom's Children: Five Long Stories*, 1938); *Eight Men*, 1961.

PLAY: *Native Son: The Biography of a Young American*, pr. 1941 (with Paul Green).

POETRY: *Haiku: This Other World*, 1998 (Yoshinobu Hakutani and Robert L. Tener, editors).

NONFICTION: *Twelve Million Black Voices: A Folk History of the Negro in the United States*, 1941 (photographs by Edwin Rosskam); *Black Boy: A Record of Childhood and Youth*, 1945; *Black Power: A Record of Reactions in a Land of Pathos*, 1954; *The Color Curtain*, 1956; *Pagan Spain*, 1957; *White Man, Listen!*, 1957; *American Hunger*, 1977; *Richard Wright Reader*, 1978 (Ellen Wright and Michel Fabre, editors); *Conversations with Richard Wright*, 1993 (Keneth Kinnamon and Fabre, editors).

MISCELLANEOUS: *Works*, 1991 (2 volumes).

BIBLIOGRAPHY

Baldwin, James. *The Price of the Ticket: Collected Nonfiction, 1948-1985*. New York: St. Martin's Press/Marek, 1985. Baldwin's essays "Everybody's Protest Novel" and "Alas, Poor Richard" provide important and provocative insights into Wright and his art.

Butler, Robert. *"Native Son": The Emergence of a New Black Hero*. Boston: Twayne, 1991. Provides an accessible critical look at the seminal novel. Includes bibliographical references and index.

Fabre, Michel. *The Unfinished Quest of Richard Wright*. 2d ed. Urbana: University of Illinois Press, 1993. Update of a work originally published in 1973 remains one of the most authoritative biographies available on Wright.

Felgar, Robert. *Student Companion to Richard Wright*. Westport, Conn.: Greenwood Press, 2000. Basic resource intended for undergraduate readers is composed mainly of biographical information and an introduction to Wright's use of literary elements. Includes a brief bibliography of Wright's works.

Kinnamon, Keneth. *The Emergence of Richard Wright: A Study in Literature and Society*. Urbana: University of Illinois Press, 1972. Valuable study of Wright's background and development as a writer. Covers his writings up to the publication of *Native Son*.

_______. *Richard Wright: An Annotated Bibliography of Criticism and Commentary, 1983-2003*. Jefferson, N.C.: McFarland, 2006. Lists more than eight thousand sources related to Wright's work, including books, articles, and dissertations on African American literature and criticism.

_______, comp. *A Richard Wright Bibliography: Fifty Years of Criticism and Commentary, 1933-1982*. Westport, Conn.: Greenwood Press, 1988. Mammoth work (one of the largest annotated bibliographies ever assembled on an American writer) traces the history of Wright criticism through the early 1980's. An invaluable research tool.

_______, ed. *Critical Essays on Richard Wright's "Native Son."* New York: Twayne, 1997. Collection is divided into sections of reviews, reprinted essays, and new essays. Includes discussions of Wright's handling of race, voice, tone, novelistic structure, the city, and literary influences.

Kinnamon, Keneth, and Michel Fabre, eds. *Conversations with Richard Wright*. Jackson: University Press of Mississippi, 1993. Collection of interviews with Wright, conducted over decades by both American and foreign journalists and scholars, provides insight into the author's views on numerous topics.

Rowley, Hazel. *Richard Wright: The Life and Times*. New York: Henry Holt, 2001. Comprehensive biography places Wright's work within the context of the events of his life. Includes bibliography, photographs, and index.

Walker, Margaret. *Richard Wright: Daemonic Genius*. New York: Warner Publishing, 1988. A critically acclaimed study of Wright's life and work written by a friend and fellow novelist. Not a replacement for Michel Fabre's biography but written with the benefit of several more years of scholarship on issues that include the medical controversy over Wright's death. Walker is especially insightful on Wright's early life, and her comments on Wright's short fiction are short but pithy. Includes a useful bibliographic essay at the end.

FRANK YERBY

Born: Augusta, Georgia; September 5, 1916
Died: Madrid, Spain; November 29, 1991
Also known as: Frank Garvin Yerby

PRINCIPAL LONG FICTION

The Foxes of Harrow, 1946
The Vixens, 1947
The Golden Hawk, 1948
Pride's Castle, 1949
Floodtide, 1950
A Woman Called Fancy, 1951
The Saracen Blade, 1952
The Devil's Laughter, 1953
Benton's Row, 1954
Bride of Liberty, 1954
The Treasure of Pleasant Valley, 1955
Captain Rebel, 1956
Fairoaks, 1957
The Serpent and the Staff, 1958
Jarrett's Jade, 1959
Gillian, 1960
The Garfield Honor, 1961
Griffin's Way, 1962
The Old Gods Laugh: A Modern Romance, 1964
An Odor of Sanctity, 1965
Goat Song, 1968
Judas, My Brother, 1968
Speak Now: A Modern Novel, 1969
The Dahomean: An Historical Novel, 1971
The Girl from Storyville, 1972
The Voyage Unplanned, 1974
Tobias and the Angel, 1975
A Rose for Ana Maria, 1976
Hail the Conquering Hero, 1978
A Darkness at Ingraham's Crest, 1979
Western, 1982
Devilseed, 1984
McKenzie's Hundred, 1985

Frank Yerby
(Library of Congress)

Other literary forms

In addition to his novels, Frank Yerby wrote poetry and short stories that are often found in anthologies of black literature. One story, "Health Card," first published in *Harper's* magazine, won a special O. Henry Memorial Award in 1944.

Achievements

Frank Yerby wrote many best-selling historical novels over a long career beginning in the 1940's. Most of his best work, however, dates from the 1960's, after he had established himself as a prolific popular novelist. Yerby excelled at creating complicated, fast-moving plots that give vivid impressions of historical eras and periods. Often the novels contradict myths and stereotypes of the periods in question. Almost every novel, too, suggests the futility of finding real truth in the universal confusion of the human condition. While Yerby's protagonists are flawed, often by ruthlessness and infidelity, they are also characterized by a fierce sense of dignity based on the worth of a human life.

BIOGRAPHY

Frank Garvin Yerby was born in Augusta, Georgia, on September 5, 1916. He received a bachelor of arts degree from Paine College in 1937 and a master of arts degree from Fisk College in 1938. Subsequently, he did graduate work in education at the University of Chicago.

From 1939 to 1941, Yerby taught English, first at Florida A&M and then at Southern University and A&M College. He married in 1941 and then worked until 1944 at the Ford Motor Company in Dearborn, Michigan, as a technician and then as an inspector at Fairchild Aircraft from 1944 to 1945. In 1944, he won an O. Henry Memorial Award for the short story "Health Card," a story that dealt sensitively with black issues. In 1945, he started work on a novel, *The Foxes of Harrow*, which he aimed to make a commercial success. Thereafter, Yerby wrote many similar melodramatic best sellers. His books have sold millions of copies and have been translated into at least fourteen languages.

Divorced in the 1950's, Yerby moved to France and then to Spain, where he died in 1991. He had four children from his first marriage. His second wife was his researcher and general manager; some of his later novels give evidence of considerable research. He traveled widely, and sometimes his travels involved investigating locales of works in progress.

ANALYSIS

Frank Yerby was a best-selling author, and much of what he wrote has clear commercial appeal, a point on which he made inconsistent remarks. His plots are intricate and involved, but in many of his novels, the characterizations are basically flat. His favorite era is the nineteenth century South, yet he wrote about many other places and times in his more than thirty novels. Occasionally, he set a novel in modern times. The reader of popular best sellers will find in Yerby's novels fast-paced narrative with appropriate amounts of violence and sex.

Yerby was more, however, than a best-selling writer. His short stories written early in his career show promise and develop radically different themes from those of his costume novels. In the 1960's, secure after many commercial successes, Yerby began to do his best work, dealing with larger issues of race and religion, which figure less prominently in his earlier novels. The characters in these later novels are no longer cardboard figures, while the backgrounds are as richly detailed and vividly re-created as ever. Yerby's historical novels must be evaluated within the context of that often unappreciated genre. His novels almost always show the conflict between two worlds or orders, as great historical novels do. Yerby rarely deals with actual historical figures but rather creates characters who have to deal with the essential conflicts of their eras. Often his novels, even the early ones, destroy widely held myths and stereotypes; Darwin Turner suggests that this revisionism might be Yerby's most significant contribution as a novelist. While extensive research is not evident in his early work, many of Yerby's later novels were thoroughly researched. Yerby was at his best in creating the color and movement of a particular era.

Yerby's typical protagonist is, in the words of his main character in *The Serpent and the Staff*, an auslander or outsider, excluded from the ruling social order. The protagonist experientially develops a philosophy that often approaches modern existentialism, an attitude that life has no answer but that people still must cope with the bleakness of human existence with both dignity and humanity. This pattern emerges in Yerby's first novel, *The Foxes of Harrow*, and is developed in three of his best novels: *Griffin's Way*, *An Odor of Sanctity*, and *The Dahomean*.

The Foxes of Harrow

The Foxes of Harrow, Yerby's first novel, is set in the South and covers the years from 1825 to just after the end of the American Civil War. Superficially, it is a novel about a clever schemer who rises to own a plantation with a neoclassical mansion, Harrow, and who has marriages to beautiful white women and a liaison with a stunning mixed-race woman. Much of the novel is composed of stock devices of pulp fiction, and Yerby himself said of *The Foxes of Harrow* that he set out to write a popular novel that would make him a lot of money, regardless of literary merit. Yerby added, however, that he became strangely involved with the writing of the novel and, despite himself, exceeded the ambitions of the pulp genre.

Stephen Fox, the protagonist, is an outsider, originally shanty Irish. He is not merely the rogue that early reviewers took him for, whose success and eventual fall conform to a predictable pulp outline. Fox sees all values and ideals slip from him, so that at the end, he is a failure despite his humanity and perception. He is superior to the southerners with whom he sympathetically deals. More than merely a novel of stock devices, *The Foxes of Harrow* is a story about the failure of a culture.

In the opening of the novel, Yerby's authorial voice establishes a pensive tone as he describes a visit to Harrow, now in ruins, in the twentieth century. Harrow is the symbol of a lost cause. Thus, for symbolic purposes, Harrow is cut off from the modern world. Bathed in moonlight, the ruins of Harrow have a decadent grandeur. The visitor feels driven from room to room and finally away from the house, never wanting to look back. The shortness of the opening, six brief paragraphs, makes the tone all the more striking, and the mood shifts quickly into the dialogue and description of the arrival of Stephen Fox in New Orleans in 1825.

Yerby was at his best in the novel in creating vivid images and scenes of the region during the forty or so years the novel spans. New Orleans appears as a lush feudalistic world where color is measured by degrees, given the novel's constant references to mulattoes, quadroons, and octoroons, references that are historically true to the setting. New Orleans emerges as a backward society that refuses to drain the marshes where the mosquitoes carrying yellow fever breed and instead fires cannon to disperse the plague. The society also destroys the creativity of freed blacks. In one case, a thoroughly educated black man returns from France and is killed for acting as if he were equal to whites. The most poignant scene occurs at the end of the novel, when the young heir to Harrow returns after the war to New Orleans to be confronted by a former slave of Harrow now in control. This former slave presents the heir's unknown half brother (by a beautiful mulatto) to his former master, who sees the image of his father as a young man—but the half brother is mentally disabled. As the scene concludes, Yerby deftly shows the social history of the next one hundred years of the South.

The former slave, now the ruler, knows that power will again return to the whites but suggests that blacks and whites can live together and respect one another. The heir, a combination of the worst of his father's roguish tendencies and the excesses of New Orleans, emphatically denies that such equality and reconciliation between the races are possible.

Yerby was weakest in his creation of character in *The Foxes of Harrow*, for the characters are one-dimensional and move woodenly through a convoluted, overheated plot. Stephen Fox is the fox, the rogue set off from southern society by his birth, whose goals are riches and the most beautiful woman in New Orleans, Odalie Arceneaux, a cold, haughty belle. Her sister, Aurore, is a foil to her, for she is warm and beautiful and in love with Stephen, who is too blind at first to see her love. As is common in pulp fiction, Odalie dies in childbirth, and Stephen then marries gentle Aurore, but only after having fathered a child by a beautiful mulatto when Odalie had spurned his strong sexual drives.

Underneath this claptrap, though, is an author working with social issues not to be found in the typical 1946 pulp novel. In one scene, a black woman recently inducted into slavery throws herself into the Mississippi rather than live in bondage. Old Calleen, a trusted slave at Harrow, later tells her grandson, Inch (the son of the drowned slave), that someday, the rightness of their freedom will be made apparent. More significantly, in understated dialogue, Stephen talks to his son, Etienne, about freeing slaves and says that the country must treat all people equally, including the blacks and the poorest whites. When his son dismisses the poor, white or black, Stephen uses history as a defense, mentioning the French Revolution, Haiti, and insurrectionist Nat Turner. It is in his sympathy and balance in treating social matters that Yerby's "moral mobility" appears, a phrase that a *Times* of London writer used in reviewing a later Yerby novel.

GRIFFIN'S WAY

Griffin's Way was published in 1962, sixteen years after *The Foxes of Harrow*, and is a departure in some respects from Yerby's work up to that time. It treats the Mississippi of the 1870's unglamorously, highlighting squalor, inbreeding among whites, and the violence of the Ku Klux Klan in a manner more characteristic of William Faulkner than of the standard best-selling author. The novel shows the paralysis of humane white society after the war, a paralysis symbolized by the central hero's amnesia and invalid status.

Much of the novel debunks the grandeur and opulence of the Old South, which Yerby himself had occasionally exploited in earlier novels. The ruined South appears first through the eyes of a northerner, Candace Trevor, a New England minister's daughter married to a paralyzed southerner and hired as a nurse for Paris Griffin as the novel opens. She despises the southern "courtesy" to which women are subjected, dismisses the neoclassical architecture in the poorly constructed homes, and comments on how most planters lived in squalor even before the war. Unlike her father, she believes in a Darwinian theory of evolution and sees the darker forces in herself as part of the "ape" still remaining in people. Candace knows that to cure Paris of his amnesia she must find the key to it from Paris's oversexed wife, Laurel. Ferreting out answers with the right leading questions, she discovers the tawdry, twisted story that led to Paris's amnesia and emotional paralysis. It is only her austere moral upbringing that allows her to control her love for Paris to use her knowledge to help him.

When Candace does cure him, Paris tries to return to his home, Griffin's Way, and to his wife, Laurel, but while his cure is a rebirth, it does not allow a return. To begin with, he has returned to a world changed by the war, a world of political corruption and violence, a world that has regressed, so that even a sixty-mile trip, once possible in three hours, now involves an arduous three-day journey because the railroads remain unrepaired even five years after the war. Three years later, with the railroad rebuilt, Paris and Laurel visit Vicksburg, where Paris, despite his humanity, appears troubled by the apparent ascendancy of blacks. Yerby balances the situation by having Paris also see the obvious corruption of the black superintendent of schools, who lives in the grand style of the Old South on money intended for the schools. Paris is thus caught between two worlds: He rejects the Klan as apes but resents a black man wearing a suit as if he is accustomed to it. Even renewed, Paris still represents the paralysis of the humane white during the Reconstruction.

Yerby titled the last third of the novel "Apocalypse," and this part has unresolved elements, unresolved on account of Yerby's honesty in dealing with his material. Paris watches the new world tumble around him, powerless to do anything. Black militants and white Klansmen fight all over the South, but Paris can only catalog the battles; he cannot change events. His moment of action does allow him to rescue Samson, a former slave, and Samson's wife by helping them escape to the North. He can do nothing to help his brother, his mulatto wife, and their children, who are burned in their house except for one daughter, who dies after being repeatedly raped, all of them victims of the Klan. He also helps a black minister escape, but only after the dynamiting of the minister's house, which killed a daughter. At his daughter's funeral, the minister delivers a stern sermon to the Klan members, who then threaten his life so that Paris must again help him. The Klan members finally back off from Paris's house when one accidentally shoots Laurel, still very much a symbol of southern womanhood.

The novel ends with dawn imagery, the night having been endured and the humane whites now waiting for the light of morning. Whether the whites threatened by the Klan can start anew is unclear. Given the implied parallel to modern events, Yerby seems to be saying that it is too soon to tell whether the twentieth century can rise above racial violence; nevertheless, the concluding imagery does suggest hope.

AN ODOR OF SANCTITY

In *An Odor of Sanctity*, Yerby is at his best as a historical novelist. It is a long, deftly paced novel that, while using many of the stock elements of Yerby's novels of the 1940's and 1950's, also deals intelligently with a religious theme. Once again, Yerby creates an outsider, Alaric Teudisson, as hero; he is set off by his odor of sanctity, a saintly force in him of which he is not fully aware for most of his life. Teudisson must deal with the complex culture of medieval Spain, a battleground for Christians, Moors, and numerous bands of marauding barbarians.

Like earlier Yerby protagonists, Teudisson is involved in many liaisons and several marriages. Teudisson is a striking blond of Visigoth extraction who, before the male hormones take effect, is so "beautiful" that at one point he is almost made a catamite. Thereafter, Teudisson has numerous sexual encounters, one unconsummated marriage, and finally a marriage to a woman who has been repeatedly raped by bandits, a marriage that shows Teudisson's magnanimity and also brings him genuine happiness and a family.

The religious motif of *An Odor of Sanctity* adds depth to what would otherwise be an entertaining but rather shallow melodrama. Despite himself, Teudisson becomes a saint by the end of the novel. As a man, Teudisson is handsome but scarred by battle, but as a boy, his beauty, so unlike the usual rough Goth face, led his mother and others to think he was marked for the priesthood. He turns from his religious impulses to lead a secular life, however, and while doing so, he finds his saintliness. In dealing with women, he shows a compassion and love that are the basis of his profound sexual appeal; at one point of seeming dissolution, he has numerous prostitutes loving him because he has talked to them and treated them as human beings and not merely as sex objects. Misused by a woman, he always responds with kindness.

By the end of the novel, Teudisson becomes the arbiter between Moor and Christian factions when a certain group of fanatic Christians wants to destroy all tolerance for the predominant Moors. Throughout the novel, Teudisson has been a genuine ecumenist. At the end, Teudisson, doubting his saintly powers because he is unable to save his wife, willingly seeks crucifixion and thus enters sainthood and legend. In losing himself, he gains sainthood. As in most of his novels, Yerby's greatest strength in *An Odor of Sanctity* is his re-creation of a time, a re-creation imbued with color and action. Again, a humane authorial voice speaks throughout the novel. The book shows that the diversity of medieval Spain is indeed its glory. While the Moorish culture encourages learning and recognizes Christ as a prophet, the contrasting Christian culture (except for Teudisson and a few Church fathers) is dark and intolerant. In showing the clash between these cultures, *An Odor of Sanctity* is first-rate historical fiction.

THE DAHOMEAN

If one of Yerby's novels is destined to last, it is *The Dahomean*, a novel unlike any of his others. It is a simple, moving tale of the life of a black man in his African culture before he was sold into slavery. Yerby neither idealizes nor sensationalizes his material but presents a story composed of love, envy, and hatred that reads as a legend, a story of characters and events drawn larger than life. The protagonist, Nyasanu, is like other Yerby protagonists because he is an alien or outsider: He is far less violent and far more handsome than most men of his society. Caught in the ugliness of the American slave system, he has the tragic quality of some of the great existentialist heroes.

Yerby begins the chronological narrative of Nyasanu as he is about to enter manhood, a passage marked by the painful ritual of circumcision. The early parts of the novel present such rituals in convincing detail. Yerby moves the reader from Nyasanu's initiation to an enemy's attempt to destroy his guardian tree to his wedding and the "deflowering" of his bride. In "A Note to the Reader," Yerby explains that the novel is based on research into the customs of the Dahomeans of the nineteenth century, but Yerby adds to his research his own respect for this African culture.

As Nyasanu moves through his period of manhood, Yerby depicts the society of the Dahomeans as a stage for the great primal emotions and forces of life. Nyasanu has encounters with numerous women, but his sexual experiences are never merely sensational: Nyasanu has a reality that sets him apart from Yerby's typical protagonists. In addition to his sexual encounters, Nyasanu has the experience of real brotherhood, for his society expects each male to have his three closest friends identified in order. Battles with warring tribes give Nyasanu the chance to show bravery and also to distinguish himself as more sensitive to violence than the average Dahomean. In addition, Yerby shows the diversity of Dahomean society, which includes both male homosexuals and Amazonian warriors.

In a moving discussion with his number one friend, Kpadunu, Nyasanu learns that the generations are all of one fabric. Each generation faces the same problems of love, the family, and death. The old priests, therefore, give answers based on the past to the young and the unsure, and—given the coherence of their society—the answers generally hold. Facing the problem of belief in the gods that these old priests try to inculcate in the young, Nyasanu realizes that their wisdom is not divine but experiential, that the past of his society answers the present needs. Ironically, his friend Kpadunu is trying to help Nyasanu rise above the control of priests by showing where their wisdom resides, yet he actually makes the skeptical Nyasanu believe more than he did, so that he must face the priestly prediction that his life will end in Dahomey but will begin again in another place.

Nyasanu does learn that he can count on the inexorability of fate and not the protection of the gods. In quick succession, he loses his friend Kpadunu, his wife in childbirth, and his father. He comes to see his heroism as mere foolishness in taking risks. Rather than listening to the gods, he simply faces life as chieftain and husband of Kpadunu's widow. Far more than the ritual of circumcision, his acceptance of life and his rejection of the illusion of divine protection mark Nyasanu's adulthood. When Nyasanu next appears in the novel, he is chieftain and has four wives. His life is successful until he is sold into slavery with the aid of his homosexual brother and rival.

The betrayal of Nyasanu has the archetypal pattern of tragedy, the hero fallen from great heights, undone by his own blindness in not facing the evil of his brother and his incestuous brother-in-law and by his pride in not following the past and living with his extended family in the same compound. He faces the guns of his attackers with his sword, only to be told to put his sword down, for in the modern era, swords are powerless against guns. First, he must watch the murder of his mother (the slavers see that she is too old to have children), the subsequent murder of all his children (the slavers know that they would die on the voyage across the Atlantic), and the subjugation of his wives, the rape of some and the suicide of one. His response is disassociation, a silence that lasts the rest of his life.

Like a classical tragedy, *The Dahomean* treats terrible despair in its conclusion but leads to an illumination, Nyasanu's enlightenment. He recognizes the evil of blacks selling blacks into American slavery, although they have no conception of the degradation of this foreign slavery, their domestic slavery being gentle and indulgent. Philosophically, Nyasanu faces the bleakness of life with the realization that there are no answers. Truth is only that there is no truth. Nyasanu acquits himself with honor; like a great tragic hero, he has his dignity, the dignity of silence in the face of the emptiness of the human condition.

Dennis Goldsberry

Other major works

SHORT FICTION: "Health Card," 1944.

Bibliography

Bloom, Harold, ed. "Frank Yerby." In *Modern Black American Fiction Writers*. New York: Chelsea House, 1994. Yerby is one of the twelve African American writers included in this book, which contains a biography, selected critical analysis of his work, and a bibliography.

Bone, Robert A. *The Negro Novel in America*. Rev. ed. New Haven, Conn.: Yale University Press, 1987. A general survey of the black novel in the United States. Bone dismisses Yerby as the "prince of pulpsters."

Glasrud, Bruce. "'The Fishes and the Poet's Hands': Frank Yerby, a Black Author in White America." *Journal of American and Comparative Cultures* 23, no. 4 (Winter, 2000): 15-21. A profile of Yerby, in which Glasrud analyzes the writer's commercial success and the challenges he encountered in his literary career. Glasrud considers Yerby a "best-selling, exceptionally popular black American author, albeit one of the most maligned and misunderstood writers of the twentieth century."

Goldsberry, Dennis. "Frank Yerby." In *Notable African American Writers*. Vol. 3. Pasadena, Calif.: Salem Press, 2006. A biographical article on Yerby that summarizes his career and analyzes his long fiction, including *The Foxes of Harrow*, *Griffin's Way*, *An Odor of Sanctity*, and *The Dahomean*.

Hill, James L. "The Anti-Heroic Hero in Frank Yerby's Historical Novels." In *Perspec-*

tives of Black Popular Culture, edited by Harry B. Shaw. Bowling Green, Ohio: Bowling Green State University Popular Press, 1990. Hill maintains that Yerby's isolation from American literary culture is crucial to understanding his fiction, in which "his great theme is the exploration of the turbulent life of an outcast who fights his way into an alien culture."

Jarrett, Gene Andrew. "'For Endless Generations': Myth, Dynasty, and Frank Yerby's *The Foxes of Harrow*." *Southern Literary Journal* 39, no. 1 (Autumn, 2006): 54-70. A discussion of Yerby's literary career, focusing on *The Foxes of Harrow*, with an examination of literary criticism of his work. Jarrett maintains that the harsh critical reviews have led to Yerby's "marginal status" in the canon of African American literature.

Osborne, Gwendolyn. "Romance: How Black Romance—Novels, That Is—Came to Be." *Black Issues Book Review* 4, no. 1 (January/February, 2003): 50-53. In this brief article, Osborne traces the origin of African American romance novels and discusses Yerby's contribution to the genre.

Turner, Darwin. "Frank Yerby as Debunker." In *The Black Novelist*, edited by Robert Hemenway. Columbus, Ohio: Merrill, 1970. Turner comments on Yerby's "painful groping for meaning" behind a "soap-opera façade."

Bibliography

Every effort has been made to include studies published in 2000 and later. Most items in this bibliography contain a listing of secondary sources, making it easier to identify other critical commentary on novelists, movements, and themes.

Theoretical, Thematic, and Historical Studies

Altman, Janet Gurkin. *Epistolarity: Approaches to a Form.* Columbus: Ohio State University Press, 1982. Examines the epistolary novel, explaining how novelists use the letter form to develop characterization, further their plots, and develop meaning.

Beaumont, Matthew, ed. *Adventures in Realism.* Malden, Mass.: Blackwell, 2007. Fifteen essays explore facets of realism, which was critical to the development of the novel. Provides a theoretical framework for understanding how novelists attempt to represent the real and the common in fiction.

Brink, André. *The Novel: Language and Narrative from Cervantes to Calvino.* New York: New York University Press, 1998. Uses contemporary theories of semiotics and narratology to establish a continuum between early novelists and those of the postmodern era in their conscious use of language to achieve certain effects. Ranges across national boundaries to illustrate the theory of the development of the novel since the seventeenth century.

Brownstein, Rachel. *Becoming a Heroine: Reading About Women in Novels.* New York: Viking Press, 1982. Feminist survey of novels from the eighteenth century through the latter half of the twentieth century. Examines how "becoming a heroine" defines for women a sense of value in their lives. Considers novels by both men and women, and discusses the importance of the traditional marriage plot.

Bruzelius, Margaret. *Romancing the Novel: Adventure from Scott to Sebald.* Lewisburg, Pa.: Bucknell University Press, 2007. Examines the development of the adventure novel, linking it with the medieval romance tradition and exploring readers' continuing fascination with the genre.

Cavallaro, Dani. *The Gothic Vision: Three Centuries of Horror, Terror, and Fear.* New York: Continuum, 2005. Study of the gothic novel from its earliest manifestations in the eighteenth century to the early twenty-first century. Through the lenses of contemporary cultural theories, examines readers' fascination with novels that invoke horror, terror, and fright.

Doody, Margaret Anne. *The True Story of the Novel.* New Brunswick, N.J.: Rutgers University Press, 1996. Traces the roots of the novel, traditionally thought to have been developed in the seventeenth century, to classical Greek and Latin texts that exhibit characteristics of modern fiction.

Hale, Dorothy J., ed. *The Novel: An Anthology of Criticism and Theory, 1900-2000.* Malden, Mass.: Blackwell, 2006. Collection of essays by theorists and novelists. Includes commentary on the novel form from the perspective of formalism, structuralism, poststructuralism, Marxism, and reader response theory. Essays also address the novel through the lenses of sociology, gender studies, and feminist theory.

_______. *Social Formalism: The Novel in Theory from Henry James to the Present*. Stanford, Calif.: Stanford University Press, 1998. Emphasizes the novel's special ability to define a social world for readers. Relies heavily on the works of contemporary literary and cultural theorists. Provides a summary of twentieth century efforts to identify a theory of fiction that encompasses novels of many kinds.

Hart, Stephen M., and Wen-chin Ouyang, eds. *A Companion to Magical Realism*. London: Tamesis, 2005. Essays outlining the development of Magical Realism, tracing its roots from Europe through Latin America to other regions of the world. Explores the political dimensions of the genre.

Hoffman, Michael J., and Patrick D. Murphy, eds. *Essentials of the Theory of Fiction*. 2d ed. Durham, N.C.: Duke University Press, 1996. Collection of essays by influential critics from the late nineteenth century through the twentieth century. Focuses on the essential elements of fiction and the novel's relationship to the world it depicts.

Lodge, David. *The Art of Fiction: Illustrated from Classic and Modern Texts*. New York: Viking Press, 1993. Short commentaries on the technical aspects of fiction. Examples from important and minor novelists illustrate literary principles and techniques such as point of view, suspense, character introduction, irony, motivation, and ending.

Lynch, Deirdre, and William B. Walker, eds. *Cultural Institutions of the Novel*. Durham, N.C.: Duke University Press, 1996. Fifteen essays examine aspects of long fiction produced around the world. Encourages a redefinition of the genre and argues for inclusion of texts not historically considered novels.

Moretti, Franco, ed. *The Novel*. 2 vols. Princeton, N.J.: Princeton University Press, 2006. Compendium exploring the novel from multiple perspectives, including as an anthropological, historical, and sociological document; a function of the national tradition from which it emerges; and a work of art subject to examination using various critical approaches.

Priestman, Martin, ed. *The Cambridge Companion to Crime Fiction*. New York: Cambridge University Press, 2003. Essays examine the nature and development of the genre, explore works by writers (including women and ethnic minorities) from several countries, and establish links between crime fiction and other literary genres. Includes a chronology.

Scaggs, John. *Crime Fiction*. New York: Routledge, 2005. Provides a history of crime fiction, explores key subgenres, and identifies recurring themes that suggest the wider social and historical context in which these works are written. Suggests critical approaches that open crime fiction to serious study.

Shiach, Morag, ed. *The Cambridge Companion to the Modernist Novel*. New York: Cambridge University Press, 2007. Essays explaining the concept of modernism and its influence on the novel. Detailed examination of works by writers from various countries, all influenced by the modernist movement. Includes a detailed chronology.

Vice, Sue. *Holocaust Fiction*. New York: Routledge, 2000. Examines controversies generated by novels about the Holocaust. Focuses on eight important works, but also offers observations on the polemics surrounding publication of books on this topic.

Zunshine, Lisa. *Why We Read Fiction: Theory of Mind and the Novel*. Columbus: Ohio State University Press, 2006. Applies theories of cognitive psychology to novel reading, explaining how experience and human nature lead readers to constrain their interpretations of a given text. Provides numerous examples from well-known novels to illustrate how and why readers find pleasure in fiction.

AFRICAN AMERICAN ISSUES AND THEMES

Abernathy, Jeff. *To Hell and Back: Race and Betrayal in the Southern Novel*. Athens: University of Georgia Press, 2003. Examines novels of Mark Twain and several twentieth century Southern writers to determine how the pattern of friendship and betrayal has helped illuminate one of the most important dichotomies of American culture: the proclamation of democracy and trends supporting racial hierarchies.

Bell, Bernard W. *The Contemporary African American Novel: Its Folk Roots and Modern Literary Branches*. Amherst: University of Massachusetts Press, 2004. Extensive historical examination of the development of African American fiction, focusing on distinctive elements and outlining the role of political and social influences in changing the focus of African American novels.

Bertens, Hans, and Theo d'Haen. *Contemporary American Crime Fiction*. New York: Palgrave, 2001. Surveys the work of crime and detective writers of the 1990's. Discusses ethnic crime literature, police procedurals, private detectives, and American fiction exploring other countries and historical periods. Special focus on the writing of women and people of color.

Hume, Kathryn. *American Dream, American Nightmare: Fiction Since 1960*. Urbana: University of Illinois Press, 2000. Surveys one hundred novels written between 1960 and 2000 that critique the idea of the American Dream and the failure of the nation to provide opportunities for happiness and prosperity to all of its citizens.

Laurence W. Mazzeno

Glossary of Literary Terms

absurdism: A philosophical attitude, pervading much of modern drama and fiction, that underlines the isolation and alienation that humans experience, having been thrown into what absurdists see as a godless universe devoid of religious, spiritual, or metaphysical meaning. Conspicuous in its lack of logic, consistency, coherence, intelligibility, and realism, the literature of the absurd depicts the anguish, forlornness, and despair inherent in the human condition. Counter to the rationalist assumptions of traditional humanism, absurdism denies the existence of universal truth or value.

allegory: A literary mode in which a second level of meaning, wherein characters, events, and settings represent abstractions, is encoded within the surface narrative. The allegorical mode may dominate an entire work, in which case the encoded message is the work's primary reason for being, or it may be an element in a work otherwise interesting and meaningful for its surface story alone. Elements of allegory may be found in Jonathan Swift's *Gulliver's Travels* (1726) and Thomas Mann's *Der Zauberberg* (1924; *The Magic Mountain*, 1927).

anatomy: Literally the term means the "cutting up" or "dissection" of a subject into its constituent parts for closer examination. Northrop Frye, in his *Anatomy of Criticism* (1957), uses the term to refer to a narrative that deals with mental attitudes rather than people. As opposed to the novel, the anatomy features stylized figures who are mouthpieces for the ideas they represent.

antagonist: The character in fiction who stands as a rival or opponent to the *protagonist*.

antihero: Defined by Seán O'Faoláin as a fictional figure who, deprived of social sanctions and definitions, is always trying to define himself and to establish his own codes. Ahab may be seen as the antihero of Herman Melville's *Moby Dick* (1851).

archetype: The term "archetype" entered literary criticism from the psychology of Carl Jung, who defined archetypes as "primordial images" from the "collective unconscious" of humankind. Jung believed that works of art derive much of their power from the unconscious appeal of these images to ancestral memories. In his extremely influential *Anatomy of Criticism* (1957), Northrop Frye gave another sense of the term wide currency, defining the archetype as "a symbol, usually an image, which recurs often enough in literature to be recognizable as an element of one's literary experience as a whole."

atmosphere: The general mood or tone of a work; atmosphere is often associated with setting but can also be established by action or dialogue. A classic example of atmosphere is the primitive, fatalistic tone created in the opening description of Egdon Heath in Thomas Hardy's *The Return of the Native* (1878).

bildungsroman: Sometimes called the "novel of education," the bildungsroman focuses on the growth of a young *protagonist* who is learning about the world and finding his or her place in life; typical examples are James Joyce's *A Portrait of the Artist as a*

Young Man (1914-1915, serial; 1916, book) and Thomas Wolfe's *Look Homeward, Angel* (1929).

biographical criticism: Criticism that attempts to determine how the events and experiences of an author's life influence his or her work.

bourgeois novel: A novel in which the values, preoccupations, and accoutrements of middle-class or bourgeois life are given particular prominence. The heyday of the bourgeois novel was the nineteenth century, when novelists as varied as Jane Austen, Honoré de Balzac, and Anthony Trollope both criticized and unreflectingly transmitted the assumptions of the rising middle class.

canon: An authorized or accepted list of books. In modern parlance, the literary canon comprehends the privileged texts, classics, or great books that are thought to belong permanently on university reading lists. Recent theory—especially feminist, Marxist, and poststructuralist—critically examines the process of canon formation and questions the hegemony of white male writers. Such theory sees canon formation as the ideological act of a dominant institution and seeks to undermine the notion of canonicity itself, thereby preventing the exclusion of works by women, minorities, and oppressed peoples.

character: Characters in fiction can be presented as if they were real people or as stylized functions of the plot. Usually characters are a combination of both factors.

classicism: A literary stance or value system consciously based on the example of classical Greek and Roman literature. While the term is applied to an enormous diversity of artists in many different periods and in many different national literatures, "classicism" generally denotes a cluster of values including formal discipline, restrained expression, reverence for tradition, and an objective rather than a subjective orientation. As a literary tendency, classicism is often opposed to *Romanticism*, although many writers combine classical and romantic elements.

climax/crisis: The term "climax" refers to the moment of the reader's highest emotional response, whereas "crisis" refers to a structural element of plot, a turning point at which a resolution must take place.

complication: The point in a novel when the *conflict* is developed or when the already existing conflict is further intensified.

conflict: The struggle that develops as a result of the opposition between the *protagonist* and another person, the natural world, society, or some force within the self.

contextualist criticism: A further extension of *formalist criticism*, which assumes that the language of art is constitutive. Rather than referring to preexistent values, the artwork creates values only inchoately realized before. The most important advocates of this position are Eliseo Vivas (*The Artistic Transaction*, 1963) and Murray Krieger (*The Play and Place of Criticism*, 1967).

conventions: All those devices of stylization, compression, and selection that constitute the necessary differences between art and life. According to the Russian Formalists, these conventions constitute the "literariness" of literature and are the only proper concern of the literary critic.

deconstruction: An extremely influential contemporary school of criticism based on the works of the French philosopher Jacques Derrida. Deconstruction treats literary works as unconscious reflections of the reigning myths of Western culture. The primary myth is that there is a meaningful world that language signifies or represents. The deconstructionist critic is most often concerned with showing how a literary text tacitly subverts the very assumptions or myths on which it ostensibly rests.

defamiliarization: Coined by Viktor Shklovsky in 1917, this term denotes a basic principle of Russian Formalism. Poetic language (by which the Formalists meant artful language, in prose as well as in poetry) defamiliarizes or "makes strange" familiar experiences. The technique of art, says Shklovsky, is to "make objects unfamiliar, to make forms difficult, to increase the difficulty and length of perception. . . . Art is a way of experiencing the artfulness of an object; the object is not important."

detective story: The so-called classic detective story (or mystery) is a highly formalized and logically structured mode of fiction in which the focus is on a crime solved by a detective through interpretation of evidence and ratiocination; the most famous detective in this mode is Arthur Conan Doyle's Sherlock Holmes. Many modern practitioners of the genre, however, such as Dashiell Hammett, Raymond Chandler, and Ross Macdonald, have de-emphasized the puzzlelike qualities of the detective story, stressing instead characterization, theme, and other elements of mainstream fiction.

determinism: The belief that an individual's actions are essentially determined by biological and environmental factors, with free will playing a negligible role. (See *naturalism.*)

dialogue: The similitude of conversation in fiction, dialogue serves to characterize, to further the *plot*, to establish *conflict*, and to express thematic ideas.

displacement: Popularized in criticism by Northrop Frye, this term refers to the author's attempt to make his or her story psychologically motivated and realistic, even as the latent structure of the mythical motivation moves relentlessly forward.

dominant: A term coined by Roman Jakobson to refer to that which "rules, determines, and transforms the remaining components in the work of a single artist, in a poetic canon, or in the work of an epoch." The shifting of the dominant in a *genre* accounts for the creation of new generic forms and new poetic epochs. For example, the rise of *realism* in the mid-nineteenth century indicates realistic conventions becoming dominant and *romance* or fantasy conventions becoming secondary.

doppelgänger: A double or counterpart of a person, sometimes endowed with ghostly qualities. A fictional character's doppelgänger often reflects a suppressed side of his or her personality. One of the classic examples of the doppelgänger motif is found in

Fyodor Dostoevski's novella *Dvoynik* (1846; *The Double*, 1917); Isaac Bashevis Singer and Jorge Luis Borges, among others, offer striking modern treatments of the doppelgänger.

epic: Although this term usually refers to a long narrative poem that presents the exploits of a central figure of high position, the term is also used to designate a long novel that has the style or structure usually associated with an epic. In this sense, for example, Herman Melville's *Moby Dick* (1851) and James Joyce's *Ulysses* (1922) may be called epics.

episodic narrative: A work that is held together primarily by a loose connection of self-sufficient episodes. *Picaresque novels* often have episodic structure.

epistolary novel: A novel made up of letters by one or more fictional characters. Samuel Richardson's *Pamela: Or, Virtue Rewarded* (1740-1741) is a well-known eighteenth century example. In the nineteenth century, Bram Stoker's *Dracula* (1897) is largely epistolary. The technique allows for several different points of view to be presented.

euphuism: A style of writing characterized by ornate language that is highly contrived, alliterative, and repetitious. Euphuism was developed by John Lyly in his *Euphues, the Anatomy of Wit* (1578) and was emulated frequently by writers of the Elizabethan Age.

existentialism: A philosophical, religious, and literary term, emerging from World War II, for a group of attitudes surrounding the pivotal notion that existence precedes essence. According to Jean-Paul Sartre, "Man is nothing else but what he makes himself." Forlornness arises from the death of God and the concomitant death of universal values, of any source of ultimate or a priori standards. Despair arises from the fact that an individual can reckon only with what depends on his or her will, and the sphere of that will is severely limited; the number of things on which he or she can have an impact is pathetically small. Existentialist literature is antideterministic in the extreme and rejects the idea that heredity and environment shape and determine human motivation and behavior.

exposition: The part or parts of a fiction that provide necessary background information. Exposition not only provides the time and place of the action but also introduces readers to the fictive world of the story, acquainting them with the ground rules of the work.

fantastic: In his study *The Fantastic* (1970), Tzvetan Todorov defines the fantastic as a *genre* that lies between the "uncanny" and the "marvelous." All three genres embody the familiar world but present an event that cannot be explained by the laws of the familiar world. Todorov says that the fantastic occupies a twilight zone between the uncanny (when the reader knows that the peculiar event is merely the result of an illusion) and the marvelous (when the reader understands that the event is supposed to take place in a realm controlled by laws unknown to humankind). The fantastic is thus essentially unsettling, provocative, even subversive.

feminist criticism: A criticism advocating equal rights for women in political, economic, social, psychological, personal, and aesthetic senses. On the thematic level, the feminist reader should identify with female characters and their concerns. The object is to provide a critique of phallocentric assumptions and an analysis of patriarchal ideologies inscribed in a literature that is male-centered and male-dominated. On the ideological level, feminist critics see gender, as well as the stereotypes that go along with it, as a cultural construct. They strive to define a particularly feminine content and to extend the *canon* so that it might include works by lesbians, feminists, and women writers in general.

flashback: A scene in a fiction that depicts an earlier event; it may be presented as a reminiscence by a character in the story or may simply be inserted into the narrative.

foreshadowing: A device to create suspense or dramatic irony in fiction by indicating through suggestion what will take place in the future.

formalist criticism: Two particularly influential formalist schools of criticism arose in the twentieth century: the Russian Formalists and the American New Critics. The Russian Formalists were concerned with the conventional devices used in literature to defamiliarize that which habit has made familiar. The New Critics believed that literary criticism is a description and evaluation of its object and that the primary concern of the critic is with the work's unity. Both schools of criticism, at their most extreme, treated literary works as artifacts or constructs divorced from their biographical and social contexts.

genre: In its most general sense, this term refers to a group of literary works defined by a common form, style, or purpose. In practice, the term is used in a wide variety of overlapping and, to a degree, contradictory senses. Tragedy and comedy are thus described as distinct genres; the novel (a form that includes both tragic and comic works) is a genre; and various subspecies of the novel, such as the *gothic* and the *picaresque*, are themselves frequently treated as distinct genres. Finally, the term "genre fiction" refers to forms of popular fiction in which the writer is bound by more or less rigid conventions. Indeed, all these diverse usages have in common an emphasis on the manner in which individual literary works are shaped by particular expectations and conventions; this is the subject of genre criticism.

genre fiction: Categories of popular fiction in which the writers are bound by more or less rigid conventions, such as in the *detective story*, the *romance*, and the *Western*. Although the term can be used in a neutral sense, it is often used dismissively.

gothic novel: A form of fiction developed in the eighteenth century that focuses on horror and the supernatural. In his preface to *The Castle of Otranto* (1765), the first gothic novel in English, Horace Walpole claimed that he was trying to combine two kinds of fiction, with events and story typical of the medieval romance and character delineation typical of the realistic novel. Other examples of the form are Matthew Gregory

Lewis's *The Monk: A Romance* (1796; also known as *Ambrosio: Or, The Monk*) and Mary Wollstonecraft Shelley's *Frankenstein: Or, The Modern Prometheus* (1818).

grotesque: According to Wolfgang Kayser (*The Grotesque in Art and Literature*, 1963), the grotesque is an embodiment in literature of the estranged world. Characterized by a breakup of the everyday world by mysterious forces, the form differs from fantasy in that the reader is not sure whether to react with humor or with horror and in that the exaggeration manifested exists in the familiar world rather than in a purely imaginative world.

Hebraic/Homeric styles: Terms coined by Erich Auerbach in *Mimesis: The Representation of Reality in Western Literature* (1953) to designate two basic fictional styles. The Hebraic style focuses only on the decisive points of narrative and leaves all else obscure, mysterious, and "fraught with background"; the Homeric style places the narrative in a definite time and place and externalizes everything in a perpetual foreground.

historical criticism: In contrast to *formalist criticism*, which treats literary works to a great extent as self-contained artifacts, historical criticism emphasizes the historical context of literature; the two approaches, however, need not be mutually exclusive. Ernst Robert Curtius's *European Literature and the Latin Middle Ages* (1940) is a prominent example of historical criticism.

historical novel: A novel that depicts past historical events, usually public in nature, and features real as well as fictional people. Sir Walter Scott's Waverley novels established the basic type, but the relationship between fiction and history in the form varies greatly depending on the practitioner.

implied author: According to Wayne Booth (*The Rhetoric of Fiction*, 1961), the novel often creates a kind of second self who tells the story—a self who is wiser, more sensitive, and more perceptive than any real person could be.

interior monologue: Defined by Édouard Dujardin as the speech of a character designed to introduce the reader directly to the character's internal life, the form differs from other kinds of monologue in that it attempts to reproduce thought before any logical organization is imposed on it. See, for example, Molly Bloom's long interior monologue at the conclusion of James Joyce's *Ulysses* (1922).

irrealism: A term often used to refer to modern or postmodern fiction that is presented self-consciously as a fiction or a fabulation rather than a mimesis of external reality. The best-known practitioners of irrealism are John Barth, Robert Coover, and Donald Barthelme.

local colorists: A loose movement of late nineteenth century American writers whose fiction emphasizes the distinctive folkways, landscapes, and dialects of various regions. Important local colorists include Bret Harte, Mark Twain, George Washington Cable, Kate Chopin, and Sarah Orne Jewett. (See *regional novel*.)

Marxist criticism: Based on the nineteenth century writings of Karl Marx and Friedrich Engels, Marxist criticism views literature as a product of ideological forces determined by the dominant class. However, many Marxists believe that literature operates according to its own autonomous standards of production and reception: It is both a product of ideology and able to determine ideology. As such, literature may overcome the dominant paradigms of its age and play a revolutionary role in society.

metafiction: This term refers to fiction that manifests a reflexive tendency, such as Vladimir Nabokov's *Pale Fire* (1962) and John Fowles's *The French Lieutenant's Woman* (1969). The emphasis is on the loosening of the work's illusion of reality to expose the reality of its illusion. Other terms used to refer to this type of fiction include "irrealism," "postmodernist fiction," "antifiction," and "surfiction."

modernism: An international movement in the arts that began in the early years of the twentieth century. Although the term is used to describe artists of widely varying persuasions, modernism in general was characterized by its international idiom, by its interest in cultures distant in space or time, by its emphasis on formal experimentation, and by its sense of dislocation and radical change.

motif: A conventional incident or situation in a fiction that may serve as the basis for the structure of the narrative itself. The Russian Formalist critic Boris Tomashevsky uses the term to refer to the smallest particle of thematic material in a work.

motivation: Although this term is usually used in reference to the convention of justifying the action of a character from his or her psychological makeup, the Russian Formalists use the term to refer to the network of devices that justify the introduction of individual *motifs* or groups of motifs in a work. For example, "compositional motivation" refers to the principle that every single property in a work contributes to its overall effect; "realistic motivation" refers to the realistic devices used to make a work plausible and lifelike.

multiculturalism: The tendency to recognize the perspectives of those traditionally excluded from the canon of Western art and literature. In order to promote multiculturalism, publishers and educators have revised textbooks and school curricula to incorporate material by and about women, members of minority groups, persons from non-Western cultures, and homosexuals.

myth: Anonymous traditional stories dealing with basic human concepts and antinomies. According to Claude Lévi-Strauss, myth is that part of language where the "formula *tradutore, tradittore* reaches its lowest truth value. . . . Its substance does not lie in its style, its original music, or its syntax, but in the story which it tells."

myth criticism: Northrop Frye says that in myth "we see the structural principles of literature isolated." Myth criticism is concerned with these basic principles of literature; it is not to be confused with mythological criticism, which is primarily concerned with finding mythological parallels in the surface action of the *narrative*.

narrative: Robert Scholes and Robert Kellogg, in *The Nature of Narrative* (1966), say that by "narrative" they mean literary works that include both a story and a storyteller. The term "narrative" usually implies a contrast to "enacted" fiction such as drama.

narratology: The study of the form and functioning of *narratives*; it attempts to examine what all narratives have in common and what makes individual narratives different from one another.

narrator: The *character* who recounts the *narrative*, or story. Wayne Booth describes various dramatized narrators in *The Rhetoric of Fiction* (1961): unacknowledged centers of consciousness, observers, narrator-agents, and self-conscious narrators. Booth suggests that the important elements to consider in narration are the relationships among the narrator, the author, the characters, and the reader.

naturalism: As developed by Émile Zola in the late nineteenth century, naturalism is the application of the principles of scientific *determinism* to fiction. Although it usually refers more to the choice of subject matter than to technical conventions, those conventions associated with the movement center on the author's attempt to be precise and scientifically objective in description and detail, regardless of whether the events described are sordid or shocking.

New Criticism: See *formalist criticism.*

novel: Perhaps the most difficult of all fictional forms to define because of its multiplicity of modes. Edouard, in André Gide's *Les Faux-monnayeurs* (1925; *The Counterfeiters*, 1927), says the novel is the freest and most lawless of all *genres*; he wonders if fear of that liberty is the reason the novel has so timidly clung to reality. Most critics seem to agree that the novel's primary area of concern is the social world. Ian Watt (*The Rise of the Novel*, 2001) says that the novel can be distinguished from other fictional forms by the attention it pays to individual characterization and detailed presentation of the environment. Moreover, says Watt, the novel, more than any other fictional form, is interested in the "development of its characters in the course of time."

novel of manners: The classic examples of this form might be the novels of Jane Austen, wherein the customs and conventions of a social group of a particular time and place are realistically, and often satirically, portrayed.

novella, novelle, nouvelle, novelette, novela: Although these terms often refer to the short European tale, especially the Renaissance form employed by Giovanni Boccaccio, the terms often refer to that form of fiction that is said to be longer than a short story and shorter than a novel. "Novelette" is the term usually preferred by the British, whereas "novella" is the term usually used to refer to American works in this *genre.* Henry James claimed that the main merit of the form is the "effort to do the complicated thing with a strong brevity and lucidity."

phenomenological criticism: Although best known as a European school of criticism practiced by Georges Poulet and others, this so-called criticism of consciousness is also propounded in the United States by such critics as J. Hillis Miller. The focus is less on individual works and *genres* than it is on literature as an act; the work is not seen as an object but rather as part of a strand of latent impulses in the work of a single author or an epoch.

picaresque novel: A form of fiction that centers on a central rogue figure, or picaro, who usually tells his or her own story. The plot structure is normally *episodic*, and the episodes usually focus on how the picaro lives by his or her wits. Classic examples of the mode are Henry Fielding's *The History of Tom Jones, a Foundling* (1749; commonly known as *Tom Jones*) and Mark Twain's *Adventures of Huckleberry Finn* (1884).

plot/story: "Story" refers to the full *narrative* of *character* and action, whereas "plot" generally refers to action with little reference to character. A more precise and helpful distinction is made by the Russian Formalists, who suggest that "plot" refers to the events of a narrative as they have been artfully arranged in the literary work, subject to chronological displacement, ellipses, and other devices, while "story" refers to the sum of the same events arranged in simple, causal-chronological order. Thus story is the raw material for plot. By comparing the two in a given work, the reader is encouraged to see the narrative as an artifact.

point of view: The means by which the story is presented to the reader, or, as Percy Lubbock says in *The Craft of Fiction* (1921), "the relation in which the narrator stands to the story"—a relation that Lubbock claims governs the craft of fiction. Some of the questions the critical reader should ask concerning point of view are the following: Who talks to the reader? From what position does the narrator tell the story? At what distance does he or she place the reader from the story? What kind of person is he or she? How fully is he or she characterized? How reliable is he or she? For further discussion, see Wayne Booth, *The Rhetoric of Fiction* (1961).

postcolonialism: Postcolonial literature emerged in the mid-twentieth century when colonies in Asia, Africa, and the Caribbean began gaining their independence from the European nations that had long controlled them. Postcolonial authors, such as Salman Rushdie and V. S. Naipaul, tend to focus on both the freedom and the conflict inherent in living in a postcolonial state.

postmodernism: A ubiquitous but elusive term in contemporary criticism, "postmodernism" is loosely applied to the various artistic movements that followed the era of so-called high modernism, represented by such giants as James Joyce and Pablo Picasso. In critical discussions of contemporary fiction, the term "postmodernism" is frequently applied to the works of writers such as Thomas Pynchon, John Barth, and Donald Barthelme, who exhibit a self-conscious awareness of their modernist predecessors as well as a reflexive treatment of fictional form.

protagonist: The central *character* in a fiction, the character whose fortunes most concern the reader.

psychological criticism: While much modern literary criticism reflects to some degree the impacts of Sigmund Freud, Carl Jung, Jacques Lacan, and other psychological theorists, the term "psychological criticism" suggests a strong emphasis on a causal relation between the writer's psychological state, variously interpreted, and his or her works. A notable example of psychological criticism is Norman Fruman's *Coleridge, the Damaged Archangel* (1971).

psychological novel: A form of fiction in which *character*, especially the inner lives of characters, is the primary focus. This form, which has been of primary importance at least since Henry James, characterizes much of the work of James Joyce, Virginia Woolf, and William Faulkner. For a detailed discussion, see *The Modern Psychological Novel* (1955) by Leon Edel.

realism: A literary technique in which the primary convention is to render an illusion of fidelity to external reality. Realism is often identified as the primary method of the novel form: It focuses on surface details, maintains a fidelity to the everyday experiences of middle-class society, and strives for a one-to-one relationship between the fiction and the action imitated. The realist movement in the late nineteenth century coincides with the full development of the novel form.

reception aesthetics: The best-known American practitioner of reception aesthetics is Stanley Fish. For the reception critic, meaning is an event or process; rather than being embedded in the work, it is created through particular acts of reading. The best-known European practitioner of this criticism, Wolfgang Iser, argues that indeterminacy is the basic characteristic of literary texts; the reader must "normalize" the text either by projecting his or her standards into it or by revising his or her standards to "fit" the text.

regional novel: Any novel in which the character of a given geographical region plays a decisive role. Although regional differences persist across the United States, a considerable leveling in speech and customs has taken place, so that the sharp regional distinctions evident in nineteenth century American fiction have all but disappeared. Only in the South has a strong regional tradition persisted to the present. (See *local colorists*.)

rhetorical criticism: The rhetorical critic is concerned with the literary work as a means of communicating ideas and the means by which the work affects or controls the reader. Such criticism seems best suited to didactic works such as satire.

roman à clef: A fiction wherein actual people, often celebrities of some sort, are thinly disguised.

romance: The romance usually differs from the novel form in that the focus is on symbolic events and representational characters rather than on "as-if-real" characters and events. Richard Chase says that in the romance, character is depicted as highly stylized, a function of the plot rather than as someone complexly related to society. The romancer is more likely to be concerned with dreamworlds than with the familiar world, believing that reality cannot be grasped by the traditional novel.

Romanticism: A widespread cultural movement in the late eighteenth and early nineteenth centuries, the influence of which is still felt. As a general literary tendency, Romanticism is frequently contrasted with *classicism.* Although many varieties of Romanticism are indigenous to various national literatures, the term generally suggests an assertion of the preeminence of the imagination. Other values associated with various schools of Romanticism include primitivism, an interest in folklore, a reverence for nature, and a fascination with the demoniac and the macabre.

scene: The central element of *narration*; specific actions are narrated or depicted that make the reader feel he or she is participating directly in the action.

science fiction: Fiction in which certain givens (physical laws, psychological principles, social conditions—any one or all of these) form the basis of an imaginative projection into the future or, less commonly, an extrapolation in the present or even into the past.

semiotics: The science of signs and sign systems in communication. According to Roman Jakobson, semiotics deals with the principles that underlie the structure of signs, their use in language of all kinds, and the specific nature of various sign systems.

sentimental novel: A form of fiction popular in the eighteenth century in which emotionalism and optimism are the primary characteristics. The best-known examples are Samuel Richardson's *Pamela: Or, Virtue Rewarded* (1740-1741) and Oliver Goldsmith's *The Vicar of Wakefield* (1766).

setting: The circumstances and environment, both temporal and spatial, of a *narrative.*

spatial form: An author's attempt to make the reader apprehend a work spatially in a moment of time rather than sequentially. To achieve this effect, the author breaks up the *narrative* into interspersed fragments. Beginning with James Joyce, Marcel Proust, and Djuna Barnes, the movement toward spatial form is concomitant with the *modernist* effort to supplant historical time in fiction with mythic time. For the seminal discussion of this technique, see Joseph Frank, *The Widening Gyre* (1963).

stream of consciousness: The depiction of the thought processes of a *character,* insofar as this is possible, without any mediating structures. The metaphor of consciousness as a "stream" suggests a rush of thoughts and images governed by free association rather than by strictly rational development. The term "stream of consciousness" is often used loosely as a synonym for *interior monologue.* The most celebrated example of stream of consciousness in fiction is the monologue of Molly Bloom in James Joyce's *Ulysses* (1922); other notable practitioners of the stream-of-consciousness technique include Dorothy Richardson, Virginia Woolf, and William Faulkner.

structuralism: As a movement of thought, structuralism is based on the idea of intrinsic, self-sufficient structures that do not require reference to external elements. A structure is a system of transformations that involves the interplay of laws inherent in the system itself. The study of language is the primary model for contemporary structuralism. The structuralist literary critic attempts to define structural principles that operate intertextually throughout the whole of literature as well as principles that operate in *genres* and in individual works. One of the most accessible surveys of structuralism and literature available is Jonathan Culler's *Structuralist Poetics* (1975).

summary: Those parts of a fiction that do not need to be detailed. In *Tom Jones* (1749), Henry Fielding says, "If whole years should pass without producing anything worthy of . . . notice . . . we shall hasten on to matters of consequence."

thematics: According to Northrop Frye, when a work of fiction is written or interpreted thematically, it becomes an illustrative fable. Murray Krieger defines thematics as "the study of the experiential tensions which, dramatically entangled in the literary work, become an existential reflection of that work's aesthetic complexity."

tone: The dominant mood of a work of fiction. (See *atmosphere.*)

unreliable narrator: A narrator whose account of the events of the story cannot be trusted, obliging readers to reconstruct—if possible—the true state of affairs themselves. Once an innovative technique, the use of the unreliable narrator has become commonplace among contemporary writers who wish to suggest the impossibility of a truly "reliable" account of any event. Notable examples of the unreliable narrator can be found in Ford Madox Ford's *The Good Soldier* (1915) and Vladimir Nabokov's *Lolita* (1955).

Victorian novel: Although the Victorian period extended from 1837 to 1901, the term "Victorian novel" does not include the later decades of Queen Victoria's reign. The term loosely refers to the sprawling works of novelists such as Charles Dickens and William Makepeace Thackeray—works that frequently appeared first in serial form and are characterized by a broad social canvas.

vraisemblance/verisimilitude: Tzvetan Todorov defines vraisemblance as "the mask which conceals the text's own laws, but which we are supposed to take for a relation to reality." Verisimilitude refers to a work's attempts to make the reader believe that it conforms to reality rather than to its own laws.

Western novel: Like all varieties of *genre fiction*, the Western novel—generally known simply as the Western—is defined by a relatively predictable combination of *conventions*, *motifs*, and recurring themes. These predictable elements, familiar from many Western films and television series, differentiate the Western from *historical novels* and idiosyncratic works such as Thomas Berger's *Little Big Man* (1964) that are also set in the Old West. Conversely, some novels set in the contemporary West are regarded as Westerns because they deal with modern cowboys and with the land itself in the manner characteristic of the *genre.*

Charles E. May

Guide to Online Resources

Web Sites

The following sites were visited by the editors of Salem Press in 2009. Because URLs frequently change, the accuracy of these addresses cannot be guaranteed; however, long-standing sites, such as those of colleges and universities, national organizations, and government agencies, generally maintain links when sites are moved or updated.

American Literature on the Web

http://www.nagasaki-gaigo.ac.jp/ishikawa/amlit

Among this site's features are several pages providing links to Web sites about specific genres and literary movements, southern and southwestern American literature, minority literature, literary theory, and women writers, as well as an extensive index of links to electronic text collections and archives. Users also can access information for five specific time periods: 1620-1820, 1820-1865, 1865-1914, 1914-1945, and since 1945. A range of information is available for each period, including alphabetical lists of authors that link to more specific information about each writer, time lines of historical and literary events, and links to related additional Web sites.

Books and Writers

http://www.kirjasto.sci.fi/indeksi.htm

This broad, comprehensive, and easy-to-use resource provides access to information about hundreds of authors throughout the world, extending from 70 B.C.E to the twenty-first century. Links take users from an alphabetical list of authors to pages featuring biographical material, lists of works, and recommendations for further reading about individual authors; each writer's page also includes links to related pages on the site. Although brief, the biographical essays provide solid overviews of the authors' careers, their contributions to literature, and their literary influences.

The Canadian Literature Archive

http://www.umanitoba.ca/canlit

Created and maintained by the English Department at the University of Manitoba, this site is a comprehensive collection of materials for and about Canadian writers. It includes an alphabetical listing of authors with links to additional Web-based information. Users also can retrieve electronic texts, announcements of literary events, and videocasts of author interviews and readings.

A Celebration of Women Writers

http://digital.library.upenn.edu/women

This site presents an extensive compendium of information about the contributions of women writers throughout history. The "Local Editions by Authors" and "Local Editions by Category" pages include access to electronic texts of the works of numerous writers, including Louisa May Alcott, Djuna Barnes, Grazia Deledda, Edith Wharton, and Virginia Woolf. Users can also access biographical and bibliographical information by browsing lists arranged by writers' names, countries of origin, ethnicities, and the centuries in which they lived.

Contemporary Writers

http://www.contemporarywriters.com/authors

Created by the British Council, this site offers "up-to-date profiles of some of the U.K. and Commonwealth's most important living writers (plus writers from the Republic of Ireland that we've worked with)." The available information includes biographies, bibliographies, critical reviews, news about literary prizes, and photographs. Users can search the site by author, genre, nationality, gender, publisher, book title, date of publication, and prize name and date.

Internet Public Library: Native American Authors

http://www.ipl.org/div/natam

Internet Public Library, a Web-based collection of materials, includes this index to resources about writers of Native American heritage. An alphabetical list of authors enables users to link to biographies, lists of works, electronic texts, tribal Web sites, and other online resources. The majority of the writers covered are contemporary Indian authors, but some historical authors also are featured. Users also can retrieve information by browsing lists of titles and tribes. In addition, the site contains a bibliography of print and online materials about Native American literature.

LiteraryHistory.com

http://www.literaryhistory.com

This site is an excellent source of academic, scholarly, and critical literature about eighteenth, nineteenth, and twentieth century American and English writers. It provides numerous pages about specific eras and genres, including individual pages for eighteenth, nineteenth, and twentieth century literature and for African American and postcolonial literature. These pages contain alphabetical lists of authors that link to articles, reviews, overviews, excerpts of works, teaching guides, podcast interviews, and other materials. The eighteenth century literature page also provides access to information about the eighteenth century novel.

Literary Resources on the Net

http://andromeda.rutgers.edu/~jlynch/Lit

Jack Lynch of Rutgers University maintains this extensive collection of links to Internet sites that are useful to academics, including numerous Web sites about American and English literature. This collection is a good place to begin online research about the novel, as it links to hundreds of other sites with broad ranges of literary topics. The site is organized chronically, with separate pages for information about the Middle Ages, the Renaissance, the eighteenth century, the Romantic and Victorian eras, and twentieth century British and Irish literature. It also has separate pages providing links to Web sites about American literature and to women's literature and feminism.

LitWeb

http://litweb.net

LitWeb provides biographies of more than five hundred world authors throughout history that can be accessed through an alphabetical listing. The pages about each writer contain a list of his or her works, suggestions for further reading, and illustrations. The site also offers information about past and present winners of major literary prizes.

The Modern Word: Authors of the Libyrinth

http://www.themodernword.com/authors.html

The Modern Word site, although somewhat haphazard in its organization, provides a great deal of critical information about writers. The "Authors of the Libyrinth" page is very useful, linking author names to essays about them and other resources. The section of the page headed "The Scriptorium" presents "an index of pages featuring writers who have pushed the edges of their medium, combining literary talent with a sense of experimentation to produce some remarkable works of modern literature." The site also includes sections devoted to Samuel Beckett, Umberto Eco, Gabriel García Márquez, James Joyce, Franz Kafka, and Thomas Pynchon.

Novels

http://www.nvcc.edu/home/ataormina/novels/default.htm

This overview of American and English novels was prepared by Agatha Taormina, a professor at Northern Virginia Community College. It contains three sections: "History" provides a definition of the novel genre, a discussion of its origins in eighteenth century England, and separate pages with information about genres and authors of nineteenth century, twentieth century, and postmodern novels. "Approaches" suggests how to read a novel critically for greater appreciation, and "Resources" provides a list of books about the novel.

Outline of American Literature

http://www.america.gov/publications/books/outline-of-american-literature.html

This page of the America.gov site provides access to an electronic version of the ten-chapter volume *Outline of American Literature*, a historical overview of prose and poetry from colonial times to the present published by the U.S. Department of State. The work's author is Kathryn VanSpanckeren, professor of English at the University of Tampa. The site offers links to abbreviated versions of each chapter as well as access to the entire publication in PDF format.

Voice of the Shuttle

http://vos.ucsb.edu

One of the most complete and authoritative places for online information about literature, Voice of the Shuttle is maintained by professors and students in the English Department at the University of California, Santa Barbara. The site provides thousands of links to electronic books, academic journals, association Web sites, sites created by university professors, and many, many other resources about the humanities. Its "Literature in English" page provides links to separate pages about the literature of the Anglo-Saxon era, the Middle Ages, the Renaissance and seventeenth century, the Restoration and eighteenth century, the Romantic age, the Victorian age, and modern and contemporary periods in Britain and the United States, as well as a page focused on minority literature. Another page on the site, "Literatures Other than English," offers a gateway to information about the literature of numerous countries and world regions.

ELECTRONIC DATABASES

Electronic databases usually do not have their own URLs. Instead, public, college, and university libraries subscribe to these databases, provide links to them on their Web sites, and make them available to library card holders or other specified patrons. Readers can visit library Web sites or ask reference librarians to check on availability.

Canadian Literary Centre

Produced by EBSCO, the Canadian Literary Centre database contains full-text content from ECW Press, a Toronto-based publisher, including the titles in the publisher's Canadian fiction studies, Canadian biography, and Canadian writers and their works series, *ECW's Biographical Guide to Canadian Novelists*, and *George Woodcock's Introduction to Canadian Fiction*. Author biographies, essays and literary criticism, and book reviews are among the database's offerings.

Literary Reference Center

EBSCO's Literary Reference Center (LRC) is a comprehensive full-text database designed primarily to help high school and undergraduate students in English and the humanities with homework and research assignments about literature. The database contains massive amounts of information from reference works, books, literary journals, and other materials, including more than 31,000 plot summaries, synopses, and overviews of literary works; almost 100,000 essays and articles of literary criticism; about 140,000 author biographies; more than 605,000 book reviews; and more than 5,200 author interviews. It also contains the entire contents of Salem Press's MagillOnLiterature Plus. Users can retrieve information by browsing a list of authors' names or titles of literary works; they can also use an advanced search engine to access information by numerous categories, including author name, gender, cultural identity, national identity, and the years in which he or she lived, or by literary title, character, locale, genre, and publication date. The Literary Reference Center also features a literary-historical time line, an encyclopedia of literature, and a glossary of literary terms.

MagillOnLiterature Plus

MagillOnLiterature Plus is a comprehensive, integrated literature database produced by Salem Press and available on the EBSCO*host* platform. The database contains the full text of essays in Salem's many literature-related reference works, including *Masterplots*, *Cyclopedia of World Authors*, *Cyclopedia of Literary Characters*, *Cyclopedia of Literary Places*, *Critical Survey of Long Fiction*, *Critical Survey of Short Fiction*, *World Philosophers and Their Works*, *Magill's Literary Annual*, and *Magill's Book Reviews.* Among its contents are articles on more than 35,000 literary works and more than 8,500 writers, poets, dramatists, essays, and philosophers, more than 1,000 images, and a glossary of more than 1,300 literary terms. The biographical essays include lists of authors' works and secondary bibliographies, and almost four hundred overview essays offer information about literary genres, time periods, and national literatures.

NoveList

NoveList is a readers' advisory service produced by EBSCO. The database provides access to 155,000 titles of both adult and juvenile fiction as well information about literary awards, book discussion guides, feature articles about a range of literary genres, and "recommended reads." Users can search by author name, book title, or series title or can describe the plot to retrieve the name of a book, information about the author, and book reviews; another search engine enables users to find titles similar to books they have enjoyed reading.

Rebecca Kuzins

CATEGORY INDEX

BILDUNGSROMAN
Baldwin, James, 14

DETECTIVE AND MYSTERY NOVEL
Himes, Chester, 91

DIDACTIC NOVEL
McKay, Claude, 128

EPISTOLARY NOVEL
Walker, Alice, 190

EXISTENTIALISM
Wright, Richard, 230

FEMINIST NOVEL
Fauset, Jessie Redmon, 74
Naylor, Gloria, 154

GAY AND LESBIAN NOVEL
Baldwin, James, 14
Naylor, Gloria, 154

HISTORICAL NOVEL
Yerby, Frank, 244

LOCAL COLOR AND REGIONALISM
Cable, George Washington, 39
Chesnutt, Charles Waddell, 50
Gaines, Ernest J., 80
Stowe, Harriet Beecher, 175

MODERNISM
Ellison, Ralph, 61
Larsen, Nella, 116

NOBEL PRIZE WINNERS
Morrison, Toni, 140

POSTMODERNISM
Reed, Ishmael, 163
Wideman, John Edgar, 211

PROBLEM NOVEL
Chesnutt, Charles Waddell, 50

PSYCHOLOGICAL REALISM
Wright, Richard, 230

RACISM
Cable, George Washington, 39
Chesnutt, Charles Waddell, 50
Himes, Chester, 91
Hurston, Zora Neale, 98
Kelley, William Melvin, 109
Lee, Harper, 122
Morrison, Toni, 140
Naylor, Gloria, 154
Reed, Ishmael, 163
Stowe, Harriet Beecher, 175
Williams, John A., 222
Yerby, Frank, 244

REALISM
Stowe, Harriet Beecher, 175

RELIGIOUS NOVEL
Yerby, Frank, 244

ROMANCE
McMillan, Terry, 134

ROMANTIC NOVEL
Stowe, Harriet Beecher, 175

SATIRE AND BLACK HUMOR
Kelley, William Melvin, 109
Reed, Ishmael, 163
Whitehead, Colson, 205

SOUTHERN AMERICAN CULTURE
Cable, George Washington, 39
Chesnutt, Charles Waddell, 50
Gaines, Ernest J., 80
Hurston, Zora Neale, 98
Kelley, William Melvin, 109
Lee, Harper, 122
Stowe, Harriet Beecher, 175
Yerby, Frank, 244

WOMEN AUTHORS
Bambara, Toni Cade, 33
Fauset, Jessie Redmon, 74
Hurston, Zora Neale, 98
Larsen, Nella, 116
Lee, Harper, 122
McMillan, Terry, 134
Morrison, Toni, 140
Naylor, Gloria, 154
Stowe, Harriet Beecher, 175
Walker, Alice, 190

SUBJECT INDEX

Aestheticism, 62
African American novel, 1-13
Allegory, 67
Angelou, Maya, 94
Angry Ones, The (Williams), 225
Another Country (Baldwin), 7, 23
Atmosphere, 86
Autobiography of an Ex-Coloured Man, The (Johnson), 4
Autobiography of Miss Jane Pittman, The (Gaines), 8, 85

Bailey's Café (Naylor), 159
Baldwin, James, 7, 14-32, 62, 94, 109, 166, 226
Bambara, Toni Cade, 12, 33-38
Banana Bottom (McKay), 132
Banjo (McKay), 131
Baraka, Amiri, 18, 166
Barrie, Sir James, 41
Beloved (Morrison), 10, 149
Biblical themes, 102, 219
Bildungsromans, 168
Black No More (Schuyler), 4
Black nationalism, 67, 130, 132
Blacker the Berry, The (Thurman), 4
Blake (Delaney, Martin), 3
Blake, William, 20
Bluest Eye, The (Morrison), 141
Bradley, David, 9
Brown, William Wells, 3
Burgess, Anthony, 177
By the Light of My Father's Smile (Walker), 201

Cable, George Washington, 39-49
Camus, Albert, 193
Cane (Toomer), 5
Capote, Truman, 123
Captain Blackman (Williams), 226
Catherine Carmier (Gaines), 83
Cattle Killing, The (Wideman), 219
Censorship, 99
Césaire, Aimé, 132
Chesnutt, Charles Waddell, 3, 50-60
Chinaberry Tree, The (Fauset), 77
!Click Song (Williams), 227
Clotel (Brown), 3
Colonel's Dream, The (Chesnutt), 58
Color Purple, The (Walker), 11, 198
Comedy, American Style (Fauset), 78
Confessions of Nat Turner, The (1832), 2
Conrad, Joseph, 179
Cotton Comes to Harlem (Himes), 95
Crime fiction, 92, 95-96
Cullen, Countée, 17

Dahomean, The (Yerby), 250
Delany, Martin, 3
Dem (Kelley), 113
Detective novels, 6, 94
Didactic novels
  Charles Waddell Chesnutt, 58
  Claude McKay, 131
Different Drummer, A (Kelley), 110
Dime novels, 169
Disappearing Acts (McMillan), 137
Douglass, Frederick, 1
Dred (Stowe), 182
Dreiser, Theodore, 236
Drop of Patience, A (Kelley), 112
Du Bois, W. E. B., 51, 118, 130
Dunbar, Paul Laurence, 3, 51
Dunfords Travels Everywheres (Kelley), 114

Ellison, Ralph
Emerson, Ralph Waldo, 63, 175
Epistolary novels, 198
Equiano, Olaudah, 1
"Everybody's Protest Novel" (Baldwin), 7
Existentialism
  Alice Walker, 193
  Richard Wright, 233
  Frank Yerby, 247

Fantastic
  Toni Morrison, 141
  Ishmael Reed, 168
Father's Law, A (Wright), 240
Faulkner, William, 16, 179
Fauset, Jessie Redmon, 5, 74-79
Feminist fiction, 11
  Gloria Naylor, 154
  Alice Walker, 193
Flashbacks, 6
  William Melvin Kelley, 112
  John Edgar Wideman, 214
Flight to Canada (Reed), 170
Foreshadowing, 53
Forrest, Leon, 9
Foxes of Harrow, The (Yerby), 247
Free-Lance Pallbearers, The (Reed), 8, 167

Gaines, Ernest J., 8, 80-90, 94, 166
Gathering of Old Men, A (Gaines), 87
Gay and lesbian novels, 12
  James Baldwin, 23
  Gloria Naylor, 157
Giovanni, Nikki, 14
Giovanni's Room (Baldwin), 7, 26
Glance Away, A (Wideman), 8, 213
Go Tell It on the Mountain (Baldwin), 7, 20
Gothic novel
  Harper Lee, 124
  Gloria Naylor, 155
Grandissimes, The (Cable), 44
Great Depression, 130
Gregory, J. Dennis. *See* Williams, John A.
Griffin's Way (Yerby), 248
Grotesque
  Ernest J. Gaines, 84
  Ishmael Reed, 168

Hardy, Thomas, 181
Harlem Renaissance, 4, 74, 98, 100, 118, 167, 169
  Nella Larsen, 116-119
  Claude McKay, 130
Harper, Francis E. W., 3
Harte, Bret, 182
Hawthorne, Nathaniel, 47, 180
Heine, Heinrich, 177
Hiding Place (Wideman), 216
Himes, Chester, 6, 91-97
Historical novels
  African American, 9
  Frank Yerby, 245
Holmes, Oliver Wendell, 175
Home to Harlem (McKay), 5, 131
House Behind the Cedars, The (Chesnutt), 55
How Stella Got Her Groove Back (McMillan), 138
Howells, William Dean, 40, 177
Hughes, Langston, 61
Hurry Home (Wideman), 214
Hurston, Zora Neale, 5, 34, 61, 98-108, 136, 190

If He Hollers Let Him Go (Himes), 6, 94
In My Father's House (Gaines), 86
Incidents in the Life of a Slave Girl (Jacobs), 1
Infants of the Spring (Thurman), 4
Interesting Narrative of the Life of Olaudah Equiano, The (Equiano), 1
Interior monologues, 213

Interruption of Everything, The (McMillan), 138
Intuitionist, The (Whitehead), 206
Invisible Man (Ellison), 64
Iola Leroy (Harper), 3

Jacob's Ladder (Williams), 227
Jacobs, Harriet, 1
James, Henry, 16
Japanese by Spring (Reed), 172
Jazz (Morrison), 150
Jewett, Sarah Orne, 176
John Henry Days (Whitehead), 208
Johnson, Charles, 9
Johnson, James Weldon, 4
Jonah's Gourd Vine (Hurston), 103
Jones, Gayl, 12
Joyce, James, 179
Juneteenth (Ellison), 72
Just Above My Head (Baldwin), 25

Kelley, William Melvin, 109-115
King, Martin Luther, Jr., 154, 226

Larsen, Nella, 5, 116-121
Last Days of Louisiana Red, The (Reed), 170
Lawd Today (Wright), 235
Lee, Harper, 122-127
Lesson Before Dying, A (Gaines), 88
Linden Hills (Naylor), 157
Local color
  George Washington Cable, 47
  Harriet Beecher Stowe, 176
Locke, Alain, 130
Long Dream, The (Wright), 240
Longfellow, Henry Wadsworth, 177
Love (Morrison), 151
Lynchers, The (Wideman), 8, 215

MacLeish, Archibald, 109
McKay, Claude, 5, 128-133
Mackey, Nathaniel, 9
McMillan, Terry, 134-139
McPherson, James Alan, 62, 166
Madame Delphine (Cable), 46
Mama (McMillan), 135-136
Mama Day (Naylor), 158
Man Who Cried I Am, The (Williams), 8, 226
Marrow of Tradition, The (Chesnutt), 3, 57
Marshall, Paule, 10
Men of Brewster Place, The (Naylor), 160
Meridian (Walker), 196
Merton, Thomas, 109
Middle Passage (Johnson), 9
Minister's Wooing, The (Stowe), 183
Modernism
  Ralph Ellison, 62
  Nella Larsen, 118
  Ishmael Reed, 168
Morrison, Toni, 10, 62, 94, 140-153, 155, 164, 166
Moses, Man of the Mountain (Hurston), 102
Motifs
  James Baldwin, 26
  Ralph Ellison, 65
  Jessie Redmon Fauset, 77
  Nella Larsen, 119-120
Mumbo Jumbo (Reed), 169
Murray, Albert, 9
My Wife and I (Stowe), 186

Narrative of the Life of Frederick Douglass (Douglass), 1
Native Son (Wright), 6, 236
Naylor, Gloria, 12, 94, 154-162
Negritude, 132
Night Song (Williams), 225
Now Is the Time to Open Your Heart (Walker), 202

O'Connor, Flannery, 193
Odor of Sanctity, An (Yerby), 250
Of Love and Dust (Gaines), 84
Oldtown Folks (Stowe), 185
Our Nig (Wilson), 2
Outsider, The (Wright), 238
Oxherding Tale (Johnson), 9

Pan-Africanism, 10, 132
  James Baldwin, 15
  Ralph Ellison, 67
Paradise (Morrison), 150
Passing (Larsen), 5, 119
Petry, Ann, 6
Philadelphia Fire (Wideman), 219
Picaresque novel, 130
Plum Bun (Fauset), 76
Poganuc People (Stowe), 187
Point of view
  James Baldwin, 22
  Ernest J. Gaines, 86
  Zora Neale Hurston, 104
  Ishmael Reed, 172
Possessing the Secret of Joy (Walker), 200
Primitive, The (Himes), 95
Problem novel
  Charles Waddell Chesnutt, 55
  Harriet Beecher Stowe, 180
Proletarian novel, 102
Pulp fiction, 247-248

Quicksand (Larsen), 5, 118

Realism
  and African American literature, 6
  George Washington Cable, 45
  Ishmael Reed, 168
  Harriet Beecher Stowe, 176
  Alice Walker, 193
Reckless Eyeballing (Reed), 171
Reed, Ishmael, 8, 135, 163-174
Religious novels, 250
Reuben (Wideman), 218
Roman à clef, 4
Romanticism
  George Washington Cable, 47
  Harriet Beecher Stowe, 178

Salt Eaters, The (Bambara), 35
Satire
  Jessie Redmon Fauset, 78
  William Melvin Kelley, 113
  Ishmael Reed, 166
Schuyler, George, 4
Senghor, Léopold, 132
Sent for You Yesterday (Wideman), 218
Sentimental novel, 75
Seraph on the Suwanee (Hurston), 103
Sissie (Williams), 225
Slave narratives, 1
  Ralph Ellison, 65
  Ishmael Reed, 170
Social realism, 166
Song of Solomon (Morrison), 144
Southern novel, 44
Sport of the Gods, The (Dunbar), 3
Sterne, Laurence, 220
Stowe, Harriet Beecher, 169, 175-189
Stream of consciousness, 138
Street, The (Petry), 6
Sula (Morrison), 143

Tar Baby (Morrison), 147
Terrible Threes, The (Reed), 171
Terrible Twos, The (Reed), 171
Their Eyes Were Watching God (Hurston), 5, 105
There Is Confusion (Fauset), 75
Third Life of Grange Copeland, The (Walker), 194

Thurman, Wallace, 4
To Kill a Mockingbird (Lee), 124
Tolstoy, Leo, 177
Toomer, Jean, 5, 193, 213
Tuohy, Frank, 109
Twain, Mark, 42, 178
Two Cities (Wideman), 220

Uncle Tom's Cabin (Stowe), 180

Waiting to Exhale (McMillan), 137
Walcott, Derek, 94
Walker, Alice, 11, 94, 136, 164, 166, 190-204
Walker, David, 3
Walker's Appeal, in Four Articles (Walker), 3
We and Our Neighbors (Stowe), 186
West, Nathanael, 168
Whitehead, Colson, 205-210
Whitman, Walt, 62
Wideman, John Edgar, 8, 211-221
Williams, John A., 8, 222-229
Wilson, Harriet E., 2
Women of Brewster Place, The (Naylor), 156
Wright, Richard, 6, 17, 61, 94, 222, 230-243

Yellow Back Radio Broke-Down (Reed), 8, 168
Yerby, Frank, 244-253